Media Literacy in Action

Questioning the Media

Renee Hobbs
University of Rhode Island
Media Education Lab

ROWMAN & LITTLEFIELD
Lanham • Boulder • New York • London

dedicated to James and Evelyn

Executive Editor: Natalie Mandziuk and Elizabeth Swayze
Higher Education Marketing Manager: Kim Lyons
Production Manager: Janice Braunstein
Cover Designer: Sally Rinehart

Credits and acknowledgments for material borrowed from other sources, and reproduced with permission, appear on the appropriate pages within the text.

Published by Rowman & Littlefield
An imprint of The Rowman & Littlefield Publishing Group, Inc.
4501 Forbes Boulevard, Suite 200, Lanham, Maryland 20706
www.rowman.com

6 Tinworth Street, London SE11 5AL, United Kingdom

British Library Cataloguing in Publication Information Available

Library of Congress Cataloging-in-Publication Data
Names: Hobbs, Renee, author.
Title: Media literacy in action : questioning the media / Renee Hobbs.
Description: Lanham : Rowman & Littlefield, [2021] | Includes bibliographical references and index.
Identifiers: LCCN 2020002687 (print) | LCCN 2020002688 (ebook) | ISBN 9781538115275 (cloth) | ISBN 9781538115282 (paperback) | ISBN 9781538115299 (epub)
Subjects: LCSH: Media literacy.
Classification: LCC P96.M4 H635 2021 (print) | LCC P96.M4 (ebook) | DDC 302.23—dc23
LC record available at https://lccn.loc.gov/2020002687
LC ebook record available at https://lccn.loc.gov/2020002688

♾™ The paper used in this publication meets the minimum requirements of American National Standard for Information Sciences—Permanence of Paper for Printed Library Materials, ANSI/NISO Z39.48-1992.

Brief Contents

Contents

PART II: JUDGMENTS ABOUT TASTE, QUALITY, AND TRUST

Contents

PART IV: MEDIA EFFECTS

Preface

This book is designed to provide you with a deep understanding of media literacy as a fundamental life skill for thriving in an information age. At a time when so-called fake news is rising and propaganda and misinformation are plentiful, this book offers an approach to analyzing media rooted in the practice of asking questions, creating media, and taking action.

The knowledge and skills you will develop by reading this book can last a lifetime. By asking questions about what you watch, read, use, play, and listen to, you will think deeply about the media messages that you encounter every day. By creating media as a way to represent your learning, you get to reflect on your own behaviors, attitudes, beliefs, and feelings. Sharing your experience of daily life may enable other people to learn from you, and it builds bonds of trust that can lead to civic engagement.

This book starts with the assumption that your own life experiences and encounters with media and popular culture are a starting point for inquiry. To guide you, this book uses a range of devices for supporting your learning. They include:

- **Definitions: Identify Key Ideas.** An advanced vocabulary for talking about media fuels critical thinking. Key ideas are italicized upon first use, and a Glossary at the back of the book offers a complete list of key terms.

- **Consider the Question.** You will find discussion questions all throughout the margins of this book. You are invited to talk over these ideas with a partner or in a small group to better reflect on your thoughts about provocative and controversial topics.

- **Intellectual Grandparents.** Each chapter introduces you to a theorist, scholar, or researcher whose work has shaped the theory and practice of media literacy. These individuals are metaphorical "grandparents" because they have influenced many people who admire their ideas and build on their work.

- **Five Critical Questions for Analyzing Media.** To show how critical analysis changes your perceptions and your experience as a media consumer, each chapter includes a model critical analysis of a media text using five questions. You can access the example provided in each chapter and practice analyzing media messages by applying this framework to any and all of the media messages you encounter in daily life.

- **Time to Reflect.** Reflection is a powerful way to engage in metacognitive thinking about your learning experience. Through sharing and contributing ideas and listening to the views of others using the power of the spoken word, you will broaden your understanding of key ideas featured in this book. Visit www.medialiteracyaction.com to access Flipgrid Inquiry, a free online asynchronous video dialogue tool. There you can view comments from other learners and contribute your own perspective.

- **Create to Learn.** In each chapter, you are invited to synthesize what you are learning by creating different types of media, including infographics, essays, image slideshows, podcasts, and more. You can share your work to a global knowledge community of media literacy learners by using the hashtag #MLAction.

- **Website Companion.** At this book's companion website, you can find links to the videos and media mentioned in this book, along with resources for learning more at www.medialiteracyaction.com.

Because this book is designed for readers who may be enrolled in a variety of different courses where media literacy is important, you will find insights from a range of different disciplines and fields, especially from the humanities, education, and the social sciences. As you read further, you will discover the power of critical questions to activate your intellectual curiosity and inspire you to want to learn more.

About the Author

Renee Hobbs is an internationally recognized authority on digital and media literacy education and the author of numerous books, digital learning platforms, and scholarly publications. As a researcher, teacher, advocate, and media professional, Hobbs has worked to advance the quality of digital and media literacy education in the United States and around the world.

She is the founder and director of the Media Education Lab and a professor of communication studies at the Harrington School of Communication and Media at the University of Rhode Island, where she codirects the Graduate Certificate in Digital Literacy. The Media Education Lab supports an online global community who aim to improve the practice of digital and media literacy education. Learn more: www.mediaeducationlab.com.

PART I

UNDERSTANDING MEDIA

Media literacy can change the way you see and understand the world

1

What Is Media Literacy?

Learning Outcomes

1. Define media literacy
2. Identify reasons why media literacy is important
3. Appreciate the diverse stakeholders who support media literacy
4. Understand the theoretical principles of media literacy
5. Analyze a media text by asking critical questions as a form of intellectual inquiry

Media literacy has sometimes been described as putting on a pair of glasses that changes the way you look at media and the world around you. It has been part of American education for a long time, but the need for media literacy gained increased visibility in 2020, when the coronavirus epidemic led to a rise in misinformation and conspiracy theories about the global public health crisis.

You may have encountered some weird opinions and ideas about the coronavirus. Some scientists told reporters that the coronavirus came to earth from a meteorite that hit the Earth! Others falsely reported that coronavirus was being manufactured by a Chinese pharmaceutical company linked to a Harvard chemistry professor. People shared social media posts that falsely claimed drinking bleach could protect people from the virus. Other posts claimed that Pope Francis had become infected. Many conspiracy theories blamed the government, individuals, or foreign leaders. One false claim even stated that the government charged people $3,000 for a coronavirus test.

Since humans are hardwired to pay attention to conflict and controversy, people can receive social rewards for being alert to impending danger. Such heightened attention can activate emotion and reduce critical thinking skills. Just as with Zika, Ebola, and AIDS, some people intentionally spread false information as a way to gain likes and shares, using the crisis as an opportunity to gain attention. In trying to make sense of chaotic, unpredictable events, conspiracy theories can help people feel like they understand what's happening. "Fake news and conspiracy theories can be seen as a coping mechanism," noted one expert (Turnnidge, 2020). People who share such information don't see themselves as intentionally causing harm. In their minds, they're expressing their emotions and offering a world view that reflects their fundamental sense of mistrust.

In describing her experience as a Chinese immigrant, Celine Tien found herself socially ostracized during the coronavirus epidemic as people acted on harmful stereotypes about Asian people. People did not stop to consider if they were hurting anyone by claiming the virus was bioengineered by Chinese scientists, sharing news about the "weird" food eaten by Chinese people, or identifying the age and race of people with new infections. She wrote, "Sensational reporting and social media were making fear more contagious than the virus itself" (Tien, 2020, SR2).

But whether people intentionally or accidentally spread inaccurate information, it can decrease trust in health professionals and lead people to make truly dangerous choices. For this reason, the World Health Organization (WHO) created the MythBusters website. There you learn that taking Vitamin C is not a cure and drinking boiled garlic water will not protect you. Cold weather and snow do not kill the coronavirus; taking a hot bath does not protect you from it.

Today you are constantly surrounded by media messages that you need to analyze and interpret. In many informal ways through daily conversation with friends, family, and coworkers, you share, discuss, and dispute interpretations of news, information, entertainment, and advertising. The inescapable role of *media culture* in people's lives is one of the reasons why Ernest J. Wilson, Walter Annenberg Chair in Communication and dean of the Annenberg School for Communication and Journalism at the University of Southern California, once described media literacy as "the new humanities" (Wilson, 2010). A media culture is any society where the consumption and production of media is an essential part of daily life, reflecting social power hierarchies and influencing public behaviors, attitudes, tastes, and values.

In this chapter, these questions will be considered:

- How is media literacy defined?
- Why is it considered important?
- How might media literacy affect our media-use habits and the quality of our social relationships?
- How does media literacy promote lifelong learning?
- In what ways can media literacy change society?

Defining Media Literacy

Media literacy can be defined as the ever-changing set of knowledge, skills, and habits of mind required for full participation in a contemporary media-saturated society. The most widely accepted definition of media literacy is "the ability to access, analyze, evaluate and create messages in a wide variety of forms" (Aufderheide, 1993). In fact, because media change so fast, media literacy is a lifelong process, not a static set of knowledge and skills. As communications media and technologies change, media literacy also changes.

People who are media literate have a heightened awareness of media and technologies that they apply in the context of their everyday life. Certain types of experiences may cause or enable people to shift their perspective on the media environment, to gain critical distance from it in order to really "see" it. You may already have noticed how your ordinary behavior has adapted in many subtle ways as a result of your everyday uses of the mobile phone. For example, researchers have found that the typical cell phone user checks his or her phone 52 times a day. It is the preferred device for reading news, checking in with friends, watching short videos, taking photos, and even banking. Two-thirds of Americans use the voice-assistant function (Deloitte, 2018). You may or may not have noticed how your interactions with your phone have changed over time. Because these changes in behavior happen gradually, you might not notice how they affect your social relationships, cultural and leisure activities, and intellectual life.

That's why heightened awareness is a key feature of media literacy. In the 1960s, Canadian scholar Marshall McLuhan developed a hypothesis to suggest that increased awareness of media might help people act more humanely. He believed that the ability to recognize what is gained and what is lost through the use of media technologies enables people to make selective, strategic use of it. Noticing how humans adapt to media environments and adjust behaviors in relationship to the available devices around us, McLuhan observed, "We shape our tools and then our tools shape us" (Culkin, 1967).

Perhaps you have noticed that this book's subtitle is "Questioning the Media." In this book, media literacy is treated as a learn-ing process that involves inquiry. Asking questions is the most direct and powerful form of informal learning that humans have for making sense of the social world. When inquiry is occurring, you will notice these features: first, questions drive the learning process. Intellectual curiosity is activated. Inquiry enables learners to have control over what they learn. They may choose to develop expertise in topics that align with their personal interests and passions or they may discover new areas of interest that they were previously unfamiliar with. As a reader of this book, you are encouraged to conduct independent exploration of the topics introduced.

Do you share or discuss how you use your cell phone with other people in your life? Why or why not?

Media literacy includes these learning processes:

Accessing. Locating and selecting appropriate and relevant content, ideas, and information, and accurately comprehending messages;

Analyzing. Using critical thinking to analyze the purpose, target audience, quality, veracity, credibility, point of view, and potential effects or consequences of messages;

Creating. Composing or generating media content using creativity and confidence in self-expression, with awareness of purpose, audience, genre, form, and composition techniques;

Reflecting. Considering the impact of media and technology on our thinking and actions in daily life and applying social responsibility and ethical principles to our own identity, communication behavior, and conduct;

Taking action. Working individually and collaboratively to share knowledge and solve problems in the family, the workplace, and the community, and participating as a member of a community at local, regional, national, and international levels (Hobbs, 2010).

When media literacy education occurs in schools, the teacher does not generally accept a single statement as an answer to a question; student-to-student interaction is valued and teachers usually avoid acting as a mediator, arbiter, or judge. Lessons develop from the responses of students and not from a previously determined "logical" structure (Postman &

Weingartner, 1969). The inquiry cycle is thus a spiral where asking questions leads to analysis and interpretation of ideas and information. When students share what they are learning by creating media, this authorship practice helps advance reflection and builds confidence about taking action in the community. This then leads back to better questions and the cycle continues again. This spiral is at the heart of authentic lifelong learning and it is never-ending throughout life.

In another type of spiral, the humanities also link the past, present, and future. Media literacy invites learners to explore the complexity of the human experience as it is represented through symbols in a variety of forms. People have long used language, literature, religion, art, music, and history to understand and record our world. For 2,500 years, people have been debating whether new forms of media emancipate or control people. This important debate began with the transition from oral to written culture. When technological innovation brought print media to mass audiences, people wondered and worried about the potential consequences of a world full of readers. In the early 20th century, as film became a highly popular form of entertainment, critics were not sure whether it would be used as a tool for liberation or oppression. Films did more than entertain, of course; they conveyed values and ideologies about living "the good life."

Each generation, it seems, struggles to make sense of rapid changes in the media and technology ecosystem. During the middle of the 20th century, with the rise of television as a dominant form of mass media, renewed interest in helping people critically analyze and create media began to grow. It seemed at the time that exploring the relationship between language, images, and other symbol systems could shed insight on perception, cognition, and the art of interpretation. In the 1990s, your parents faced the rise of the 500-channel universe, growing competition between news media organizations, and the commercialization of the Internet. To make sense of it all, they needed to understand the business of media. Today, your generation must come to terms with Instagram influencers, video game streamers, so-called fake news, the rise of a surveillance society, and much more. Media literacy can help you be prepared for an unknowable future.

Life in a Media-Saturated Society

People have many choices, and their use of media and technology is becoming more and more effortless. Virtual reality, podcasting, social media, memes and other forms of digital culture bring potential opportunities and risks, as algorithms, disinformation, propaganda, artificial intelligence and machine learning become key features of our everyday media experience.

In part, because there is a proliferation of print, visual, audio, and digital media content to choose from, people easily recognize that content is not the only feature that matters. Media messages come in a wide variety of forms and formats. For example, a novel is a form of entertainment that encourages a particular way of telling a story; certain kinds of cultural expressions can occur in a novel that are not possible in an infographic or a social media post. Each form of expression and communication has its own characteristic strengths and limitations. For this reason, people benefit from gaining knowledge about various genres, forms, and formats. News, advertising, film, television, the Internet, and social media all make use of highly specialized genres that help audiences understand and interpret the author's intended purpose and meaning.

Because media interact with nature and culture to shape society, it is important to understand how media and communication affect human perception, understanding, feeling, and values. Media organizations interact with social institutions, including the family, school, workplace, marketplace, and public square. Media also influence other social institutions, including law enforcement, politics, and the economy. It is important to understand how digital tools and technologies themselves (not just the content they deliver) shape many aspects of our day-to-day lives, attitudes, and social interactions. For this reason, media literacy is aligned with the study of media as an environment: this is sometimes called *media ecology.*

Today, people often select media experiences based on their interests and their need to be part of a community. Niche communities may enable people to enjoy media "alone together"—participating in social networks of fandom. In 2018, for example, 330 million people used Reddit in more than 150,000 active communities where people share opinions, ideas, and information on a wide range of topics in often playful ways (Smith, 2018). People's access to media is now shaped more by the people in their social networks than by professional editors or producers. The 20% of Facebook users who have more than 500 friends receive a river of content just from what people post and share online each day.

New voices and points of view continue to emerge in the contemporary media landscape. Ryan Kaji has not yet had his 10th birthday but his unboxing videos at "Ryan's World" have made him the highest-earning YouTuber in 2020, with $26 million in income from digital advertising, sponsored content, and merchandising tie-ins (Suciu, 2020). Many of his fans comment and respond to each of his videos, and some people may even enjoy reading the comments as much as watching the videos. As people make choices about what kinds of media to use, they participate in different types of cultural conversations. Because people have a continually increasing set of choices available, media literacy education aims to be relevant to people's lived experience.

A Practice of Lifelong Learning

As a form of everyday learning that connects the classroom to the living room, media literacy education can inspire people to be intellectually curious in engaging with the people and ideas they encounter throughout life. When people have media literacy competencies, they can recognize the biased information that surrounds them. Media literacy advances your

Consider the Question

What does the term *media literacy* mean to you and why it is important in your life? How might your media literacy competencies affect your social relationships, your family life, your work and career, and your responsibilities as a citizen?

sense of *autonomy* and brings a deeper appreciation for quality media. Autonomy is a major part of being media literate: it means you can think for yourself, without having to be dependent upon the interpretations and opinions of others.

You may have been exposed to media literacy education when you were younger. Perhaps you remember learning to evaluate sources by determining factors associated with credibility. Or perhaps a teacher used a film analysis activity where you learned to recognize the grammar of film. Your science teacher may have shown you how to analyze science news in the newspaper in order to judge whether the study was quality or junk. Or perhaps you created a blog to post your responses to literature, or been assigned to create a video, infographic, or animation project. When students get opportunities to analyze, create, and produce media, they develop confidence in self-expression.

Why do students benefit from opportunities to collaborate, analyze, and create media?

As you read this book, you will encounter some of the pedagogical practices of media literacy, including close analysis of media texts, cross-media comparison, keeping a media diary, and *multimedia composition*. Instructional practices like these help learners build awareness of the constructedness of the media and technology environment and help people deploy questioning strategies that can be useful throughout life.

Project-based learning is an important instructional practice for the development of media literacy competencies. When students make media, they take responsibility for their own learning. Some instructors feel this is a better way to measure growth in learning than traditional assessment measures like tests.

When students activate intellectual curiosity while responding to a YouTube video, a news story in *The New York Times*, an ad, or a social media post, they ask "how" and "why" questions to interpret messages. They use search strategies to gather additional information and gain context on an unfamiliar topic. They compare and contrast evidence and take note of omissions to recognize a message's point of view. Then, they create media to demonstrate what they have discovered and learned. They reflect on the work they created and consider intended and unintended consequences of their efforts. This work is often so compelling that, when published, it finds an authentic audience so that others can benefit from it.

For the most part, educators advocate for, implement, and develop media literacy programs based on their own interests and motivations for media literacy. Learners also may benefit from this flexibility. For example, one student may focus on the genre of hip-hop while another may examine the mathematics of *Minecraft*. Still another may concentrate on the history of romance novels or study the current business models for photojournalists. Other students may examine how the Internet can support local small businesses or learn how people can protect themselves from malware and scams.

What topics and issues activate your most engaged and focused attention?

Skynesher/iStock

This book, rooted as it is in asking questions about media, helps you, as a learner, to generate questions and explore answers. Because media are so diverse, media literacy education may include focus on the Internet, advertising, news, music, sports, or entertainment media. Critical analysis of media is generally paired with some form of production activity, including blogging, vlogging, podcasting, or video production.

An Expanded Form of Literacy

Media literacy involves asking critical questions about what you see, watch, listen to, and read. Because media literacy focuses on interpretation, questioning, and creative expression, some people see it as an expanded conceptualization of literacy. Literacy is generally understood as reading, writing, speaking, and listening. but in this book, *literacy* is defined more broadly, as the sharing of meaning through symbols. Concepts like *author*, *text*, *audience*, *message*, *meaning*, and *representation* help people analyze all forms of expression and communication, not just the printed word.

A number of related terms tap into the powerful concept of literacy. The diversity of these terms has emerged because of the range of people, academic disciplines, and knowledge communities who have come to see the value of new competencies for navigating the media-saturated society of the 21st century. Related terms include:

Visual literacy: the competencies required to understand and create photography, images, and graphic design;

Information literacy: the competencies needed to search for, find, and evaluate the quality of information sources;

News literacy: the acquisition of critical-thinking skills for analyzing and judging the reliability of news and information;

Digital literacy: the skills, habits of mind, and competencies required for active participation in the use of the Internet and social media;

Data literacy: the knowledge and competencies associated with understanding, using, critically analyzing, and working with data in all its many forms.

In this book, you will find elements of all of these approaches. As the sharing of meaning through symbols, literacy is expanding because it involves making sense of and using medium-specific features, a growing number of which are digital in nature. For example, the skills and competencies of reading and writing in print are not the same as the skills of viewing or creating a video documentary. But editing a print document and editing a video documentary both involve reading, analysis, organization, and strategic thinking.

You understand this intuitively, of course, if you have ever noticed how the process of reading from a mobile phone is different than reading from a laptop screen, which is different from reading from a printed page. Each form of media places different expectations upon the reader, viewer, listener, or user. Figure 1.1 shows some of the broad, general competencies, habits of mind, and skills of digital and media literacy. These are some of the competencies that you will activate by reading this book and completing the suggested learning activities.

Today, the competencies of print and online reading and writing are perhaps more important than ever before. In the context of information-age, technology-intensive jobs, high levels of reading comprehension and good writing skills help you advance in your career.

Reading and writing are an important part of home and family life, as people read and respond to social media and interact with family and friends using informal literacy practices. Because social media tools and platforms have enabled group collaboration and community dialogue, we use writing and reading practices in the context of our family and social relationships. For example, when you text with friends and relatives, you are using practices of writing and reading. You create media when you create profiles, strategically authoring your online identities, making decisions about how to represent yourself using images, language, sound, and multimedia.

For these reasons, it is easy to see that media literacy is an expanded conceptualization of literacy. The concept of *text* is similarly evolving to mean all the ways we share meaning via symbols. With choices of expression including words, images, gifs, emojis, digital voice, and more, literacy is no longer confined to the domain of printed language. Although print-based text is in no way endangered, it now "interacts with digital

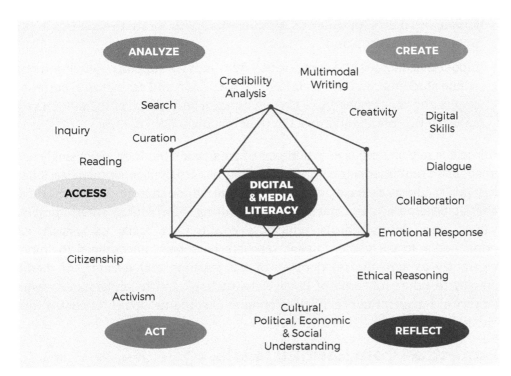

Figure 1.1
Some Digital and
Media Literacy
Competencies

technologies and multimodality to create more complex texts" (Carrington & Robinson, 2009: 5).

Organizations including the National Council of Teachers of English (NCTE) have long understood media literacy as a part of literacy education. In 2019, the NCTE issued a resolution on critical literacy in politics and media, calling for educators to promote pedagogy and scholarly curricula in English and related subjects that instruct students in analyzing and evaluating "sophisticated persuasive techniques in all texts, genres, and types of media, current and yet to be imagined." They also urge members to:

- support classroom practices that examine and question uses of language in order to discern inhumane, misinformative, or dishonest discourse and arguments;

- prioritize research and pedagogies that encourage students to become critical thinkers, consumers, and creators who advocate for and actively contribute to a better world;

- provide resources to mitigate the effect of new technologies and platforms that accelerate and destabilize our information environment;

- support the integration of reliable, balanced, and credible news sources within classroom practices at all levels of education;

- resist attempts to influence civic discussion through falsehoods, unwarranted doubts, prejudicial or stereotypical ideas, attempts to shame or silence, or other techniques that deteriorate the quality of public deliberation; and

- model civic literacy and conversation by creating a supportive environment where students can have an informed discussion and engage with current events and civic issues while staying mindful and critical of the difference between the intent and impact of their language. (NCTE, 2019)

Politicians rely on language as a means of persuasion but they increasingly use images and multimedia to communicate key ideas to their constituencies. Since the 1970s, educators have acknowledged that although nonprint media have already become a major means of transmitting information, entertainment, values, and cultural ideals, educators continue to focus exclusively on print media. In particular, English teachers have been encouraged to "more vigorously explore the relationship of the learning and teaching of media literacy to other concerns of English instruction" and to understand media literacy as it may influence the development of students' ability "to control and direct their own lives" (NCTE, 1970).

Protection from Harmful Media

Media literacy has been examined as an intervention to address some of the problems caused by media content or media use, and this approach to media literacy has been called *protectionism*. When their children are young, many parents provide informal media literacy learning experiences in the home by selecting programs that embody good values, or by setting limits on the amount of time that their children use media. Other parents may comment on specific aspects of problematic content like violence, bad language, or gender stereotypes, modeling for their children the practice of "talking back to media."

Media literacy has been shown to offer a type of protection, according to researchers who have studied this topic from different points of view. Both media effects researchers and those working in the cultural studies tradition of media studies have adopted the idea that media literacy may provide immunity from the harms and dangers associated with media culture.

Researchers who study *media effects* examine the impact of media on attitudes, beliefs, and behaviors. Social science researchers from the disciplines of psychology, communication, and public health have conducted a number of empirical investigations of media literacy interventions, and many of these demonstrate meaningful effects on targeted attitudes and behavior. For example, some researchers have explored how media literacy education may help people make decisions about the use of dietary supplements and other performance- and appearance-enhancing substances, including those that athletes use as a form of illegal doping. In one study, researchers developed a school-based program where, through dialogue, students talked with communication experts who discussed how media messages can promote dysfunctional beliefs about sports and body image. They met with pharmacology experts, who described the side effects of dietary supplements and other substances, including a focus on the persuasive misinformation offered on television and through social media. Dialogue with athletes and sports psychologists focused on exploring the moral and ethical implications of doping substances use and offered a set of mental strategies to counteract temptations toward doping use. As part of this work, students created anti-doping public service media messages to demonstrate their understanding of key ideas. Over 6 months, this health media literacy program contributed to attitude changes in students' views of illegal doping and even led to decreased self-reported use of legal dietary supplements (Lucidi et al., 2017). Other important work has shown the value of media literacy in addressing issues like nutrition, sexual behavior, aggressive behavior, underage drinking, tobacco and drug use, and other topics (Kistler, Kallman & Austin, 2017).

Why might media literacy offer a form of protection against potentially harmful media messages? Researchers who have gathered data have observed that some types of audiences are particularly vulnerable to negative media messages because they develop *expectations* about reality from what they see, watch, and read in the media. Rooted in social psychology, this idea is sometimes called *expectancy theory*. In thinking about how media literacy serves as a form of protection, the reasoning goes like this: people form expectations about reality based on real-life and media experiences. If people have more awareness of their media choices, more knowledge about how media are constructed, and a sense of control over their interpretations, they are less likely to see media representations as useful for forming expectations about real life (Pinkleton et al., 2012). This shift in thinking can minimize the potentially negative consequences of media violence, sexual depictions, cyberbullying, stereotyping, or the lures of consumer culture.

Are you desensitized to violence? Why or why not ❓

For these reasons, media literacy is associated with increased *resilience* of children and youth, which is a key factor in health and human development. Media literacy has proven effective in a wide variety of contexts and learning environments. Some programs may consist of only one or two short sessions, and other programs are a semester or longer in length. Some focus on one issue (violence, advertising, alcohol) while others address many different topics (Martens, 2010). For example, researchers have found that:

Get Milked

- Adolescents with higher levels of media literacy show lower levels of smoking behavior and intent to smoke;
- Children's fears about terrorism can be reduced by having parents attend a media literacy program to learn about how news is constructed;
- College students can recognize and resist the "thin ideal" presented in the depiction of women's bodies in movies, magazines, and media;
- People can recognize and critique racial, gender, and occupational stereotypes;
- Teens can create anti-tobacco campaigns to discourage the use of tobacco or alcohol.

In such work, researchers have found that media literacy minimizes the potential harms of media usage and exposure. In a comprehensive meta-analytic assessment of 51 studies of media literacy interventions, Jeong, Cho, and Hwang (2012) discovered a substantial overall effect size of media literacy interventions on outcomes including media knowledge, criticism, perceived realism, influence, behavioral beliefs, attitudes, self-efficacy, and behavior. Media literacy interventions can have a significant impact on knowledge, attitudes, and behaviors. Researchers have observed that the magnitude of intervention effects does not vary much by agent, target age, setting, audience involvement, topic, or country. As a result, media literacy education appears to be effective with a variety of different types of people on a wide range of issues.

Despite this evidence, some scholars reject the idea of media literacy as a form of protection. Debates about the relative value of media literacy have been vigorously discussed for more than 20 years (Hobbs, 1998). Critics who dislike the idea of media literacy as protection think it implies that, without media literacy, people are deficient, helpless, or incapable. But advocates say that media literacy education is a form of positive protection that can help address people's natural human tendencies to actively imitate and uncritically accept the behaviors and values presented in mass media and popular culture.

Advancing Citizenship in a Democracy

Some people examine how media literacy education embodies the practice of citizenship, and the concept of the *active audience* is central to this argument. In the *American cultural studies* tradition, audiences are conceptualized as engaged in the creative and active work of making meaning. Rather than see users as vulnerable victims, the active audience theory perceives viewers, readers, and media consumers as making choices and constructing interpretations that meet their needs.

The study of highly engaged audiences, including fans, has been critical to the development of this line of argument. Some scholars even suggest that media fans are a perfect model of an active audience. Because fans interpret, comment, critique, and create media to represent their relationship with their favorite media (whether that be *Harry Potter*, *Game of Thrones*, or the *Star Wars* franchise), they participate in the collaborative creation of culture.

Some people consider media literacy a type of advocacy or social movement. *Social movements* arise in response to changing social norms and values as a form of political participation where people engage in a sustained public effort to make social change, using communicative action to raise awareness, build strategic alliances, and, ultimately, to challenge and reform some aspect of contemporary culture.

Those who see media literacy as a social movement are generally motivated by a belief that changes in audience behavior can bring about larger changes in the media industry—and in society overall. The argument goes like this: if people have better skills at distinguishing fact from opinion, they may come to prefer high-quality journalism. If people learn to recognize elements of cinematic art, perhaps they will come to appreciate independent films. This approach is sometimes conceptualized as *demand-focused media literacy*, and it is rooted in the idea that developing media literacy competences will improve or raise consumers' expectations for media products.

The idea of media literacy as a form of *empowerment* is embodied in the belief that culture is produced by ordinary people, not just from powerful institutions like mass media. Both the rise of user-generated content and the use of digital platforms for creating and sharing ideas have validated this approach (Bulger & Davison, 2018). As a form of empowerment, educators engage learners by asking them to respond to popular culture, including blogging, message boards, and video production. The engagement that results from interest-driven learning promotes lifelong learning skills in youth from a variety of ethnic and cultural backgrounds (Ito et al., 2013).

Another important form of empowerment is civic and political participation. Exposure to media literacy education may help people be more motivated to seek out information on relevant social, cultural, and political issues. Paul Mihailidis, in his book *Civic Media Literacies*, notes how, as people are increasingly beholden to the algorithms of their smartphone technologies, it has become harder to engage in meaningful community dialogue (Mihailidis, 2018b). He shows how media literacy learning experiences can cultivate care, imagination, critical consciousness, persistence, and a liberating sense of freedom. As people gain skills to evaluate the quality of available information, and as they engage in dialogue with others to form coalitions, they shift away from the spectator position. Some may even become empowered as activists themselves, using the power of information and communication to make a difference in the world.

How are values and points of view embedded in the images you create ❓

Media literacy has proved a useful lens for promoting dialogue about many current social, economic, and political challenges, including climate change, immigration, and the rise of populism, xenophobia, and nationalism (Ranieri, 2016). Media literacy educational initiatives also create opportunities for cross-national dialogue. For example, the Mind Over Media digital learning platform enables high school and college students to view and discuss propaganda from around the world. (Hobbs, 2020). Educational programs like the Salzburg Academy on Media and Global Change offer summer learning opportunities to undergraduate and graduate students and faculty from multiple countries (Mihailidis, 2018a). UNESCO has developed a global teacher education program, the Media and Information Literacy Curriculum for Teachers, designed to support member states in their continuing work to advance media and information literacy.

Research has shown that media literacy education is effective in supporting the habits of mind associated with citizenship in democratic societies. In one study, researchers found that nearly half of high school students from 21 high schools in California had previously engaged in various classroom activities designed to support media literacy competencies, including critically analyzing the trustworthiness of websites, using the Internet to get information about political or social issues, and creating content for the Web. Young people who had media literacy education in school had higher rates of politically driven online activities (Kahne, Lee & Feezell, 2012). Other research has shown that students with media literacy education are better at critically analyzing media messages aligned with their existing beliefs. Most people uncritically accept messages that reinforce what they already believe. But a quasi-experimental design study with a large sample of California youth, those with greater levels of exposure to media literacy education outperformed others in their ability to recognize the bias embedded in a political media message that aligned with their preexisting beliefs (Kahne & Bowyer, 2017). Clearly, when people acquire media literacy competencies, they are better prepared to revise or change their opinions as they gain new knowledge.

The National Association for Media Literacy Education (NAMLE) in the United States is the largest membership organization for media literacy in the world, and it engages in advocacy to raise awareness of the importance of media literacy by hosting "Media Literacy Week" each November. Other organizations show their support for media literacy by aligning their efforts. For example, the Girl Scouts have long included media literacy as a part of its education program, even creating a Truth Seeker Badge as part of its media literacy advocacy efforts. To earn the badge, girls learn to judge sources on credibility, accuracy, reasonableness, and support for claims. Activities help them evaluate sources, investigate what experts say, be a wise consumer, find truth in everyday life, and become a citizen journalist.

In a number of U.S. states, concerned citizens have lobbied their state governments for laws that support media literacy, putting pressure on state departments of education and local school districts to enable media literacy education to reach more learners. In the State of Washington, legislation passed in 2016 that required the state school board to convene an advisory group to identify successful practices and to recommend media literacy and digital citizenship improvements statewide. They made recommendations including revisions to district policies to better support digital citizenship, media literacy, and Internet safety in schools and improving the capacity of school librarians to lead digital citizenship and media literacy programs across all grades and content areas.

Members of Congress have also been involved in advocating for media literacy. In 2019, the Digital Citizenship and Media Literacy Act was introduced in the Senate, which would authorize $20 million for media literacy initiatives in elementary and secondary schools. The initiative was inspired by concerns about the continuing threat of Russian disinformation and election interference. At other points in time, politicians have talked about the value of media literacy as a solution to different types of social crises. However, at the present time, no federal law provides fiscal support for media literacy education in the United States. Each community or school must pay for media literacy initiatives using existing resources.

Some media organizations have taken leadership roles in bringing media literacy programs into schools and communities. The New York Times Learning Network offers lesson plans, videos, and other resources to help students develop media literacy competencies in responding to news and current events. A public broadcasting station in San Francisco, KQED, offers a variety of media literacy workshops and programs, including a certification program for educators. Former journalists created the News Literacy Project to develop curriculum resources and offer school-based programs.

Hundreds of other nonprofit organizations work to advance media literacy education in the United States, helping to increase visibility and inspire social action.

A large number of university–school partnerships have developed that involve undergraduate students bringing media literacy learning experiences to younger children in local schools. At Johns Hopkins University, Julian Owens created a six-lesson curriculum rooted in hip-hop music and culture for Baltimore teens, teaching them to deconstruct music by collaborating, communicating, reading closely, thinking critically, conducting research, and taking useful notes while listening (Owens & Smith, 2016). As a culturally relevant approach to address education disparities and improve educational engagement among young people who have not

TO CREATE **A BRIGHT FUTURE**, WE NEED **HARDWARE** AND WE NEED **SOFTWARE**

BUT WE ALSO NEED **MORALWARE.**

MIL strengthens your moral compass online and offline.

#MILCLICKS

UNESCO MIL CLICKS

Why might media literacy strengthen your "moral compass" online and offline❓

experienced success in traditional academic programs, programs like this can be understood as a form of social activism for media literacy.

Some activists see media literacy as a fundamental human right (O'Neill, 2010). Access to quality media and information content and participation in media and communication networks are necessary to realize Article 19 of the Universal Declaration of Human Rights regarding the right to freedom of opinion and expression (UNESCO, 2013). Working under the auspices of UNESCO, organizations like Global Forum for Partnerships on Media and Information Literacy (GAPMIL) involve representatives from more than 80 countries, developing concrete partnerships to drive global media literacy development and impact. In higher education institutions around the world, media literacy is seen as a transdisciplinary area of study that includes scholars with expertise in communication and media studies, education, public health, and human development, as well as the social sciences, arts, and humanities.

In Europe, the need for media literacy is recognized through activism and engagement in both the government and the nongovernmental or civil society sectors. For example, the British government has mandated media literacy as a provision for all the people of the United Kingdom through its important *media reform* of regulations and policies. OFCOM is the name of the agency that regulates the post office, radio, television, and broadband services. The agency has developed an evidence base to measure the use of electronic media among children and adults.

Recognizing the increased competitive environment of the audiovisual sector that results from an inclusive knowledge society, the Council of Europe has noted that the education system must better support people's ability to access, understand, evaluate, create, and communicate media content as part of lifelong learning. In Europe, the inclusion of media literacy within the Audiovisual Media Services Directive at the European Commission has made it more visible in the 27 nations of the European Union. Media literacy is framed within a regulatory policy designed to safeguard the public interest and promote cultural diversity, the right to information, and the importance of media pluralism, including consumer protection, as well as the protection of minors and other vulnerable audiences. But critics note that some approaches to media literacy emphasize the ethical responsibilities of the individual media consumer without focus on the institutional structures that maintain the status quo.

A Critique of Institutional and Social Power

We tend to take for granted that media will focus on the sensational yet troubled lifestyles of the rich and famous. Media vividly represent stories about crime, violence, and law enforcement because these stories can be exciting and dramatic. Some narratives address the genuine delights of ordinary daily life, including relationships, careers, and family matters. Other stories focus on the many challenges they face, such as unemployment, mental health problems, poverty, addiction, and more.

Media shape our understanding of reality. It is a profound form of social power. After all, we have only three ways of understanding the world: we learn from direct experience; we learn from listening to and observing others; and we learn from media representations.

Because your life experience is inevitably limited, you rely on media for an understanding of the world. The term *representation* captures this idea, examining how books, television shows, movies, video games, music, and social media represent lived experience. This is why some scholars point out that media institutions shape social reality.

To examine this form of social power, you can look for gaps between the media representation and the more complex reality. This practice may reveal how patterns of storytelling and news coverage can distort people's understanding of real events, situations, and people.

For example, take the case of the Flint water crisis, where Michigan residents pay $200 per month for access to water for drinking, bathing, and cooking. When city officials switched the source of drinking water in 2014, the water was treated improperly, causing lead from the pipes to leach into the water supply, leading to extremely elevated levels of this poisonous substance that damages the brain. A research study examining press coverage of the case found that reporters covering the crisis trusted city officials more than local residents. People complained about the color and taste of the water. Local authorities said the water was safe. For a long time, the news media ignored the story of how the people of Flint, who were largely poor and African American, took proactive political steps to address the water problem in their community. Researchers explain that "Newspapers and networks missed the many months of people showing up at city hall and meetings to complain about the water and the rashes and illnesses. The media missed a story about citizen action that cut across racial and class lines" (Jackson, 2017).

Some were surprised when the topic of Flint's water crisis was raised again in 2018, when comedian Michelle Wolf ended her comedy performance at the White House Correspondents' Association dinner on a serious note, reminding reporters, "Flint still doesn't have clean water." It was intended to shame and stun the members of the press by reminding them of their inattention and lack of vigilance on issues of public concern. Wolf was calling attention to *structural (or systemic) racism*, the complex system by which racism is developed, maintained and protected. It involves institutional practices, cultural representations and other social norms that work to reinforce racial inequities. In all the hype about presidential politics, had members of the press forgotten their social obligation to keep an eye on abuses of power that hurt ordinary citizens? People who are media literate try to notice those topics and stories that do not get media attention of contemporary journalism. By studying media representations, people come to recognize that all media messages are selective and incomplete.

But issues of representation are not limited to news and journalism. Advertising and entertainment present us with a stream of stereotypes and depictions of people, events, and experiences that shape our understanding of the world. Are snipers as ruthless as they appear in Hollywood movies? Are Wall Street executives as low-class, sneaky, and manipulative as they look in TV shows? Are British people as obsessed by the royal family as it seems from watching entertainment news shows like *Access*, *Extra*, and *The Insider*? Sometimes, without us even being aware of it, media representations have a significant role in shaping our expectations about people, events, and ideas.

We may look around at the many choices of media content available to us as consumers and think that people have access to diverse messages, but that may be an illusion. Studying media industries in the 1970s, Herbert Schiller recognized that media companies were major profit centers for American industry. He wrote about how U.S. media corporations were dominating business and cultural life around the world, especially in developing nations (Schiller, 1976). Ben Bagdikian describes the rise of media conglomerates, arguing that a "private ministry of information" emerged as a concentration of ownership narrowed the range of ideas available to the public (Bagdikian et al, 2004).

Have you ever participated in a public protest? Why or why not?

Jim West/Alamy Stock Photo

The role of media conglomerates may be beneficial or harmful to consumers, and we explore that more fully in Chapter 10, but one thing is certain: media ownership shapes the kinds of ideas expressed in publishing, movies, television shows, and music. Have you ever noticed how many websites target men and women as separate groups? Because media companies rely on financing from Wall Street banks and investment firms, they must embrace capitalism and consumer culture, where established and traditional ideas about gender targeting is an expected norm.

Researchers and scholars working in the *cultural studies* tradition value media literacy as a means to inform the public about the institutions that control the creation and dissemination of media messages. By gaining deeper levels of knowledge about media organizations and media economics, people can better understand the *culture industry*, to examine how economic and political factors shape information and ideas.

Critics of institutional power note that the culture industries create media messages that inevitably reproduce power relations in favor of those who have economic control. Audiences find the products of the culture industry (social media platforms, movies, music, and the like) both irresistible and inescapable. After all, they have been carefully designed to keep users engaged. But media products may also alienate the masses from the means of production of their own culture and suppress critical thinking on the part of the audience by producing spectacles that make no demands on the viewer beyond mere attention.

Guy Debord voices his concern that *spectacle* has replaced lived experience in his 1967 book *The Society of the Spectacle*, which is a call to arms against passive spectatorship. As images and sensations replace genuine human interaction, Debord observes, media messages define for people what they should need and want in order to feel fulfilled in life. Debord recognizes that the nature of the spectacle is hard to define, as it constantly shifts from moment to moment. He notes the rise of *appearance* as a central human value and fears its development into an ideology similar to religion in shaping people's understanding of "the good life" (Debord, 1967/1995).

Even when audiences see through the spectacle, Debord contends, people may still like the pleasures of feeling superior to the slick appeal of mass media and popular culture. After all, recognizing media spectacles as superficial and trivial makes people feel smart. Todd Gitlin states, "Collectively, we are in thrall to media—because they deliver to us many of the psychic goods we crave, and we know no other way to live" (Thompson, 2003).

Indeed, people experience deep pleasure in consuming media. But critical theorists sometimes scorn this pleasure, positing that it produces a *false consciousness* in the mass audience, causing oppressed groups to be unaware of the reasons for their oppression. While the pleasure of consuming media can be intense, people also may simultaneously experience resentment and anxiety when considering the many variations of depravity, triviality, and inhumanity that are depicted in ordinary forms of media entertainment. As we will see in Chapter 13, as pornographic content enters into mainstream public life, it may shape how people understand human sexuality as a feature of personal and social identity.

Other critiques of institutional power address the pervasive sexism, racism, and misogyny in mass media culture. Media literacy educators want to help learners discover how to recognize and resist the many distorted representations they encounter in advertising, news, and entertainment. In *Reading in a Participatory Culture*, Jenkins and Kelley recognize the value of examining media representations as a means to "embrace those changes that deepen and enrich human consciousness and push back on those that trivialize and distract" (Jenkins & Kelley, 2013: 17). Through analyzing media representations, people not only resist them; they can also transform them so that they more truly reflect our diverse society.

A Theoretical Framework for Media Literacy

Certain key ideas can help people of all ages develop media literacy competencies. To help people internalize the inquiry process, key ideas have emerged from decades of multidisciplinary scholarship in the

How does social media content represent reality? How might it reinforce or disrupt the institutional power of mass media?

humanities and social sciences. The theoretical framework presented in this book incorporates ideas from five major fields of inquiry: *aesthetics*, a branch of philosophy that explores the nature of art, beauty, and taste; *semiotics*, the study of signs, symbols, and meaning-making; *sociology*, the study of the structure and function of human society; *psychology*, the study of the human mind and human behavior; and *political economy*, the study of how media and technology goods and services are enabled through law, business, and government.

As a result of the growth of the field of media and communication and the rise of hyperspecialization, scholars and researchers have developed expertise that may focus on just some of these big ideas. The field of media studies uses categories developed in the mid-20th century, organizing scholarship with terms like health communication, visual or political communication, public relations, news, and journalism. Within these specialty areas, researchers may spend a lifetime focusing on just one of the media literacy concepts described in the pages that follow. For example, a researcher may specialize in the political economy of video games or the effects of advertising on children. Specialization is how new knowledge is created. Yet one of the great benefits of media literacy as an approach is its big-picture perspective, which offers ideas that can be practical and useful for consumers, creators, researchers, educators, policymakers, and the business community.

The major concepts of media literacy have been discussed and debated for more than 20 years, and ideas have emerged through transdisciplinary dialogue and discussion. In 2006, several members of the NAMLE board and other media literacy leaders met to draft a framework for thinking about and implementing media literacy education. The group, facilitated by former NAMLE president Faith Rogow, delved into the deep and often delicate discussion among colleagues as to the exact language and terms for communicating to the world what media literacy education means in the United States. The group emerged from this meeting with the Core Principles for Media Literacy Education. The meeting came to be known as the "Queens Meeting" since it took place in Queens, New York. In defining the fundamental practices of media literacy education, these key ideas emerged:

Media Literacy Education
1. Requires active inquiry and critical thinking about the messages we receive and create;
2. Expands the concept of literacy to include all forms of media (i.e., reading and writing);
3. Builds and reinforces skills for learners of all ages. Like print literacy, those skills necessitate integrated, interactive, and repeated practice;
4. Develops informed, reflective, and engaged participants essential for a democratic society;

Intellectual Grandparent:
Neil Postman

When Neil Postman's book *Amusing Ourselves to Death* was published in 1985, television was at the peak of its cultural power. In those pre-Internet days, the growth of the cable television industry gave television viewers a 500-channel universe that kept them glued to the many television sets in their homes. Postman was a professor of education at New York University whose books on teaching, including *Television and the Teaching of English* (1961) and *Teaching as a Subversive Activity* (1969), resonated with a lot of people during the 1960s. Postman was an early advocate for media literacy, believing that all students benefit from opportunities to critically analyze and reflect on the media and popular culture that surround them. Neil Postman contributed the following key ideas to media literacy.

Learning needs to be relevant. Postman worried about traditional approaches to teaching media and communication in higher education that were, in his eyes, "shallow, brittle and even profoundly irrelevant," producing only technological cheerleaders (Postman, 2000). Postman understood the importance of making learning relevant to learners. He had a deep understanding of the need to empower learners to take charge of their own learning. Early in his career, he explained that "there is no way to help a learner to be disciplined, active, and thoroughly engaged" without the learner himself or herself "perceiving a problem to be worth learning" and taking an "active role in determining the process of solution" (Postman & Weingartner, 1969: 71).

Everyone can be an informed media consumer. Postman trusted in the ability of ordinary people to analyze and critique media. Although people sometimes see Postman as having hostile attitudes toward media, he was a pioneer of sorts, developing

5. Recognizes that media are a part of culture and function as agents of socialization;

6. Affirms that people use their individual skills, beliefs, and experiences to construct their own meanings from media messages.

Various scholars around the world have developed *core concepts* to represent their understanding of the big ideas embedded in the practice of media literacy. This book presents 10 fundamental theoretical concepts that shape the process of accessing, analyzing and evaluating, creating, and reflecting on media and technology in society and culture. They have broad application to the social practice of literacy, and they also apply to a wide range of media, from advertising, music, publishing, video games, social media, movies, and more.

In this book, these 10 concepts are grouped into three broad categories called domains: authors and audiences (AA), messages and meanings (MM), and representations and reality (RR). Table 1.1 shows the main theoretical claims of media literacy.

an educational television program that offered college credit in communications as part of the Sunrise Semester in the 1960s. This was one of the earliest distance learning programs in media/communications, and it was produced as a collaboration between WCBS-TV in New York and New York University. This program offered advanced communication studies for many people who would never otherwise have had exposure to higher education.

Like Marshall McLuhan, a Canadian media theorist whose work influenced Postman a great deal, Postman took on a humanist identity that led to a unique approach to teaching media and communication. He believed that people should discuss and debate how media and communication technologies shape the development of rational thought and democratic processes. He stimulated many people to consider how media may influence human capacity for goodness, compassion, and morality.

Media can trivialize the human experience.
Postman was skeptical about the benefits of media and technology that were touted by the media industry. In *Amusing Ourselves to Death*, he argued that television was at its most dangerous when attempting to take on serious subjects, like news, education, religion, and politics (Postman, 1985). As Postman understood it, television alters the meaning of being well informed by promoting sensational and misleading information. Such knowledge leads people to think they know something, but it actually leads them away from knowledge that acknowledges and honors complexity. Postman wrote, "When a population becomes distracted by trivia, when cultural life is redefined as a perpetual round of entertainments, when serious public conversation becomes a form of baby-talk, when, in short, a people become an audience, and their public business a vaudeville act, then a nation finds itself at risk; culture-death is a clear possibility" (Postman, 1985: 156).

If Neil Postman has influenced your thinking about media, you can share a comment on the Grandparents of Media Literacy website at www.grandparentsofmedialiteracy.com.

Authors and Audiences

1: Authors create media for different purposes. Media and communication are tools for self-expression, sharing information, persuasion, and entertainment. People also create media messages for social influence and/or profit.

AUTHORS & AUDIENCES

2: Authors target specific audiences. Authors cannot please everyone: to design effective communication, they mentally visualize a group of individuals with common characteristics, attitudes, or beliefs, targeting that audience with a carefully designed message they hope will grab attention and be perceived as valuable.

3: People interpret messages in relation to the context in which they experience them and the context in which they were produced.

Media messages are dependent on audience members' interpretation of their meaning. When you view old movies, you consider the time period of its production as you interpret it. But you also consider its meaning in the present era. If you have ever been in a large group of people where the whole room laughs together at the jokes in a video standup routine, you appreciate how audiences can have a shared understanding. But ask people in the room about the joke, and you may find that people have different nuances of meaning that occur as they interpret the comedy and apply it to their own lives.

4: Both authors and audiences add value to media messages as part of an economic and political system. Audience attention is a highly valuable commodity. Knowledge about the political, economic, and business contexts of media industries and institutions can improve your understanding of how and why media messages circulate in culture. Those who are identified as authors may (or may not) receive financial compensation for their creative work. The scale and importance of the media industry in a global economy is undeniable. Your media use behaviors have value in the marketplace as both a consumer, creator, and citizen.

Messages and Meanings

5: Production techniques are used to construct messages. The sharing of meaning occurs through the creation and interpretation of symbols. Each genre and form of communication uses different production techniques to attract and hold audience attention. For example, in a photo, the use of color, lighting, distance from the lens, and the position of the subject depicted may all be strategic choices deployed by the photographer. In a film, dialogue, characters, plot, action, and special effects are production elements that help the filmmaker accomplish the purpose of narrative storytelling. In writing, an author uses sentence structure, vocabulary, and narrative devices to develop ideas.

MESSAGES
& MEANINGS

6: The content of media messages contains values, ideology, and specific points of view. Every word choice you make as writer suggests what matters to you, what you value. Your point of view is embedded in the works of art, expression, and communication that you create, even when you attempt to be unbiased and adopt a disinterested, neutral tone.

7: Messages impact people's attitudes and behaviors. Authors invest time and money to create media because they have a particular goal in mind; they know that information, entertainment, and persuasion all have undeniable social influence that affects people in different complex but important ways. Such influence may be an emotional sensation that is momentary and superficial (you laugh, or perhaps you cry) or it may be substantial and life-changing (a film, song, celebrity, or news event that serves as a touchstone for your whole life).

Representations and Realities

REPRESENTATIONS
& REALITIES

8: Messages are selective representations of reality. A famous saying expresses this theoretical idea: "The map is not the territory." This expression, developed by Alfred Korzybski, the founder of general semantics, encourages people to distinguish between symbols and the things that symbols stand in for. This idea celebrates the need for a heightened awareness of the differences between media representations and the realities that we inhabit. Because you depend on media representations for many topics (especially when lacking direct experience of the world), it is easy to confuse the map with the territory.

9: Messages use stereotypes to express ideas and information. Because they are selective and incomplete, messages rely on stereotypes to express ideas and information. Stereotypes are a form of media representation that depicts people, events, and experiences using widely shared but oversimplified ideas. Stereotypes can be harmful because they distort people's understanding of the world around them. Filmmakers and writers may use stereotypes because they provide an effective shorthand for depicting personalities, relationships, events, and experiences quickly. Some creative authors play against the stereotype by creating characters that may seem stereotypical but then break with expectations in interesting ways. Once you recognize stereotypes, you can analyze their rhetorical functions in news, advertising, information, literature, video games, films, and other media.

10: People judge the credibility of media messages using features like authority and authenticity. We value media messages that are credible and trustworthy because they help us develop a more accurate understanding of the world. Trustworthy and believable media messages extend your perception and widen your view of a topic. You may make judgments about whether a message is believable or not without much awareness. When you encounter an Instagram post, you judge it for authenticity, deciding within a few seconds whether filters have been used. You may judge whether or not it has been created by an influencer who has been paid to promote the product. When you see a video that uses facts and statistics that come from reputable sources, you may be more likely to believe it because the message has authority. Authority is established through community norms about what counts as expertise. Understanding how authority and authenticity are expressed in news, advertising, and entertainment can lead to better discernment of the quality and value of media messages.

5 critical questions about *Crash Course*

Media literacy inquiry involves asking critical questions through a process called deconstruction, and it can reveal important insights on both the content and the form of a media message. Each chapter includes a model of the practice of critical analysis, exploring a particular media message using five critical questions of media literacy. At the website www.medialiteracyaction.com you can view the media example described and analyzed here.

In this 10-minute YouTube video from **Crash Course** *entitled "Introduction to Media Literacy," hip-hop critic Jay Smooth offers an introduction to media literacy. Using five critical questions of media literacy, you can analyze this media message to gain insight on its meaning and value.*

Google and the Google logo are registered trademarks of Google LLC. used with permission.

Introduction to Media Literacy: Crash Course Media Literacy #1
146,960 views   👍 6.5K   👎 98   ➔ SHARE   ⊒₊   ...

1. **Who is the author and what is the purpose?** This video is the first in a series produced by Hank Green and John Green, the creators of the famous *Crash Course* video series, a YouTube channel that offers fast-paced summaries of academic subjects on a wide variety of topics. As executive producers, the Greens fund the program and take responsibility for distributing the videos through their YouTube channel, which has nearly 8 million subscribers. This video series features hip-hop critic Jay Smooth as the host, and the program's creators include a producer, director, editor, writer, script editor, educational consultant, and sound designer. All of these people have shaped the content and the unique format of the show. Like all *Crash Course* videos, the purpose of the show is to use a combination of entertainment and information to introduce people to new ideas. In this case, the value of developing media literacy competencies is emphasized. Because the series was launched immediately after the so-called fake news scandal in the fall of 2017, we may assume the producers intended the show to be relevant to contemporary challenges people are experiencing specifically in relation to news and information they receive from social media.

2. **What techniques are used to attract and hold attention?** The video uses verbal humor, animation, and text on screen as three major components for attracting and holding attention. For example, as Jay Smooth gives the definition of media, viewers see the definition written on the screen. As he lists

the many types of media, he includes silly ones like "embarrassing but cute photos of your childhood that you post on Throwback Thursday." As he speaks, we see the words #TBT Childhood Photos on the screen. Throwback Thursday is an Internet phenomenon where, using the hashtag #TBT, people post images of themselves from the past. Interspersing serious and silly examples appeals to the attentive listener who is familiar with Internet culture.

3. **What lifestyles, values, and points of view are depicted?** The video assumes that people are always interacting with mass media and popular culture, and it depicts media literacy as a process of accessing, analyzing, evaluating, and creating media. The video suggests that people might not always engage actively in critical thinking about media. When the video distinguishes between media content and media effects and introduces viewers to the work of British sociologist Stuart Hall, it explains encoding and decoding using an example from a boyfriend and girlfriend who are texting about a dinner date. From this, we get the idea that this show encourages young people to reflect and deepen their understanding of their own uses of media.

4. **How might different people interpret the message?** This video, like all *Crash Course* videos, is heavy on talk, with a fast-paced narration that conveys a lot of content in a brief period of time. At first glance, it might not seem like educational media, but it is. The combination of serious ideas with silly animation might be off-putting to some viewers who are more familiar with public broadcasting's style of educational media. These viewers might not see this video as appropriately "serious." Still others will be enamored with the charm of Jay Smooth, the host of New York City's longest-running hip-hop radio program on WBAI. Many people will delight in the show's references to popular culture, which may make them feel like insiders when they recognize the references. For example, when the idea of being an active interpreter is described, the host says, "You're not just a helpless sponge. [...] [Y]ou have the ability to see what messages are coming at you, and decide whether you want to catch them, pass them, or drop them completely." During this sequence, we see an animated image of a wiggling Pokemon ball. People unfamiliar with Pokemon may not understand the metaphorical use of the image.

5. **What is omitted?** The host admits that the viewers watching this video are probably already media savvy, and he urges them to share what they learn with others. But he does not offer any ideas on practical strategies people can use to help others develop media literacy competencies.

Table 1.1
Media Literacy Theoretical Framework

DOMAINS	CONCEPTS	CLAIMS
Authors and Audiences (AA)	*Author* *Purpose* *Audience* *Usage* *Interpretations* *Context* *Systems*	1. Authors create media messages for different purposes. 2. Authors target specific audiences. 3. People interpret messages in relation to the context in which they experience them and the context in which they were produced. 4. Both authors and audiences add value as part of an economic and political system.
Messages and Meanings (MM)	*Ideas* *Emotions* *Techniques* *Ideology* *Effects*	5. Production techniques are used to construct messages. 6. The content of media messages contain values, ideology, and specific points of view. 7. Messages impact people's attitudes and behaviors.
Representation and Realities (RR)	*Representation* *Stereotypes* *Authority* *Authenticity*	8. Messages are selective representations of reality. 9. Messages use stereotypes to express ideas and information. 10. People judge the credibility of media messages using features like authority and authenticity.

What the future may hold: Media Literacy

Media literacy is constantly evolving as the media environment changes. For example, with the rise of video games as a part of culture, play may become a media literacy competency. Some who advocate for media literacy want people to learn how to code and program as a way to better understand the digital environments we use every day. Others emphasize that media literacy is a fundamental part of learning and education, occurring first at home and then continuing far beyond it.

Some worry that, because media literacy is rooted in asking critical questions about what you see, watch, read, use, and listen to, it will cultivate disbelief and cynicism. Others wonder whether democracy can flourish if people are not active and engaged as critical thinkers. As people become empowered to ask questions and demand answers, their deeper engagement in the political process may present a profound challenge to the status quo establishment. As media literacy education becomes more widespread, its potential influence on social and political processes is yet to be seen.

TIME T🧠 REFLECT

Reflect on one or more of the reasons why media literacy matters to you. Use the video reflection tool Flipgrid to consider these questions as you plan your informal extemporaneous response:

- How is media literacy relevant to your life?
- Which of the different motivations for media literacy make the most sense to you?
- How might people think and talk differently about media as they develop media literacy competencies?
- What unintended consequences might media literacy bring?

As you read this book, you can share your ideas about what you are learning in the Flipgrid Inquiry by contributing a brief oral presentation. You can also view and respond to comments of other people who have offered thoughtful reflections on media literacy. Visit www.medialiteracyaction. com to contribute your ideas.

CREATE T▶ LEARN

Make a Media Literacy Meme

Use what you learned in this chapter and use a simple online meme generator to create a meme that expresses your thoughts and feelings about some of the key ideas of media literacy. Post and share your meme to your social network using the #MLAction hashtag.

Media offer a world of ideas, stories, relationships, and opportunities

Why Are Media Important?

Learning Outcomes

1. Define media and understand how and why they have changed over time
2. Understand how media use is deeply embedded in people's daily lives
3. Appreciate five different reasons why people use media
4. Consider media's role in constructing culture and society
5. Reflect on your own patterns of media use and your reasons for using them

He cannot sing, dance, or act, but he is perhaps one of the most famous people in the world. It has been said that he is rewriting the rules about being a celebrity. He has been called the pied piper of YouTube, and his fans are so absurdly dedicated and loyal that some even hacked into the *Wall Street Journal*'s website after the newspaper wrote a critical news story about him.

He is Felix Kjellberg, also known as PewDiePie, a Swedish man whose 110 million subscribers love his 4,200-plus YouTube videos, most of which show him commenting on memes, talking about Reddit users, playing video games, and being goofy. You may even find his pleasantly confident personality addictive, as he regularly mixes self-assurance with vulnerability in an unpolished way that can be charming—and a little gross—all at the same time. He can be very funny, and he gives attention to YouTubers, gamers, and other up-and-coming talent.

Who is your favorite YouTube personality and what features of their work do you admire most?

But not everyone finds PewDiePie amusing. Some are baffled by the genuine weirdness of his work, which includes frequent profanities. One researcher counts an average of three swear words per minute on his videos, observing that he generally swears to demonstrate his annoyance with his own poor performance as he plays a video game, as a way to connect with and entertain his viewers (Beers Fägersten, 2017).

PewDiePie's offbeat humor and lack of inhibition suggests the very kind of intimacy and informality that people experience in a face-to-face relationship with a close friend. Researchers call this a *parasocial relationship* between a performer and an audience. The term emerged in the context of television, radio, and film, where psychiatrists Horton and Wohl (1956) describe the pleasure people get from feeling connected to media performers and personalities. For YouTube viewers, many of whom watch PewDiePie on their cell phones in the free moments between school, work, and life, his videos offer a continuing relationship that "duplicate the gestures, conversational style, and milieu of an informal face-to-face gathering" (Horton & Wohl, 1956: 216). For many, PewDiePie is simply a hilarious online friend.

A whole genre of YouTube videos now offer the pleasure of watching a video game player comment on his play, recreating the vicarious experience of visiting your trash-talking older cousin. PewDiePie gleefully pushes the boundaries of good taste in ways that delight his fans, who call themselves the Bro Army, which includes a large number of boys and young men ages 13 to 24 (Grossman, 2016). In 2019, he earned $13 million from merchandise and brand sponsorships as game companies pay him to play their games in his videos.

But when the *Wall Street Journal* documented nine instances of PewDiePie making anti-Semitic remarks, it angered fans who believe that their friend Felix does not have a hateful bone in his body. Felix himself said his intent was not to spread hate, and even as he issued his apology video, the sense of connection between him and his audience was evident. It makes for compelling viewing. Indeed, it feels quite raw and electric, and quite a contrast to the faux authenticity of reality television. The rise of YouTubers raises many interesting questions about the dynamic nature of entertainment culture today.

Media are constantly changing and transforming to create novelty that commands audience attention. The pressures of keeping an audience entertained may lead some media authors toward *transgression*, the state of "going too far" beyond accepted social norms and conventions. In this chapter, we set the stage for critically examining all forms of media by asking questions like:

- What are media?
- Why do people use media?
- Why are media changing so fast?
- Why are media considered so important?
- How do media help to change society or reinforce the status quo?

Media: A Definition

What are media? *Media* can be defined as the forms, formats, structures, and interfaces for disseminating symbolic content (Couldry, 2012). Symbols are any mark used to stand for something else. For example, letters of the alphabet represent the sounds that make up words. Photos and videos stand in for the people, events, and situations they represent. When some people hear the word "media," they think of television and movies, but it also includes books, newspapers, magazines, video games, radio, recordings, podcasts, advertising, social media, videos on YouTube, and other content on the Internet.

What are some of the different locations where you use media in your daily life❓

Today, because so much of the symbolic content we use comes via a digital form, the lines are blurring between *mass media* (communication that reaches a larger audience) and *interpersonal communication* (communication focused on maintaining social relationships). As we see with PewDiePie and other online

Drazen_/iStock

celebrities, social media blur the boundaries between the two concepts. You use, create, and share highly customized digital content with friends, family, coworkers, acquaintances, and strangers, and you also read, view, listen to, and use content provided by institutions and corporations.

Media are deeply intertwined with life, and for an increasing number of us, we live *in* media, rather than *with* media (Deuze, 2011). No two people have exactly the same set of attitudes and beliefs about media because our attitudes are based on our experiences, and no two people have had exactly the same kinds of media exposure. For many of us, it is not always easy to notice or appreciate the profoundly individualized role media play in our everyday lives. Media use is *ubiquitous*. It surrounds us and is present and available to us for most of our waking hours.

Some people do not actively experience media use as a set of choices—rather, it's just part of everyday life. You may check social media upon waking up and you may drive to school or to work while listening to Spotify. As you drive, you see advertising billboards on the highway. News comes to you through friends who share content on social networks. At school, you may read books and view movies or videos for learning purposes. When you go shopping, you encounter screens, images, and advertising in every store. When you are not working (and sometimes while you are at work), you may watch YouTube videos, listen to music, play a video game, or watch sports, network TV shows, or movies.

Many people also regularly create symbolic content, sometimes without even recognizing it. You compose text messages, forward links to online content or digital files through email, and create, edit, and upload photos to social media platforms. In all these activities, you are creating media. The sheer normalcy of these activities enables them to disappear from people's active awareness. You may not think about yourself as an author or producer, but you are.

Scholars use the term *mediatization* to describe how the media and everyday life have fused together (Hjarvard, 2008). Media experiences co-exist with everything else we do in life. To deepen awareness of media's role in society, then, requires a new way of looking at everyday life. You cannot focus only on your experiences in the present time period either. Think about the many changes that have occurred with media and technology in your lifetime. Because media change so quickly, to notice media's complex influence on society, it must be examined across decades or even centuries.

Consider the Question

Your parents, relatives and family have all witnessed changes in media and technology. Compose some questions that you could ask your parents and grandparents that would help them explain to you how media have changed over their lifetimes. For example, what do you think they loved most about media when they were younger? What do they miss most about how they used media when they were younger?

Why Are Media Changing So Fast?

Using a cell phone, you can read a book, play games, check out the weather, download files from the Internet, take photos, edit video, play music, send a text message or gif, and make a phone call. On your television, you can play YouTube videos, access your email, or stream movies. With a voice-activated digital assistant like Siri or Alexa, you can perform an Internet search, keep a grocery list, or check out movie schedules. You have literally millions of choices of media content available at any waking moment through the use of print, visual, sound, and digital media. Since the rise of the Internet, *convergence* connects media, technologies, industries, markets, genres, and audiences. Convergence enables us to use all kinds of media on all kinds of devices.

Convergence is being brought to us by several trends. First is the ability for anyone to publish and share ideas online for very little cost. This has led to an exponential growth of content. Media critic Todd Gitlin (2007) calls it a torrent of content that rains down volumes of entertainment, information, and persuasion in a huge array of forms and formats. The abundance of media content is so substantial that scholars once calculated that people have more than 1,000 choices of content for any given minute

Milestones in Media History

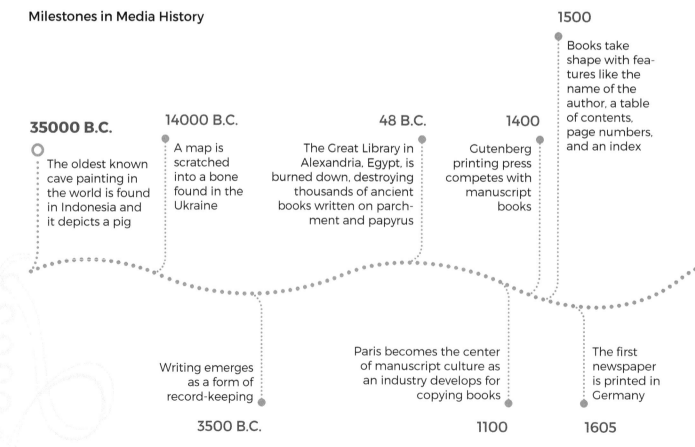

35000 B.C.
The oldest known cave painting in the world is found in Indonesia and it depicts a pig

14000 B.C.
A map is scratched into a bone found in the Ukraine

48 B.C.
The Great Library in Alexandria, Egypt, is burned down, destroying thousands of ancient books written on parchment and papyrus

1400
Gutenberg printing press competes with manuscript books

1500
Books take shape with features like the name of the author, a table of contents, page numbers, and an index

Writing emerges as a form of record-keeping
3500 B.C.

Paris becomes the center of manuscript culture as an industry develops for copying books
1100

The first newspaper is printed in Germany
1605

(Neuman, Park & Panek, 2012). But because even that number was based on data from 2005, before the use of social media and the Internet, it's clear that the availability of media content is an unknowable but very large number.

Second, the technological power of digitization enables all kinds of information and content to be encoded into zeros and ones so that computers can store, process, and transmit it. For example, when you visit a doctor's office, information about your health is stored in a form that enables a physician to access it from anywhere. With the rise of digitization, data become more important in decision-making and more jobs now require the use of computers as automation changes many aspects of work and business practices. This process is transforming the world of work, leading nearly every industry to require digital skills of employees.

A third factor influencing convergence is the rise of multinational media conglomerates. Companies like Facebook, Amazon, Google, Apple, and Netflix have become the most important corporations in the world, it seems, with their value ever spiraling upward over that of companies in every other type of industry, including health care and manufacturing. For many people, Google and Facebook are now the first stop for news.

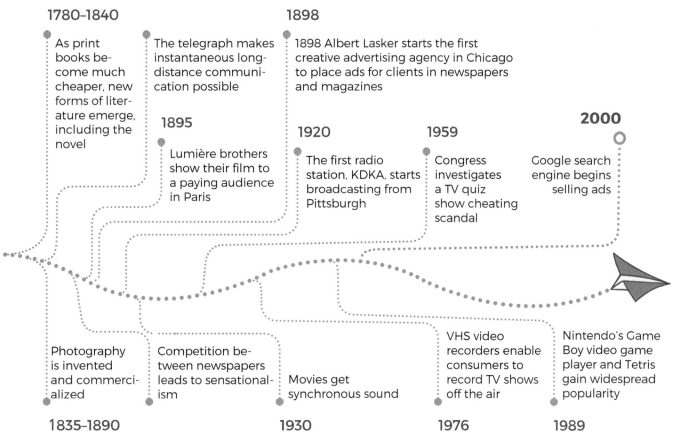

1780–1840
As print books become much cheaper, new forms of literature emerge, including the novel

The telegraph makes instantaneous long-distance communication possible

1898
1898 Albert Lasker starts the first creative advertising agency in Chicago to place ads for clients in newspapers and magazines

1895
Lumière brothers show their film to a paying audience in Paris

1920
The first radio station, KDKA, starts broadcasting from Pittsburgh

1959
Congress investigates a TV quiz show cheating scandal

2000
Google search engine begins selling ads

Photography is invented and commercialized

Competition between newspapers leads to sensationalism

Movies get synchronous sound

VHS video recorders enable consumers to record TV shows off the air

Nintendo's Game Boy video game player and Tetris gain widespread popularity

1835–1890

1930

1976

1989

Amazon is now the first stop for more than one-third of consumers, making it by far the world's largest retailer, bigger than all other retail companies put together (including Walmart). While there are more websites than ever before, *page views* are becoming more concentrated and less diverse. While in 2001, the top 10 websites accounted for 31% of all page views in America, by 2010, the top 10 websites accounted for 75% (Reich, 2015). It is ironic that although the world's information and entertainment are literally at our fingertips, our choices are more restricted to a few giant digital platforms.

Finally, convergence has been spurred on by government deregulation of media, which has increasingly allowed media conglomerates to own different kinds of media (e.g., television and radio stations and newspapers) in the same communities (Post, 2015). One of the biggest media companies is NBC Universal, which earned $32 billion in 2017 from its broadcast and cable television networks (including E! Entertainment Network, USA Network, MSNBC, and Hulu as well as DreamWorks and Universal Pictures). NBC Universal, which provides media content, is owned by Comcast, which is not only the biggest cable television company in the United States but also the biggest broadband company, providing Internet access to more than 30 million households. Comcast is not only the largest Internet service provider in the United States. It is also the second-largest media company in the world.

Corporate convergence enables companies to reduce labor costs, to use media content across different platforms, and to provide advertisers with package deals, making it difficult for smaller companies to compete. When Comcast Corporation tried to buy Time Warner Cable in 2014, government regulators had concerns about the centralization of media ownership. Critics recognize that corporate convergence may affect the quality of journalism by diminishing public access to a wide range of diverse viewpoints. Conflicts of interest may also occur when one company can have disproportionate control over the business of other firms.

How Much Media Do People Really Use?

Using media is such a natural part of life that we do not generally even recognize how much time we spend using them. Although people use a lot of media, they are not glued to the screen. Multitasking with media is common, as you may watch TV while cooking or listen to music in the car when you drive. In 2016, Americans spent an average of 10 hours and 39 minutes using these forms of media. For about two-thirds of our waking hours, it seems, media are part of our lives (Neilsen, 2018).

The typical American will watch 5,000 movies in a lifetime. Although people go to only five films a year at the movie theater, the average Netflix subscriber spends 2 hours per day watching movies. People like to binge-watch a series—watching several episodes in one sitting—in order to complete a series in an average of 5 days. Most Americans watch 5 hours of broadcast television per day. In many households, the TV is always on.

During the school years, reading is an important form of media use, and lots of people read books for school, work, and pleasure. Among adults, researchers have found a decline in print book reading. But there has been an increase in the use of e-books and audiobooks. In 2019, 72% of adults reported reading one or more books within the previous year. On average, people read 12 books per year. More than 65% of people read books in print format and 28% read e-books. One in five college graduates has listened to an audiobook in the past 12 months (Pew Research Center, 2019).

Throughout life, people use entertainment and information media. For people of all ages, the amount of time spent consuming media—watching TV, surfing the Web on a computer, using an app on a phone, listening to the radio—is on the rise. People 24 years old and younger are watching less live TV programming per week. If you have visited your grandparents recently, you might have noticed: people over the age of 50 watch by far the most TV. Figure 2.1 shows a Nielsen chart that documents media use as measured in a representative sample of U.S. households. This chart shows data from the 2017 and 2018 Nielsen ratings, revealing that we spend about 11 hours per day using media. That is almost half a day!

Figure 2.1

Hours and Minutes Spent, per Adult per Day

SOURCE: Nielsen, 2018

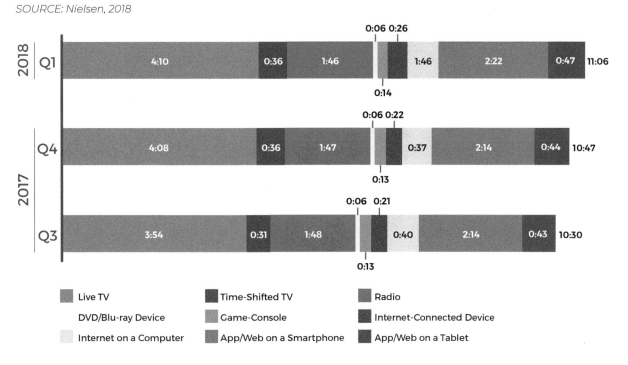

Web Historian

Let us face it: we all have a complex love–hate relationship with the Internet and social media, with many people having highly mixed feelings about them. With more than 2 billion active users, Facebook is clearly appreciated and valued by many people, and yet a recent poll shows that 32% of the public would like to, as the survey put it, "kill it and hope it dies" (Molla, 2018).

Because people have a nuanced set of attitudes about media that include both appreciation and critique, these opinions can be leveraged as part of the media literacy inquiry process. Studying your own behaviors, thoughts, and feelings about media is often a first step in the practice of media literacy. For example, you may enjoy checking out potential local dates on Tinder while at the same time feeling guilty for judging people in such a superficial manner. You might be fond of sharing photos of your restaurant meals on Instagram, but you might also resent the excessive ads, the confusing chronology of content, and the promotional merchandising that crowds out the photographers whose work you enjoy.

Using Web Historian, you can examine patterns in your use of the Internet so as to reflect on your uses of digital media. The chart shown in Figure 2.2 reveals the times of day and the days of the week when my Internet use is heaviest and lightest. From the chart, I can see that Wednesday is when I am the most active online, and I also see evidence of late-night Internet searching (Friday at 3:00 a.m.!). Sunday is a media fast day for me as I try not to use digital devices on that day.

Figure 2.2
Web Historian Reveals Personal Patterns of Internet Use

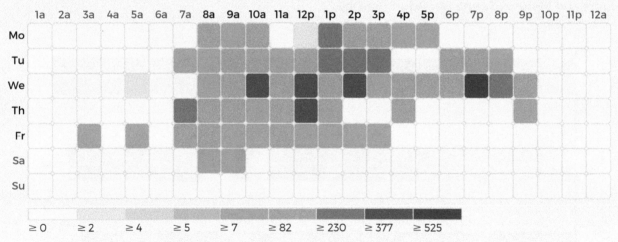

Who Uses Smartphones?

Because the smartphone is a digital device connected to the Internet, most people rate it as the device they value most highly. Why? Perhaps you value smartphones because of their size and portability; perhaps you value them because you use this device as both a media consumer and a media creator. After all, people receive content including text messages, digital content, and interactive voice communication—and they also create images, videos, and text messages to share with others.

Jovanmandic/iStock

How old were you when you first started using a smartphone? What do you remember about the experience❓

Most people now grow up with smartphones and keep using them throughout life. You may have gotten a smartphone in middle school or high school. But children today grow up in households where they see members of the family using smartphones. Children in many Western democracies start watching videos on a smartphone or tablet as babies and toddlers, playing with apps, watching cartoons, and listening to music on them. By age 10, more than 50% of American children already have a smartphone of their own (Howard, 2017).

Smartphone use also varies greatly from country to country. As Figure 2.3 shows, globally, 43% of adults own a smartphone. In some countries, they seem ubiquitous, and in other countries, smartphones are less central to daily life. For example, 88% of South Koreans but only 39% of Japanese have a smartphone. Age, education, and income seem to explain most of the variation. Important differences in smartphone use have emerged between older and younger people, and, as expected, people with greater levels of education and income are more likely to own smartphones (Silver, 2019).

If you are like most people your age, the mobile phone is the one piece of digital technology you could probably not live without. Whether you have a Huawei Mate XS, an iPhone, a Samsung Galaxy, or some other brand, half of the global population has a cell phone already, and researchers expect that 3.8 billion people will have a smartphone by 2021.

Most of the time, we are not very aware of how much time we spend interacting with the cell phone. Researchers who monitored how often people touched their phones over a 5-day period were surprised to find that people touch the phone thousands of times per day. Using special software that measures activation of the phone by touch, the researchers discovered that users averaged 2,617 daily touches of their smartphone, with 87% checking their phones at least once between midnight and 5:00 a.m. (Dscout, 2016).

Figure 2.3
Percent of Adults Who Own a Smartphone
SOURCE: Pew Research Center, 2019

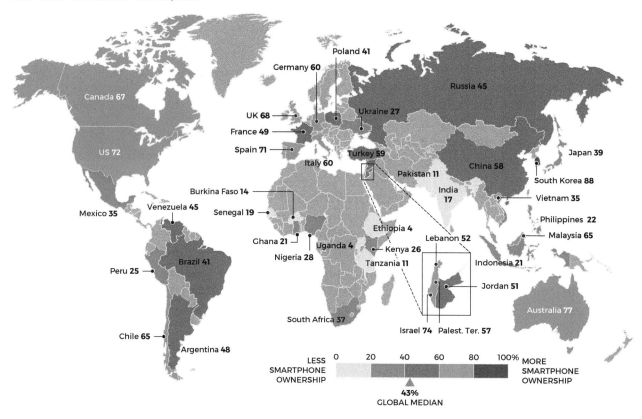

Still, most people are not glued to their smartphones. In fact, long periods of smartphone use are quite unusual. Most people use their handheld digital devices for a few minutes at a time, throughout the day. But this adds up. One study found that people use their smartphones for a little more than 2 hours per day (145 minutes per day on average), using it in 70–130 separate sessions during the day (Meyer, 2017).

Uses and Gratifications

The study of people's reasons for using media is not new, but as media change, our reasons for using them change as well. In 1972, researchers Jay Blumler, Joseph Brown, and Denis McQuail proposed four uses of media: for diversion, to support personal relationships, as a means of expressing personal identity, and as a form of surveillance. This theory of media use is sometimes called *uses and gratifications theory*. It argues that the medium that provides the most satisfaction for a person will be used more often than other types. Researchers generally recognize these different types of human needs:

Affect. People use media to experience feelings. Using media to arouse emotions such as happiness, fear, or excitement is a form of pleasure;

Cognition. People use information to support thinking and action in the world around them. Media use supports lifelong learning;

Surveillance. People monitor events in their neighborhood, their region, their country, and around the world in order to be aware of their surroundings and make decisions based on changes in the environment;

Status. People use media to promote a personal identity or express priorities, interests, or reputation, or as a means of expressing social power and value;

Social. People use media as a means of sharing social experiences with others;

Escape. People use media to gain relief from the stresses and pressures of the real world. People use media as catharsis or as a form of escape.

People may share a common media experience but use it to fulfill very different needs. For example, a grandfather may enjoy watching the 2018 Netflix remake of *Lost in Space* so as to activate nostalgic emotions, remembering his own childhood by enjoying the family space drama series. His adult son may like the same show for social reasons, appreciating the chance to sit near his mom and dad and spend time together as a family. His wife's brother, who lives nearby, may enjoy *Lost in Space* because he has a reputation as an expert on sci-fi. He tries to stay current on all the newest science fiction media. The grandaughter may identify with the attractive young adult characters. For her, the show offers a window on how people act when faced with crisis and conflict. Her mother, who is not a great fan of sci-fi, may simply enjoy the show as an escape from the demands of work-related email.

When it comes to news, you may listen to podcasts or use search engines to gather news about what is happening in the world. Or perhaps your surveillance of the world is distributed across your friend and family network, as people simply tell you about important current events that are noteworthy. You may listen to news on the radio. Your parents may read a daily newspaper online, watch TV news, or read content they find on Facebook. If they are retired, your grandparents may listen to talk radio or sit in front of a TV news channel, watching people discuss, argue, and interpret current events in real time as they unfold.

Your purposes for using media vary across the life span and are aligned with your identity position within a family or community. Your orientation may be either selfish or social, and these patterns are frequently learned in childhood. For example, when hanging out with friends, you may watch sports because the experience of rooting for the team deepens feelings of social cohesion. When alone, you may listen to music so as to manage your moods and emotions, feel less lonely, or even deepen the enjoyment of being alone. When facing an unresolved question, you may use Google to find answers and gain information. When you are bored, you may use media to fill time, experiencing a variety of emotions from entertainment media. You may be more or less attentive to media depending on the context and situation. In many cases, your media choices are not so much a matter of individual choice. People use media in ways that are expected and conditioned by their social identity and social roles.

Why Are Media Important for Individuals and Society?

Media are important because of the purposes they serve in our society. Building upon the work of Denis McQuail (2010), a British media scholar, five basic functions of media for individuals and society can be identified: (1) diversion and entertainment; (2) connecting past, present, and future; (3) sharing knowledge; (4) the symbolic power to construct reality; and (5) mobilization for social action. These five different functions are easy to spot in personal and social life.

Diversion and Entertainment. One of the best things about going to the movies is the feeling of escape that occurs when you enter the movie theater. In the darkened room, surrounded by a giant screen, vivid colors, action, and sound, your reality is displaced by another reality.

Media use can create an altered state of mind. Some people feel this pleasurable experience of escape when they read a novel, as the mental images of the story play out in the mind's eye. Others get the feeling when playing a video game, experiencing a visceral thrill of being "in" another world. The feeling of being inside a story is familiar to many people, which is why some people can be annoyed when theatergoers talk during a movie, as it shifts their attention from the world they are experiencing on-screen to the dark room they are actually sitting in. On the other hand, if it is a bad film, you might explain the viewing experience to a friend by saying, "I just couldn't get into it." What you mean by this is that you did not experience an altered state of mind during the viewing experience.

But sometimes stories that are frightening, dark, or depressing can also serve as a meaningful form of entertainment, enabling us to explore unpleasant emotions, such as fear, sadness, and rage through a *vicarious experience*. The release of tension through diversion and entertainment is considered part of healthy human development. People experience this sense of diversion in many different ways:

- For some, it is a matter of a getting a laugh from a short YouTube clip, from a favorite comedian or a cute puppy video;

- First-person shooter games can create a rush of emotion that comes as you temporarily leave reality behind;
- Listening to music can create intense moods that activate memory and imagination.

There is no doubt about it: all media, including films, books, music, and video games, can create an altered mental state. Researchers have called it *flow*, or optimal experience (Csikszentmihalyi, 1997). A flow state occurs when people experience a deep sense of enjoyment in activities that completely absorb all of their attention. When concentrating on a film or reading a novel, people may lose track of time or fail to notice events occurring around them because of their focused involvement in the world of the narrative. For these reasons, most people truly enjoy the many choices of media available on television, tablets, laptops, and cell phones.

Connecting Past, Present, and Future. Throughout human history, people have shared their experience of being human through direct observation and stories. Storytelling and music are the oldest cultural forms, and they clearly have supported human survival. To thrive in any culture, you need to learn from direct experience and from your tribe through well-coordinated cultural participation. Thus, education can be understood as a process of formally learning what previous generations have discovered.

Carl Mydans/The LIFE Picture Collection/Getty Images

What type of media have you used recently that creates the feeling of being connected to the past?

Through media, we inherit virtually free of charge the wisdom of preceding generations. Throughout the 1.8 million-year cycle of ice ages called the Pleistocene era, there have been more than 85,000 generations of our ancestors. Although we do not know for certain, anthropologists believe that the capacity for speech dates back more than a million years. The hominids who emerged 20,000 generations ago certainly used language of some sort, given their highly coordinated social actions, including hunting, tool-making, and funeral rituals. Being a good storyteller might have been a status symbol within the tribe, offering sexual advantages that increased the likelihood of producing offspring. After all, storytellers do charm audiences with colorful, brilliant, and poetically polished prose, and "when storytellers use ornament and plumage to draw attention to their tales, they inevitably draw eyes themselves" (Vanderbes, 2013: 1).

Storytelling also supports people's critical thinking skills. *Counterfactual thinking* is a concept in psychology that involves the human tendency to create possible alternatives to life events that have already occurred; something that is contrary to what actually happened. In stories, you can explore alternate endings to events and imagine "what if?" hypotheticals. For example: What would happen if the leader of the tribe was killed? What if I encounter a bear while searching for berries today? What if my spear would have hit the water buffalo instead of missing it? Exposure to a rich array of stories may have given some people an evolutionary advantage by preparing them for the unexpected and unknowable future.

Indeed, communications media and technologies actually shape how social change occurs. In studying the history of communication technologies, Canadian economist Harold Innis introduced the concept of the *monopoly of knowledge*, the idea that the ruling class maintains political power through control of key communications technologies. Once laws were written down, for example, a powerful form of social control could be exercised over a long period of time. Writing provides an important form of continuity across generations. As Innis understood it, when a new communication technology is created, the group who uses it can acquire knowledge in a way that offers advantages over those from previous generations (Tremblay, 2012).

Media and communication enable people to both understand the past and feel empowered to change their culture for the better. Older communications media (like book publishing, newspapers, and magazines) are like sedimentary layers that gradually adapt and change in relation to

How do apps and platforms amplify the voices of the most powerful and most popular in society?

Bigtunaonline/iStock

dominant technologies over a long period of time, as Figure 2.4 shows. Reflecting on these ideas in the 1960s, Marshall McLuhan shifted his originally pessimistic stance toward the rise of television. He came to see television as "reshaping patterns of social interdependence," forcing people to reconsider older more tribal knowledge that they had gained from the family, and neighborhood (as quoted in Tremblay, 2012: 564).

Sharing Knowledge. Through media, we learn about events, people, and ideas outside of our direct experience. As we move through the day, we encounter *data*, which can be observations encoded as facts or figures, images, or sounds. When data are organized, they become *information*, which is collected and curated for a particular purpose. As David Weinberger explains it, "Information is to data what wine is to a vineyard: the delicious extract and distillate" (2012: 2).

When people make sense of information and apply it to their own life context, it becomes *knowledge*. With knowledge, people can apply information to solving problems. Knowledge is a synthesis of information that is linked to a particular purpose or goal. It is an ongoing process of inquiry in every domain, field, and topic. For example, Charles Darwin used information about animals and their habitats around the world to generate knowledge about evolution and natural selection. Media researchers used observations of people's behavior to synthesize knowledge about uses and gratifications. Even the guy who repaired your cracked iPhone constructed knowledge from a combination of reading, observation, and practice.

Figure 2.4

Estimated Media Supply to Home in Minutes per Day, 1960–2020

SOURCE: Adapted from Neuman et al. (2012)

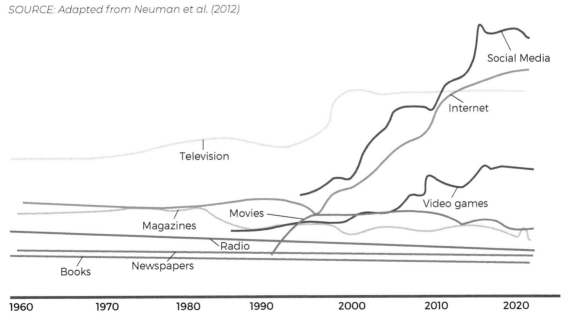

Forsman. Kresten/CartoonStock

"The secret to finding all knowledge is to use exactly the right keywords when you google."

CartoonStock.com

This cartoon features a guru offering his wisdom. Do you agree with his advice? Why or why not?

Over millennia, knowledge has accelerated through education and sharing. When people share knowledge, they create *knowledge networks*, by freely collaborating and sharing ideas, new data, information, and knowledge. When knowledge is widely shared by groups of individuals, beliefs are formed. People do not form beliefs lightly. They develop over time and cohere into a world view. Over time, knowledge can transform into wisdom, as people develop the ability to generalize knowledge accumulated through life experience and share insights that serve as guides to life.

Book publishers, libraries, and universities deserve a lot of credit for the thousands of years of knowledge produced through the process of sharing ideas in writing. But publishers, libraries, and universities did not just gather up information; they also filtered out stuff that was not considered "good enough." In general, the filtering process was social, as teams of people made decisions about which books to publish, or which books to purchase for the library. Note that this sort of filtering happened to the author at the front end of the process. If an author was lucky enough to make it through the first filter (getting a book published), the author then had to hope to get through the second filter (getting the book into a library), and then the third (getting someone to read it).

Today, there is still a filtering process, but it happens in a different way. Since anyone can publish anything, with no editorial gatekeepers, as David Weinberger (2011: 11) explains, "Filters no longer filter out. They filter forward, bringing results to the front." Since anything can be published, authors increase their likelihood of reaching audiences if their work is findable. Consumers can find content in a lot of ways, including through metadata, data used to describe another item's content. For example, if you search for the phrase "crime fiction," you will find only content tagged with that phrase.

But findability can also be increased through a variety of editorial processes. For example, when you read a newsmagazine article about 10 great new works of crime fiction, you may be presented with hyperlinks that give you the opportunity to read excerpts from each of those books on Amazon. These 10 books have been selected from among a much larger collection of crime novels in an editorial process called *content curation*,

How do you encounter and interact with ideas that have been curated by others?

Kevin, CC BY 2.0

a way of filtering information that provides people in a knowledge community with content that has been created by others and collected to reflect the curator's particular point of view.

Whenever possible, it is important to be aware of the curator's point of view and how it may affect your interpretation of information. Five common curation practices include: (1) aggregating similar content together, (2) distilling ideas to present only the most important material, (3) highlighting content by elevating it to be more visible than other content, (4) mashing up older content to create a new message, and (5) organizing content in chronological order so as to show change or continuity over time (Bhargava, 2011).

Because experts of all kinds have the ability to share their personal filters with each other, expertise is becoming increasingly decentralized in a lively *marketplace of ideas*, where truths and falsehoods sit side by side. We can see this as a problem or an opportunity, but it is a reality of life in a digital age. There is no putting the genie back into the bottle now that everyone, everywhere has the power of digital authorship.

Philosophers have long reminded us that knowledge cannot be understood separately from the social context in which it exists. Everywhere we see how experts disagree on the facts. Is the stock market inflated or headed for a crash? Will reducing carbon emissions slow down extreme weather events? Does eating bacon cause cancer?

This "conspicuous inevitability of disagreement" requires that people develop media literacy competencies, according to David Weinberger, which, he emphasizes, includes learning the conventions of how to participate effectively in knowledge communities, how to evaluate knowledge claims,

South_agency/iStock

How do you depict your identity as a member of a family or group❓

and, perhaps most important, "learning to love difference" (2012: 183)—that is, embracing the opportunity to encounter and interact with ideas and information outside your comfort zone. Through developing these habits of mind, we can benefit from the abundant knowledge networks of the world.

Symbolic Power and the Construction of Reality. The control of wealth and militaries has always enabled the formation of social hierarchies, with kings at the top and peasants at the bottom. But even in ancient times, people appreciated how communication was another form of symbolic power: good storytelling could create heroes, giving visibility and public respect to people for their valor or their deeds.

The power to construct people's understanding of social reality is the most profound reason why media are important to individuals and society. Many of the ties that connect people as members of a group are media representations that depict social relationships. Everyone in my family has a set of expectations about my identity, which can lead to feelings of social pressure. In my personal identity as a "daughter," I am tied to all the movies, TV shows, books, and other stories that I have encountered that feature daughters. These stories present ideas about how I am expected to behave and act. Everyone in my family has a set of expectations about my identity that are rooted in their own experience with media messages. In this way, mediated social relationships serve to define and maintain the status quo, our experience of "reality." This is sometimes called *symbolic power*, the capacity to influence the actions of others and to create reality through producing and transmitting symbols (Couldry, 2012).

But this power is not evenly distributed in society. Because TV and movie producers tend to tell the stories that are familiar to them, we see upper-middle-class white people overrepresented and fewer stories that feature people of color. Because journalists consume a lot of media themselves as they interact with political sources and public relations professionals, they tend to recirculate messages previously developed by politicians and the press. This concept is sometimes called *self-referentiality*. As Nöth and Bishara (2007: 1) explain, instead of depicting people's experience with reality, the press, advertising and creative professionals are "referring more and more to what has been seen previously in the arts or to what the media themselves have more recently reported." Through symbolic power, the

https://en.wikipedia.org/wiki/Joan_of_Arc

E! Entertainment Television/Photofest

What do Joan of Arc and Kim Kardashian have in common? How are they different❓

social world is shaped in particular ways that make some stories common and other stories quite rare.

How do some people get access to the important visibility that media provide? The storyteller's rhetorical skills can add gloss to a person who is seeking authority, social power, or influence. The history of fame offers insight on the careful construction of *social identity* and how it can lead to symbolic power that constructs and shapes reality (Braudy, 1997). Consider the story of Joan of Arc, the French peasant girl living in the Middle Ages who had a vision from God that inspired her to lead the French to military success. Through the repetition of stories about Joan across society, she became famous and achieved a type of social power separate from wealth or military might.

In the present day, we might think of Kim Kardashian, who first gained media attention as a friend of Hollywood socialite Paris Hilton. She leveraged social identity through the distribution of a sex tape created with her former boyfriend. Her 2007 TV show *Keeping Up with the Kardashians*, her marriage to Kanye West, and her Instagram selfies have all contributed to her identity as a celebrity who is famous for being famous and who has a form of social power that has led to wealth and influence. Recently, she has began to use her social power on behalf of criminal justice reform.

The people, groups, and ideas left unrepresented by media spectacle may feel deprived of public attention and feel that the process of media representation is essentially unjust. The invisibility of not being famous can be painful (Couldry, 2012). Some people seem to suffer a type of hidden injury that can be healed only through participation in media culture. Because of the human need for social validation, some people may gravitate to participating in competitive performance shows like *American Idol*. Others may join YouTube to "live within the spaces of the media system" as "ordinary members of mediated societies" (Couldry, 2012: 95). Such beliefs may contribute to the rise of *competitive individualism*, the social belief system that positions effort and ability as defining features of success and the perception that competition is an acceptable means of distributing limited resources and rewards.

Mobilization for Social Action. Why are media important for individuals and society? Media and communication are the engines of social change. In

5 critical questions about smartphones and health

In this Facebook post, we see a startling question: "Is it true that smartphones cause head cancer?" Using five critical questions of media literacy, you can analyze this media message to gain insight on its meaning and value.

1. **Who is the author and what is the purpose?** This post was created by Medicine.net. Reviewing the About Us page, we learn that it is an online health care media publishing company that provides easy-to-read, in-depth, authoritative medical information for consumers via its robust, user-friendly, interactive website. From the information provided, which includes the name of the medical doctor who reviewed the content for accuracy, it seems like the company values the provision of reliable information. The purpose of the post may be to drive Facebook users to the Medicine.net website to access information about cell phones and health. Once there, they might look at other health articles and see ads for products including Lysol (which you can use to remove germs from your smartphone).

2. **What techniques are used to attract and hold attention?** The content of the headline is designed to create fear, and the image

his book *Democracy and Education*, American philosopher John Dewey explains that a democracy is more than a form of government: it is the practice of communicating our experiences to others. By carefully considering our own deeds and actions in relationship to those of others in the society, we break down "the barriers of class, race and national territory," which keep people from "perceiving the full import of their activity." Through public discourse, we discover our common interests (Dewey, 1944/2004).

Today, there are real challenges to democracy, including a lack of participation stemming from social inequalities and systemic racism as well as the abuse of power by people with narrow and self-interested motivations who lack principles of ethical behavior. Despite these challenges, democratic self-governance is possible and it depends upon effective communication in the *public sphere*. This concept was developed by Jurgen Habermas who acknowledged it as the process of exchanging ideas and opinions in public so as to identify common interests and problems, and using imagination and compromise to brainstorm possi-

(featuring the hand and the smartphone) is attractive, simple, and compelling. Although the headline refers to cancer, most of the dangers of cell phones described in the slideshow itself concern texting and driving, eye strain, hand and wrist pain, and, of course, germs.

3. **What lifestyles, values, and points of view are represented?** This social media post appeals to people who are worried and concerned about their health. It seems to value the process of learning more about health as an important social value, but it also taps into people's existing fears about the impact of technology.

4. **How might different people interpret this message?** Some people may ignore this post and see it as irrelevant to their lives while others (who may be experiencing eye strain

or pain in their thumbs) will find it useful. A medical professional is likely to believe that the simple sentences contain insufficient information.

5. **What is omitted?** Information is not provided about how many people are affected by other medical problems related to smartphone use. While mobile phones emit electromagnetic radiation, which can be absorbed by tissues close to the phone, hand injuries caused by excessive use of smartphones are much more common health problems. Surprisingly, the most life-threatening health risk of cell phones is omitted from this post. Texting while driving is implicated in many fatal automobile accidents, and research has shown that distracted drivers have four times greater chance of an accident.

What is the most important change needed in society now? What ideas and policies need more visibility ❓

ble solutions (Habermas, Lennox & Lennox, 1974). It is obvious: people need to interact with others in order to make sense of the world.

The Internet has become a tool and venue for political groups of all kinds, as high-profile events on national and global stages have been used to motivate citizens to take positions without much deliberation and discussion. Perhaps you saw a meme that made you angry and you found a website where you were asked to join to receive a newsletter. Perhaps you shared a link to the newsletter with your friend on social media. Then you

Intellectual Grandparent:
Sonia Livingstone

Sonia Livingstone watches people use mobile phones, TVs, and computers. A professor of social psychology in the Department of Media and Communications at the London School of Economics, she takes a comparative, critical, and contextual approach to examining media audiences, media literacy, and media regulation, with a particular focus on the opportunities and risks of digital media use in the everyday lives of children and young people. Professor Livingstone conducts large-scale survey research and she also looks at children and teens' media behaviors using ethnographic research methods. Sonia Livingstone contributed the following key ideas to media literacy.

Careful examination of how families use media can inform government policy. There is plenty of fear among parents and policymakers about the role of smartphones in the lives of young children and teens. In a 2018 report entitled "In the Digital Home, How Do Parents Support Their Children and Who Supports Them?" researchers first conducted in-depth qualitative interviews and fieldwork with parents, childcare providers, educators, children, and young people from 73 families and in learning sites across London. This information helped Livingstone and her colleagues to design and implement a nationally representative survey of U.K. parents. They gathered data from 2,032 parents of children aged 0–17 in late 2017. The research team identified many participants through online recruiting, but they also reached out to non-Internet-using

Vesnaandjic/iStock

got an email urging you to call your senator about impending legislation. Maybe you called or maybe you did not. For many people, that is the extent of political participation.

And perhaps that is how democratic mobilization for social change actually begins. Jenkins and his colleagues describe *civic imagination* as the capacity of people to "envision alternatives to current conditions and develop new pathways into political and civic engagement" (Jenkins, Shresthova, & Gamber-Thompson, 2016: 296). Through networked communities, young activists use fan fiction and other creative strategies to engage people's emotions about the plight of new American immigrants, including those called DREAMers, the undocumented youth who were born outside the country but raised here since they were very young children. For many young people who have been alienated from traditional political discourses, a focus that connects their identities as fans and their idealism as potential activists seems more meaningful and authentic as a way to raise awareness about the need for political action.

parents, who were interviewed in person. In this study, researchers report two major findings:

Smartphones bring families together, but in different ways. Parents of young children use smartphone messaging apps and video chat to connect with family members, while parents of teens are more likely to use social media. High-income families tend to create music, photos, or videos together, giving children a chance to develop an identity as digital authors.

Although parents try to enable children's online opportunities and address risks, they lack support for dealing with digital dilemmas. How much screen time is too much? What is the right age for a child to get a smartphone? Should there be a computer, TV, or digital device in the bedroom? These questions are an ongoing

source of conflict in some families. When parents have questions about media use in the family, they generally search online or figure it out on their own. Today's young parents do not feel that they can ask their own parents for advice about parenting in a digital age. This may create a generation gap that leaves parents unsupported when it comes to important parenting issues. Most U.K. parents also perceived that other sources of support, like friends and relatives, health professionals, or a child's school, are not useful.

If Sonia Livingstone has influenced your thinking about media, you can share a comment on the Grandparents of Media Literacy website at www. grandparentsofmedialiteracy.com.

In her study of global activist movements in Turkey and Egypt, Zeynep Tufecki (2017) points out that, as a result of social media, activists can organize without organizations, building momentum for increasing awareness rapidly in response to particular events. For example, after the high school massacre in Parkland, Florida, the #Parkland hashtag was used to summon protesters to protest gun laws in Washington, D.C. But Tufecki points out how a variety of Internet activists around the world have struggled with tactical maneuvering after they achieved initial visibility. Her research shows that social change movements built without the longer-term process of collective decision-making can be quite fragile.

Media and communication have the potential to support the never-ending processes of social change, but the Internet alone is insufficient for the job. Digital technology offers the *amplification* of existing tensions, problems, and paradoxes in society. Digital tools can help people access documents critical to demonstrate abuses of power. For example, after the murder of George Floyd by Minneapolis police in 2020, the live stream depictions of police brutality activated strong emotions among the general public. At the same time, misinformation and fraudulent news was created and shared to sow division.

Using social media's audience-targeting capabilities, messages can be designed for specific groups as a means to alienate them from participating in the democratic process. For example, a 2016 survey showed that almost a third of Americans remembered seeing such social media posts, but only one in five people who remembered those stories could tell that they were fake (Tufecki, 2017).

In a networked public sphere, social movements do not need to rely on thought leaders, elites, or editorial gatekeepers. But in a landscape where anyone can be an author, there is "a lack of broad agreement about who is an expert or what constitutes expertise, combined with the lack of the usual indicators of expertise provided by gatekeeping institutions" (Tufecki, 2017: 273). The breakdown of consensual acceptance of "what counts as knowledge" and "who has expertise" can have profound consequences, intensifying partisanship and social divisions.

What the future may hold: Social Credit Systems

Media forms, formats, and genres—and the ways we use them—are in a constant state of change. But although media technologies, genres, and formats change, the pleasures we get from using media are likely to remain stable and consistent. Maybe the mobile phone will migrate to a pair of glasses or even a small implant with tiny sensors that offer a type of virtual intelligence. Perhaps someday we'll be able to manipulate our smartphones by simply thinking, with no fingertip action required. Facial recognition technology may help us identify people we have met—or even recognize those we have not seen for years.

But we can see that media offer both significant opportunities and substantial risks. It is easy to imagine that the smartphone could be programmed to monitor our every move. In a sense, this is already a reality in the United States. The National Security Agency (NSA), a highly secretive part of the U.S. government, collects phone records for millions of American customers, regardless of whether they are suspected of any wrongdoing (Gorman, 2008). Under the Patriot Act, telecommunication companies must release to the government unlimited phone metadata that enable the government to know the identity of every person with whom an individual communicated electronically, how long they spoke, and their location at the time of the communication.

Once those data are available to a government, it is quite tempting for political leaders to use it to achieve policy goals. Already, the Chinese government is testing a social credit system where people's digital and face-to-face behavior is documented and consequences can be levied for bad actions. According to an official planning document, the system will "allow the trustworthy to roam everywhere under heaven while making it hard for the discredited to take a single step" (Mistreanu, 2018: 1).

A *social credit system*, facilitated by the smartphone, could do more than penalize bad civic actors. It could also provide incentives for specific types of socially desirable behavior. For example, to promote public health, diabetics who use a food intake app to document their eating might get a price break on their medication. In the near future, if you shout at another driver or display aggression while interacting with a police officer, you might not be granted access to a bank loan or a job. Thus, it is possible that smartphones could enable companies or governments to reward and shape the way people think and act.

When it comes to media, the future is truly unknowable. But as we have seen in this chapter, it is important to ask questions about different forms of media and reflect deeply on why we use them. Through reasoning about both the affordances and the potential risks associated with the media we use, we are likely to be able to balance the opportunities and the dangers, both now and in the future.

CREATE T► LEARN

Infographic on Your Media Life

Over a 3-day period, monitor your media usage in half-hour increments. From the time you wake up to the time you fall asleep, create a chart that shows how much media use occurs. If possible, make notes to identify your moods and feelings, as well as the context and situation of the use. If you like, you can use a simple behavior-tracking app to record patterns in your use of media, creating categories that are specifically relevant to you.

Then create a simple infographic to analyze the patterns and illustrate the variety of media choices you made. Your infographic might use a combination of data, images, and language to show how much time you spend using media, and where and when your media use takes place. Visit www.medialiteracyaction.com to learn more about how to create infographics and access free digital platforms for making them. Post and share your work online using the #MLAction hashtag.

TIME T◉ REFLECT

After charting the media in your daily life, it is time to reflect on some of the pleasures and annoyances they cause. Consider these questions as you plan your informal extemporaneous response for the Flipgrid Inquiry:

- What patterns did you notice when charting your own media use?
- Describe some features of print, visual, sound, or digital media that you really appreciate and value. Explain why they are important to you.
- Describe some features of the same media that are annoying, troubling, or have negative consequences or impact on yourself, others, or society. Explain why they are important to you.
- How do you balance the positives and the negatives when it comes to the media you use most?

You can share your ideas about what you are by contributing ideas to the Flipgrid Inquiry. You can also view and respond to comments of other people who have offered thoughtful reflections on media literacy. Visit www.medialiteracyaction.com to learn more.

Algorithmic search may be both a blessing and a curse

How Do Search Engines Work?

Learning Outcomes

1. Understand how the Internet has changed over time
2. Learn why data are important to the economy
3. Consider the impact of algorithms on individuals and society
4. Reflect on the consequences of search personalization
5. Consider how data surveillance affects people's privacy and freedom

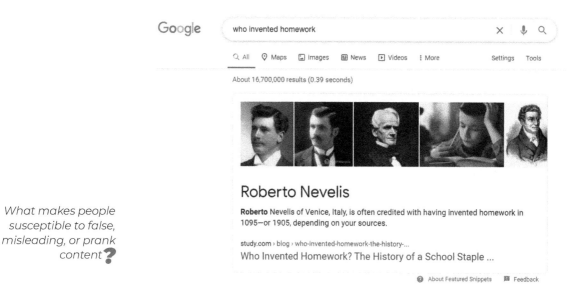

Search and ye shall find, goes the ancient saying. Have you ever wondered who invented homework? Type that phrase into Google or Bing and you will find the answer.

Roberto Nevilis invented homework, one Google result reveals. No wonder he is reviled by millions of students around the world!

But if you look closer, this search result raises several red flags. It says the history of homework goes back to 1095 in Venice, which places it squarely in the Middle Ages, when cathedral schools existed to train boys to read, write, and speak Latin, preparing them for the clergy. Because manuscript books were so expensive, students generally memorized their teachers' lectures. It is hard to imagine what kind of homework might have been necessary back then, and the date of 1095 makes the accompanying photo seem absurd. After all, photography was not invented until 1835. The gentleman depicted looks like he might have been photographed in 1905. Even though this information is presented in the special box called the Google Knowledge Graph, it simply does not make sense.

The source of this information is Quora, a crowdsourced question-and-answer website where questions are asked, answered, edited, and organized by a community of users in the form of opinions. *Crowdsourcing* is a form of information gathering that is only as good as the people who contribute it. Looking more closely into the Quora site on the question "Who invented homework?" we find 28 answers as of September 2018, offering a wide range of opinions. The photo of the man depicted is credited with a website—9gag.com—whose motto is: "Go Fun the World." It is a website where 150 million young users view and upload funny videos featuring animals, pranks, and other silly stuff. More searching reveals little additional information, so although hundreds of websites have republished the paragraph under examination, the absence of other sources makes it seem *bogus*. Bogus information is fake.

The Internet now shapes nearly all forms of media that we use in daily life. In this chapter, we explore the technology, politics, and economics of search engines. We consider questions like:

- How has the Internet changed over time?
- How do search engines actually work?
- How can people detect the bias of search engines?
- How will we protect against new forms of discrimination that might emerge in a data-driven society?

Because Google controls two-thirds of all Internet searches, we focus on that company. Other search engines include Microsoft's Bing and privacy-protected search engines like Duck Duck Go. In this chapter, we show how information literacy skills help people become better, faster searchers, exploiting the amazing power of the search engine for work, leisure, citizenship, and learning. We examine the architecture and design of the Internet in order to understand how search engines work and we learn why some information is more "findable" than other information. Demystifying how Internet search engines work helps people recognize the built-in biases, limitations, and affordances of these technologies. By reading this chapter, you will gain knowledge that will improve your ability to find, access, and critically evaluate all the content you encounter online.

Internet Technology 101

Yes, the Internet is a network of interconnected computers, but how are they connected? When children are asked to draw a picture of how the Internet works, some draw a picture that shows the placement of their computer or

How does online surveillance affect personal freedoms?

Peopleimages/iStock

laptop in their home, with the drawing depicting the many wires connecting the keyboard, the router, and the computer. Others show how Wi-Fi works, depicting a router and the wireless invisible signals transmitted to mobile phones, tablets, and laptops. These are good representations. But the most accurate drawing of the Internet looks like a spiderweb of computers all linked together.

Today, the easy availability of Wi-Fi makes the Internet seem magical to many. Wherever you go, it is just there. But it is not magic: even when radio waves are used to transmit data, there is always a wired access point, which is generally a set of copper or other type of wires connecting to underground wires that link together a network of interconnected computers.

When you use the Internet, your device becomes part of it. The signals you send by swiping or clicking transmit information at light speed. When you play a video game, your clicks on the joystick are converted (or encoded) as bits (usually 0 for released and 1 for pressed). The same is true for typing on a keyboard or speaking into a microphone.

Data move at a speed of nearly five times around the earth per second, through wires and airwaves, in a continual stream of zeros and ones called *packet switching*. This is a mode of data transmission in which a message is broken into a number of parts sent independently, over whichever route is fastest for each packet, and reassembled at the destination—your computer, tablet, or smartphone (Halavais, 2017).

When you upload pictures, watch movies, or listen to music, you access *servers* usually located in *data centers*, which are a giant factory of interconnected computers that communicate to each other. When you want to access a website, a kind of question is sent to these computers, which then deliver information back to you using a specific *IP address*, which is the unique set of numbers that identifies your specific machine. All devices connected to the Internet have a unique IP address.

Because people prefer names over numbers, a *domain name* is used, with the help of an address registry, to identify the location of the servers on which data and information are stored. A *domain name server* (DNS) stores all the IP addresses of the servers. When you type in a domain name, your query goes to the DNS and sends back the IP address, and then your computer goes to the computer with that IP address.

Five Eras of the Internet

The Internet has changed very quickly over 30 years, and it is expected to continue to change in the years ahead. Its dynamic quality is a key feature of this form of media and communication. To really understand the future of the Internet, it is worthwhile to get a sense of its past. You have experienced much of this history just in your lifetime. Doug Belshaw (2014), a digital literacy expert, identifies five eras within the history of the Internet:

- **The Information Superhighway**. In the early 1990s, the Internet made information available to users, instantly and for free. Suddenly, it seemed, there was an explosion of available content. More information professionals were beginning to use email, and the Internet was generally used primarily for accessing information.

- **The Wild West.** By the late 1990s, it was possible to look at websites using a *browser*, a software application (like Internet Explorer, Firefox, or Safari) that displayed websites and made them easier to view on a computer terminal. Many people built websites during this time, and companies experimentined with offering consumers a variety of entertainment services including online games, pornography, shopping, and chat rooms.

- **Web 2.0**. By 2003, new programming languages made it possible for programmers to create software applications that enabled users to "write the Web" in the browser itself. With little technical knowledge, people could create wikis, websites, and games, and easily contribute to and comment on websites. Because users wanted to make their digital creations more findable, YouTube, Facebook, and Twitter became major destinations for social life.

- **The Platform and App Era.** As the Internet became easier to use and smartphones became more common, a shift toward platforms and apps enabled companies to have more control over users' online experiences. Around 2008, users began sharing content, not on their own devices, but on "the Cloud," privately owned platforms. Since everyone's content was already online, some people could and did seek to stand out from the crowd by choosing to "resist, reconfigure, and/or reformulate" digital spaces. In fact, programmers and hackers themselves helped people develop critical mindsets to identify how values shape the design of digital tools (Santo, 2011).

- **The Post-Snowden Era.** By 2013, data privacy issues became more acute when Edward Snowden leaked classified information about the legal but top-secret surveillance programs on American men and women by the U.S. and other governments with support from telecommunications and computer companies. During this time, the public also grew more aware of how online data is commodified and sold. As more services were offered to users for free, the public gradually gained a greater understanding of how businesses and governments use the Internet for marketing and surveillance. Public concern increased about the accumulated power of the FAANG companies, which are Facebook, Amazon, Apple, Netflix, and Alphabet (Google), because of the collective impact these companies have on society.

- **The Future.** We do not know what is next, but it may involve more (or less) centralization of ownership, virtual reality, machine learning, surveillance, and increased industry regulation. In order to adapt to all of these changes, it will be important for consumers to continue developing digital and media literacy competencies so as to explore and address the new topics that arise.

How Search Engines Work

Many science fiction movies rely on the common stereotype of the intelligent agent, a computer that knows what we want or need based on a simple request. Today, we may use a horizontal search box to type in our keywords or we may use Siri or Alexa to speak a natural language *query*, which is the term used for the keyword or other information users provide when initiating a search. Some people take such searches for granted, without giving much thought to how they actually work. But today, everyone needs to understand "what is under the hood" when it comes to utilizing search engines.

First, Google collects data from the Internet using Web-crawler software (called *spiders*). The software finds Web pages by connecting to hyperlinks, and content from Web pages is copied and stored in an index. Since this Web-crawling process is more or less continual, the index changes over time. This is why a search conducted on April 15 will likely yield different results than one conducted on August 15. When you type your query, Google uses the words you type to guess your purpose. An autocorrect function will correct your spelling and offer you results for what it thinks you meant to type.

After you query a search engine, a *search engine page of results* (SERP) is offered to you that includes both organic results and paid-for (or sponsored) results. Each result (which are sometimes called *hits*) includes a title, a short description, and a hyperlink, and these are generally presented in order of their perceived relevance to your query. These results are the product of an *algorithm*, a set of computer programming instructions that Google engineers design, refine, and improve based on evidence from user behavior and strategic business goals.

The process of using a search engine is now so easy that it conceals a deeper truth: humans have distinctly different strategies for finding and using information depending on their existing knowledge, purposes, and goals. To address this issue, the Association of College and Research Libraries (ACRL) has identified some important concepts that it describes as portals to being a lifelong learner (ACRL, 2015). Consider the following ideas as a way to reflect on your own approach to Internet searching.

Search as Strategic Exploration. When you use a search engine, sometimes you know exactly what you want. For example, if you type in "hotel rooms in New York City," you will get a list of websites and ads for companies that provide hotel booking. But sometimes when you use a search engine, you do not exactly know what you want. If you are new to a subject, you might not even know which words to use for a keyword search. The search process is then more like a type of discovery. Through trial-and-error learning, which includes careful reading, listening, and viewing, over time people develop knowledge that leads to more skillful Internet searching. As beginners to a topic, they use search to "learn how to learn" about the topic when they lack background knowledge or access to an expert as their guide.

This type of search *discovery process* is iterative. Experienced searchers know that generating keywords requires a process of trial and error over a period of time. You try a word, review the results, and then try a different word, learning as you go and gradually getting closer to your goal. Users know that very distinctive keywords can help narrow and focus a search. They use quotation marks to search for a specific phrase. They may use the minus sign to exclude certain results. For example, when someone is searching for a particular type of music competition, typing in *bass competition – fish – fishing* can filter out unwanted results. Using the advanced search option on Google, it is easy to narrow and refine a search. Using a reverse image search, you can locate the original source of an image, find a high-resolution version, track down the photographer, or get more information about an image. Users looking for information, reports, publications, and other rich content sometimes add the words "filetype:PDF" to their search so as to produce a limited list that contains only PDF documents.

Search as an Ongoing Conversation. When you explore any topic using search engines, you automatically join a *learning community*, relying on people who have engaged in sustained discourse on it over time. Information needs to be understood in historical context. Competing perspectives and interpretations emerge as more people choose to explore and learn about a particular topic.

Big controversies rage in every field of study because knowledge is not fixed and static; it changes as a result of human inquiry. The ACRL (2015) points out that this idea can be embodied by the phrase, "scholarship is a conversation." With Google Scholar and other social scholarship tools, users can access scholarly works and see *citation metrics* on the papers that other scholars have most frequently mentioned as influential. Beginning researchers can use social data like citation metrics as indirect evidence of quality. After all, if many other people found this work valuable, then it might be valuable to them as well.

Search as a Prelude to Purchase. Today, the practice of search is not limited to the search for knowledge and information. In fact, search is deeply integrated

What special strategies do you use when searching the Internet?

FeelPic/iStock

into our consumer behavior. Many people purchase many things online, and the rise in e-commerce is another reason why searching has become such an essential life skill. E-commerce sales in 2019 were estimated at more than $600 billion, representing 11% of total sales (U.S. Department of Commerce, 2020). When you begin your search for a new car, a new video game, or a new pair of shoes, you may start with Amazon or Google. Others search on EBay or Etsy to find products. People looking for a new restaurant may turn to Yelp. Other people shop by responding to ads shown to them on social media.

The nature of purchasing has been transformed as a result of the Internet. Online shopping is a worldwide phenomenon, and it is rapidly changing and adapting based on consumer response. The world's biggest online shopping website is in China. Taobau.com has more than 1 billion products available for sale and more than 618 million active users.

On each of these platforms, the search algorithms are different because each search engine has a particular set of biases built into its programming code. For example, on Yelp, the search filter hides many restaurant reviews. Yelp screens out users who are not very active as a way to minimize fake reviews. When you visit a restaurant page on Yelp, you are likely to see an ad promoting a competing restaurant, which can create confusion. Business owners believe that Yelp displays more reviews to companies that advertise on Yelp, but Yelp disputes this. Most reviews on Yelp are negative.

The Yelp algorithm has been shown to have a big impact on the fate of local businesses. Independent research has found that for every added star on Yelp, local restaurants (but not chain restaurants) experience a 5–9% increase in revenue. Consumer response to a restaurant's average rating is more affected by the number of reviews and whether the reviewers are certified as "elite" by Yelp (Luca, 2016). By conducting an experiment where some restaurants received free advertising, researchers showed that advertising led to a 25% increase in Yelp page views, which they estimated is equivalent to an 8% revenue gain. They also found that once the advertising stops, the benefit also stops (Gerdeman, 2017).

Why are most reviews on Yelp negative ❓

© Yelp Inc

When it comes to media, our purchase habits are also transforming. Instead of making one-at-a-time purchases of music or media, more people now purchase goods and services using a *subscription model*, where users pay a monthly fee. In 2020, Netflix had 183 million subscribers and Spotify had 250 million subscribers. For the purpose of comparison, consider that *The New York Times* had 6.5 million subscribers in 2020. The subscription model was originally developed by magazines and newspapers, but it is now used to sell movies and music, as well as wine, clothing, shoes, makeup, video games, technology, and more.

User Experience

The search process can be examined from the point of view of the author or from the point of view of the audience. The challenge for content creators is to get their message found, since people have only a limited attention span for searching. At the simplest level, digital media creators need to consider the *user experience (UX)* throughout the design and development process. Information architect Peter Morville (2014) notes these criteria for creating content that meets users' needs:

- **Useful**: Content should be original and fulfill a need;
- **Usable**: Content must be easy to use;
- **Desirable**: Image, identity, brand, and other design elements are used to evoke emotion and appreciation;
- **Findable**: Content needs to be navigable and locatable onsite and offsite;
- **Accessible**: Content needs to be accessible to people with disabilities;
- **Credible**: Users must trust and believe the content provided.

If you have a message to share, you probably want to make your content findable. The number of clicks and the time spent on a page can be a metric of quality because it measures how much people actually use the content. Since most people look at only the top one or two results of a search, a whole industry called *search engine optimization* helps companies get their websites to the top of a search engine result list.

If you use a social media platform like Instagram or Twitter, you probably already know about the power of the hashtag to make content more findable. A hashtag is a type of metadata represented with the hashtag symbol (#) plus a phrase, as in #medialiteracy. It allows ordinary people to create their own organizational systems for finding information on a specific topic. In Chapter 8, we will discuss the origins of the #OscarsSoWhite hashtag. Although anyone can create a hashtag, hashtags become useful only when a lot of people use them. Hashtags may enable networked special interest communities to form and organize to take coordinated action.

Is Searching Too Easy?

Has Internet searching become too easy? The average individual searches the Internet four times each day, or about 1,200 searches each month. Today, search results generally include rich snippets, which may consist of images, video, news, or other content chosen by an algorithm. When Google introduced the Knowledge Graph in 2012, the box with basic information that pops up on the page when you search for a topic, many people loved it. But others hated it.

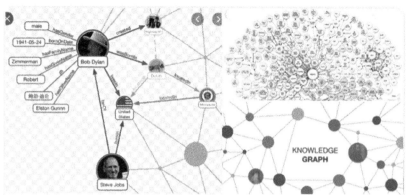

Google and the Google logo are registered trademarks of Google LLC, used with permission.

Knowledge Graph

The Google Knowledge Graph is a knowledge base used by Google and its services to enhance its search engine's results with information gathered from a variety of sources. The information is presented to users in an infobox next to the search results.
Wikipedia

How many times a day do you use a search engine **?**

The Knowledge Graph combines information from websites that other Google users have found useful, like the answer to the question, "Who invented homework?" Now, for many topics, Google presents you with "the answer" to your query. You do not even need to click on a external website link. The Knowledge Graph relies on an artificial intelligence algorithm to construct these summaries.

Why is the Knowledge Graph controversial? As this type of information becomes instantly available to users without the need to seek out external websites, users will not bother visiting individual websites at all. If people get used to getting "the answer" from Google without a real understanding of how that knowledge was constructed and selected, they may become vulnerable to forms of bias and propaganda that can be embedded in algorithms. They may lose track of the key media literacy idea that all media messages are constructed, and that it is messages are always selective and incomplete.

Consider the Question

What are the pros and cons of getting instantaneous answers through search engines? Discuss this question with a partner or in a small group and generate a list of advantages and disadvantages. Think about potential advantages and disadvantages from the point of view of children, teens, adults, and older people. Be sure to consider both short-term and longer-term potential consequences and unanticipated impacts as well.

Keyword Prediction with Autocomplete

To make searching easier, Google offers its users a set of predictive choices based on the most common searches. The autocomplete function is designed to make searches faster and more efficient, reducing typing by up to 25%, according to Google (2018). Like search, *autocomplete* predictions are algorithmically generated based on users' search activity and interests.

During the 2016 presidential campaign, conservative critics complained that Google's search engine was suppressing autocomplete predictions for information about Hillary Clinton's health. When users typed in "Hillary Clinton's," Google did not show the result "Hillary Clinton's health problems," but this result was found at the top of Microsoft's Bing search engine. When users typed in the query "Are Jews," the Google autocomplete prediction offered the phrase "Are Jews evil?" In 2016, if users typed in "did the hol," the Google autocomplete prediction produced the question "Did the Holocaust happen?" (Laposki, 2018).

In 2017, when Devin Kelley killed 26 people and injured 20 more at a Texas church, many Google users who searched for Devin Kelley 24 hours after the killing found that the autocomplete function offered "Devin Kelley Antifa." Immediately after the news broke, right-wing agitators had tweeted the killer's name and the word "antifa," which refers to a loose group of left-wing antifascist organizations that monitor the activities of American Nazis and others spreading hate speech (Collins, 2017). Conspiracy theorists like Alex Jones and anonymous websites like 4chan falsely blamed left-wing political groups as inspiration for the mass murder.

Although Google claims that it does not exert editorial control over the content users see, Google engineers tinker a lot with the algorithms in order to please a wide variety of powerful interests. Investigative journalism by the *Wall Street Journal* revealed that Google makes algorithmic changes to autocomplete so as to filter out inflammatory results on high-profile topics (Grind, Schechner, McMillan, & West, 2019).

Google also manually overrides the autocomplete algorithm in order to avoid users experiencing shock or distress with unwanted or unexpected predictions. The company removes sexually explicit predictions, violent or hateful predictions against groups and individuals on the basis of race, religion, and several other demographics, and predictions that refer to dangerous or harmful activity.

Danny Sullivan, Google's public search liaison, explains, "While some predictions may seem odd [or] shocking or cause a 'Who would search for that!' reaction, looking at the actual search result pages sometimes provides needed context." For example, when we look at the autocomplete results generated in 2018 for the phrase "school shootings are," we find as the first result "school shootings are not as important as the wall," followed by "school shootings are funny" and "school shootings are good." Sullivan notes that when you learn more about the information context, these phrases make more sense. The phrase "school shootings are not as important as the wall" refers to a critique of President Trump's press agent not mentioning the school shooting in her news briefing. The phrase "school shootings are funny" stems from a satirical news story on the Cracked.com website (Google, 2018). The company contends that "even if the context behind a prediction is good, even if a prediction is infrequent, it's still an issue if the prediction is inappropriate" (Google, 2018).

Algorithmic Personalization

It is true: Personal data are the oil of the 21st century, "a resource worth billions to those who can most effectively extract and refine it" (Dance

5 critical questions for Me and Google

This meme depicts a post on Tumblr and uses the Google search box to make a comment on people's relationship with Google. Using the five critical questions of media literacy, analyze this media message to gain insight on its meaning and value.

a Google search, with the words "Me and Google are so close we finish each others sen" followed by the word "sentences" as an autocomplete suggestion. It seems primarily designed to entertain and amuse. A Google reverse image search produces no results, but at Know Your

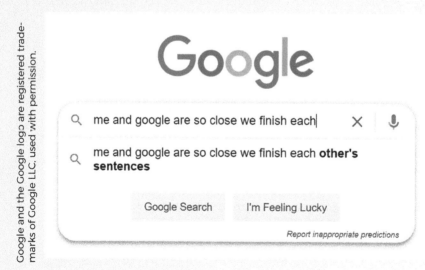

Google and the Google logo are registered trade-marks of Google LLC, used with permission.

1. **Who is the author and what is the purpose?**
   This is a meme that looks to have been created by a Google user in Australia. The meme depicts

Meme, this is considered part of the "Did You Mean?" series, which includes memes exploiting Google's spell-check or autocomplete function. The graphic design of the dialogue underneath

et al., 2018: 22). But because most of us do not watch other people interact with the Internet, we do not fully understand how *algorithmic personalization* affects daily life. When two people from different parts of the country or demographic groups search using the same keywords, their search results will likely differ. That is because search engines are increasingly personalized, based on information users provide.

For example, type in "pizza" in New York City and your results will be far different than if you use the same keyword in Atlanta. After you type in a keyword, a results list is presented, constructed by algorithms designed to offer relevant and quality sources. Google makes algorithmic inferences about *user intent* in order to refine results. Within one

---

looks to be from Tumblr; a search there reveals the original author to be Grace, age 19, whose Tumblr is http://thebestdaysofmy-flerm.tumblr.com. She posted this in 2014 and it received more than 600,000 shares.

2. **What techniques are used to attract and hold attention?** The meme relies on visual parody and wordplay that enable the query box to appear to be talking to the user. The Tumblr dialogue at the bottom uses the "Did you mean..." formula and the humor is accomplished with the wordplay that connects "sentences" and "sandwiches." Both are things that friends might feel comfortable finishing.

3. **What lifestyles, values, and points of view are represented?** The meme is commenting on people's tendency to use the Google search box playfully and experimentally. It may also be making fun of people's dependence on search personalization itself. The meme also seems to suggest the deep connection that Tumblr users often feel to their online community. In the meme, we see two discourses: one that features a user and Google, and the other that features a dialogue between kingdomworlds

and kingdomandlionhearts. This meme may be commenting on the value of using the query box to ask intimate or personal questions that are hard to bring up in face-to-face situations. It may be depicting the genuine intimacy that can be experienced between online friends who share an intense and personal connection.

4. **How might different people interpret the message?** Those unfamiliar with Tumblr might not understand that this meme depicts a type of relationship that develops among Tumblr users. People whose native language is not English might not recognize the idiom "We're so close we finish each other's sentences."

5. **What is omitted?** Those unfamiliar with Tumblr may not be aware that reblogging, or sharing content, is the major activity and that Tumblr documents the chain of sharing back to the original post. This meme may make people wonder whether research has been conducted to measure people's feelings of emotional connectedness to Google Search specifically or to the search process in general.

browsing session, if you search for "Trump" and then, a few minutes later, you search for "gun control," the results you get for your latest search may be influenced by your former previous search.

The Google algorithm determines which results to present through personalized searches, using these elements:

- your geographic location;
- which digital device you are using;
- the keywords you used recently;
- your previous searches, including the results you clicked on;
- all the websites you have ever browsed;
- information you provided about your identity when using social media like Facebook, YouTube, Twitter, or Instagram;
- the content of your emails.

Many media companies employ algorithmic personalization, and it continues to be adapted to increase profits. Now that you know that Google uses this kind of information in calculating which information to provide you in a search may affect, your future online behavior may change.

As we will learn in Chapter 10, algorithmic personalization is a very profitable business strategy. For this reason, how search works is a trade secret, and platform companies release very little information about it (Hannak et al., 2013). You may like to think that the algorithm is optimized for you, but it's really optimized for advertisers (Sandvig et al., 2015).

Social Media Search

Facebook and Instagram also have personalized algorithms that shape what you experience when using these platforms. On Facebook, you can search for people, posts, photos, videos, places, pages, groups, apps, and events. Facebook search results are ranked based on a combination of your activity on Facebook and that of the Facebook community in general. You can filter through friends, friends of friends, and the general public.

On Instagram (which is owned by Facebook), you can use the Explore tab, which whittles down billions of images to just those that align with your online behavior. Instagram uses machine learning to identify the content of images. When you click on an image, the Instagram algorithm immediately picks up metadata from that image (including hashtags and captions) and from your behavior, drawing a complex map of your behavior and the people you follow. The algorithm tries to predict your behavior by ranking the images in terms of how likely they are to be relevant to you (Titlow, 2017).

Partnerships between Facebook and other companies create opportunities for your data to be used for purposes that you are not aware of. In 2018, members of Congress questioned Mark Zuckerberg about the release of Facebook user data that were used without permission from users. For example, data were shared with Cambridge Analytica, the company that used Facebook data to build tools to influence the 2016 presidential election. Facebook also secretly allowed Microsoft's Bing search engine to see the names of virtually all Facebook users' friends—without user consent—and granted Netflix and Spotify access to users' private messages. The release of social media data under *third-party data-sharing agreements* allowed Facebook to grow by selling access to their users' data. They gave access to some companies and prevented access to other Silicon Valley companies (Dance et al., 2018).

Algorithmic personalization creates substantial challenges for privacy. For example, the Facebook Graph Search allows others to discover information about you that you may not have intended them to find. Making Facebook content discoverable means you become more vulnerable to those seeking to find you.

Users don't expect that their social media posts to family and friends will be used to define their identity for marketers. As Global Voices Advox (2013) explains, "There's a big difference between posting information for anyone to find and posting information to be searched and sorted." When Facebook came under the eye of the Federal Trade Commission in 2011, both the public and the regulators had the impression that third-party data sharing was a thing of the past. But the controversy is ongoing because it seems that Facebook is still not transparent about its business relationships with its partners (Zhou, 2019).

How Algorithms Reproduce Racism

As corporate advertisers tried to game the search process through search engine optimization so as to get their brands displayed on the first page of results, they were counting on the fact that the general public intuitively trusts those results, seeing them as highly credible sources. Most people do not know how companies pay to influence search results.

As a form of automated decision-making, algorithms are not neutral: They have a point of view. Safiya Noble started investigating Google Search in 2009 and was dismayed to see that searching for the phrase "Black girls" called up an enormous amount of pornography. Searching for "Asian girls" and "Latina girls" produced the same kind of pornographic results. For women of color, the consequences of this kind of misrepresentation are significant as it reinforces and deepens stereotypes that affect social identity, with the potential to affect how we respect and value others (Noble, 2016).

How do search engines amplify some voices and silence others? When Kabir Alli typed in "three Black teenagers" and looked at the top result, it was a montage of police mug shots of youth placed under arrest. Then he typed in "three white teenagers" and got glamorous stock photography of teens at play (Allen, 2016).

How do search engines amplify some voices and marginalize others **?**

Austin Police Department

Why did this occur? The explanation is in the tags used in machine learning algorithms. Images are tagged in different ways to be findable online. *Alt tags* are the descriptive words that producers attach to an image or article that help a search engine produce results. Google also offers a service for web developers that allows them to automatically identify the content of images, using machine learning to detect faces, landmarks, brand logos, and more.

For Kabir Alli's particular search, the images that appeared came from two sources: news sites and stock photography firms that sell images for marketing purposes. The newspapers had uploaded the police mug shot as part of the crime reporting process. Both groups had created tags for their images as a way to increase their findability. When Alli posted the results to social media, a kerfuffle erupted on social media, but then Google tweaked the algorithm so that the results also showed white teens under arrest.

Does this problem have a solution? Platforms are not required to be transparent about how algorithmic decision-making actually works, and they naturally do not want to release their actual code. But regulatory models offer some ideas for how transparency could be mandated legally. For example, American companies have a regulatory tradition of supplying consumers with information about how banks make decisions about lending money. The Fair Credit Reporting Act requires that people be given a specific reason if they have been denied a loan. Perhaps a similar procedure could be implemented for people to request the modification of algorithmic decision-making.

Experts also say that, as a society, we also need to decide what data should be allowed for producing algorithms. According to Louise Matsakis

(2018: 1), "Discrimination laws may prevent using categories like race or gender, but it is possible that proxies for those same categories are still utilized, like zip codes. Corporations collect lots of types of data, some of which may strike consumers as invasive or unreasonable." She wonders whether a furniture retailer should be allowed to take into consideration the model of a consumer's smartphone when determining whether that customer receives a loan. Should Facebook proactively use information from a person's *social graph* to detect when it thinks that user is feeling suicidal?

Silicon Valley may want to persuade people that intelligent agents and algorithms offer better critical thinking than people can achieve on their own. But media literacy educators generally reject that idea, arguing that the increasingly common use of artificial intelligence in everyday life must not encourage people to abdicate their thinking, reasoning, and decision-making to machines.

The Politics of Filter Bubbles

Algorithmic personalization may make Internet searching easier and more effective, but it may also have unexpected and dangerous consequences. Filtering search results based on users' previous searches strategically limits their exposure to new ideas and information. The *filter bubble* is the idea that digital media algorithms and recommendation engines limit and narrow people's exposure to information and ideas by offering results that the search engine considers relevant to a user's profile (Pariser, 2011).

How do these filter bubbles develop? One factor is the rise of *information cascades*, which happen when Internet users make decisions to share content based on their perception of what others are doing. When it seems like *everyone* is talking about Kanye West (or coronavirus or Donald Trump or fill in the blanks with other current examples), it is possible that an information cascade has flooded the cultural environment with that particular information. Such cascades may warp people's understanding of what's really important. Information cascades are a new form of social pressure that may shape people's attitudes without their awareness.

Personalized search may also affect how people make political decisions. The algorithmic ranking process that returns relevant items for any particular query can be biased. Results of an Internet search that may appear neutral and authoritative can be shaped by data from the inputs to the ranking system, or by the ranking system itself (Kulshrestha et al., 2018). As a result, people may only get news on subjects they are interested in and with the perspectives they already identify with. This creates more insulated and polarized communities, with a potentially negative impact on democracy.

Some people believe that algorithmic personalization may also affect whether people see news and current events information at all. For example, younger Internet users may get most of their news from social media. They may choose to avoid political news altogether, which could lead to a widening knowledge gap. Recommendation engines may contribute to the development of *counter-publics*, the marginalized social groups that situate themselves outside of the mainstream public discourse. The rise of QAnon and other conspiracy theories may be evidence of the changing information ecosystem brought about by search engine algorithms (Waterson & Helmore, 2018).

The political impact of search personalization may vary from country to country. In the United States, concerns about political polarization and propaganda are influencing the policy agenda in relation to questions of how the Internet should be regulated. In August 2018, President Donald Trump accused Google of bias against him, tweeting that Google suppresses conservative voices and "news that is good." He was referring to a comment by Lou Dobbs on Fox News, who mentioned a blog post that claimed that a majority of Google News results for the president came from left-leaning outlets. The site used a bizarre classification from conservative pundit Sharyl Attkisson that ranks almost every mainstream news outlet (other than Fox News, the *Wall Street Journal*, *The Economist*, and DailyMail.com) as left wing. But after Trump's tweet, Google had to respond. It did by saying, "When users type queries into the Google search bar, our goal is to make sure they receive the most relevant answers in a matter of seconds. Search is not used to set a political agenda and we don't bias our results toward any political ideology" (Waterson & Helmore, 2018). As we will see in Chapter 10, tension between the press and the executive branch of government raises concerns that may impact on the practice of democratic self-governance.

What benefits and harms may result from the widespread use of facial recognition technologies ❓

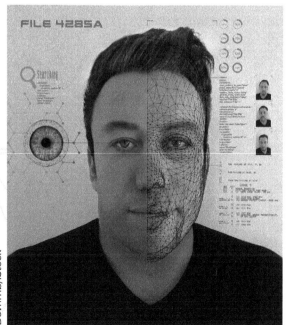

Devrimb/iStock

Censored Search

Should American technology companies create news aggregation and search engine services in countries where government censorship restricts access to information? The Chinese government blocks information about political opponents, free speech, sex, news, and many forms of academic scholarship. It bans websites about the 1989 Tiananmen Square massacre and references to "anticommunism" and "dissidents." Users of Weibo, a Chinese social media website, cannot discuss books that show the dangers of authoritarian governments, like George Orwell's *Nineteen Eighty-Four* and *Animal Farm*. Western social media sites like Instagram, Facebook, and Twitter, as well as American news organizations such as *The New York Times* and the *Wall Street Journal*, are not accessible in China.

At the present time, Google is also blocked in China by a form of censorship called the *great firewall*. In order to advance their global business interests, Google is creating a search engine designed to comply with Chinese government regulations. On some topics, the search engine will produce results that say, "Some results have been removed due to statutory requirements." The search engine will also blacklist sensitive queries so that no results will be shown at all when people enter certain words or phrases.

Some fear that such actions may become a template for many other nations. An Amnesty International spokesperson calls it "a big disaster for the information age," noting that when the world's biggest search engine obeys China's censorship rules, "it sends a signal that nobody will bother to challenge censorship any more" (Gallagher, 2018).

Surveillance Society

Because algorithmic personalization depends on data, everyone who uses the Internet provides a massive amount of information to technology companies, governments, and other businesses each day. Now that you know that Google reads the content of your email and tracks the purchases you make online in order to determine how to customize searches for you, this naturally raises concerns about privacy.

As we have seen in this chapter, personal and collective data can be used for a variety of purposes and are having a significant impact on how we learn and gain information, use media, and buy products. By spending 3 or more hours online every day, people are producing gigantic volumes of data that can be used for monitoring and surveillance. In fighting crime, law enforcement professionals can use web crawlers to learn who posts on which websites, who they interact with, and what they post. Facial recognition technology can, with a high degree of accuracy, identify an individual in a picture, and much can be learned about an individual's daily behavior from social media.

In general, the American public is aware that the government has access to personal information and that a vast quantity of user data is made available to advertisers who wish to promote their products and services to targeted audiences. Governments are eager to access these data as well. As we learned in Chapter 2, the Chinese government has been creating a social credit system that includes data about people's shopping habits, social behavior, and friendships. Those with low scores may be blocked from booking a flight or buying a train ticket. As personalization has become more profitable, data collection has increased, and without regulatory controls, data collection can be abused.

The term *privacy paradox* describes the apparent trade-off between the benefits of personalization and the potential harms of data misuse. In general, most people are willing to share their data for better service. Some will even say, "I have nothing to hide, so I have nothing to fear."

The onslaught of digital marketing abuses has increased people's desire for new types of algorithmic personalization that do not compromise trust. As Merijn te Booij (2018) puts it:

> If I buy a pair of shoes, by all means, remember my shoe size. But don't pester me to buy another pair immediately and everywhere I turn for the next three months of my life. Just because I looked at something online today doesn't mean I want to be looking at it again tomorrow and the next day and the day after that.

Whether we like it or not, traditional ways of thinking about privacy may interfere with genuine inquiry. Digital platforms like Google and Facebook generally present the topic of privacy as a matter of *individual choice*, suggesting it is all about personal responsibility. This belief leads some people to withdraw from social media, obscure information, or use pseudonyms. But these actions only make things worse. Researchers who conducted interviews and focus groups with youth of low socioeconomic status (SES) in New York City found that they were highly aware of the risks of sharing information online. Many poor people work in the service industry, where persistent surveillance occurs;

Intellectual Grandparent:
Michel Foucault

Bettmann/Getty Images

Michel Foucault was a French philosopher, historian of ideas, social theorist, and literary critic. Foucault's theories primarily addressed the relationship between power and knowledge, and how social control is enacted through societal institutions and processes. His ideas have influenced academics and educators in sociology, cultural studies, literary theory, and critical theory.

Before Foucault, scholars thought about power as something that individuals exercise through political strategy or military force. They thought about power in relation to individual, masculine authority, as in the power of the medical doctor in relation to the needs of his patient, or the role of the father in relation to the needs of his children (Taylor, 1984).

Foucault's work has relevance for the kind of social power that is embedded in search engines because power needs to be treated as a relational concept. A relational perspective on power looks at power by mapping the social relationships that underpin the power of institutions or entities. Some key insights from Foucault include:

Power is socially constructed. By examining the intellectual history of institutions including prisons and mental institutions, Foucault showed that power is not primarily something that works at the individual level. It is more diffuse than that, more like a process of constraining discourse. Foucault used the term *power/knowledge* to signify that power is constituted through accepted forms of knowledge, scientific understanding, and "truth":

> Truth is a thing of this world: it is produced only by virtue of multiple forms of constraint. And it induces regular effects of power. Each society has its regime of truth, its "general

they may also live in communities with high police presence. By opting out of digital media as a result of fear, uncertainty, and doubt, they may stay under the radar screen in ways that diminish their own life opportunities. That is why some researchers believe it is not helpful to conceptualize privacy as simply a matter of individual choice. Marwick, Fontaine, and boyd (2017) write:

> Essentially, we tell young people that many governmental and institutional actors are mining personal information, and it is up to individuals to prevent this through their own actions, regardless of their structural position. We never mention that this is impossible. Our mental model of young people as selfie-taking narcissists desperate for attention from anonymous audiences makes it possible to blame them for privacy violations, rather than passing legal protections which would protect young people from the prying eyes of governments, educational institutions, and employers (p. 10).

Recently, the public is beginning to recognize the value of privacy and the harms of surveillance as structural matters in a global society. Regulation may be needed to balance the rights of individuals and companies so as to advance the public interest.

politics" of truth: that is, the types of discourse which it accepts and makes function as true; the mechanisms and instances which enable one to distinguish true and false statements, the means by which each is sanctioned; the techniques and procedures accorded value in the acquisition of truth; the status of those who are charged with saying what counts as true. (Foucault, cited in Taylor, 1984: 180)

Power is necessary and productive for societies. For Foucault, although power is a major source of social conformity, it can also be a necessary, productive, and positive force in society. For example, Foucault showed how people learn to conform to the "disciplinary power" of schools. The rules and procedures developed in these institutions for people to interact with each other have a force of their own, as people willingly adapt their behavior to reproduce institutional values and accepted norms of expertise and authority (Foucault, 1991).

Social media may subtly control and limit personal freedom. Foucault never wrote about the Internet. But other scholars have used his ideas to examine the power of search engines, which organize and make useful the world's information. Because, as Michael Zimmer puts it, "the quest for the perfect search engine requires the widespread monitoring and aggregation of a users' online personal and intellectual activities," this practice itself threatens the very "values the perfect search engines were designed to sustain" (Zimmer, 2008: 77). When you use personalized search tools without understanding how businesses monitor your behavior, this creates a type of power/knowledge "cage" that may subtly control and limit your autonomy and personal freedom.

If Michel Foucault has influenced your thinking about media, you can share a comment on the Grandparents of Media Literacy website at www.grandparentsofmedialiteracy.com.

What the future may hold: **Monetizing Your Data**

As digital devices proliferate, more of them will be used to collect data in the service of advertisers. Lessons learned from search engine personalization are likely to influence cell phones and other digital devices.

People generally think of their cell phone data as private. In the United States, Internet service providers (ISPs) can record and sell your browsing history, and collect information about which apps and services you use. They do not have to tell you what they collect or who they sell it to beyond what they volunteer to say in their privacy policy. But some telecom companies disguise their surveillance goals.

During the Obama administration, Verizon was fined $1.3 million by the U.S. Federal Communications Commission (FCC) for using a super cookie tracker to target its advertising program. But other companies, or even intelligence agencies, could leverage the super cookies to track wherever people went online. As part of the fine, Verizon agreed it would use *opt-in* strategies for any data collection efforts. Opt-in strategies ask customers to freely choose to accept data collection, monitoring and tracking.

Verizon uses a different way to get data from customers by offering rewards for those who opt in and agree to give up their privacy. It offers coupons and other rewards for every $300 consumers spend on their monthly bill. The program has attracted only 10 million of Verizon's more than 116 million customers. To participate in the special offer, users click a link that installs an ad-tracking program that collects personal data from their mobile device. Those data are then shared with Verizon and a host of other companies, who are called "partners." As one writer put it, "So, in plain English, Verizon is saying: let us use your browsing, location, interests and other personal data for marketing purposes—and we'll let you participate in our earn-rewards program" (Lomas, 2017).

In the future, companies may simply bet on the idea that consumers love price discounts and special deals so much that they do not mind that their activities are mined as sources of data for targeted advertising (Turow, 2017). Some evidence of this possible future is already evident. Only 1 month after a Facebook data breach was announced in 2018, when information from 50 million user accounts was hacked, Facebook announced the release of Portal. Portal is a device that looks to be an intriguing combination of a smart speaker and a video chat device. It uses artificial intelligence to automatically detect and follow people as they move throughout the frame on a video call. The marketing slogan says, "If you can't be there, feel there."

According to the website, Facebook does not listen to, view, or keep the contents of video calls and it does not use facial recognition technology. But although Portal does not have ads, it collects information with which to target ads on Facebook and Instagram (Wagner, 2018). From a business point of view, the biggest benefit of Facebook placing a digital device in users' homes is that it provides the company with another data stream for its ad-targeting business. As more digital devices include microphones and video cameras, regulations that protect consumer privacy may become even more important.

TIME T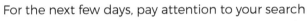REFLECT

Reflect on your typical search process when you are trying to buy something online. When you are online, you might take on the following roles:

- *Navigator:* You use menus to find what you are looking for.
- *Scroller:* You like reviewing a lot of images to search for things.
- *Searcher:* You use keywords to type in the name of things you are looking for.
- *Shopper:* You use reviews from other shoppers who provide hyperlinks to products and services.

For the next few days, pay attention to your search processes as you engage in online shopping, and then reflect on your own patterns. Consider the advantages and disadvantages of each of these four roles and consider how and why you may mix these strategies at different stages of your shopping process.

Consider these questions as you compose an informal video response:
- In what kinds of shopping situations have you found yourself using search engines?
- Do you notice any patterns about typical ways that you use search engines for shopping purposes?
- Can you describe one of the best experiences searching for something and one of the worst experiences you have had?
- Based on your experience, do you have any tips, tricks, or advice for other people who might want to improve their online shopping skills?

Use the Flipgrid Inquiry online video dialogue tool available at www.medialiteracyaction.com to share your views. You can also view and respond to comments by other people who have offered their own thoughtful reflections on this question.

CREATE T▶LEARN

Curate Knowledge

Curation is a process of carefully selecting information to increase knowledge. When a list of online sources is carefully curated and annotated, it can be valuable to others. After reading this chapter, use a search engine to explore a topic of search engines and social media interest to you and create a "Top 10" list of resources on the topic.

In creating your own annotated list of online resources, make a list of the search terms you will use to find diverse perspectives on this topic. When deciding which results to include in your list, be sure to select diverse genres and types of media, including at least one video, one news story, and one scholarly article. See if you can find information from people who have different perspectives or professional expertise, including ordinary people, scholars and researchers, company executives, activists, and other voices with something to say about your topic. Share your curated list by simply publishing your Google Doc to the web, using the hashtag #MLAction with links to the content you have selected along with a short description of each resource.

Fierce competition in the news industry has had unexpected consequences for American society

How Do People Get the News?

4

Learning Outcomes

1. Understand how people access news and journalism today
2. Identify the many different forms of news and journalism that consumers use
3. Appreciate the professional journalistic practices involved in reporting news about war, crime, and conflict
4. Consider how framing shapes news coverage and current events in certain predictable ways to make information more salient to audiences
5. Reflect on how economic pressures affect news values and increase news partisanship

When Christopher Hebert decided to stop reading, listening to, and watching news for 1 whole year, it was a dramatic decision. After all, he was an English professor at the University of Tennessee, and in his line of work, being knowledgeable about current events is considered a civic duty. But he recognized that he was spending so much time consuming news that he "didn't have any energy or emotion left to do anything about it" (Hebert, 2018).

Why do some people watch the news and others seek to avoid it completely? What difference do news coverage and journalism really make in our lives, after all? Few topics are more polarizing these days than current events and news. Some people are news junkies and others feel overwhelmed by the 24-hour news cycle and the constant barrage of bad news, with its focus on conflict and controversy. Other people feel compelled to watch Fox News or CNN every day while others tune in mainly for the local weather report. Some people have complex feelings about Sean Hannity or Rachel Maddow. Others read *The New York Times*, the *Wall Street Journal*, or the *Washington Post*. Still others learn about the news from talking with friends and from the posts that their friends share on Twitter or Facebook.

Some young people are not much into the news, it seems. In one comprehensive study of college students' news consumption, nearly half of the participants agreed it is difficult to tell the most important news stories on a given day. They reported that they learn about current events primarily from discussions with peers and professors and via social media. Most young adults claim that they are simply overwhelmed by the sheer volume of news (Newman, 2018). College students do engage with news topics that are important to them; however, they do not define news by traditional standards, and they do not necessarily assign authority based on the platform or authors from which news comes. A large majority of students agree that news has fallen short of the standards of accuracy, independence, and fairness (Head et al., 2018).

In this chapter, we examine the changing practices of contemporary journalism in order to explore the question "How do people get the news?" In this chapter, we explore how news is constructed and the changing nature of journalism in the digital landscape. We consider questions like:

- How are editorial decisions made about what news to cover?
- How is news aggregation affecting the practice of journalism?
- How is journalism both reflecting and shaping the growing political partisanship in the United States?
- How can the practice of journalism reconcile its ideals with the messy realities of today's competitive news environment?

It is easy to say that news about politics, current events, crime, science, and community events helps people make good decisions as citizens in a democratic society. Of course, that is the message you probably expect to find in a book about media literacy. You hear people claim that it is a civic duty to stay informed. Most people say: "I need to know what is going on in the world" or "We cannot just ignore the issues." More broadly, the argument goes like this: "News is vital for democracy. It serves as a check on the government and big corporations in order to protect the public from abuses of power."

But let us face it: for most people today, a powerful tension exists between what we want journalism to be and what it really is. While the American public knows that news coverage is necessary in a democracy, they are also aware that it falls short when it comes to accuracy, independence, and fairness (Bennett, 2016). Misinformation, public relations, partisanship, errors in journalism, clickbait, political manipulation, and sponsored content all contribute to the public's distrust of news coverage.

To restore public confidence in the role of the press in American democracy, we first need a better understanding of how editors, producers, and reporters report the news. As we see in in this chapter, a competitive business environment makes it difficult for, journalists and business leaders to engage with all sectors of the American public as they develop new business models that may enable journalism to thrive in a digital age.

Reading, Watching, and Listening to News

About 70% of American adults claim to be active news consumers, engaging in *direct discovery* of the news through intentionally reading, listening to, or watching news coverage. But people are not watching TV news or reading newspapers as much as they used to. They are getting their news from Facebook, Twitter, or other types of social media. Only about 34 million households receive a print newspaper at least once a week. In just 1 year, circulation statistics are down 10%, which is worrying for the industry. Broadcast TV news coverage is holding on to a mostly elderly audience. About 50% of American households watch television news programming on a regular basis. The average audience for the evening newscasts for ABC, CBS, and NBC decreased by 7% in 2017, down to 5.2 million, compared with 5.6 million in 2016. Viewers of

What sources do you use to access news about current events **?**

CNN, Fox News, and MSNBC also decreased 12% from 2016 to 2017, down to 1.2 million (Pew Research Center, 2018).

Listening to the radio is a well-established habit for many people. Many people get their news from the radio because it is convenient to listen as part of the daily commute to work. More than 29 million people listen to National Public Radio (NPR), and 87% of them report that they discuss topics they have learned about on the radio with friends and family (NPR, 2018).

Big differences in reading, listening to, or viewing news coverage have always existed based on age and education. Younger adults are less likely than older adults to watch local, national, or cable newscasts. For example, just 8% of those ages 18–29 often get news from network TV, compared with 49% of those 65 and older. Adults who have completed college are less likely to watch local and national news coverage than those with no more than a high school degree. As Figure 4.1 shows, young adults ages 18–29 spend less time consuming news than any other age group. One study found that, for

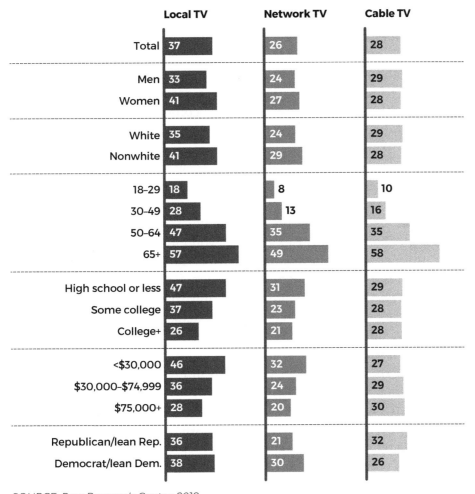

	Local TV	Network TV	Cable TV
Total	37	26	28
Men	33	24	29
Women	41	27	28
White	35	24	29
Nonwhite	41	29	28
18–29	18	8	10
30–49	28	13	16
50–64	47	35	35
65+	57	49	58
High school or less	47	31	29
Some college	37	23	28
College+	26	21	28
<$30,000	46	32	27
$30,000–$74,999	36	24	29
$75,000+	28	20	30
Republican/lean Rep.	36	21	32
Democrat/lean Dem.	38	30	26

Figure 4.1
Demographic Characteristics of Audiences for Local, Network and Cable News

SOURCE: Pew Research Center, 2018
Data are expressed in percentages

young people, social media, online news websites, and apps were considered the most helpful in learning about the 2016 presidential campaign. For this age group, print and network television news coverage were considered the least helpful (Gottfried et al., 2016).

We do not have as clear a picture about how much news people are consuming through digital platforms on their phones and computers. One study by the Reuters Institute for the Study of Journalism found that nearly two-thirds of young people rely on *distributed discovery,* an approach to news consumption through which people find, access, and navigate information through platform services, including social media like Facebook and search engines like Google (Newman, 2018). Many large news organizations, including the *Washington Post,* do not publicly report their digital circulation statistics. But digital advertising has been financially important to news organizations. It accounted for 35% of all newspaper advertising revenue in 2017, having grown significantly since 2011 (Pew Research Center, 2018).

Avoiding the News

One in three American adults say that they do *not* intentionally read, listen to, or watch national and local newscasts, according to the Reuters Institute. This finding is similar to evidence from across Europe, Asia, and Latin America (Newman et al., 2017). Media researchers have not generally studied this group of people, but the collapse of local journalism and the rise of digital platforms like Google and Facebook has begun to change that.

Researchers have conducted in-depth interviews with people called *news avoiders,* people who believe that "the news finds them" or that "the information is out there" (Toff & Nielson, 2018). Because information is perceived to be "in the air" as an ambient part of daily life, these people feel they can absorb it rather than actively seek it out. Beyond incidental exposure while using the Internet and social media as part of daily life, they also employ Internet searches as a way to get information for daily decision-making. News avoiders also rely on friends and family, using interpersonal communication to talk about news events, which helps them maintain a sense of connection to the public sphere without depending on intentional news consumption (Edgerly, 2017).

Some claim that the quality of their lives improves when they kick the news consumption habit. For example, Rolf Dobelli was once a news junkie who focused on the news every single day. He gradually discovered that news and journalism consumption became a waste of time and had other negative effects on his life. After choosing to stop consuming news, Dobelli came to see news reports as full of distracting material with no lasting value. He became more aware that because the news industry thrives on competition for public attention, politicians are encouraged to be outrageous, leading to bad public policies. Journalists work too quickly to be the first to report news, leading to inaccuracies in reporting. Because it emphasizes primarily novelty and conflict, news coverage offers an inaccurate representation of what is happening in the world, he thought. Dobelli found that he actually learned more about the world from reading and viewing non-news content, including books, documentaries, magazines, websites, documents, and even novels.

Canadian writer David Cain also quit consuming the news, and he experienced relief from choosing to not watch the daily tragedies and disasters unfold. News coverage increases people's fears about people, places, and things. He noticed that dramatic images of police brutality or car crashes may provide a rush of excitement but offer no real insight or explanation for social, cultural, and political problems. Superficial awareness of current events may help you chat with colleagues, but "when you quit playing the current events game, and observe others talking about them, you might notice that almost nobody really knows what they're talking about" (Cain, 2017).

Most troubling, Cain points out that when we consume news, "we can remain uninvolved without feeling uninvolved." He observes that while "being informed" sounds like an accomplishment, the hobby of monitoring the state of the world does not actually improve the world. This distinction is important to underline. When he escaped from the superficial, sensational world of news coverage and journalism, which seemed designed more to agitate than inform, Cain was able to make better choices about alternative sources of information and to use his reading and viewing time more productively.

News Values

What makes news coverage and journalism different from other forms of information? Journalism makes truth claims specifically about current events. Editors and reporters use *news values* as criteria to determine whether particular information they discover is newsworthy (Fuller, 1996). To determine what to publish in a newspaper or to report on a television news story, journalists use one or more of these five criteria:

Proximity. News is relevant to the geographic locale of the audience.

Timeliness. Events that happened recently are more likely to be considered news.

Relevance. Information that helps people make decisions about voting, public policy, jobs, the economy, and even topics like food, technology, and travel can be newsworthy.

Conflict. Significant disagreement between people or groups is newsworthy because people want to know about conflict. Crime, tragedy, and bad news are more newsworthy than good things that happen in the community every day.

The US politics sketch Donald Trump

Wounded by media scrutiny, Trump turned a briefing into a presidential tantrum

President lashed out at reporters, swiped at Biden and refused to accept that he had put a foot wrong in coronavirus response

How do news media outlets communicate a point of view through the choice of headline and image **?**

The Guardian https://www.theguardian.com/us-news/2020/apr/13/trump-coronavirus-meltdown-media-authority

Human Interest. Entertainment news coverage about celebrities and ordinary people offers information that is shocking or surprising—or even just insightful and emotionally appealing.

The Forms of News

Today, the terminology for different types of news coverage and journalism has become more complicated because of the vast array of available choices. While we once categorized news media by their method of delivery (print, broadcast, digital), today all forms of news and information are digital, even when they are printed or broadcasted.

Here is a list of some of the many choices people have for getting news and current events today:

- **Legacy Media:** This is the term used for the major national newspapers and broadcast television stations like *The New York Times* and the *Washington Post* or national news organizations like CBS, NBC, ABC, PBS, Fox News, CNN, and MSNBC. News agencies like Reuters and the Associated Press are also part of legacy media as are traditional book and newsmagazine publishers.

- **Local Media:** This term refers to newspapers like the *Boston Globe* and the *Los Angeles Times* as well as free metro papers that you find in major cities. It also refers to local television stations that are affiliates of a network and provide geographically specific news.

- **Citizen Journalism:** This term is used for video, photos, and other media produced by ordinary people who document natural disasters, police brutality, protests, or other public events.

- **News Aggregators:** These are websites like Google News, Vox, or Yahoo News or portals like MSN that algorithmically curate (or aggregate) content from a range of sources and use human editors and freelancers to (re)write news from other sources. In China, the aggregation service Toutiao has more than 120 million users.

- **Original Digital News:** These are "born digital" news publications like *Huffington Post*, *BuzzFeed*, *Vice*, *Salon*, and *Slate* or blogs that produce original content specifically on news, current events, and journalism. Blogs may also offer opinion and commentary, and some provide in-depth reporting on political, social, or cultural issues. Most target younger audiences with niche topics (technology, music, media, politics) that appeal to them.

- **Content Publishing:** Some companies and bloggers publish magazines and/or websites on topics of more general interest to people, including science fiction, health and wellness, personal finance, and lifestyle choices. Examples include *Scientific American* and Gizmodo. Some of these publishers rely on *content marketing* or *sponsored content* to produce content and they gain revenue by publishing content that advances a public relations goal of a business or company.

- **Analysis and Investigation:** Some media organizations like *The New Yorker* and ProPublica engage in investigative journalism, dig deep into important issues, and specialize in analyzing and uncovering abuses of power and betrayals of public trust. Some blogs also feature reporting of this type.

- **Meta-journalism:** Some news coverage focuses on the news industry itself, examining the business of journalism, news reporting, and technology. Publications of this type include the *Columbia Journalism Review*, *Nieman Reports*, and NPR's *On the Media*. This type of reporting about reporting also includes blogs like Jeff Jarvis's *Buzz Machine* and websites like The Information.

In using these news sources, consumers must apply different expectations to them based on their format. For example, when you see a video of a breaking news story, you may check to see if it has been produced through legacy media or citizen journalism. When you stumble across a news story about dangerous dog food, you may look closely to see what type of news it is, checking whether it has been sponsored by a pet food company or written on a veterinarian's blog, or if it is a science news story from the *Washington Post*.

Which forms of news do you use most often? Why do you prefer them **?**

All about News Aggregation

The term *news aggregation* refers to services that gather up news and information from many different sources and package it for their readers or viewers. News aggregation can be done algorithmically, and this is becoming a more common way for people to receive news. For example, consider the News 360 app, which personalizes a news feed for users. After you select topics of interest, the app uses algorithms to select news you might be interested in. As you use it, the quality of the content seems to improve because the algorithm uses your choices to modify its selections. Today, a growing variety of news aggregation services use algorithms to curate the news.

But news aggregation can also be done manually, by human curators. In fact, as Vox's Ezra Klein (2015) reminds us, *Time* magazine began its life as an aggregator as it originally reprinted excerpts from other daily news publications. One way that journalists discover news is by reading the work of other journalists. Members of news organizations may republish bits and pieces of what they learn from their colleagues around the world, sometimes under a collaborative financial agreement like the Associated Press, sometimes directly by copying and pasting, and sometimes by reworking or revising content and giving it a different spin. Former *New York Times* editor Bill Keller (2011) once explained that aggregation can mean "smart people sharing their reading lists, plugging one another into the bounty of the information universe."

But important controversies surround the work of news aggregation services. The most critical concern is that news aggregation may contribute to filter bubbles, as discussed in Chapter 3. In 1995, MIT Media Lab director Nick Negroponte described an imaginary news aggregator he called "The Daily Me" so as to make the point about the dangers of hyperspecialization in the presentation of news and current events.

Yet another controversy comes around the issues of respecting copyright and intellectual property. When it comes to infographics and data visualizations, Klein (2015) explains, some editors think that, instead of merely copying them, news aggregators should remake or redo them. Klein sees that as an effort to "hide the original intellectual authorship." He points out correctly that the most challenging aspect of creating an infographic is not creating the chart—it is coming up with the idea for the chart.

Perhaps the most important problem with news aggregation is that, in retransmitting the work of others, news aggregators are essentially compromising financial incentives for the original creator. We explore this further in Chapter 10 when we examine media economics. Some journalists object to aggregation when it involves "taking words written by other people, packaging them on your own Web site and harvesting revenue that might otherwise be directed to the originators of the material" (Keller, 2011). The news industry has not yet figured out a solution to this important ethical and economic problem.

Framing the News

News coverage influences how people understand the world. The public depends upon the news media for information about local, national, and international events. But as an *infotainment society* has developed (Kellner, 2008: 11), the representation of crime and violence has shifted ever more toward entertainment. Of course, stories about crime and criminality have always been popular and profitable for news organizations. But a close look at crime news also reveals quite a bit about the way journalists make sense of complex realities and turn them into compelling news stories with heroes, victims, and villains.

The term *framing* is used to explain how journalists select some aspects of perceived reality and make them more salient and accessible to the reader, expressing them in a way that connects to the existing knowledge, beliefs, and attitudes of the audience. Depending on the target audience, media frames embody different values and ideologies and they articulate a point of view. Noticing framing in the news helps people understand how news coverage is constructed and how it selectively presents reality (Entman, 1993).

Journalism scholars have conducted a considerable amount of research on framing in the news. In one study, researchers examined local television news media portrayals of perpetrators, victims of crime, and law enforcement officials in Los Angeles by comparing them with official government crime records. TV news portrayals of Los Angeles officers were compared with employment records published by the Los Angeles Police Department (LAPD) and the Los Angeles Sheriff's Department. The researcher analyzed 117 news programs randomly selected from the UCLA Communication Studies News Archive, which contains a population of hundreds of thousands of news programs digitally captured since late 2006. After coding for the race, ethnicity, and gender of the perpetrators, victims, and law enforcement officials, researchers discovered that perpetrators of crime are accurately depicted on local TV newscasts. Blacks in particular were portrayed as perpetrators, victims, and as police officers in ways that aligned with the actual data from crime and employment records. Although Latinos were accurately depicted as perpetrators, they were underrepresented both as victims and as police officers. There were fewer TV news stories that featured Latino crime victims or police officers as compared with their overall proportion in the city of Los Angeles. In local TV news, whites were overrepresented both as victims and police officers (Dixon, 2017). Thus, it seems that TV news producers make choices in the presentation of facts about crime and law enforcement in ways that are responsive to their presumed target audience. These strategic choices create a distorted perception of reality for viewers.

Most of the time, people are unaware of how frames work to shape their thoughts and feelings about news events. To make sense of the world, people rely on a number of *heuristics* (or mental shortcuts) that speed up the processing of information but also leave them vulnerable to framing. In his 2011 book *Thinking Fast and Slow*, Daniel Kahneman describes research he conducted to show how the language embedded in news stories shapes interpretation, memory, and attitudes. Researchers asked people to read brief passages about crime in a hypothetical city named Addison. Some participants read a passage that said that crime was a "beast preying" on the city of Addison. Some participants read a passage that called crime a "virus infecting" the city.

As the researcher explains, "Although the passages were nearly identical, those exposed to the 'beast' metaphor were more likely to believe that crime should be dealt with by using punitive measures, whereas those exposed to the 'virus' metaphor were more likely to support reformative measures" (Rathje, 2017: 1).

Researchers found that changing the metaphor in this passage influenced people's beliefs about crime. Weirdly, when participants were asked about what influenced their decision, no one seemed to notice the metaphor. Because frames can be activated by simple phrases and metaphors, it is wise for us to slow down as readers and viewers and engage more deeply with political news coverage in order to notice how it is constructed and how its framing may influence us.

The power of frames and framing may even help us understand public reaction to school shootings. Consider the case of school shootings, including those at Parkland, Columbine, Virginia Tech, and Sandy Hook, just to name a few of the most noteworthy of the many that have occurred over the past 20 years. When public interest in a story is high, journalists present school shooting news through different frames over a series of days. You are already familiar with this, of course. First is the breaking news story with video footage of the event. Then come press briefings with local police officials and school leaders. There will (inevitably) be a focus on the mental health of the perpetrator, for example, or on the good qualities of the victims. A story may follow on the type of weapons used, the role of the media in promoting violence, and (of course) the policy issues associated with access to guns and the need for gun control.

How does news coverage of school shootings usually present potential solutions to the problem?

The familiarity of these frames and the selective emphasis on different angles of a news event have been called *frame shifting*. Frame shifting allows the media to highlight different facets of a news event in order to capitalize on public interest in the news (Reese, 2007). By selecting some aspects of reality and giving those aspects distinct emphasis, journalists define a social problem, interpret it, evaluate it, provide moral insight, and offer recommendations for policy action (or inaction). Such frames may contribute to a public perception that solutions are impossible to the most difficult problems we face in our society.

In a study of how news media cover school shootings, researchers have found differences that depend upon the level of public attention and interest in a particular event (Schildkraut, 2012). More broadly, researchers have also discovered that even people's *moral judgments* about violence and crime in general can be affected by the framing and point of view journalists take, as well as the sequence in which they offer information. For example, crime news can be presented from the victim's or the perpetrator's point of view; it can focus on the context and circumstances, or highlight the perpetrator as a type of victim (Cerulo, 1998). Each of these decisions about how to present or frame the crime has consequences for how people interpret and understand the event.

The concept of framing is an important idea in media literacy. But researchers have not yet discovered whether learning to identify news frames through the process of media literacy education changes people's knowledge, attitudes, and beliefs (Bulger & Davison, 2018). Being cognitively active in identifying media frames takes a lot of practice. It may be difficult for a single learning experience alone to alter culturally dominant interpretations of media messages that result from frames that are congruent with the audience's existing attitudes and beliefs.

The Living Room War

He was called "the most trusted man in news." Walter Cronkite began his career covering World War II as a wire-service reporter before becoming the anchor of *CBS Evening News* in 1962. During this time, broadcast television reporting on U.S. involvement in Vietnam was taking full advantage of newly available lightweight film and sound equipment, which made it possible for reporters to get closer to the fighting as they covered the events of specific battles (Lehmann, 1989).

Journalists stationed in Vietnam found themselves frustrated by U.S. government officials, who claimed that the war was designed to root out communist guerilla fighters in South Vietnam. It was not officially a war: government officials explained that their purpose was to encourage the "hearts and minds" of the people to reject communism. But to journalists who were there, it looked like the United States was waging war against ordinary people, not soldiers. For example, in 1965, CBS News correspondent Morley Safer and his colleagues followed Marines into the little village of Cam Ne.

How has TV news coverage of war changed over time?

Reporting Vietnam: Cronkite's Vietnam Editorial

16,696 views • Feb 26, 2016

👍 28   👎 5   ➤ SHARE   ≡₊ SAVE   •••

They expected to find Viet Cong guerrilla fighters; instead, they encountered friendly fire. The Viet Cong were nowhere to be found. But the Marines burned down 150 houses in the little village using flamethrowers and cigarette lighters. In his report, Safer sympathetically explained the profound significance of the significant loss of property to the Vietnamese villagers (Newseum, 2016).

For the first time, television enabled American viewers to gain access to information about the Vietnam War that showed the war effort in a negative light. The horror of those images was a rare scene at that time. Cronkite's nightly newscasts helped shape public opinion about Vietnam, which became known as "the living-room war" (Arlen, 1997/1969). As the war dragged on, Americans saw more of these vivid and gut-wrenching examples of the deadly impact as the death toll on both sides continued to climb.

Unlike during World War II and the Korean War, journalists covering the Vietnam conflict did not have to submit their stories to military censors for clearance. Although the military leaders in Saigon considered imposing censorship, American political leaders believed that censorship would prove politically unpopular (Lehmann, 1989).

By 1968, during the Tet Offensive, when the Viet Cong launched surprise attacks all across the country, Walter Cronkite decided to leave the anchor desk and see for himself what was happening on the ground. During this time period, hundreds of American soldiers were dying every week. Cronkite went to Hue, where the fighting was intense. Viewers saw him as he left the ancient imperial city in a military helicopter with the remains of 12 Marines in body bags.

In true journalistic fashion, CBS News included the point of view of U.S. military leaders when it aired the "Report from Vietnam: Who, What, When, Where, Why?" But in the closing moments of the show, Cronkite shared a subjective opinion with the American public. Although the Viet Cong suffered a military defeat, he explained, overall the Tet Offensive was a stalemate, with neither side gaining a winning position. "It is increasingly clear to this reporter that the only rational way out then will be to negotiate, not as victors, but as an honorable people who lived up to their pledge to defend democracy, and did the best they could. This is Walter Cronkite. Good night" (Pach, 2017).

There is no definitive research showing whether or how the news media coverage of the Vietnam War affected public opinion. The United States did not withdraw from Vietnam until 1975. Reflecting on the impact of Vietnam on the state of American journalism, to took more than a decade to understand the evolution of government deception, for example. Pressure from editors to get vivid images distorted public opinion because journalists did not have time to understand or explain the larger context of news events.

Press coverage of the Vietnam War revealed the biases embedded in their own routines of *hit-and-run reporting*, the practice of getting news and pictures of the latest firefight by riding helicopters in and out of the battlefield the same day. Andrew Pearson (2018) contends that perhaps the most important legacy of the Vietnam War was that "the best young reporters have learned […] to question authority and find out for themselves what's really going on."

Eyewitness Reports

In your lifetime, you have experienced the power of police brutality videos, a form of crime reporting or *citizen journalism* that shows the point of view of friends, family, bystanders and sometimes even the victims themselves. On YouTube, there are many thousands of videos that depict police officers shooting and beating unarmed Black people. Beginning in 2009 with the shooting of Oscar Grant, these videos have stirred widespread public outrage for 10 years, leading to federal investigations and nationwide #BlackLivesMatter protests. Many of these videos are short, graphically explicit, and brutal, focusing precisely on the events leading up to the moment of death.

When people first encountered such videos in 2009, they had many questions about the identity of the filmmaker. Was this person a bystander who merely recorded the tragic event, or should they be grateful for the individual's efforts to document reality in pursuit of justice? Sadly, some people even felt inspired to violently retaliate against the police after seeing these videos (Antony & Thomas, 2010). Clearly, police brutality videos, offered as citizen journalism, provide a frame of interpretation that positions police officers as perpetrators of violence, a frame rarely used in journalism and mainstream media.

How might exposure to police brutality videos affect people in different ways ❓

Although people respond in different ways to these videos, watching people die on cell phone video at the hands of a police officer can be psychologically traumatic. The spectacle of media violence as depicted in police brutality videos is compelling. TV news organizations may replay them because they are "driven to construct tabloid spectacles in an attempt to attract maximum audiences for as much time as possible" (Kellner, 2008). Sadly, however, because the media framing of police brutality has become so familiar to news consumers, people have likely become desensitized to the horror of these tragic events. *Desensitization* is a media effect that occurs when repeated exposure

Akabei/iStock

lessens the emotional intensity of reader or viewer response. As the number of police brutality videos has grown, available via YouTube and shared and reshared by people on social networks, critics like Jamil Smith (2015) note, "Increased awareness has not translated into prevention and policy. [...] The surge of video evidence has only made our society increasingly numb to the spectacle of Black death."

Thankfully, not everyone was numb. In 2020, there were nationwide (and worldwide) mass protests against police brutality and structural racism in law enforcement and society. On a single day in June, more than 500,000 people marched in hundreds of cities and towns across the United States. Survey researchers have found that between 16 and 26 million people reported that they participated in a protest event in 2020, in the largest protest movement in American History (Buchanan, Bui & Patel, 2020). Although millions of people demonstrated through peaceful protest, news media generally emphasized violent incidents.

Trust but Verify

Journalists make important decisions about what to include and what to exclude from their news coverage—this is the practice of *gatekeeping*, a term introduced in 1951 to describe the complex decision-making involved in the newsroom (Entman, 2005). This concept supports a key concept of media literacy, which is that all media messages are selective and incomplete. Today, with the 24/7 news cycle, time pressures are intense and journalists must manage their limited time well in choosing what kind of content to publish. As news organizations struggle financially for survival, pressures associated with resources, staffing, and the need for business revenue also influence the construction of news reporting (Nimmo & Geyer, 2017).

At the heart of journalism is the relationship between reporters and sources, a relationship that includes trust but that also is characterized by mutual self-interest. Journalists pay special attention to information that comes from *reliable sources*, experts who can offer information that a responsible person uses as the basis of a decision or action. Journalists often rely on government officials, members of law enforcement, and business leaders to inform their understanding of reality. Reporting the statements of people in authority is one of the many *journalistic routines*, the practices used to manage the inevitable limitations of time and organizational resources in the newsroom. Other journalistic routines involve creating balance through presenting two opposing perspectives on an issue and defining news events around a focus on conflict and controversy.

But journalistic routines can sometimes distort news and information. For example, a community has a meeting to discuss new plans to develop a new hotel. Almost everyone at the meeting thinks this is a great idea, but a couple of citizens speak out against it. A journalist from a local news outlet is present at the meeting, capturing footage. When editing the story, the producer wants to be objective, so she shows one person speaking in favor of the hotel and one person speaking against it. She frames the story as a choice of one option or the other, giving the impression to viewers that the two sides are equal—even though they were not equal at the event. The aim to be objective created a distortion of what happened. Similar types of distortion resulting from misplaced efforts to balance news coverage have affected topics like climate change, income inequality, health care, and other important issues.

In the field of journalism, institutional practices help to reinforce the difference between news and entertainment. For example, news organizations separate news workers from those responsible for entertainment and advertising. Journalists engage in information gathering through a mix of structured and unstructured techniques. Structured techniques include press conferences, interviews, and analysis of evidence such as photos, videos, and documents. Unstructured techniques traditionally refer to observations and background research using Google, telephone inquiries, and other methods.

When seeking reliable sources, journalists value *independent sources* with no financial, personal, or intellectual stake in a particular outcome. They collect information using interviewing and traditional research processes. In a few stories, they may rely on a single source. In most stories, at least three people are interviewed. In other forms of investigative journalism, journalists may interview dozens of people, piecing together the information they receive so as to understand an event, a trend, or a cultural phenomenon.

Journalists highly value *accuracy*, working hard to ensure that basic facts are described in a way that most people would agree are truthful. When reporting crime and other tragic or unexpected events, they understand that eyewitness accounts are sometimes unreliable and can be clouded with emotion. Journalists generally insist upon *accountability* and document their sources by name, only occasionally granting anonymity under circumstances where sources may face harm.

As a mode of inquiry, journalism evolves over time, with information revealed gradually as a result of newly found evidence and changing circumstances. In the 2015 award-winning film *Spotlight*, directed by Tom McCarthy, viewers see a team of investigative journalists at the *Boston Globe* work tirelessly to uncover the long-standing scandal of child sex abuse by priests in the Catholic archdiocese. Through interviews and document analysis, they discover the scale of the cover-up by Cardinal Bernard Law.

Journalists are also expected to be transparent about potential *conflicts of interest*—both from their sources and from their own organizations. In 2018, NBC News ran a story about the 25th-anniversary release of the award-winning film *Schindler's List*, a film directed by Steven Spielberg that dramatizes a true story about a German business owner who rescued numerous Jews from the gas chambers and protected them by employing them in his factories. After featuring an interview with the director about why the film remains relevant today, the anchor, Lester Holt, ended the broadcast by noting that the film is owned by NBCUniversal, the parent company of NBC News. Because journalists are expected to be transparent about the potential conflicts of interest of sources used in their reports, Holt's statement was significant. He invited his viewers to consider how NBC's reporting on the rerelease of the film actually served as a type of advertising or promotion. As a few giant media companies control more media outlets, this form of journalistic transparency is more important than ever before.

Partisanship and Journalistic Objectivity

Journalists emphasize the value of reliable information on which the public can make informed decisions. When Fox News retired its famous slogan "Fair and balanced" in 2017, it replaced it with the phrase "Most watched, most trusted." The marketing slogans of news organizations suggest how they communicate their values to the general public:

- *New York Times*: "All the news that's fit to print"
- CNN: "The most trusted name in news"
- *Washington Post*: "Democracy dies in darkness"
- *USA Today*: "We deliver news, not noise"

News media organizations have not always valued being unbiased and impartial. Back at the beginning of our nation's history, *partisanship* was the norm. In the early 19th century, the type of press the First Amendment protected was not neutral—it was filled with opinions, gossip, and rumors, as well as advertising and blatant untruths. Newspapers were openly affiliated with political parties and many news stories were constructed in order to support a favored political friend or to damage a political foe. Newspaper editors sometimes worked part time for members of Congress or state legislators. If the editors did not like the news, they sometimes simply kept it out of the paper. For example, as journalism historian James Baughman (2011) explains, when Democrat Grover Cleveland was elected president of the United States in 1884, the Republican *Los Angeles Times* simply did not report the news for several days!

In the early 20th century, radio broadcasting, newspapers, and newsmagazines gradually began to adopt a spirit of neutrality, capitalizing on their power and authority with elites in government and business. Many cities had two newspapers, competing to bring the latest news to citizens. Over time, and with the arrival of television, declining circulation led most American cities to have only one. Within a local community, newspapers were generally a monopoly with little competition. Until the late 1970s, most of the employees of American news organizations were male and white. In order to attract the maximum number of readers, journalists avoided identification with particular political orientations. Aiming to attract readers, listeners, and viewers from all political parties, they embraced a focus on accuracy, fairness, and balance.

The *ethic of journalistic objectivity* was enacted through three journalistic practices:

1. providing facts and neutral information substantiated by experts or officials;

2. avoiding interpretation and using language in ways that minimize a perception of bias; and

3. maintaining independence from political parties and insulating journalists from advertising pressures.

News professionals have political opinions and biases, of course. In the 1950s, Edward R. Murrow, the distinguished CBS broadcaster, emphasized the separation of fact from opinion but also said, "It is not, I think, humanly possible for any reporter to be completely objective, for we are all to some degree prisoners of our education, travel, reading—the sum total of our experience" (Wertenbaker, 1953).

How does journalism's past affect its future ❓

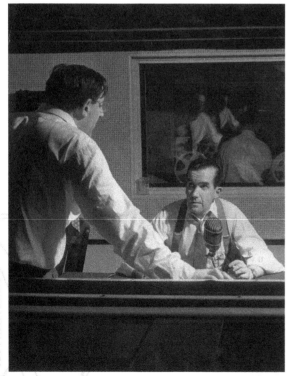

CBS Photo Archive

A belief in objective reporting held firm during the 1940s and 1950s until leaders of media organizations learned firsthand of the dangers of "straight" reporting—that is, simply reporting what politicians and government officials say, without analysis or interpretation.

During the Cold War, Senator Joseph McCarthy launched an anticommunism campaign, using the press to spread lies and whip up fear, uncertainty, and doubt. In 1950, for example, a first-page story in the *New York Journal American* said that the government was planning to "round up 4,000 Reds," that communists had taken over the State Department, and that 100 scientists were Russian spies protected by the U.S. government (Bayley, 1982). Senator McCarthy generated massive amounts of news coverage (using false claims, name-calling, and little evidence or information) because he knew that the press thrives on conflict and controversy. McCarthy was skillful in manipulating the press by exploiting deadline pressure, releasing his accusations just minutes before wire services sent out their releases, leaving reporters with no time to investigate. Each day brought new accusations, making it difficult for reporters to do more than simply report the senator's claims.

In 1954, Edward R. Murrow critically examined the senator's anticommunist accusations in a one-hour episode on the CBS news show *See It Now*. This influential form of documentary long-form journalism helped give viewers more informational context through which to understand McCarthy's strategy of destroying people's careers by false accusations. In 1954, a congressional hearing during which the U.S. Army accused Senator McCarthy of false accusations was televised—the first time congressional hearings were televised in American history. For 36 days, the American public could see the congressional investigation "live" on TV. Although Senator McCathy's personality showed him to be deceitful, ill-mannered, and bullying, eventually McCarthy was cleared of the charges, with his reputation in ruins.

The press and the public learned from this experience and gradually, news media organizations began to include more *analysis and interpretation* in their news coverage. It was considered necessary to help people make sense of current events. During the 1960s and 1970s, there was much experimentation with new approaches to journalism, including "new journalism," which used a subjective, first-person voice and immersive reporting techniques. Many of these works were published in magazines, not in newspapers. Truman Capote even wrote an entire nonfiction novel about a murder in his 1966 bestseller *In Cold Blood*. It was a sensation: it used extensive detail to describe the lives of the murderers, the victims, and other members of a rural community, and it was both a form of literary journalism and an example of a new genre in true-crime writing.

Interpretation and analysis have another benefit, of course. They enable news organizations to differentiate themselves from their journalistic competition. When the Fox News Channel debuted on cable television in the United States in 1996, it had more opinion and commentary than other national television news broadcasts (Taub, 2017). It announced a political identity by claiming, "For 3 out of 4 Americans who believe the news is biased, we present something quite rare: a news network dedicated to pro-

Alamy

Why has news partisanship been increasing?

viding fair and balanced coverage" (Hallin & Mancini, 2004: 1). Clearly, partisanship is in the eye of the beholder.

When it launched, Fox News was considered the embodiment of partisan news. Partisan news is not fair and balanced—it proudly defends an ideological point of view and offers an interpretation of news and current events from a distinct perspective. The founder of Fox News, Roger Ailes, understood that opinions are cheaper to produce than reporting and investigations. People prefer information that confirms their existing beliefs and world views. He also saw that advertisers, who once sought out a mass audience, now aim with more precision at niche audiences. Rather than try to reach everyone, media entrepreneurs focus on reaching subgroups of readers or viewers. So *Fox and Friends* cultivated a niche audience of conservatives (Stelter, 2020).

In countries like England, Germany, France, Spain, Italy, Brazil, and in other parts of the world, news media have always been partisan, and readers are expected to understand that news reporting comes with a bias or point of view attached. There, newspapers and magazines differentially value the interests of labor unions, business owners, and intellectuals. For example, in Italy, the newspaper *La Repubblica* offers an explicitly center-left perspective on the news, and it "doesn't pretend to follow an illusory political neutrality, but declares explicitly that it has taken a side in the political battle" (Hallin & Mancini, 2004: 1). Like the rest of the Italian press and broadcasting, *La Repubblica* reports on the world from a distinct political point of view. In Italy, as in other countries in Europe, newspapers are easily recognized as having different ideological flavors, and government-controlled radio and television broadcasts offer the position of the government in power. Journalists play an outside role in elections in many parts of Europe because paid political advertising is strictly limited, and election campaigns last for only a short period. In Europe, governments grant free airtime to political parties instead of requiring political candidates to raise vast sums of money to pay for television and digital advertising (Hallin & Mancini, 2004).

Consider the Question

Who benefits and who is harmed by news partisanship? Discuss this question with a partner or in a small group and generate a list of advantages and disadvantages. As you discuss, consider this question from multiple points of view, including aspiring politicians, government, business and media leaders, public interest activists, and citizens. Be sure to consider both short-term and longer-term potential benefits, harms, consequences and unanticipated impacts as well.

Virality and Sensationalism in News

Sensationalism has always been part of the media, and with good reason. You can't inform, entertain or persuade people until you have first grabbed their attention. Whenever there is intense competition among media organizations, they need to find ways to stand out in a crowded field. It's a matter of business survival. During the 1980s, when cable television intensified competition, broadcasters

FBI WARNS ABOUT HIGH-TECH TOYS

Why does local TV news use sensationalism to attract views?

attracted audiences by relying on a time-honored approach: they used stories featuring sex, violence, children, animals, and UFOs, a practice known as *sensationalism*. Local television news producers constructed breathless, suspenseful teasers designed to pique people's curiosity (and motivate them to stay up for the 11:00 p.m. local newscast). Airing during evening primetime hours, usually during *sweeps week*, when local news is measured by Neilsen ratings, these *news teasers* included lines like these:

- Could your house be making you fat?
- The ingredients in shampoo that make boys grow breasts—Tonight at 11.
- Some say a popular drug can turn you into a compulsive gambler.
- Could frequent hiccups be a sign of cancer?
- Were you poisoned by a Big Mac?

How effective is sensational journalism? Dutch researchers conducted an experiment during which they gave viewers a chance to freely watch 90-second news videos that included negative content (like fires, accidents, crimes, or riots) or neutral content (like culture or economics). Half of these news videos were structurally sensational in nature, where production features (including camera shots, sound effects, music, and editing techniques) are used to make the news content more compelling. This style of composition is sometimes called *tabloid packaging*.

Researchers found that audiences watch negative content for twice as long as neutral content. They watch structurally sensational stories on neutral topics for somewhat more time than similar stories without tabloid packaging. But researchers also found differences by age and gender, finding that female and older viewers dislike sensationalism, choosing to stop watching such content (Vettehen & Kleemans, 2017).

The rise of the Internet has enabled sensational content of all kinds to spread widely. The term *virality* is used to describe stories that are widely shared through email and social media. What makes something go viral may depend on the type of message content, the timing and context, the design or packaging of the story, and the target audiences. In a study of *The New York Times* health news articles, researchers found that the most viral content was positive, emotionally evocative, with familiar (not novel) content (Kim 2015). During the 2016 presidential election, researchers discovered that a very small subset of conservative viewers did most of the sharing of so-called fake news (Guess et al., 2018).

5 critical questions about who gets to be a U.S. citizen

This video from AJ+ asks the question "Who Gets to Be a U.S. Citizen?" After viewing the video at www.medialiteracyaction.com, use the five critical questions of media literacy to analyze this media message and to gain insight on its meaning and value.

Youtube Screenshot

1. **Who is the author and what is the purpose?** This is a 12-minute YouTube news segment entitled "Could Your Citizenship Be Taken Away?" It is produced by AJ+, which is the new media division of Al Jazeera America. Al Jazeera is a television network that is sponsored by the government of Qatar, in the Middle East. AJ+ is designed to reach young people by releasing news video segments directly to social media. This particular news segment is informative. It exposes the Trump administration's use of denaturalization as a political tool against legal immigrants. The policy strips people of citizenship rights if they have "cheated the process" by using food stamps or benefiting from other government programs before acquiring citizenship. To explain the policy, the segment also offers a brief history of immigration law and denaturalization processes, including "fast track" laws, created in the 1990s, that make naturalized citizens less equal than people born in the country. Because the story explains this policy as it was developed under both the Trump and Obama administrations, it does not appear persuasive or partisan.

2. **What techniques are used to attract and hold attention?** The reporter who explains the story speaks directly to the camera, providing information about the denaturalization process. The segment also

Do virality and sensationalism really matter for the future of journalism? Sensationalism is likely to increase as people compete for scarce human attention in a crowded information landscape. Critics worry that if the sensational storytelling news style replaces rational, considered, and critical analysis in news coverage, then people may be less critical of the techniques typical of tabloid style and their attention may be more easily manipulated by sensational production techniques. As the distinctions between the different genres of digital content blur, it could become more difficult to defend the unique role of mainstream journalistic news organizations in modern society.

features interviews with knowledgeable experts who offer information and opinions. A *music bed* makes the story seem important and exciting. Unlike in a traditional news story, the reporter asks viewers to subscribe to the AJ+ YouTube channel at two different points. Graphic elements include an animated depiction of the 18-page immigration application form, with the many pages of the form flying across the screen. Near the end of the segment, the reporter calls attention to the shift in the tone of the music with a clever *meta-reference*, saying, "Ted, hit 'em with a tempo change." This technique actually increases viewer awareness of the use of music as it is intended to deepen people's emotional connectedness to the news.

3. **What lifestyles, values, and points of view are represented?** The news segment includes the point of view of Donald Trump, new immigrants, and immigration lawyers. The reporter points out that President Obama was the first to address immigration fraud but notes that immigration has become increasingly technical and difficult, even for lawyers. The news segment seems to *balance* several different points of view.

4. **How might different people interpret the message?** Some viewers will be shocked to learn that people can be deported for incorrectly filling out the immigration form, with even a very trivial error, years after they have been in the country working and paying taxes. Immigrants will be happy to learn that the government has the burden of proof to pursue a denaturalization case. This story seems to offer useful information both to people who support immigration and those who oppose it.

5. **What is omitted?** The positive aspects of "two types of citizenship" are not described. Surprising, the news segment does not include the story of an actual individual directly affected by this policy or present the stereotype of new immigrants as victims.

Intellectual Grandparent:
Walter Lippmann

Walter Lippmann was an influential Pulitzer Prize–winning American journalist, news analyst, and commentator whose book *Public Opinion*, published in 1922, is considered a classic work in the field of communication. He wrote a syndicated column called "Today and Tomorrow" for the *New York Herald Tribune* as well as 20 books of political commentary. Throughout his long career, he influenced a generation of politicians and journalists. Lippmann deeply understood the role of the press in the democratic process. To sustain democracy, he claimed, three elements are essential: (1) protection of the sources of the news, (2) organization of news coverage so as to make it comprehensible, and (3) education of human response (Clark, 2018). Thus, he was one of the earliest thought leaders to anticipate the value of media literacy as a means to both empower and protect.

Lippmann understood both the strengths and the limitations of journalism as practiced in the United States. He was careful to distinguish between news reporting as the signifier of an event, while truth is the larger picture of the world upon which human beings can act. Lippman identified several ideas that serve as key contributions in analyzing the news media and its role in society:

Stereotypes are in our heads. Lippman used this phrase to describe the distorted pictures or images in our minds that come not from personal experience, but from stories and information received through family, friends, and media. We can have *stereotypes* of groups of people, events, places, and ideas. Because they are passed down culturally from one generation to the next, stereotypes are resistant to change. In times of war or economic hardship, governments have used stereotypes to activate us-versus-them polarization, "which ultimately enables members of the in-group to tolerate or even rationalize harming members of the perceived out-group" (Woods & Barna, 2010: 1). Because stereotypes are charged with strong emotions and make us feel safe, they are a defense mechanism, and "any disturbance of the stereotypes seems like an attack upon the foundations of the universe" (Lippmann, 1922).

Reporter–source relationships shape the news. A peculiar dependency exists between reporters and sources, and Lippmann, who was closely connected to Democratic politicians like President Franklin Delano Roosevelt, understood this phenomenon well. He was highly aware that reporters cultivate relationships with people who have information to share, including government officials, eyewitnesses and informants. Lippman knew from experience that journalists who are "openly hostile to those in authority" might inevitably lose access to news sources and be unable to do their jobs. Thus, the complex interplay between the press and the powerful is maintained through mutual self-interest. Journalists serve the needs of the powerful even as they attempt to make the powerful accountable to the public.

Agenda setting occurs through opinion leadership. Although Lippmann did not use the term *agenda setting*, he explained the core idea, noting that the topics and issues the press identifies as important come to be thought of as important in the minds of the general public. How does this happen? Because of people's lack of access to information and their cognitive biases as a result of stereotypes, Lippmann did not believe that ordinary citizens could be adequately informed on all the many complex issues of the day. For example, many people are not willing to invest the time and effort to be truly knowledgeable about climate change. They rely on friends and colleagues who are passionate and interested in the topic and trust their interpretation and analysis of the facts.

Lippmann recognized that some individuals in a society serve as opinion leaders, and these individuals are the most deeply influenced by the information and messages they receive from the news media. They, in turn, influence the people in their social network, creating what Katz and Lazarsfeld (1955) call a *two-step flow of influence*. Lippmann believed that thought leaders can work for the benefit of the public interest. He appreciated the multifaceted nature of influence, realizing that news media channels are but one of many ways people come to form opinions about public affairs.

When suggesting that thought leaders and experts shape public opinion, Lippmann recognized the growing role of experts in the complex decision-making required for policy on topics like health and welfare, regulation of business, foreign policy, and other matters. Other philosophers of the time period, including John Dewey, offered critiques of this perspective, seeing it as elitist and technocratic. The debate continues today: Can the public rely on experts or must people be fully capable of using public communications to make informed decisions?

If Walter Lippmann has influenced your thinking about media, you can share a comment on the Grandparents of Media Literacy website at www.grandparentsofmedialiteracy.com.

Talking Back to the News

News should inspire public dialogue and discussion. Through talking with others, we make sense of the media content we consume and publicly debate major political and social issues. So when technology companies developed commenting platforms that could be embedded in news websites, there was much celebration. What a great tool for audience engagement, thought the editors of news organizations. They imagined this would create stronger connections between content creators and consumers. Plus, this kind of innovation—enabling readers to respond to and discuss news stories—could even strengthen the role of the news organization in supporting the democratic process.

But in 2016, when National Public Radio (NPR) closed down its reader commenting system, it concluded that the comment sections were not providing a useful experience for most users. NPR found itself overwhelmed by *trolls*, anonymous contributors who use offensive, mean-spirited, and inappropriate submissions to gain attention and shred authentic discussion and debate. In 2013, the Popular Science website shut down its comments section after it learned that comments were affecting readers' perceptions of science. The presence of nasty and negative comments at the end of an article makes many readers less trustful of the main content (Finley, 2015).

To better understand the nature of readers who comment on news stories, researchers who examined more than 9 million comments from *The New York Times* published online between 2007 and 2013 found that 2%

Why do people pay so much attention to controversy and conflict **?**

Alamy

of comments included swear words and 10% contained uncivil language including name-calling (using words like dumb or hypocrite), discrimination (using words like racist or bigot), or references to misinformation (using words like distort or mislead). Partisan words (like Democrat, Republican, GOP) were present in 24% of comments. Comments that included both uncivil *and* partisan words received the most engagement from news audiences, leading people to upvote the comment to increase its visibility.

Perhaps we should not be surprised that people seem to like controversial, conflict-laden, and highly partisan comments. Researchers have concluded that professional news values that emphasize conflict and controversy work hand in hand with the cognitive biases of readers to "tacitly encourage particular types of incivility in the comment section" (Muddiman & Stroud, 2017: 607).

Until recently, *The New York Times* manually moderated online comments and did not allow online commenting on articles dealing with particularly controversial issues. In 2017, it began using a machine learning digital tool called Moderator, developed by Google, which uses algorithms to prioritize user comments, assigning them values that make them more or less visible to readers. Will algorithmic monitoring of comments on news and current events improve or degrade the quality of public discourse?

People need to rethink their responsibilities as participants in public discussion. Carolyn Marvin and Philip Meyer (2005: 407) point out that engaging people in dialogue and discussion is essential for democracy to thrive. "The public needs a journalism sophisticated and generous enough to relinquish the patronizing notion of a passive citizenry."

Journalism: Challenges Ahead

It has been an open secret for a long time: the news business faces real challenges to its survival. Declines in the number of people reading, viewing, and listening to news—and the radical increase in alternatives to journalistic content—pose threats that will shape the industry's future. In a 2018 *Washington Post* article, Douglas McLennan and Jack Miles put it this way: "Newspapers have been dying in slow motion for two decades now" (McLennan & Miles, 2018). People working in the profession identify a variety of problems leading to declines in the number of jobs for journalists. In a study of more than 10,000 alumni of 22 journalism schools conducted by Tom Rosenstiel and colleagues for the American Press Institute, participants identified a variety of problems facing the field, but two common concerns were prevalent. Rosenstiel asked the question: What do you think are the biggest challenges facing journalism in general today?

Top 10 Press Pressures

1. Too much opinion and false information on the Internet
2. The economic model for news
3. Media owners focused too much on profits
4. The public doesn't care about quality journalism
5. Media owners don't believe quality will sell
6. Traditional media have not adapted well to new technology
7. Journalism education isn't preparing people for the future
8. Technology monopolies control the Internet
9. The 24-hour news cycle
10. The public does not trust journalists

Adapted from Rosenstiel et al (2015)

Two big trends are evident. Most participants named the flood of opinion and false information on the Internet as a significant problem. One in four participants did not think legacy media would be able to adapt to the technological changes needed to compete with non-journalistic sources of information. However, only a small number of journalism graduates appeared concerned about technology companies holding a monopoly.

The second most common concern revolved around the "broken business model" that relies primarily on advertising and subscription revenue. Forty-four percent of participants identified this as a problem, with one-third saying that media business owners are too focused on profits. Note that some journalism graduates even blame the public, saying that the public does not care enough about the quality of information, while others blame owners who do not believe that quality will sell.

TIME T🧠 REFLECT

Think about the Top 10 Press Pressures and, after reading this chapter, respond to the question:

- In your opinion, which of the challenges on this list are most important? Which of the challenges on this list are least important?
- What other challenges not shown on this list seem important to you?

Consider the top three most important issues facing the future of journalism. Make an informal extemporaneous response by using the Flipgrid Inquiry online video dialogue tool available at www.medialiteracyaction.com to share your views, offering description and examples, and using reasoning and evidence to support your top three choices. You can also view and respond to comments by other people who have offered their thoughtful reflections on this question.

CREATE T▶ LEARN

Analyze and Comment on a News Story

Find a recent news story that interests you. Perhaps you will choose something from legacy media, digital content, meta-journalism, or any of the categories discussed in this chapter. You may choose news radio, television, print, or online news. As you review the work you have selected, discuss some of the following questions with a partner and take notes of key ideas that emerge. Then write an essay about your ideas, answering each of the questions below in a paragraph. Use evidence from the news story you selected to support your reasoning process. Post and share your work online using the #MLAction hashtag.

- **Message:** What is the content and main ideas of the information being expressed?
- **Rationale:** Why did you select this example? What makes it interesting to you?
- **News Values:** Why was it published? Which news values are most relevant to this particular story?
- **Audience and Context:** Who is the target audience? What kind of prior knowledge is needed to make sense of this news story?
- **Construction Techniques:** How are language, images, and sound used to construct this news story? How are metaphors, symbols, and rhetorical strategies used to attract audience attention and activate emotional responses?
- **Context:** Where, when, and how have people encountered this message? How might this affect its interpretation?
- **Credibility:** What type of news media message is this, and what distinctive features are used in the story to communicate credibility?
- **Omissions:** What questions do you have after reading and analyzing this story?
- **Judgment:** How does the information in this story make sense to you? What do you see as the strengths and limitations of this story?

VM/iStock

The blurry lines between advertising, public relations, and propaganda create challenges for media consumers and creators.

5

What Is the Difference between Advertising, Public Relations, and Propaganda?

Learning Outcomes

1. Understand the similarities and differences between advertising, public relations, and propaganda

2. Appreciate how advertising is regulated around the world

3. Recognize how propaganda can lead people to bypass critical thinking

4. Consider the reasons for the blurring of journalism and public relations

5. Reflect on spin as a duel of interpretations in the social construction of reality

Advertising is everywhere. When you watch a YouTube video, you watch advertising—or wait a few seconds before you can click the ad away. Highway billboards and online banner advertising are obvious, and TV commercials fill 10 to 16 minutes of every hour of programming.

Advertising is also a form of entertainment. During the 2018 Super Bowl, a unique Tide campaign demonstrated people's awareness of the many conventions of Super Bowl advertising. In a creative strategy never used before, Tide took over the whole event by featuring David Harbour, an actor on the Netflix science fiction horror series *Stranger Things*. He served as an omniscient narrator who invited viewers to question every ad they see. In the ad, Harbour seems to enter many stereotypical advertising worlds. As viewers watch, they discover that what they are watching is not actually what they think they are watching. Numerous short ads appear for cars, beer, deodorant, perfume, insurance, jewelry, razors, mattresses, dietary supplements, prescription drugs, cleaning products, technology, and more. Each of these mini-ads is perfectly crafted to be familiar in light of real products advertised frequently. In each, David Harbour is there, and viewers experience a pleasurable surprise reveal when they discover each ad is really a Tide ad.

Like Rod Serling in *The Twilight Zone*, Harbour mysteriously asks, "Is every Super Bowl ad a Tide ad?" In another segment, he claims, "If clothes are clean, it's a Tide ad." This campaign acknowledges that for many viewers, watching and discussing the Super Bowl ads is at least as much fun as the game itself.

2018 Super Bowl "Tide Ad" Commercial Compilation

589,313 views • Feb 4, 2018   6.1K   100   SHARE   SAVE   ...

What is the most memorable ad you have encountered recently?

Let's begin with some definitions. The terms *advertising*, *public relations*, and *propaganda* are a interconnected. Over time, these terms have evolved to reflect changes in culture and society:

- **Advertising** lets people know what is available in the marketplace and persuades them of the value of products and services. Advertisements are *paid placements* in other media, including television, radio, magazines, newspapers, the Internet, and social media. Advertising ties products and services to human needs, like love, acceptance, status, and power. The advertising industry includes all the professionals who work to create and place ads on behalf of their clients.

- **Propaganda** is the use of media symbols in a systematic effort to influence attitudes, reinforce or change beliefs, and inspire action among a large number of people. Propaganda is carefully designed to tap into people's hopes, dreams, and fears, and it is commonly used in politics, business, and activism.

- **Public relations (PR)** is the practice of influencing public opinion on behalf of a client in order to reach desired business objectives. Generally PR involves *unpaid placements* in media. The PR industry includes people who create and place news stories that put their clients' goods and services in the best possible light. Sometimes PR takes the form of publicity or promotion.

How have your attitudes and beliefs been influenced by advertising, propaganda and public relations?

More than 40 brand marketers, agency executives, PR executives, and lawyers worked on the 2018 Tide Super Bowl commercial, and they even watched it live together, huddled around a TV monitor as the ad reached 100 million people. The company spent $15 million on the campaign for 90 seconds of total placement (Johnson, 2018).

It might not be obvious how the 2018 Tide Super Bowl ad involved propaganda and PR. But of course, through creative use of symbols, the Tide ad was a form of propaganda, aiming to reshape people's impressions of the company.

After all, Tide desperately needed an image makeover after the large volume of negative media coverage it had received about the Tide Pod Challenge, a cultural phenomenon that emerged in 2015, when the satirical publication *The Onion* published an essay about a child seeking to eat one of the candy-colored packets of laundry soap. When a YouTuber made the first version of the Tide Pod Challenge, he depicted himself in a video eating

Juanmonino/iStock

a Tide pod and dared others to try it. This inspired many other YouTubers to follow suit in order to increase the size of their audience or just as an adolescent dare. Children and teens began to imitate these videos. The U.S. Poison Control Center reported more than 13,000 accidental poisonings from laundry detergent pods in 2017.

Proctor & Gamble, the parent company of Tide, had been aware that young children were eating Tide pods for a long time. It responded by marking the product with "Keep Out of Reach of Children" and "Do Not Ingest" labels. Then its PR team worked hard to get mainstream news media to cover the problem, with earnest stories like this:

Tide's parent company, Procter & Gamble, told CNN in a statement that "nothing is more important to us than the safety of people who use our products. We are deeply concerned about conversations related to intentional and improper use of liquid laundry pods and have been working with leading social media networks to remove harmful content that is not consistent with their policies," said a company representative (Kowitt, 2019).

But many people responded to this PR message with a duh-type response. After all, it seems obvious that people should not eat laundry detergent. In the minds of the marketers, the hilarious new Superbowl ad was a good strategy to wipe away all the unpleasant memories of the Tide Pod debacle.

As we will see in this chapter, important similarities and differences exist between advertising, PR, and propaganda. They are all forms of persuasion, which is the practice of social power that occurs when people try to influence others using language, images, and other symbols. Clearly, consumer culture does more than sell products. It promotes ideas and values that shape people's personal, social, and cultural identity, affecting the fabric of global society. We consider these questions:

- Why do brands spend so much money on advertising?
- How does advertising shape ideas about gender and identity?
- How does PR affect journalism?
- How do advertising, PR, and propaganda affect the democratic process?
- How does online personalization affect users' experience of advertising?

Consumer Culture

Advertising, PR, and propaganda drive the economic engines of capitalism and shape important aspects of the political and social process of culture and everyday life. Global spending on advertising exceeded $650 billion in 2020, with digital media accounting for nearly 50% of that spending. The U.S. share of this spending is 37%, closely followed by the Asia-Pacific region,

How do ads depict "the good life"?

which is expected to outpace the United States by 2022 (E-Marketer, 2018).

Most people understand that advertising is a form of communication designed to promote the sale of goods and services. Advertising is a part of the *marketing process*, which includes everything a company does to facilitate an exchange between itself and its clients. In an analysis of the changing definitions of advertising, scholars have observed how many definitions of advertising emphasize the way in which attention is sought for a mutually beneficial exchange between a buyer and a seller (O'Barr, 2015). In this sense, then, advertising is a form of salesmanship. But to truly understand the purpose of advertising, we must see beyond the mere goal of earning money or increasing sales.

Advertising works by building metaphorical connections between goods and services and human emotions and values. Advertising creates a link between a product/service and a set of feelings. To create an enduring link between products and feelings requires a systematic and long-term approach to communication. A *brand* is defined as a specific and particular set of messages that create a coherent set of feelings and ideas:

- Nike: doing your best
- H&M: trendy
- Coors: refreshing cold mountains

By linking products to treasured ideas and feelings, brands increase people's trust in products and services. Companies know that if customers are happy with the feelings they get from buying a product, they will return again and again to purchase it, and recommend it to others.

Companies offer value to consumers through advertising that delights and entertains, imbuing the purchase of goods and services with meaning. Raymond Williams, a British cultural studies scholar, famously defined advertising as "the official art of capitalist society" (Williams, 1960: 50). This definition expresses the idea that, in any society, art is linked to the interests of the powerful.

The important connection between art and commerce goes way back in history. For example, during the Renaissance, the Medici family in Italy were patrons of artists like Michelangelo and Leonardo da Vinci. Today, artworks by David Hockney, a British painter, have sold for more than $8 million. While much art is inaccessible to ordinary people, advertising makes visually stunning images available for free. The striking and memorable visuals of most contemporary advertising demonstrate the still-powerful role of art in upholding capitalism and the values associated with status, power, and wealth. Corporations now spend great sums to create clever and entertaining Super Bowl commercials that Americans talk about and comment on every year. Indeed, the ability to purchase a Super Bowl ad has become a type of status symbol for companies and brands.

Frank Baker

How many of the 26 brands do you recognize in this brand alphabet?

Get Them While They Are Young

Ads do not just communicate ideas about products. Advertising places an emphasis on positive values like pleasure, excitement, love, and loyalty—and on darker values like immediate gratification, conformity, gluttony, lust, and self-indulgence. They also communicate distinct messages about gender and identity, telling boys how to be boys and girls how to be girls. Ads offer a glimpse of a product-filled "good life" that is unattainable for many people.

Consider the Question

List three brands that you are familiar with and write down three adjectives or phrases to describe the feelings you associate with these brands. Then imagine that you ask a friend to do the same thing with the brands you selected. What is your prediction? Will your friend's list of words be mostly similar or quite different from yours?

Now try the experiment in real life and see what happens. Because ads are designed to connect products to feelings, the choice of words people use to describe their feelings should be carefully scrutinized. People's feelings about brands may reveal aspects of their own personal and social identity—and this illustrates the power of advertising to link products to people's feelings and values.

Antonel/iStock

People are so familiar with advertisements that they often do not really notice them. But they are an inherent part of the cultural environment, so pervasive that even very young children can read the logos of ads they see every day. By the age of 3, children can recognize, on average, about 100 brands. This is not that surprising since young children see more than 40,000 ads per year just from watching television and videos online; 60% of children under the age of 3 watch online videos, and one in four mothers allows her children under age 2 to interact with her cell phone (Braiker, 2011).

Ads for food are highly attention-getting and effective, as anyone who has had a late-night pizza craving while watching TV can attest. Children respond to ads much in the same way as adults do: they develop strong preferences for toys, food, candy, and fast food as a result of exposure to advertising. Although children start to recognize brand logos on products as early as age 3, older children have difficulty recognizing an ad when it is presented on a Web page (Guernsey, 2012).

Critics of advertising say that children need special protections in the marketplace. Children are considered vulnerable to manipulation due to their lack of understanding of the persuasive intent of advertising. Many children lack the cognitive skills needed to critically analyze advertising and develop skepticism only gradually as a result of disappointing experiences (Chu et al., 2014).

In particular, parents, educators, and public health professionals have been concerned about food advertising for more than 50 years, and this concern has grown as the rate of childhood obesity has risen dramatically in just the past 5 years. Since 2010, more than 40% of all the food ads children

How is color used to signal the gender of the target audience for children's toys?

see are for sweet or salty (non-nutritious) snacks. Many highly nutritious foods do not receive advertising to promote their consumption. Think about it: have you ever seen a TV commercial for an apple, a banana, or a box of blueberries? Advertising images of food may negatively influence people's nutrition and exercise behaviors.

In many families, parents help children understand advertising. They counteract potentially undesirable advertising effects by actively talking with their children about it. But as children use more media on personal digital devices, there is less opportunity for viewing or using media as a family.

For generations, parents and consumer advocates have been concerned about pairing advertising and entertainment for young audiences. But many parents do not recognize common advertising practices like *advergames*, which use online forms of product placement and in-game advertising that integrate branded products or logos into preexisting online video game platforms. Branded games may feature logos, trade characters, or advertising messages, and playing them creates strong emotional connections with a product or brand.

Back in the 1990s, *Chexquest* was a first-person shooter game in which players rescued people from alien invaders. It looked and played like a child's version of the video game *Doom*, although it was less violent and scary. Because of the high level of interactivity and immersion, marketers consider this form of advertising far superior to TV spots.

Advergames remain popular. In 2014, eager to reach the 13–24-year-old market, Gatorade hired Usain Bolt, the fastest man in the world, as a spokesperson and created an advergame called Bolt! Users maneuvered the Bolt avatar along a running course, gathering up Gatorade and avoiding water along the way. With the help of its PR team, Gatorade got celebrity

NI QIN/iStock

Why are advergames effective in influencing children's attitudes and behaviors ❓

endorsements from Justin Bieber and other high-profile young stars. Within months, Gatorade had 4 million online fans, more than 87 million plays, and 820 million *brand impressions*, which is a measure of the number of times a particular page is located and loaded.

But then the attorney general of California took notice, suing the company under the state's *false advertising laws*. What was the problem? Throughout the race, water was inaccurately and negatively depicted as hindering the sprinter's performance. Water would slow down the Bolt character's performance while Gatorade increased its speed. When users played the game, a fuel meter depicted water as decreasing the athlete's fuel while Gatorade increased it. The game tutorial even stated: "Keep your performance level high by avoiding water." Think about the potentially dangerous impact of this highly inaccurate statement on the beliefs and attitudes of children. The case was settled; Gatorade paid $300,000 to the State of California and agreed to avoid marketing or advertising apps that send misleading messages about water in relation to athletic performance (CSPI, 2014).

Regulating Advertising

Global concerns about the potential harms of advertising to children have translated into policy in many countries, where regulations limit advertising to young children. Overall, two-thirds of all countries around the world have such regulations. Table 5.1 shows examples of laws addressing the timing and placement of advertising in media aimed at children from countries including Australia, Belgium, Brazil, England, Germany, Italy, Russia, and the United States.

This is not a new phenomenon. Nearly 40 years ago, Quebec passed a law restricting marketing junk food to kids under 13 years old in print and electronic media. As a result, fast food expenditures decreased by 13% and child obesity rates there are low. In 1991, Sweden placed a ban on television and radio advertising targeted at children under the age of 12. In 2013, food companies in Sweden agreed to self-regulation that bans all marketing of unhealthy food and drinks for children under 16 years old (DLA Piper, 2016).

In the United States, back in the 1970s, the Federal Communications Commission (FCC) recommended an end to *host selling*, where ads containing program characters are placed near or adjacent to content with those same characters (Evans et al., 2013). But when the Federal Trade Commission (FTC) proposed banning advertising to young children, a firestorm of controversy

Table 5.1
Sample of International Laws Concerning the Timing and Placement of Advertising

COUNTRY	LAWS
Belgium	• Alcohol-related ads are forbidden directly before or after children's programming. • Ads may not interrupt children's radio and TV programs. • Ads deemed unsuitable are not allowed to start 5 minutes before or after children's programs.
Brazil	• Product placement in children's programs is forbidden. • Ads for children cannot be presented in a journalistic format.
Australia	• For children's shows between 7:00 a.m. and 4:30 p.m. from Monday to Friday, advertising is strictly prohibited. • At other times, no more than 5 minutes of advertisements is permitted in each 30 minutes of broadcasting. • Ads may not be repeated more than once during any 30-minute period.
Russia	• Advertising can be aired in certain children's television and radio programming up to 6 minutes per program. • Ads can be shown twice, once at the beginning and once at the end of the show.
Sweden	• Children and young people should not be portrayed in unsafe situations or engaging in actions harmful to themselves or others. • Products unsuitable for children should not be advertised in media targeted to them. • Advertising to children under the age of 12 is strictly prohibited. • Cell phone apps directed to children and that contain an invitation to purchase are prohibited as improper marketing. • Marketing may not be a part of games, social media, or websites directed to children.
United States	• In children's television programming aired on broadcast, cable, and satellite networks, advertising is limited to 10.5 minutes per hour on weekends and 12 minutes per hour on weekdays. • In California, websites directed at persons under 18 cannot include ads for alcoholic beverages, firearms or ammunition, aerosol paint, tobacco products, dangerous fireworks, ultraviolent tanning equipment, certain dietary supplements, lottery games, branding or permanent tattoos, or e-cigarettes.

SOURCE: DLA Piper (2016).

erupted, with many parent groups in favor and many businesses opposed. As part of the rulemaking process, officials investigated the nature and quantity of television commercials directed to children and studied children's responses to television advertising. They heard from leaders of parents' groups like Action for Children's Television about the annoying "gimme gimme" mentality that children developed from watching toy advertising. Medical professionals spoke about the nutritional, dental, and health problems resulting from excessive sugar consumption.

But broadcasters, product manufacturers, and advertising agencies also offered their own reasons opposing a proposal to ban advertising to children. They noted how rules limiting advertising may negatively affect business and perhaps violate the First Amendment. The rulemaking process was especially controversial because some people perceived the government as taking on a role of an overprotective "nanny," limiting people's freedom. To stop the regulatory process, Congress first allowed the FTC's funding to lapse and then passed a law prohibiting the FTC from adopting any rule in children's advertising rulemaking that uses the concept of unfairness (Beales, 2004).

During the Obama administration, the FTC identified companies that made false claims about products marketed to children. For example, in 2010, a Kellogg's cereal box claimed that Rice Krispies cereal "now helps support your child's immunity," with "25% Daily Value of Antioxidants and Nutrients—Vitamins A, B, C, and E." The back of the cereal box stated that "Kellogg's Rice Krispies has been improved to include antioxidants and nutrients that your family needs to help them stay healthy." The FTC did not have the authority to issue fines; instead, Kellogg's was simply warned not to make health claims about a product that cannot be substantiated with evidence (Nestle, 2010).

Today, commercial speech in the United States is fully protected by the First Amendment, but it was not always considered worthy of that protection. In the 19th century, courts believed advertising had little social value. But over time, courts have granted it more protection. Today, the First Amendment provides strong protection to advertisers. When the State of New York tried to limit condom advertising back in the 1970s, the courts claimed that commercial speakers have a right to free speech, with Supreme Court Justice William Brennan noting, "the fact that protected speech may be offensive does not justify its suppression" (Stone, 1990). In the *Edenfield* v. *Fane* case in 1993, the Supreme Court explained the reasoning:

> The commercial marketplace, like other spheres of our social and cultural life, provides a forum where ideas and information flourish. Some of the ideas and information are vital, while others are of little worth. So even communication that merely proposes a commercial transaction is entitled to the coverage of the First Amendment. The general principle is that the speaker and the audience,

not the government, are responsible for assessing the value of the information presented. (Stone, 1990).

Today, the government cannot restrict advertisements or other commercial speech except when (1) the advertising is misleading, (2) the government interest in regulation is substantial, (3) the regulation directly advances that interest, and (4) the regulation is not more extensive than necessary (Johnson, 2002). As a result, local communities who have tried to regulate casino, gun, or alcohol billboard advertising have found it difficult to limit such forms of expression. But although First Amendment protections are strong, they are not absolute. The First Amendment does not stand for "the proposition that all speech is equally worthy and should be uttered or encouraged, or that speakers should not be condemned for the speech that they make" (Drumwright & Murphy, 2004: 12).

Then and Now

The two print magazine ads shown below link the featured products to the values of elegance, status, and beauty. On the left is a Germaine Montiel perfume ad from 1943 and on the right is a Dior J'adore perfume ad from 2018. Notice the similarities in the use of visual symbols and of color to represent wealth and status. Notice the placement of the women's bodies, the depiction of hair, and even the direction of the women's gaze. Notice the fashion and consider where and when such clothing would be worn in real life during the time periods represented. Do you see where the product is located on the page? Advertising professionals like to place the product on the lower outside corner of a magazine so that users have to symbolically touch the product in order to turn the page.

What similarities and differences do you notice in these ads?

Advertising's Unreal Realities

She is a legend on the college speaking circuit: Jean Kilbourne has changed the way many people see advertising. Her books *Can't Buy My Love* and *So Sexy So Soon* as well as her film *Killing Us Softly: Advertising's Image of Women* have garnered international acclaim. Jean Kilbourne shows how advertising portrays women by using examples from magazines, movies, and television shows and explains the power of marketing ideas about gender to children and young people.

Even though most people feel immune to the effects of advertising, they believe it influences the attitudes and behaviors of other people, a phenomenon researchers have called *the third-person effect*. The majority of people believe ads do not affect them and they have the ability to "tune them out." Although ads may not always affect sales, multiple researchers who have studied ads find that they increase brand awareness. Still, 93% of women think that portraying women as sex symbols is harmful.

Looking at the history of the representation of women in advertising for beauty products reveals a certain set of visual tropes that is repeated across the generations. Using dramatic examples, Kilbourne shows how images of women present unattainable beauty through image manipulation, where inches are trimmed and wrinkles are removed. Researchers have found that the views of both women and men are influenced by these beauty images. In her presentation, Kilbourne reveals how advertisements even make sexual violence seem erotic. She notes, "Violent images make some people more violent, they make all of us more callous to violence and more likely to blame the victim. But the worst thing to do is to link sex and violence." Violence against women is a serious problem in the United States and around the world, where one in four girls is sexually abused during childhood, battering is the single greatest cause for injury of women in America, and a third of all women killed in America are murdered by their husband or male partner (Kilbourne, 2012).

When advertising appeals to female empowerment, is it helping improve society or exploiting feminism for commercial purposes❓

Advertisers and publishers are often criticized for editing pictures of already beautiful women into impossibly perfect images. When *AdWeek* airbrushed a cover image of actress Kerry Washington in 2016, she said she barely recognized herself. "It felt strange to look at a picture of myself that is so different from what I look like when I look in the mirror. It's an unfortunate feeling," she wrote on Instagram.

In part because of Kilbourne's efforts at raising media literacy, advertising agencies are developing

Dove Self-Esteem Project

☐ boy?
☐ babe?

campaignforrealbeauty.com Dove

marketing campaigns that empower women and girls rather than perpetuating harmful gender stereotypes. These campaigns have been called *femvertising*, and they reflect the marketing power of women, who control 85% of household purchases. Seventy-one percent of women want ads to promote positive messages to women and girls, and 81% believe that pro-female ads are important for younger generations to see. For example, after Dove launched its Campaign for Real Beauty, its sales jumped from $2.5 billion to $4 billion.

Such moves by beauty product manufacturers signal an interest among companies to be socially responsible in the way they represent girls and women. CVS Health announced in 2018 that it will stop touching up its beauty images because it recognizes the dangers of unrealistic body images for girls and young women. CVS said it will not materially alter photos used in stores, on websites, and on social media by changing a model's shape, size, skin or eye color, or wrinkles. Because marketers and advertisers seek to cultivate consumer trust, such efforts are good for business in the long term.

Defining Propaganda

How might propaganda be beneficial in some ways and harmful in other ways?

When people hear the word *propaganda*, some see it as dangerous and immoral. Many think that propaganda is always harmful. But actually, the word has not always had this negative connotation. Consider this definition of propaganda, created by the U.S. Holocaust Memorial Museum in conjunction with the special exhibition entitled "The State of Deception," about the history of Nazi propaganda:

> Propaganda appears in a variety of forms as strategic and intentional communication designed to influence attitudes, opinions and behaviors. Propaganda can be beneficial or harmful. It may use truth, half-truths or lies. To be successful, propaganda taps into our deepest values, fears, hopes and dreams.

Propaganda can be understood as persuasion in the public sphere, where it is designed to reach large numbers of people about issues related to the public interest and social welfare, politics, and the wider world.

Each generation has offered definitions of the term propaganda that apply to the context and public culture of the time period. At the turn of the 20th century, Edward Bernays, author of the classic book *Propaganda* (1928), understood it as part of the practice of democracy. Like later communication scholars, including Walter Lippmann and Harold Lasswell, Bernays

Universal History Archive/Universal Images Group/Getty Images

Intellectual Grandparent:
Roland Barthes

Advertising uses symbols and emotions to bypass critical thinking. In the 1950s, Roland Barthes started writing about popular culture at a time when few people thought it was worthy of serious study. Roland Barthes was not your typical French academic scholar. Far from it. In a series of short essays collected in book form and titled *Mythologies,* he explored the cultural significance of toys, photography, fashion, wrestling matches, wine, and even detergents, observing how mass media now supply the myths that once came from religion and faith. Some key ideas include:

Media restructures reality. Barthes used the practice of semiotics to study how advertising puts a gloss on reality in order to tap into people's fantasies, dreams, and desires. As the study of meaning-making, *semiotics* includes a focus on words, signs, symbols, representation, metaphor, and even objects that communicate meaning. Barthes helped people see the visual symbols of advertising in everyday life in a new and different way.

Barthes was interested in discovering how meaning is conveyed through the skillful use of language and other nonlinguistic practices, such as font, color, image choices, and even the sound of a voice. In analyzing advertising, Barthes recognized that symbols build enduring connections between objects and feelings.

Ads can be interpreted politically. Barthes showed how ordinary cultural phenomena like advertising can be interpreted in relation to social power and the demands of capitalism. He wanted to reveal how one powerful social group can use signs and symbols at the expense of others. He saw advertising as an abuse of the process of signification (Garlitz, 2015). For example, when he analyzed advertising images, he noted the gap between what the image actually depicted (denotations) and what larger ideas and messages were suggested (connotations). He believed that a great variety of such symbols function as myths—

viewed propaganda as the way in which large numbers of people are induced to act together. For example, during the Great War, propaganda posters were used to inspire young men to join the military to help defeat the enemy.

By the 1960s, people began to recognize propaganda's uncanny ability to tap into people's deep-seated drives and needs. As psychoanalytic theories explored how fears of sex and death affect human functioning, French theologian and philosopher Jacques Ellul defined propaganda as a form of information that panders to our insecurities and anxieties in his 1962 book *Propaganda: The Formation of Men's Attitudes.* By the 1980s, with the rising professionalism of PR and political communication, propaganda came to be understood as a type of transaction between author and audience, as "the deliberate, systematic attempt to shape perceptions, manipulate cognitions, and direct behavior to achieve a response that furthers the desired intent of the propagandist" (Jowett & O'Donnell, 2012).

making ideas about capitalism and colonialism seem natural and acceptable as "the truth." In his view, advertising helps maintain the status quo because ideas that are considered "natural" will not be resisted or fought against. Indeed, they will not even be noticed. This is how visual symbols in the everyday environment contribute to maintaining the stability of society, including its long-standing inequalities. Barthes's work became important worldwide because of the way his writing connected "the practices of mass culture and its appeal to a very modern theoretical apparatus" with a rigorous interpretive methodology that anyone could learn to use (Polan, 2016: 70). His ideas have become foundational to the practice of media literacy.

Culture jamming is a form of civic activism.
Later in his career, Barthes became fascinated with how signs and symbols take on an almost mystical authority. After traveling to Japan, he wrote about how culture and history intersect. As history is told through written accounts, it is codified in a system and represented as the truth. Later scholars, influenced by Barthes, also wanted to question that process. Scholars and activists continued to demonstrate how "the dominant culture utilizes media to promulgate the notion of the commodity as the highest form of existence" (Ewen, 1976). Barthes and other media critics inspired activists to draw upon the cacophony of visual images in advertising as a means to demonstrate their frustration with capitalism's narrow vision of humanity in seeing people as merely consumers. Following in Barthes's footsteps, *culture jammers* like Kalle Lasn of *Adbusters* magazine used symbolic sabotage of the rhetoric of consumer culture, seeking to create a movement critical of capitalism through the rejection of advertising's mythologies (Harold, 2007).

If Roland Barthes has influenced your thinking about media, you can share a comment on the Grandparents of Media Literacy website at www.grandparentsofmedialiteracy.com.

Propaganda can be difficult to detect. When Neil Postman (1979) examined the rise of media technologies that shape and limit human freedom, he defined propaganda as intentionally designed communication that invites people to respond emotionally, immediately, and in an either-or manner. By emphasizing how propaganda activates emotions and simplifies information, he recognized key features that distinguish propaganda from other forms of communication and expression. Propaganda can disable the practice of critical thinking about media, which is why people need to develop media literacy competencies.

More recently, scholars have defined propaganda by noting how carefully audiences are targeted for ideological, political, or commercial purposes through the controlled transmission of one-sided messages, which may or may not be factual (Nelson, 1995). Based on these broader definitions of propaganda, advertising is a form of propaganda, as are PR, news management, and strategic communication.

Laura Ingraham ✔
@IngrahamAngle

Check out the sign in Times Sq.! Thanks to
@JobCreatorsUSA!

10:35 AM · Feb 20, 2019 · Twitter for iPhone

9.7K Retweets   1.5K Quote Tweets   25.7K Likes

Who is the target audience for this propaganda? What is its purpose ❓

The term propaganda is situational and contextual, and it adapts in response to changes in technology and society. In the countries of Eastern Europe once ruled by Communism, the concept of propaganda has different meaning than it does to people who live in more traditionally democratic nations like Great Britain or The Netherlands.

The primary ethical challenge propagandists face concerns propaganda's stance toward truth and truthfulness, knowledge and understanding, according to Walter Cunningham, author of *The Idea of Propaganda* (2002). Public relations practitioners aim to be ethical by acknowledging the political nature of their activities and being aware of the power relations inherent in their work. Because PR professionals have a strategic communication objective to influence attitudes, emotions, knowledge, and beliefs, it is important for them to maintain a policy of transparency with their audiences.

But not all PR professionals honor the spirit of transparency. When an organization that calls itself the Job Creators Network put up a giant billboard in Times Square that blamed U.S. House Representative Alexandria Ocasio-Cortez for Amazon's decision to pull its new headquarters out of New York City, it got a lot of attention in the news media (Ma, 2019). Some New Yorkers were persuaded by it. The Job Creators Network is part of a network of *astroturf* groups that pose as defenders of "Main Street." But they actually represent the interests of billionnaires who are attacking a politician interested in limiting corporate power. Astroturf groups are fake grassroots groups that disguise their propaganda goals behind a nonprofit organization. It's not easy to detect such highly deceptive forms of propaganda. Since propaganda can be found everywhere, in journalism, advertising, PR, government, education, entertainment, religion, and activism, people need to learn to identify some of its hallmark features.

How to Recognize Propaganda Techniques

Propaganda appears in a variety of forms, but four common techniques make it relatively easy to spot:

Activating Strong Emotions. Propaganda plays on human emotions—fear, hope, anger, frustration, sympathy—so as to direct audiences toward the desired goal. In the deepest sense, propaganda is a mind game: the skillful propagandist exploits people's fears and prejudices. Successful propagandists understand how to psychologically tailor messages to people's emotions in order to create a sense of excitement and arousal that suppresses critical thinking. The recipient is emotionally moved by the message. Labeling is another weapon of choice for the propagandist. What emotions are important for those who create propaganda? Fear, pity, anger, arousal, compassion, hatred, resentment—all these emotions can be intensified by using the right labels.

Simplifying Information and Ideas. Propagandists may employ accurate and truthful information, or half-truths, opinions, lies, or falsehoods. Successful propaganda tells simple stories that are familiar and trusted, often using metaphors, imagery, and repetition to make them seem natural or "true." Simplification is an art and many forms of media rely on it. Oversimplification occurs when catchy and memorable short phrases become a substitute for critical thinking. Oversimplifying information does not contribute to knowledge or understanding, but because people naturally seek to reduce complexity, this form of propaganda can be effective.

Responding to Audience Needs and Values. Effective propaganda conveys messages, themes, and language that appeal directly, and many times exclusively, to specific and distinct groups within a population. Propagandists may appeal to its audience as a member of a family, or through racial or ethnic identity, or even with hobbies, favorite celebrities, beliefs and values, or even personal aspirations and hopes for the future.

Is it fair to call propagnda a weapon? Why or why not?

Sometimes, universal values are activated—the need to love and be loved, to feel a sense of belonging and place. By creating messages that appeal directly to the needs, hopes, and fears of specific groups, propaganda becomes personal and relevant. When messages are personally relevant, people pay attention and absorb key information and ideas.

Attacking Opponents. Propaganda can serve as a form of political and social warfare to identify and vilify opponents. It can call into question the legitimacy, credibility, accuracy, and even the character of one's opponents and their ideas. Because people are naturally attracted to conflict, a propagandist can make strategic use of controversy to get attention. Attacking opponents also encourages "either-or" or "us-them" thinking, which suppresses the consideration of more complex information and ideas. Propaganda can also be used to discredit individuals, destroy their reputation, exclude specific groups of people, incite hatred, or cultivate indifference (Hobbs, 2020).

Public Relations

To thrive in the marketplace, businesses need to be responsive to their customers and to the larger society. As a part of business management, PR practitioners offer knowledge and strategies that enable a two-way flow of ideas and information from the business to the society, and from the society to the business. Public relations can generally be understood as a type of *reputation management*, and it has been notoriously difficult to define. Still, most people agree that it encompasses these practices:

* maintaining two-way communication between a company and its publics;
* representing the company's goals and actions to the public in a way that builds goodwill and supports the bottom line;
* anticipating social trends and informing a company about changes in public opinion that may affect the firm;
* inspiring company management to serve the public interest;
* responding to business problems by using the power of communication in an ethical manner.

Public relations professionals think about audiences or *publics* widely, including customers, employees, investors, politicians and regulators, neighbors, and business partners, including distributors, suppliers, and others (Franklin et al., 2009).

The origins of the field of PR are closely tied to the emergence of propaganda in the early 20th century. Edward Bernays actually positioned himself as the "father of public relations," arguing that the term public relations is more attractive and professional-sounding than the older terms publicity agent or propagandist.

As the field developed, inspired by leaders including Bernays, Raymond Miller, and others, the ideals of PR were conceptualized. Public relations can be an ethical practice when public communication is used to enact a *social conscience*. Public relations professionals, by helping to communicate with the public and listening to public needs, are in a good position to influence decision-making at all levels of business. They communicate and interpret the company's goals and actions in ways that draw support from other stakeholders, including politicians, competitors, and customers. By using the power of communication to build *goodwill* between business and community, they "preserve a responsible society which provides an optimum economic and social climate" (Neilander & Miller, 1951: 13).

Today, PR professionals think of themselves as storytellers for the firms they speak for. They help put a public face on an organization, whether it is a company, educational institution, hospital, government agency, or individual. Through compelling stories, PR professionals try to encourage the public to take on board the point of view they represent.

One of the most significant ways that PR influences the public is through journalism. Most estimates suggest that a minimum 50% of news content is now written and provided by PR practitioners, and scholars have long noted that PR techniques have come to dominate the public sphere (Habermas, Lennox & Lennox, 1974).

The products PR professionals create include:

- Press releases and *video news releases*;
- Speeches;
- Email *pitches* that attract the attention of journalists;
- Special events;
- Market research;
- Networking events and sponsorship programs;
- Writing and blogging for diverse audiences;
- Crisis strategies for handling negative publicity;
- Social media promotions and responses to negative opinions online;

Related to the practice of PR is *corporate lobbying*. Lobbyists represent the interests of their companies or organizations to influence state and federal legislators and members of regulatory agencies. Their goal is to shape the proposal, passage, defeat, or amendment of laws or regulations to their benefit.

The term *grassroots lobbying* is used to describe the work of activists or volunteers who aim to promote certain policy goals on behalf of the public interest. Lobbyists use their specialized knowledge of the legislative process to educate and influence lawmakers and to shape public policy. Today, most large corporations employ a large number of people engaged in *public affairs*, which is a specific form of PR focused on influencing government officials and government policy.

However, over time, the practice of PR has also acquired the reputation of being used to hide, mask, or redirect public attention away from social problems caused by business interests. Critics see PR as fundamentally undemocratic because it creates an unlevel playing field, enabling large corporations and business to influence public opinion through well-funded campaigns that give them an unfair advantage.

The Blurring of Journalism and Public Relations

The city of Davenport, Iowa, was struggling with getting information out to residents. In many municipalities across the United States, with the decline of advertising revenue, local news organizations have few journalists available to report on local community events. School boards and city coun-

Does Public Relations Help or Hurt Democracy?

Democracies work through deliberations in which people discuss and resolve their disagreements over matters about which a decision must be reached. Ideally, all those entitled to participate should have equal access and status and arguments should lead to a rational consensus. Review the arguments below and decide for yourself whether or not public relations helps or hurts democracy.

.**Good for Democracy.** The process of democracy is difficult to imagine without PR as a way for organizations and groups of all kinds to generate publicity for their positions. After all, in the real world, self-interest defines many forms of expression and communication, not just corporate interests. Plus, people express ideas and make decisions not just through the examination of logic, reasoning, and evidence; they also use emotions and feelings in the process of deliberation. Because PR helps ensure that ideas circulate to a wide range of interest groups, "no single group can dominate deliberative engagements and decisions are based on the broadest possible set of relevant information" (Edwards, 2016: 70). Because PR professionals listen carefully and respond to the many publics they address, many voices can be heard in debates that concern them.

Bad for Democracy. Publicity encourages engagement among wider audiences, which is why journalism is considered essential for the democratic process to function. But with so much journalism being shaped by PR, the disguised self-interest of corporations and businesses, rather than the common good, comes to dominate the sources of information available to the public (Edwards, 2016). Even worse, there are many examples of PR campaigns that work against democracy by misleading the public. Through PR, disasters are reframed as opportunities. On issues of public concern, opposition voices can be shut down, compromised, or co-opted. Critics note, "The vast majority of public relations is carried out to serve vested commercial and political interests such that the ability of the wider public to have an effective voice in debates about the public interest is reduced" (Edwards, 2016: 66).

cils may not get a reporter to attend their meetings, and when reporters do show up, they naturally focus on controversial issues rather than the positive developments public officials want to publicize.

In an attempt to resolve some of these issues, in 2016, the City of Davenport created a website called Davenport Today. It looked like an online news website, but it was actually created by the city itself.

In an editorial on the matter, the state's major newspaper, the *Des Moines Register*, called it "a taxpayer-funded propaganda machine" (*Des Moines Register*, 2016). But even as it critiqued the practice, the *Des Moines Register* admitted that it had itself published taxpayer-funded propaganda disguised as news. In reporting on the city's school district, the newspaper intentionally disguised the authorship of one particular article, using the term "staff writer" to hide the fact that the school district's PR team actually wrote the article.

The *Des Moines Register* noted in an editorial that "the average person may find it impossible to differentiate between independent journalism and government self-promotion," and this problem has substantial implications for the future viability of the news business. After taking down the website, the city officials who created it justified their work, saying, "Local media like to report on planes that crash. We were reporting on the planes that land."

The blurring of journalism and PR has led to new forms of promotional communication, which have emerged as part of the rise of the Internet and digital culture. *Content marketing* (which is sometimes also called *sponsored content*) is a form of advertising that matches the form and function of the platform or media on which it appears. For example, as a way to sell gas grills, the Weber grill company offers advice on how to barbeque chicken or make the perfect smoked ribs. Instead of being something that interrupts our media use experience, advertising is positioned as a type of information that offers value to consumers. For this reason, marketing professionals talk about content marketing as a way to develop a personal relationship with customers.

What are the social, political, and economic consequences of the blurring of journalism, propaganda, and public relations?

© Medium

When people are exposed to content marketing, they may interpret it as information, or even as news. This is because the content is intentionally designed to blend in with the other information on a particular website. But make no mistake about it: sponsored content always has a explicit marketing goal. Clients seeking to get their message across in a subtle way use it because it is perceived as more credible than advertising. Journalistic organizations accept content marketing because they have no choice, especially given the decline of financial support for traditional advertising (Cooper, 2017).

For these reasons, content marketing has become a mainstream part of journalism. But most of the American public is unaware of it. Did you know that even *The New York Times* engages in content marketing, helping brands tell stories to readers? *The New York Times* launched the T Brand Studio in 2015, which hires editors with backgrounds in journalism. Clients include banks, embassies, and even countries. In 2018, Netflix paid *The New York Times* to develop an article and interactive graphics for a story about women in prison. Netflix produces a popular prison drama, *Orange Is the New Black*. In this case, the sponsored content was clearly labeled with the phrase "Paid Post."

Did readers understand that it was a new form of advertising? Researchers at the University of Georgia showed that roughly two-thirds of subjects fail to recognize sponsored content as a form of persuasion. When labels are provided and people do recognize it, they perceive the content as less credible and are less likely to share it with their social networks (Wojdynski & Evans, 2016).

Why do people find sponsored content appealing?

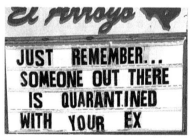

[Gallery] 35 Witty Signs That Make The Best Of The Situation

www.domesticatedcompanion.com

[Photos] Confirmed: This is The Deadliest Snake on Earth

Ice Pop

New York Post – Outbrain

A Fast Way To Pay Off Up To $10,000 In Credit Card Debt

NerdWallet

[Gallery] 29 of the Best Trail Cam Photos In Human History

Lifestyle A2Z

The practice of creating sponsored content is very profitable for media companies. Facebook-sponsored content may look like a video, news, or other content. In reality, it is an ad meant to be clicked on. For example, when I visit CNN.com, I see something that says "More Stories." This content is generally all sponsored. One headline down at the bottom catches my eye: "When Jimi Hendrix Opened for the Monkees." This shows up because I have provided digital clues from my browser history reflecting my interest in the awesome music of the 1960s. When I click on it, I see that I have left the CNN website and moved to another website. If I study this website closely, I see that it is labeled with the phrase "brand storytelling."

It is not clear how many people interpret this phrase or this content as a form of advertising. One thing is certain: sponsored content intentionally blurs the line between advertising, information, and entertainment, which helps disguise its real purpose as propaganda. The phenomenon of content marketing may be on the rise because journalists are torn between their "loyalty to journalistic ideals and loyalty to the economic advancement of the media organization for which they work" (Dalhgren, 2001: 80).

The Duel of Interpretations

Spin is a vital part of the political process: it is the cacophonous mixture of advertising, debates, conventions, speeches, polls, news releases, and hype that is part of the election process. The horse race of politics is experienced as a media spectacle that people either love or hate. It may be exhilarating to see how politicians craft their talking points to reach desired audiences, or their speeches may seem like nothing more than empty promises and lies.

While detractors sometimes criticize the way politicians and policies are sold to the public like laundry detergent, spin has always been

What are some of the different reasons why politicians use advertising, public relations, and propaganda **?**

The Summer of Winning

53,143 views • Sep 3, 2019   👍 3.2K   👎 671   ↗ SHARE   ⊟₊ SAVE   ...

part of the democratic process. In the United States, the presidency derives its power directly from the support of the American public, and so the White House has long used political communication strategies to interact directly with the public. Advertising, propaganda, and PR all come together seamlessly in modern political campaigns.

In Robert Greenberg's 2016 book *The Republic of Spin*, he traces the history of political communication from the founding of the country to the present era, and he emphasizes the process as a type of duel of interpretations. Of course, the history of political communication has its roots in ancient rhetoric. But the duel of interpretations was particularly noticeable during and after the

5 critical questions about Diet Coke and Taylor Swift

Using five critical questions of media literacy to analyze advertising and propaganda reveals insights on its meaning and value.

1. **Who is the author and what is the purpose?** Cola-Cola created this ad in 2013 in order to promote its brand ambassador, Taylor Swift, a pop star singer-songwriter. The purpose of this ad is to link the product to people's feelings about the celebrity, thus building a relationship between the product and the customer. Fans of Taylor Swift seem to be the target audience as viewers are expected to recognize her easily. Swift is a highly popular musician. In 2012, she earned $35 million and won six Grammy Awards. In 2013, Coca-Cola spent $26.1 million to advertise Diet Coke.

2. **What techniques are used to attract and hold attention?** Although the can of Diet Coke is in the center of the image, Swift's slender legs are the focus of the ad. "The perfect duet" is meant to link the product and the celebrity, and the word "duet" also resonates with the word "diet." The use of the red color clearly links together the product logo, Swift's lips, the heart-shaped straw, her guitar, and the phrase, "Stay Extraordinary."

3. **What lifestyles, values, and points of view are represented?** The slogan suggests that people and products go together. Fans will appreciate the focus on the value of the duet, because Swift is well known for performing duets with other musicians, including Faith Hill, Katy Perry, Justin Bieber, Nicki Minaj, Justin Timberlake, and Selena Gomez. The "Stay Extraordinary" message can mean many different things, depending on the context. For people in their 30s, it might mean "Stay Young." For people struggling with weight control, it might mean "Stay Slim." For celebrities, it might even mean "Stay Famous."

4. **How might different people interpret this message?** Fans of Taylor Swift will have

2016 presidential election, when the public became increasingly anxious about the types of political persuasion used by Russian organizations that interfered with the election. Utilizing an online social media campaign, Russian trolls created false U.S. personas and operated social media pages and groups designed to attract Americans. They focused on divisive political and social issues, including racism, gun control, immigration, terrorism, and many other topics.

During the 2017 congressional hearings on Russian influence on the election, observers learned that more than 3,500 advertisements were purchased and more than 80,000 posts were viewed by more than 126 million Americans.

background knowledge that may affect how they interpret the message if they read about her genuine love of Diet Coke or have seen the TV ads where she is depicted writing lyrics while composing the hit song "22." Activists and medical professionals have criticized Swift for endorsing Diet Coke, which contains aspartame, a chemical that has caused cancer in animals. The Center for Science in the Public Interest (CSPI) responded to the Diet Coke campaign with its #shakeoffaspartame social media propaganda campaign. Noting that Taylor Swift has donated money to cancer-related charities, CSPI disseminated a public letter to her that says, "To the extent that your endorsement encourages them to begin drinking Diet Coke, or to drink more, your endorsement is likely increasing your fans' risk of cancer." This activist organization also created propaganda aimed at increasing awareness of the risks of aspartame. In its campaign, CSPI exploited the popularity of Swift's hit song "Shake It Off," which had 470 million views on YouTube as of January 2015 (Horovitz, 2015). Activists have pointed out that celebrities are free to endorse whatever they want, but should not use their influence to market junk foods. You may see this as beneficial propaganda in the public interest, or you may see it as harmful to the image and reputation of the celebrity and the brand.

5. **What is omitted?** Advertising professionals know that another Diet Coke campaign featuring Taylor Swift called "You're On" featured people drinking Diet Coke just before stressful situations. This campaign was pulled after social media critics wrote posts with headlines like "Is Diet Coke Dabbling in Drug References in Its Ads?" and "Diet Coke Trying to Act Like This Isn't a Cocaine Joke." Just because a famous person is involved in an advertising campaign does not guarantee it will succeed.

Center for Science in the Public Interest. Taylor Swift Urged to "Shake Off" Aspartame.

#ShakeOffAspartame

AMERICA WILL GO ALL THE WAY ACROSS THE OCEAN TO FIGHT TERRORISTS

BLACKTIVIST

BUT WILL IGNORE ALL THE TERRORISTS HERE

Have you shared propaganda with the people in your social network? Why or why not?

The goal was simple: to create conflict among voters in the U.S. political system, discouraging some from participating and riling up others to activate hatred of the so-called establishment.

Russian propaganda directed at American audiences was powerful because it activated strong emotions that inspire and deepen us-vs.-them thinking and in-group tribalism. In the meme shown here, the image of KKK marchers is paired with a verbal claim that suggests the United States is more interested in foreign terrorists than in homegrown ones. It suggests that American attention to ISIS and wars in Iraq and Afghanistan deflected attention away from national forms of terrorism like the KKK.

What made memes like these spread so widely is a phenomenon called *moral contagion*, a concept that refers to how moral emotional language and ideas can spread across communities. Researchers examined more than half a million social media communications about gun control, climate change, and same-sex marriage, looking at the use of moral-emotional words like bad, blame, hateful, destroys, attacks, safety, peace, and wrong. They found that the presence of moral-emotional words in messages increased their chance of spreading by 20% (Brady et al., 2017). The researchers discovered that moral-emotional language also stays within liberal and conservative networks, and is less likely to cross between them.

Political polarization can emerge from the moral and emotional language people use on their social networks, and it can also be cultivated by political leaders. It is easy to exploit people's tendency to form in-groups by attacking opponents. The deep antagonism between Republicans and Democrats can be seen as *affective polarization* that results in growing incivility and high levels of distrust. Political propaganda arouses strong emotions that influence attitudes and behaviors. When this occurs, opposing views can be perceived not as different interpretations, but as morally wrong choices (Zittel, 2018).

Today, some critics see democracy as endangered. Why? The legitimacy of democracy itself is challenged when political leaders rely on *charisma* alone for their legitimacy. Disrespect of the procedural aspects of modern democracy can be dangerous. As flawed as democracy may be, it relies on people valuing accurate information, appreciating the checks and balances provided by the three branches of government, respecting the due process of law, and acknowledging the political process as a set of compromises and negotiations.

What the future may hold: Surveillance Capitalism

Today, the rapid expansion of advertising, propaganda, and PR has increased the supply of information and entertainment that consumers can access. But advertisers and propagandists do not just want to tell their story in a way that affects consumers' emotions and, ultimately, their behavior. They also want to collect detailed information about consumers. Of course, they want this information in order to connect to people more directly across the devices and platforms people use. But they also want to collect detailed information in order to more effectively influence and persuade.

In the political realm, data science companies have tried to identify Americans' biases and craft political messages designed to trigger their fears and anxieties to influence voting. Both the Republican and Democratic parties have developed digital campaign tools to gather as much information as possible on potential voters. In 2012, when President Obama directed TV ads to consumers based on data collected from cable set-top boxes, it was considered cutting-edge political communication. In 2016, Republicans used i360, a $50 million initiative that offered incredibly detailed information on potential voters. Political campaign strategists had access to shopping habits, credit status, homeownership, and religious affiliation, with voting histories, social media content, and any connections users might have had with advocacy groups or other campaigns (Halpern, 2018).

It has been called *surveillance capitalism*: the use of data extraction and analysis through computer monitoring and automation. By personalizing and customizing goods and services to users of digital platforms, companies carry out continual experiments on users and consumers without their awareness (Zuboff, 2016).

Online, many ads are personalized to users' actual needs, which is why users may perceive them as less bothersome, annoying, and intrusive than before. But in his 2011 book *The Daily You*, Joseph Turow, a professor at the Annenberg School for Communication at the University of Pennsylvania, worries that personalization is actually a form of social profiling that leads to discrimination. For example, if marketers think you buy your clothes at H&M, you probably will not see too many designer clothing ads from Saks Fifth Avenue. Today, much of the media content you experience online is shaped by choices made by marketers, based on what they know about you. Over time, your digital identity may become increasingly calculated by your value to marketers.

Mobile phones are becoming a more powerful device for customizing advertising and propaganda directly to individuals. Because a cell phone is constantly relaying data about its user's location, it can also gather information about the Internet-connected devices nearby. Pervasive tracking of online activity is something that most people have already become accustomed to. But people have different levels of acceptance of online surveillance. Researchers have found that Americans feel differently about online surveillance depending on their political affiliations. In one survey, Republicans were more pleased about surveillance than were Democrats (Singer, 2018).

New debates about surveillance and privacy are emerging in the context of the *Internet of Things*. This term refers to the dramatic rise in the types of products connected to the Internet: TVs, cars, toys, clothing, fitness monitoring watches and jewelry, home security devices, refrigerators and household appliances, and much more.

How do marketing practices affect your identity and your privacy❓

Cristiano Babini/iStock

New forms of advertising called *proximity marketing* include targeting mobile-device users with personalized content based on how close they are to a specific location. Using GPS data, advertisers can now send advertising messages to the phones of customers who are within a range of only 3 feet of a specific location.

Such marketing practices raise substantial concerns about protecting consumer privacy. Recently, one of the world's largest manufacturers of Internet-connected televisions was fined $2.2 million by the Federal Trade Commission when it installed software on its TVs to collect viewing data on 11 million consumer TVs without consumers' knowledge or consent.

Understanding digital marketing practices is now becoming an essential media literacy competency. Proximity marketing, consumer loyalty programs, and retailer apps can be coordinated to build profiles of individuals based on their behavior. In a radio interview, Professor Joseph Turow explains, "We are allowing companies to simply profile us and treat us based upon ideas about us that we have no conception of. They're taking data about us, making these profiles and we have no notion of what they're doing." According to Turow, retailing surveillance is training us in the belief that "to get along in the 21st century we have to give up data" (Gross, 2012). A media-literate individual must ask, "Whose interests are served by this point of view?" As digital devices are used for surveillance purposes, consumers must develop considerably more knowledge about how marketing practices affect their identities and privacy.

TIME T◉ REFLECT

REFLECT

After reading this chapter, reflect on the ideas you encountered, integrating them with your experiences with advertising, propaganda, and PR. Then respond to the following two questions by composing a short video reflection:

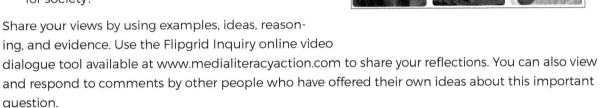

- How are advertising, propaganda, and PR beneficial for society?
- How are advertising, propaganda, and PR harmful for society?

Share your views by using examples, ideas, reasoning, and evidence. Use the Flipgrid Inquiry online video dialogue tool available at www.medialiteracyaction.com to share your reflections. You can also view and respond to comments by other people who have offered their own ideas about this important question.

CREATE T▶ LEARN

Create a Video to Comment on Propaganda

Advertising and propaganda are timeless and yet constantly changing. Explore the Mind Over Media online platform (www.mindovermedia.gallery), which includes a gallery of thousands of examples of contemporary propaganda from all over the world. If you like, you can upload an example of advertising, propaganda, or PR to the website.

After selecting a specific example that interests you, work individually or with a partner to discuss the following questions:

- **The Message:** What is the content of the information and ideas being expressed?
- **Techniques:** What symbols and rhetorical strategies are used to attract audience attention and activate emotional responses?
- **Environment and Context:** Where, when, and how do people usually encounter this message?
- **Means of Communication and Format:** What is the genre of the message and how does this particular form influence audiences?
- **Audience Receptivity:** How are people likely to think and feel about the message and how free they are to accept or reject it?

Using concepts from the chapter and with your own reasoning and evaluation, put your ideas together in a short video presentation, using Adobe Spark, a free media production tool that enables users to use text, images, spoken language, and music to create moving image media. Post and share your work online using the #MLAction hashtag.

Stories transform the most challenging and difficult aspects of human experience into pleasure

6

Why Are We Attracted to Characters and Stories?

Learning Outcomes

1. Understand how fictional stories can create unreal realities that convey emotional truths

2. Appreciate the efforts of authors who create fictional works

3. Examine how character archetypes enable stories to be time-less and universal

4. Consider how well-designed narrative structure can create high levels of engagement for readers, viewers, and players

5. Analyze how reality TV structures characters and conflicts in order to produce drama

Language, images, and sounds are used to structure and represent human experience and feeling, transporting us to new places and providing new experiences through the power of narrative. When done well, media storytelling captures our imagination. It can represents people, events, and ideas in ways that help us understand human experience. When done poorly, media stories seem boring, superficial, or a waste of time. At their worst, they can make destructive values seem appealing, misrepresent information, and foster harmful stereotypes. To explore the question "Why are we attracted to characters and stories?" we must learn more about how the essential features of story content, structure, and form can be used for different purposes.

Take for an example Scandinavia's favorite TV show, *Skam (Shame)*, a Norwegian series that epitomized the best characteristics of the teen drama. *Skam* featured the everyday lives, struggles, and insecurities of teenagers as they experienced issues of love and romance, mental illness, sexuality, family problems, and religious identity. Each season, one of the characters' lives was highlighted.

Because the show was posted online in weekly episodes (not all at once like on Netflix) and the characters all had Instagram accounts, the show used *transmedia storytelling* to increase viewers' sense of identification. Transmedia (or multiplatform) storytelling is the technique of telling a story across multiple platforms and formats using multiple digital technologies. *Skam* viewers could learn more about characters by visiting their Instagram pages, where snippets of text messages would be posted each day. Scenes from the show were posted on Facebook during the week to create the illusion that the drama was occurring in real time (Jakupsstovu, 2018). This novel format increased the appeal of the show.

When Facebook Watch launched in 2017, why did it immediately feature a large number of teen dramas ?

© Facebook, Inc

But the writers and producers were not the only ones to create transmedia for *Skam*. As the show grew in popularity, fans took the initiative to post episodes to a Google Drive network, where Norwegian fans voluntarily added subtitles to the episodes so that people from all over the world could enjoy the show. But they did not stop there. To engage with the story themselves, fans also created podcasts and Facebook groups to discuss and interpret the characters and the conflicts they experienced as part of the drama.

The show's international success has inspired an adaptation for the United States. In 2018, the producer, Julie Andem, created an American adaptation featuring a fictional group of teens from Austin, Texas. Instead of creating a traditional 30-minute TV show, clips and segments are released on Facebook Watch. Viewers can piece together the network of social relationships in order to understand the characters' history. According to television critic D. T. Max, "Collectively, the video clips, photographs, and comments imbued the characters with a depth that not even flashbacks provide in conventional TV" (Max, 2018: 1).

But critics also note that *Skam* creates unreal realities that blur the boundaries between actors and characters and between fiction and reality. Because Facebook has an interest in representing teenagers as constantly engaged in using social media, *Skam* is an ideal project for Facebook to support. The show depicts Facebook's ideal consumer as a teen scanning and studying people's social media profiles minute by minute throughout the day.

Comedians are influential storytellers. Which comedians do you admire most **?**

To achieve a certain semblance of reality, the show's producers created fictional Facebook profiles for the characters, with faked backdating of posts to show the characters' personal history. But this action intentionally violated the Facebook terms of service. Producers intensified the perceived realism of the fictional show in ways that made it very difficult for viewers to distinguish between fiction and reality.

This case study of *Skam* naturally makes us wonder: how do stories shape the way we understand the world? As we learn in this chapter, some stories are powerful enough to change the world. To understand and analyze their potential power, we consider these questions:

Redsnapper/Alamy Stock Photo

- Why are stories so good at attracting and holding attention?
- What have stories contributed to social and political change?
- How and why do fictional stories activate strong emotions in people?
- What elements of storytelling must the storyteller master?
- How is reality TV structured to attract audiences?
- How do fans contribute to the storytelling experience?

Storytelling and Social Power

Through *storytelling*, we make sense of the complexity of lived experience. You may have experienced the pleasure of telling stories about your own life experience, like when you accidentally got on the wrong bus and arrived late for a job interview or broke your leg while on a camping trip. Storytellers transform life experience into something that is meaningful for the audience who encounters the story.

Think about how you do it: as the protagonist of your story, you describe the situation, telling listeners about where and when it happened. Then you describe the problem, trouble, or difficulty you experienced. As you notice people's heads nodding in sympathy, you may embellish the description, offering little details that help the listener to imagine and visualize the experience. As you talk, you may decide to explain other little problems, working your way up to the big one. Or you might put the big problem first, followed by a series of (hilarious or awful) smaller problems that happened afterward. Then you reveal how the problem was solved. In the resolution of the conflict, you might reveal how you rescheduled the interview or were rescued by a fellow camper who helped you get to the hospital. Finally, you are likely to offer a comment that helps your listener understand your feelings and emotions or see what you learned about yourself from a difficult experience.

Sometimes we cannot really understand our actual life experiences until after we have transformed them into a story. This is why people seek out opportunities to talk over even the most mundane events of their day, explaining "what happened" and getting a reaction from a trusted and caring friend.

Stories are at the heart of the human experience. As we grow up, we encounter thousands and thousands of stories, told by our family members and our friends. Researchers have found that parents who share family stories with preschool children (especially when they tell those stories in a detailed and responsive way) help children become good storytellers themselves. As a result, these children also have a better understanding of other people's thoughts and emotions (Reese, 2013).

Experience with storytelling supports listening and reading *comprehension* and even helps kids get along with their peers. Teens whose families collaboratively discuss everyday events and family history have higher self-esteem and stronger self-concepts than teens whose family members do not share stories. And adolescents with a stronger knowledge of their own family history even have lower rates of depression and anxiety (Reese, 2013). But the benefits of storytelling extend beyond the experience of the teller. Listeners and viewers also benefit from storytelling as they gain new information through vicarious experience and deepen their sense of connection to others.

Truth be told, people simply like imagining what happens when others face complicated situations. Consider some of your favorite stories from the perspective of a hypothetical question. See if you can recognize the famous story embedded in these questions:

- What if dinosaurs were real again?
- What if wizards lived among us, but we did not know it?
- What if a most humble creature had to save the world?
- What if you had to rescue your father and ended up falling in love with the one who kidnapped him?

Did you recognize the essential questions of *Jurassic Park*, *Harry Potter*, *The Hobbit*, and *Beauty and the Beast*? Literary critic Roland Barthes (1974) has called these types of questions the *hermeneutic code* of a narrative. Early on in a story, a fundamental problem is introduced that raises questions in the mind of the reader, listener, or viewer. This part of the story initiates feelings of tension, which motivate interest and attention. Then, as the story progresses, suspense is created through conflict and action. The hermeneutic code is essentially the many unknowns (or mysteries) embedded in a story through its narrative structure. Through reading, viewing, or listening, these mysteries are gradually revealed.

Storytelling also has important cultural functions that support or maintain a society over time. Cultural historians, anthropologists, and scholars of literature have demonstrated for centuries that storytelling builds consensus and helps to create a common culture of shared understandings.

The majority of stories in a culture align with the values of the majority, reinscribing social power. For example, in American culture, stories often illustrate both the power and limitations of law enforcement, science, technology, magic, and love. Stories often depict people whose use of violent force seems justified by the circumstances. Stories make sense to us when they embed values that are part of our cultural heritage.

But stories can also shatter complacency and challenge the status quo. They can be told from the point of view of the underdog, the lowly one who offers a potent critique of those who are on top or who hold power. As Richard Delgado (1989: 2431) explains, "Stories open new windows into reality, showing us that there are possibilities for life other than the ones we live."

For example, in 1852, when Harriet Beecher Stowe wrote *Uncle Tom's Cabin*, her book depicted the lives of slaves in a compassionate way. But today's readers cringe at the stereotypical characters presented in the book, including Uncle Tom, the African American who is too eager to please others; Mammy, the dark-skinned and affectionate mother character; Sam, the lazy guy; and Topsy, the empty-headed small Black child. But Stowe's compelling portrait of people who face physical or psychological assault also offered readers a novel and alternative point of view in the 1800s. Reading the book intensified people's rejection of slavery and increased their passion for abolishing it. The book quickly sold well over a million copies in the United States and Britain. Abraham Lincoln, upon meeting Harriet Beecher Stowe, acknowledged the author's important role in helping to abolish slavery. To address the problem of racial injustice in American society required the development of the ability to tell stories from multiple points of view. Through deepening people's empathy with others, stories can inspire social change.

What are some other examples of fictional stories that have inspired social change?

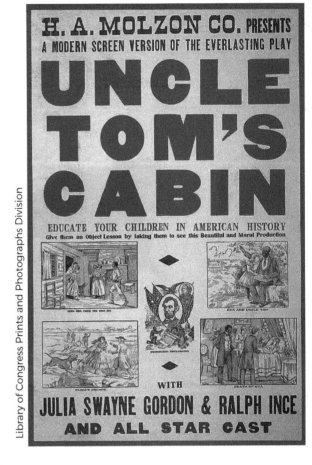

Library of Congress Prints and Photographs Division

Telling Emotional Truths through Fiction

When you begin watching one of the *Harry Potter* films, you enter a world of unreal reality. As strange as this alternative world is, you do not find yourself doubting the plausibility of the events, characters, and situations. This has been called the *willing suspension of disbelief*, an idea developed by Samuel Taylor Coleridge in 1817, who wrote about creating a story that offers a "semblance of truth." One way of explaining this phenomenon is that we experience genuine emotions because the fictional story provokes thoughts about real people and situations. For many, fiction can feel more authentic than nonfiction because of its capacity to reveal *emotional truth*. Stories are powerful because people accept the reality of imaginary worlds.

When you are watching a movie (or reading or listening to a book) and you feel a visceral, heartfelt connection to a character through the unfolding of narrated conflict, you have experienced the power of fiction to activate strong emotions. When you feel this, you have the sense that the characters are real, even though you know they are invented by an author or screenwriter. Your empathy toward the character is activated through feelings of love, disgust, anger, or even fear. Feeling a strong emotional resonance after reading or viewing a fictional story is a meaningful form of pleasure.

Which fictional characters activate your strong emotional response❓

We may also enjoy such feelings for their own sake, feeling gratitude that we can feel a wide range of emotional experiences. Researchers have found that watching fictional TV dramas also improves people's ability to read the thoughts and feelings of other people, a skill known as *emotional intelligence*. In an experimental study, researchers randomly gave people one of three experiences: some watched an episode of *The Good Wife*, others watched a documentary, and the third group did not watch television at all. This award-winning CBS television show has been noted for its insights on social media and the role of the Internet in society, politics, and law, along with the exceptional performances of the show's cast, including Julianna Margulies and Christine Baranski.

After viewing, people who watched *The Good Wife* episode performed better on a test that asked people to identify the emotions conveyed in photos of human faces. In the test, people viewed 36 pairs of eyes, one at a time, choosing the best word from among four choices to describe the emotion depicted in the photos (Black et al., 2015). Watching film and TV drama activates the practice of reading facial expressions to detect underlying emotions

Our emotional response to fiction seems to be a bit of a paradox. It seems that "truth," "reality," or "existence" is not needed in order for us to be moved emotionally by narrative. After all, from a strictly logical point of view, our emotional response to fictional characters and stories is "irrational, incoherent, and inconsistent" (Radford, 1975: 75). Indeed, fictional stories can move us emotionally in ways that are often more powerful than for true nonfiction stories, human interest news and current events.

Often, while you are engaged in reading or viewing fiction, the actual truth status of a story becomes irrelevant as you vicariously identify with the character. When Albert Camus said, "Fiction is the lie through which we tell the truth," he recognized that the most important reasons why we are attracted to fictional characters and stories is that they have been carefully crafted to reveal something that's honest and authentic about complex human experience.

The Paradox of Tragedy

The ancient Greeks valued tragedy for its capacity to create *catharsis*, or a purge of negative emotions. After all, people tend to feel better after crying. The emotional truth of storytelling actually leads people to enjoy tragic fictional stories with unlikable characters and unhappy endings. It has been a staple of drama since ancient times, and William Shakespeare created many memorable unlikable characters, including Lady Macbeth, Hamlet, and King Lear, to name just a few.

This has been called the *paradox of tragedy*. We can experience this paradox in a number of different types of stories, not only those with unhappy endings. Any media message may activate sadness, pity, heartache, loneliness, disappointment, guilt, shame, or regret. Even comedies can have moments when readers and viewers experience disgust, shock, distress, or anger. Music can create these types of distressing feelings too.

Scholars have noted that the depiction of death, dying, and suffering acknowledges our awareness of the passage of time, the loss of youth, and the inevitability of death. Death and loss are painful—but such loss matters. People find stories about death and loss significant because they are an aspect of life worth honoring and exploring through art.

For example, consider the 2009 black comedy-drama *A Serious Man* by the Coen brothers. The film tells the story of Larry, a Jewish professor living in Minnesota in 1967. From the moment we meet him on screen, bad things start happening to Larry. His wife asks for a divorce, his brother gets in trouble with the law, and a student tries to blackmail him so as to get a better grade. All these problems are piling up and Larry is overwhelmed. Trying to understand his problems, Larry seeks out rabbis for advice, who offer him a range of clichés and parables. Larry himself tries to explain the meaninglessness of life through mathematics, while other characters use drugs, listen to music, or even believe in mystical maps. But a deep anxiety lurks beneath the jokes, and although the film is written and structured like a farce, it feels like a horror movie (Scott, 2009).

The film invites viewers to consider the dread of a world that cannot be interpreted—a meaningless world. As Evers and Deng (2015: 344) explain, "Part of the appeal of these sequences lies in their acknowledgement of feelings of meaninglessness and religious doubt as significant events in people's lives." Stories are perhaps among the most accessible ways for humans to confront and reflect upon the deepest and most difficult aspects of the human experience.

Who Is the Author?

Our culture is saturated with storytellers, only some of whom we call *authors*. Each medium, genre, and form may use different terms to identify authors. Sometimes the people who create stories are highly visible and easy to recognize. For example, Stephen King, the prolific writer of horror stories, including *The Shining* (1977) and *Pet Sematary* (1983), is well known by readers who eagerly await his forthcoming books and are confident that they will provide the expected thrills and chills. Other times, authors are not widely

Six to Start and Naomi Alderman

Why do apps and games include narrative elements **?**

recognized or noticeable. For example, most video game players would not recognize John Romero, who was responsible for much of the classic first-person shooter video game *Doom* (1993) and who has received numerous awards for his creative talents in the industry. Other distinguished writers have created multimedia content too. Consider Naomi Alderman, author of a critically acclaimed book entitled *The Power* (2018). She also created an immersive running game, *Zombies, Run!,* where runners take on a series of missions during which they run and listen to audio stories as part of their daily exercise.

Media-literate individuals value the concept of authorship, but it is a challenging topic to address across diverse forms of media because each medium, genre, and form has a set of norms and conventions about how authorship is conceptualized and credited. All forms of media are more or less collaborative. Although a book lists only a single individual as the author, a whole team of people were involved in its creation. The author is the one identified as the primary creative force behind the project, and the editors, copyeditors, graphic artists, and marketing team are not identified. Movies rely on even larger teams of collaborators. In film, we distinguish between screenwriters, producers, actors, animators, film crew members, special effects experts, actors, and others who help to create a film. We might not call all of them "authors," but they all made vital contributions to the creative product.

The norms and conventions for identifying authorship in film and music have changed. In the early part of the 20th century, movies did not identify the names of any of the people who created them. Over time, credits began to appear at the beginning of films, usually in three or four title cards acknowledging the cast and principal technical players, including the producer, the director, and sometimes the cinematographer. As films became digital, credits got longer. The credits for the 2013 film *Iron Man 3* include 3,700 names (Murphy, 2017)! Generally speaking, though, only some of the people who worked on a film get their names in the credits.

Video games involve many different types of creative people: art directors, animators and artists, programmers, writers, quest designers, and more. It is often difficult to identify the role individual storytellers or computer programmers play in the creation of video games, "because games are more highly industrialized even than film" (Thevenin, 2019: 74). In a fascinating video, Evan Puschak, creator of the Nerdwriter YouTube channel, explains the development of music for Super Nintendo, where we learn how musicians needed a lot of creativity to manage processing limitations. Music and sound play an important role in structuring emotion in film and video games, and the creative work of musicians is deeply linked to the hardware and software tools and technologies they use.

Most video games display credits, and sometimes they do it with quite a bit of creative flair. For example, inside the action role-playing game *The Witcher 3* (2015), there is a place called Toussaint, where you can find a cemetery. On one gravestone, it reads "Martina Lippin'ska, engineer and pug lover. Solved the most obtuse technical problems in all the duchy with the grace of a ballerina." Another headstone reads, "Natalie Mrooz. Duchess Ademarta's court sorceress. Granted the wishes of the common folk." Certain important people are being honored for their contribution to the creative project. These headstones seem out of place in the video game world, but they do "seem to nod to tales of the people behind a game that's already all about stories" (Wiltshire, 2016). In both film and video games, closing credits show a sense of deep respect for the magic of creative collaboration.

Characters Count

When writers and screenwriters are developing stories, they sometimes imagine how a particular character would react under a stressful situation, like being stuck in an elevator. Would they pound their fists or stamp their feet? Cry or yell? Stand patiently, waiting for help? Imagining how different characters might respond to a stressful situation can help in the creation of memorable, complex characters.

In general, you are more likely to be entertained by a flawed character than a virtuous one. We enjoy flawed characters because they give us something to talk about and discuss. We also like seeing a character who makes bad decisions and learns from the experience. Consider this list of unlikeable characters:

- Frank Underwood in *House of Cards*;
- The Hound in *Games of Thrones*;
- Frank Castle in *Daredevil*;
- The Penguin in *Gotham*;
- Carl Grimes in *The Walking Dead*;

Storytellers use stereotypes in the creation of story worlds. The word stereotype was introduced earlier in this book. In the context of storytelling, it refers to anything that is conventional, formulaic, and oversimplified, or conforming to a set image or type. Gender, race, occupational, and ethnic stereotypes are familiar to the audience and so everyone recognizes the fast-talking salesman and the manipulative, sexy female angling for attention. Stereotypes can simplify the process of storytelling since not all characters can be fully developed as three-dimensional characters, especially in time-based media like television and film.

But what makes some characters seem so real, so easy to relate to, and so appealing to a mass audience? Nineteenth-century social theorist Emile Durkheim wanted to understand what makes people act in similar and predictable ways. He developed the concept of *collective consciousness* when he observed that people's individual behavior is influenced by being part of a cultural group.

Through collective consciousness, you learn to become aware of the social norms and conventions of the people around you. Characters who struggle to fit into society embody this essential human challenge. After all, to thrive in contemporary society, people need a mix of "standing out" and "fitting in." You may be familiar with the popular genre of film that is often called a coming-of-age story, where the story focuses on the growth of the protagonist from youth to adulthood. In these stories, we see how characters navigate developing an individual identity while learning how to get along with the people around them. Such stories embody the concept of collective consciousness.

Another psychologist, Carl Jung, also recognized how shared cultural myths and stories shape expectations about the self, others, and the human experience overall, from birth to death. Jung contended that people respond to certain characters more than others. He developed the concept of the *archetype* to describe the characters of human experience that he saw as universal. According to Jung, archetypes are psychological structures that enable and support people's mental functioning. Among media professionals, however, the term archetype is used more generally, as a means to both analyze and create characters that take on the roles of hero, villain, victim, and helper.

The Archetypes of Storytelling

Hero

- THE WARRIOR. Tough and courageous, overcoming obstacles and able to handle challenges.

- THE SEEKER. Sometimes different from others, and must brave loneliness and isolation in order to seek out new paths.

- THE CREATOR. Constantly generating new ideas and projects and fosters an imaginative perspective on reality.

Villain

- THE RULER. Values order, structure, and hierarchy, seeking to gain or maintain social power.

- THE DESTROYER. Enraged by structures that no longer serve life and seeks power through delivering death.

- THE SHADOW. Discontented and full of self-hatred, which causes hate for others.

Victim

- THE INNOCENT. The trusting person who fears abandonment but gains support from others.
- THE ORPHAN. The wounded individual who seeks to regain love, support, and empathy.
- THE FOOL. Lowly and sometimes taken advantage of, this character is also able to offer wisdom through humor and play.

Helper

- THE SAGE. Offers valuable knowledge and advice that helps to solve problems.
- THE CAREGIVER. Moved by compassion, generosity, and selflessness to help others.
- THE MAGICIAN. Tries to transform situations, influence people, and make visions into realities.

Since the time of Jung, theorists from many different disciplines have used the concept of archetypes to understand literature, popular culture, marketing, and media. In her book *The Hard Facts of the Grimm Fairy Tales* (2003), Maria Tatar, a scholar of folklore who has examined the sex and violence in the Grimm brothers' fairy tales, shows how these old stories, which the Grimm brothers collected from German peasants, were not really designed for children at all. Instead, she shows how they offered up moral tales for the many complexities of adult life.

Movie superheroes embody some archetypal traits while reflecting the particular cultural values of the present time. Of the best-selling Hollywood films of 2017, 7 of the top 11 feature superheroes who embody the values of contemporary society, notes novelist and author Mark Bowden. Superheroes are characters with god-like powers, who transcend the laws of nature.

In many of today's superhero movies, "rule of law and the importance of tradition and community" are missing and "institutions and human knowledge are useless. Religion is irrelevant. Governments are corrupt and/or inept, when not downright evil.

How do stories reproduce cultural beliefs at a specific point in time❓

SNOW WHITE AND HER SEVEN PEOPLE

Roz Chast/CartoonStock

CartoonStock.com

The empowered individual is all" (Bowden, 2018: 1). Stories are not neutral: they reproduce the existing beliefs in a particular culture at a specific point in time.

Narrative Conflict

In literature and film, the structure of a story can be the difference between success and failure. How do you attract and hold the attention of a reader or viewer all the way through the entire story? Many stories activate universally relatable emotions through putting obstacles and conflicts in the way of the protagonist, culminating in a climax where conflicts are resolved. The plot includes the specific events in the story, and the way the overall plot points are structured is called the *narrative arc*.

The ancient Greeks first documented the importance of conflict in storytelling. The Greeks used the term *agon* to refer to a struggle or contest. This could be a contest in athletics, in chariot or horse racing, or in music or literature at a public festival.

All stories put characters in trouble in order to see what happens. Writers imagine characters and conflicts and shape them into stories. And the shape of the story really matters. In good stories, the characters experience increasing conflict until finally the struggles are resolved in an interesting or surprising way. Writer Kurt Vonnegut, author of *Slaughterhouse Five* (1969), once showed the timeless shape of stories by drawing a chalkboard diagram (Vonnegut, 2010), as shown in what follows.

In the Arc of the Story chart, the horizontal line represents time and the vertical line represents good fortune at the top and bad fortune at the bottom. In one type of story, a character with a good life gets into trouble and then eventually gets out of it. The other line shows a character whose life is bad. Over time, it starts to get better until something wonderful happens. But then, suddenly, something terrible happens. Finally, another good thing happens, creating a happy ending. Looking at the lines in the chart, can you tell which of the two lines represents the story arc of the classic fairy tale of Cinderella? Although Cinderella was hated by her stepsisters, her fairy godmother performs magic that enables her to meet the prince. But at midnight, the spell is broken. Eventually, though, the prince finds Cinderella and marries her. The narrative arc of a story, and the way in which characters experience conflict, can increase audience engagement.

Which of the two lines best represents the story of Cinderella❓

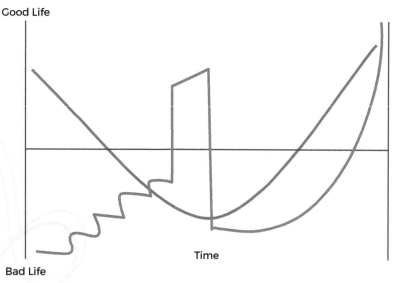

Good Life

Time

Bad Life

Such dramatic conflict can change characters. In some stories, a villain transforms into a hero, and in others, a victim becomes a villain, depending on the circumstances. Types of dramatic conflict include:

- **Person vs. Person**: A protagonist and an antagonist struggling with each other over something or someone that matters;
- **Person vs. Self**: An internal conflict that an individual experiences between their ideal self and their actual behavior;
- **Person vs. Fate/God**: A conflict that occurs when circumstances seem to pile up for a protagonist who cannot control what happens;
- **Person vs. Nature**: A conflict between a protagonist and the physical environment, natural world, or animals;
- **Person vs. Society**: A conflict that occurs when a protagonist's society is harmful or dangerous;
- **Person vs. the Unknown**: A conflict that is generated by an alien, mysterious other;
- **Person vs. Technology**: A conflict where a protagonist is challenged by machines or technologies that are controlling.

In film, planning tools like *scripts* and *storyboards* enable storytellers to shape stories. When it comes to well-told stories, animated films are often more compelling than big-money action blockbusters. Because "special effects workshops often have to start building a movie's big action set pieces years before its release date, a complete script can be a rare luxury when a movie is actually filming" (VanDerWerff, 2018: 1). For animated films, when writers and artists work on the story, they create *animatics*, which are roughly drawn approximations of the story sequence using hand-drawn sketches. In the 2018 animated film *Ralph Wrecks the Internet*, story editors used animatics to test out plot points in the narrative. In order to ensure audience attention, editors make tough decisions to delete scenes when they do not advance the narrative arc.

Which types of conflict are most likely to engage your interest and attention?

Finally, although stories are primarily shaped by authors and editors, in the world of book publishing, *agents* also help to shape stories for maximum appeal. In seeking authors whose stories can be published or produced in the commercial marketplace, they receive and review a great number of stories, but most stories

Wreck-It Ralph Deleted Scene - Vanellope's Volcano (FULL)
735,786 views · Feb 13, 2013

they encounter are quite boring. Agents are actually in the business of rejecting stories created by authors. But when they find a story or an author with promise, they generally help to develop their work by improving the structure of the story so that it keeps the attention of the reader or viewer all the way from the beginning to the end.

Seven Basic Plots: Narrative Analysis

Narratives can be analyzed in many different ways, since they are found in virtually all forms of media, including entertainment, information, and persuasion. Scholars throughout time have wondered about the consistent, repeated patterns that exist in story structures. In books, movies, and television shows, stories display general patterns, according to Christopher Booker, author of *The Seven Basic Plots* (2004). His approach builds on the work of scholars including Vladimir Propp, Rollo May, and Joseph Campbell, to name just a few.

Authors plan and develop their stories by imagining characters and considering what happens to them. They use these basic plot patterns, composing and arranging the characters, situations, and conflicts so as to provide a satisfying experience for readers, viewers, players, or listeners. Sometimes, when you watch a bad movie or read a dull book, you can use narrative analysis to understand how the limitations of the story's structure may have contributed to your response. When you apply narrative analysis to a book, film or video game you admire, it can also reveal mind-blowing insights that deepen your appreciation for the creativity and artistry involved in structuring a story. The recurring plot patterns shown in Table 6.1 suggest universal themes that have allowed humans to pass on to the next generation the wisdom gained from living.

Structuring Conflicts and Characters

Reality TV is a style of television programming consisting of nonactors placed in challenging and often competitive situations. It combines elements of documentary with elements of scripted drama or comedy. The use of nonactors lowers the production costs involved to create the television series and makes these cheaper to produce than scripted television programming. A network pays far less for a reality show as compared to a scripted comedy or drama. Reality TV (now sometimes called *unscripted programming*) is a popular genre: 50 different shows were in production as of March. When this number is compared to the nearly 500 scripted TV shows in production in 2018, it is clear that, while reality TV once dominated the television world, today it is a relatively small part of the landscape.

All sorts of conflicts can be embedded in reality TV shows. For example, the Discovery Channel's *Deadliest Catch*, a long-running reality TV series, features the lifestyle of Alaska crab fishermen and includes documentary elements

Table 6.1

Seven Basic Plots

PLOT	FILM EXAMPLE
Overcoming the Monster. These stories feature a hero who encounters and battles with a monstrous figure of evil.	In the horror film *It* (2017), a group of bullied kids band together to destroy a shapeshifting monster, which disguises itself as a clown and preys on the children in a small Maine town.
Rags to Riches. These stories feature the life of an insignificant person who is revealed to be someone quite exceptional.	In the drama *The Shape of Water* (2017), we meet a lonely janitor who forms a unique relationship with an amphibious creature held in captivity at a top secret research facility in the 1960s.
The Quest. These stories feature a hero who struggles through an obstacle-filled journey in order to achieve an objective.	In the animated Disney film *Inside Out* (2015), a young girl is uprooted from her Midwest life where her emotions (Joy, Fear, Anger, Disgust, and Sadness) experience challenges as she learns to navigate a new city, house, and school.
Voyage and Return. These stories feature a protagonist who is thrown into a strange, unfamiliar, or abnormal world and must eventually escape.	In the action-adventure film *Jurassic World* (2015), a new theme park, built on the original Jurassic Park site, creates a genetically modified hybrid dinosaur that escapes containment and goes on a killing spree.
Light Conflict. These stories are about relationships between people, where misunderstandings and confusion lead to conflict, which is eventually happily resolved.	In the comedy musical *La La Land* (2016), a pianist and an actress fall in love while attempting to reconcile their aspirations for the future while living in Los Angeles.
Dark Conflict. These stories feature a protagonist who is impelled into something that is forbidden or taboo and then experiences an increasing series of consequences where things get out of control, leading to destruction.	In the horror film *Get Out* (2017), a young African American man visits his white girlfriend's parents for the weekend, where his simmering uneasiness about their reception of him eventually reaches a boiling point.
Rebirth. These stories feature a protagonist who is impelled into something that is forbidden or taboo and then experiences an increasing series of consequences where things get out of control. But instead of destruction, a rescue brings wholeness.	In the science fiction film *Arrival* (2007), a linguist is recruited by the military to communicate with alien life-forms after 12 mysterious spacecrafts land around the world.

Adapted from: Booker, *The Seven Basic Plots* (2004)

about the real challenges of that very dangerous job. This is sometimes called a "person against nature" plot. But the show also includes manufactured competitive events in order to increase dramatic tension between people, in a "person

ABC/Photofest

Which reality TV characters and conflicts have been most memorable to you? Why ❓

against person" plot. For example, in several episodes, tension is depicted between new fishermen and the more experienced ones, where we see that bullying is common.

Reality TV shows examine issues of weight loss, plastic surgery, hoarding, or social media hoaxes and present characters and conflicts in ways that evoke strong emotions and address serious social issues. Perhaps you enjoy watching *Keeping Up with the Kardashians*, *The Bachelor*, *Ultimate Beastmaster*, *America's Next Top Model*, or *Top Chef*. Reality TV producers say that one of the great challenges of producing reality TV is making the characters likeable. After all, the casting process attracts narcissists "willing to cash in their dignity for a shortcut to fame and notoriety" (Callenberger, 2016: 1).

While reality TV producers do not generally write lines of dialogue, they carefully plan episodes to feature characters in conflict. Without characters in conflict, the audience has little motivation to maintain their interest. As screenwriting guru Robert McKee (1997) says, "A protagonist and his story can only be as intellectually fascinating and emotionally compelling as the forces of antagonism make them."

Reality TV shows have been part of television programming since the early days, when Alan Funt's *Candid Camera* debuted on ABC in 1948, offering a range of hidden-camera gags that entertained audiences for more than 1,000 episodes. Ted Mack's *The Original Amateur Hour*, a talent search program, ran from 1948 to 1954. Audiences were invited to vote on the winner, who was invited to appear on the next week's show. Three-time winners were eligible for the annual championship, and at that event, the grand-prize winner received a $2,000 scholarship (Devolld, 2011).

Getting a chance to see real people engaged in everyday conflict was a pioneering idea in 1973 when PBS aired a documentary series called *An American Family*, produced by Craig Gilbert. It featured the Loud family from Santa Barbara, California. The family of seven was filmed as they went about their daily routines. In episode one, for example, we are introduced to the family as they prepare for the New Year's Eve party they are planning. Over the course of 12 episodes, more than 10 million people watched this strange new form of television, watching the parents' marriage dissolve and the young adult son Lance come out as gay.

Although reality TV is carefully constructed, many people seem unaware of how such construction occurs. When it was released, *An American Family* attracted a lot of attention for its depiction of family conflict, but, in general, it did not stimulate widespread discussion about the complex way that film represents reality. When the show was released, all the focus was on the marital conflict between Pat Loud and her husband, Bill, and the controversy surrounding Lance's coming out. Most reviewers failed to acknowledge any distinctions between representation and reality. *Newsweek* wrote: "In the presence of 10 million Americans, Pat Loud will tell her husband of twenty years to move out of their house." But by the time this episode aired, the Louds had already been divorced for 6 months. One scholar explained, "The review, like many others, collapsed the difference between story time and broadcast time, implying that viewers saw the events not as they had happened, but as they were happening" (Ruoff, 1996). The story in this documentary was created in the editing room as months of filming ordinary life were boiled down to highlight the conflicts and controversies.

Today, of course, many people understand the tricks and devices used to construct compelling reality TV. They understand how time is compressed and events are resequenced to intensify dramatic tension. The scripted drama *Unreal* that airs on the Lifetime network even offers a gritty inside look at the production process of creating reality TV. In the series, you see how contestants are baited in order to produce *sound bites* that serve the pre-planned story arcs the producers have created. As contestants experience repeated humiliations, you see how producers actually put people's mental health at risk in making a TV show.

Fandom, Copyright, and Creativity

Fans of popular culture can be storytellers too. *Fandom* is the social community of fans, a group of people who enjoy a particular story. Generally, people who participate in fandom are entranced by the worlds created by other storytellers. There are Harry Potter fans, J. R. R. Tolkien fans, Batman fans, *Ghostbusters* fans, and Disney Princess fans. Sometimes, fans are not satisfied with a story ending or the feature of a particular character. At other times, they seek to bring together characters from one story into the world of another story. One form of fandom includes the practice of fan fiction (often

How might recommendation systems on Netflix cultivate fandoms❓

AA Film Archive/Sportsphoto/Alamy Stock Photo

Intellectual Grandparent:
Vladimir Propp

He respected the power and the beauty of stories. Vladimir Propp (1895–1970) was a Russian folklorist who studied the underlying structure of Russian folktales. During the 19th and 20th centuries, scholars observed the rapid rate of industrialization and became interested in documenting the traditions of rural, mostly uneducated peasants in Europe. At a time of rapid cultural change, many of their stories and cultural traditions were beginning to die out.

Propp's major work, *Morphology of the Folktale*, was published in 1928 and became a cornerstone of *structuralism*, a theoretical paradigm in the fields of sociology, anthropology, and linguistics. Structuralist theory suggests that all aspects of human culture and identity can be defined by their place in a structure. This idea opened up a range of important scholarship in the study of languages, the humanities, and the social sciences by scholars such as Ferdinand de Saussure, Roman Jakobsen, Claude Levi-Strauss, Roland Barthes, and others. Here are some key ideas from Propp's work.

Conflict is essential to storytelling. Propp used the term *villain* to describe one of the key characters in stories, but he emphasized that a villain is not necessarily "bad" or "evil." In many stories, the character or personality of the villain doesn't really matter. The villain simply has to oppose the hero. The villain's primary function is to be a source of conflict for the hero. The same is true for heroes: they do not have to be good, and in fact they usually have many flaws. The main job of the hero is to struggle against an adversary toward a resolution.

called *fanfic*), which is one type of creative work made by a fan. Fan work can occur in any medium if it uses elements from another work not merely in passing, but as a central theme or purpose. Some fans even compose fictional stories about celebrities and real people from the present and past!

One of the most popular activities for fans is to write romantic or sexual stories that connect two characters who are not in a relationship. The practice is called *shipping*, which is shortened from the word "relationship." A shipper is a fan who engages in this activity. Shippers sometimes disagree about who should couple with whom; they use the phrase OTP (which stands for "one true pairing") to indicate their favorite pairing. The most famous of these is the large number of stories written about a gay romantic relationship between Spock and Captain Kirk from the *Star Trek* franchise. Stories are published on websites including Archive of Our Own, Wattpad, and others (Romano, 2016).

Fandom can be controversial and there is a dark side to fan culture. For example, after Kelly Marie Tran starred in *The Last Jedi* (2017), a film in the *Star Wars* franchise, she received ruthless online abuse from so-called fans who objected to an Asian woman cast in a leading role. Some people see fan fiction as creatively lazy, a superficial form of authorship. Some au-

Narrative tension matters for momentum. Propp also noticed that fairy tales always include heroes who receive warnings and yet ignore them. Propp called this *interdiction* and violation. The interdiction occurs when a helper character warns the hero about something, and the violation occurs when the hero ignores the warning. For example, in the story of Little Red Riding Hood, her mother warns her to stay on the path to Grandmother's house, but the wolf successfully tempts her off the path. In *Star Wars*, Luke's uncle warns him not to search for R2D2, but he does so anyway. Interdiction and violation increase the narrative tension that compels the interest of readers, listeners, and viewers. These techniques can be used over and over to make a story longer and more interesting. In the 19th century, writers like Charles Dickens discovered how to use interdiction and violation to create long, complex stories that hooked readers into buying his serialized stories every week. Today, we see this structure in place in many episodic dramas on Netflix.

Stories express cultural stability and values. Stories are both timeless and timely. Propp himself was part of a movement of scholars across Europe who were inspired by feelings of nationalism and wanted to validate peasant language, folk stories, fairy tales, and songs. Propp and other scholars noticed how the stories the peasants told embodied values, lifestyles, languages, and traditions that predated Christianity. Stories are stabilizing; they connect us to the past. As the world changes faster and faster, stories are an important way we stay connected to or reclaim the values of tradition in an increasingly global and digital age.

If Vladimir Propp has influenced your thinking about media, you can share a comment on the Grandparents of Media Literacy website at www.grandparentsofmedialiteracy.com.

thors are offended when fanfic authors create new stories with their characters. As George R. R. Martin, author of *Game of Thrones*, has said, "My characters are my children. I don't want people making off with them, thank you" (Grossman, 2011). As a result, some authors have sued fanfic authors for copyright violation.

Fortunately, for fans who want to create such works, the doctrine of fair use may provide some legal protection. When fans create new work based on copyrighted material, they might be sued. In such a case, a judge must decide if the newly created work is *transformative*. When you create a new work that uses copyrighted concent, it might (or might not be) transformative. A transformative work makes use of copyrighted content by repurposing the original content or adding something new (Aufderheide & Jaszi, 2018). To decide if your use of copyrighted material is transformative, you can ask these questions:

- Did you add value to or repurpose the copyrighted material?
- Did you use only the amount needed?
- Could the new work be a substitute for the original?

Because copyright infringement is decided with sensitivity to a specific context and situation, each case must be analyzed for its unique features. But if you use characters and stories from the work of another author in ways that are not transformative, your work may be a copyright infringement. Work that takes a single character and simply places that character in a different setting might be a copyright violation, because the character is an original creation of its author. Courts do not always protect authors' copyright on characters, but they may when those characters are fully fleshed out and complicated in relationship to the story being told (Schwabach, 2018). If you create a story that is too similar to the original and could be a substitute for it, this new work might not be transformative.

5 critical questions about Dante's *Inferno* and *Willy*

After viewing this YouTube video at www. medialiteracyaction.com, use five critical questions of media literacy to gain insight on its meaning and value.

1. **Who is the author and what is the purpose?**
   This video is part of a Web series, *In Theory*, created by Erik Campbell (the animator) and Jimmy Martinez (the illustrator). They create videos with strong visual imagery using ideas from online fans and critics. In this case, the episode seems designed to both entertain and inform. Looking more closely at the opening of the video, we see a credits section that acknowledges the creative work of Lou Anders (in 2005) and

Willy Wonka And The Chocolate Factory Fan Theory | In Theory
158,764 views · Jan 24, 2017
👍 1.6K 👎 54 ➡ SHARE ➡ SAVE ···

Willy Wonka fan theory

Many people are unaware that copyright law acknowledges the role of borrowing and reworking the creative works of others as part of the process of creating new knowledge. Scientists use, rework, and build upon the creative work of other scientists to create new knowledge. All human creativity is combinatorial. For most of human history, people have created stories by building upon, extending, and revising stories that people were familiar with. Writers have long borrowed characters and plots from all sorts of sources and turned them into new stories. When Virgil wrote *The Aeneid*, for example, which is a story of the Trojan hero Aeneas, he took a minor character from Homer's *The Iliad* and moved him to Italy for new battles and adventures. Shakespeare's *Hamlet* is a reworking of a Norse legend from the early Middle Ages (Romano, 2016).

Wonka and the Chocolate Factory

Amanda DiMarco (in 2015), the people who developed the central ideas of the video. They developed the detailed comparison between the Roald Dahl story and the classic Italian poem depicted in the video. This video is produced by Uproxx, a media company with the slogan, "The Culture of Now." Its website is filled with engaging stories about entertainment media and popular culture. According to the company's chief operating officer, Benjamin Blank, fresh digital content inspires target audiences to share it.

2. **What techniques are used to attract and hold attention?** The video starts with a compelling question: "Is Willie Wonka's chocolate factory actually Dante's Inferno?" The animation and illustration technique involves the use of illustration and a stop-motion process, which creates an impression that the images are being drawn in real time, right before your eyes.

3. **What lifestyles, values, and points of view are depicted?** This video assumes that you think it is a good idea to compare popular culture to classic literature. To appreciate this video, you are expected to be generally familiar with both the Roald Dahl story (and film) and the classic Italian poem. By detailing the similarities between the two, the video seems to flatter audiences who are familiar with both works. Thus, we can infer that the target audience is college-educated people with an interest in popular culture, literature and history.

4. **How might different people interpret this message?** Fans of Roald Dahl, Gene Wilder as Willy Wonka, Dante, and classic literature more generally may be more likely to enjoy this video. Critics may say that this video trivializes and exploits a popular story for profit.

5. **What is omitted?** Although it may be that any story with a certain structure and theme will loosely mimic a classical predecessor, the viewer does not really learn much about the full range of stories that could be considered in alignment with Dante's Divine Comedy.

Sarah Edwards/WENN Rights Ltd/Alamy Stock Photo

As we have seen from the study of archetypes, stories have qualities that are both particular and universal at the same time. Critics have noted that *Hamilton*, the famous Broadway musical by Lin-Manuel Miranda, is a type of fanfic in its creative reworking of Ron Chernow's biography of Alexander Hamilton. It creates an alternative universe by changing something about the main character, in this case, his race. In doing so, *Hamilton* both celebrates the Founding Fathers and critiques them by blending past and present in creative ways.

It has been said, "There are no new ideas under the sun." Do you agree or disagree? Why ❓

By exploring American history by considering those who were left out of it, the musical *Hamilton* reimagines the actual historical figure to create something new, as Miranda pointedly notes in his lyrics: "I'm passionately smashing every expectation/every action's an act of creation." (Romano, 2016: 1).

In a sense, fandom also offers an important way for authors to connect with audiences. If you draw pictures of Bart, Marge, Homer, and Lisa, people who like *The Simpsons* might see them. If you make a podcast about the space explorers who pilot the giant super robot Voltron, your work might reach other fans of Voltron. As Burt (2017: a1) points out, "If you can work your memories, hypotheses, or fantasies about living away from home, or about gender transition, or about retirement, into a story about Bruce Wayne and Dick Grayson, maybe the many people who care about Batman and Robin will care about your thoughts and experiences, too." In a world where most of the stories we encounter have been capitalized through a commercial economy driven by profit, fandom levels the playing field for ordinary people to be storytellers.

Consider the **Q**uestion

Does fan fiction deserve more respect? Working with a partner or in a small group, discuss your thoughts and opinions about fan fiction, using reasoning and evidence to defend your ideas. Then create a chart to address your perspective on these two different claims:

- Fan fiction is an important form of authorship that deserves respect.
- Fan fiction is less creative than other forms of authorship.

What the future may hold: AI for Video Game Storytelling

Everyone is embracing storytelling these days, it seems. Marketers use storytelling to make people fall in love with products and services. Other creative people are seeking new ways to give video game players more *agency*, or the ability to have personal control over actions. Video games allow players to control characters through branching narratives, where a choice made by the player leads to different plot elements.

But what if video games could have endless stories generated and fully controlled by users themselves? Chet Faliszek, a video game writer for games including *Half Life* and *Left for Dead*, is exploring the possibility of using machine learning and artificial intelligence for storytelling (Academy of Interactive Arts and Sciences, 2018). Perhaps the future of storytelling will include action video games where player-driven characters can choose to do anything they like within the context of the story world. Machine learning may enable people to be the heroes of their own stories.

To reflect on this possible future, we must reflect on the differences between choice and agency. For those of us who grew up playing games where you routinely choose between options given to you by an unknown programmer or designer, this might come to seem like a normal part of game play—and a normal part of life. Choices give people an illusion of control. They are not equivalent to the fuller freedoms of agency. When playing *World of Warcraft*, you can select talents for your avatar, choosing between Unholy Blight or Bursting Sores, and these choices affect your gameplay. Having the choice of different options that are basically equal in value feels empowering to users.

Ian Dagnall/Alamy Stock Photo

But when players have agency, they interact with other players and engage in play not specifically designed into the game. When players make decisions to take actions that change the world they interact with, they have agency. A number of multiplayer games provide users with feelings of agency. When people experience the power and pleasure of agency in game worlds, it can produce feelings of satisfaction that they may not experience in the real world.

TIME T◯ REFLECT

Reflect on one of your favorite books, TV shows, movies, or video games and use the concepts from this chapter to analyze it. Consider these questions as you plan your informal extemporaneous response:

- What media text did you select and why do you like it?
- Describe a key character, explaining how his or her personality and actions demonstrate the characteristics of one or more archetypes.
- How does the story use one of the seven basic plots?
- What kinds of conflict do characters experience in this media text? How are the conflicts resolved?

You can share your work in the Flipgrid Inquiry by contributing your ideas in a brief oral presentation. You can also view and respond to comments of other people who have offered thoughtful reflections on media literacy. Visit www.medialiteracyaction.com to learn more.

CREATE T▶ LEARN

Storytelling with a Narrative Arc

Select a familiar story that interests you or tell an original one of your own. Working individually or with a partner, share the story's main plot points. Then draw a narrative arc, using the visual structure graph developed by Kurt Vonnegut and shown earlier in this chapter. Make sure your drawing includes a horizontal axis for time and a vertical axis for good fortune and bad fortune.

Using ideas from the chapter and with your own reasoning and evaluation, add annotations to your drawing to explain your work, helping a reader to see which story elements correspond to the line's changing shape. You can use Google Drawings or another free media production tool to create your narrative arc. Post and share your work with the global community of media literacy learners using the #MLAction hashtag.

PART II

JUDGMENTS ABOUT TASTE, QUALITY, AND TRUST

People balance the need for novelty and familiarity when choosing media

Why Do People Prefer Different Kinds of Music, Movies, and TV Shows?

Learning Outcomes

1. Examine why people like diverse types of media as a result of differences in aesthetic judgment and taste

2. Understand how novelty, familiarity, and repetition affect people's liking of media content

3. Discover how media genres, codes, and conventions help people comprehend and interpret media content

4. Appreciate how recommendation engines structure people's choices of movies and TV shows

5. Reflect on how features of the media environment shape everyday life and behavior

You have noticed, surely, that people may grow up in the same family but have very different preferences and tastes when it comes to music, movies, and media. Consider the various choices of a brother and a sister. When Roger was 13, he saw *Ocean's Eleven*, a heist film directed by Steven Soderbergh and featuring an ensemble cast including George Clooney, Brad Pitt, Matt Damon, Don Cheadle, Andy Garcia, and Julia Roberts. It captivated his imagination like no movie he had experienced before. Later that summer, he began reading heist fiction, starting with *The Hot Rock* by Don Westlake, a comic masterpiece of crime writing written in 1970. He watched a lot of crime movies too, discovering some of the distinctive features of the heist. Every summer, it seems, there is a new heist film to enjoy. In 2017, it was a hillbilly drama called *Logan Lucky*; in the summer of 2018, it was *Oceans 8*, an all-female heist film featuring Danny Ocean's sister. In 2019, it was *Triple Frontier*, starring Ben Affleck. Each of these films includes a montage depicting the elaborate planning process, a tension-filled change-in-plans sequence when something goes wrong, and of course, a high-speed getaway. These timeless features help make heist crime dramas a popular genre.

But Roger's sister could not care less about crime films. Rachel has always been a fan of fantasy: when she was a teen, she was enamored with the *Harry Potter* books and films, and she read *The Hobbit* by J.R.R. Tolkien. As a young adult, Rachel prefers the fantasy genre, and she is a big *Game of Thrones* fan. She loves the dragons, but she is also fascinated with the complicated characters, some of whom she loves to hate. She has read *The Song of Ice and Fire* trilogy by George R. R. Martin and she even checks in on the *Game of Thrones* subReddit. Fantasy is sometimes combined with other genres, as in the 2020 film *Artemis Fowl*, based on the book by Eoin Colfer and directed by Kenneth Branagh, which combines crime and fantasy in the tale of a 12-year-old criminal mastermind.

Roger and Rachel grew up in the same family where neither of their parents nor other family members read, watch, or enjoyed either crime or fantasy genres. Where did this brother and sister get their taste preferences? When it comes to music, what factors explain why some people enjoy acoustic and others prefer death metal, hip-hop, Christian rock, folk, jazz, or electronica?

This chapter introduces fundamental concepts for understanding how audiences develop taste preferences and make choices of media content. With more choices available than ever before, deciding which types of media to use (and when not to use them) is an important one. By being metacognitive about how and why we choose to pay attention to some forms of media content and not others, we can make choices that are truly in our best interests. After all, when it comes to your body, we know that choices in what you eat and drink can affect your health. When it comes to your mind, the choices you make can affect the quality of your mental health, social relationships, and career prospects. Taking time to reflect on your media choices is part of the lifelong practice of media literacy.

In this chapter, we explore how people, profit, and platforms shape the choices we make using all forms of media. To reflect upon and analyze our choices, we consider these questions:

- How do parents and siblings affect the development of musical tastes?
- Can repetition make something popular?
- How are new media genres created?
- How do recommendation engines structure viewers' choices of movies and TV shows?
- Why is media awareness important?

How Do Musical Tastes Develop?

No doubt you have heard the phrase, "Beauty is in the eye of the beholder." Questions about whether *taste* (also called aesthetic judgment) is subjective or objective have been vigorously debated for hundreds of years. Philosophers like Emmanuel Kant and David Hume began debating the concept of taste during the Enlightenment, when in the late 17th and 18th centuries, society underwent a shift away from tradition toward ideas that emphasized reason and individualism. Since then, artists, musicians, and philosophers have been exploring the complex nature of aesthetic judgment.

Three different perspectives have emerged on the topic. Some see taste as (1) the identification of inherent properties of an object, artifact, sound, or experience. Others see taste as (2) a specific characteristic of the individual who listens, views, reads, or appreciates works of art and media. Differences in perceptual processes may occur in how individuals perceive beauty, for example. Certain rhythms, chords, and combinations of musical sounds may be especially pleasing to some ears, but not to others. Finally, some assert that (3) social class and status shape taste judgments more than any special ability to experience

What explains why people like different types of media?

International Artists/Alamy Stock Photo

and appreciate the sensory, aesthetic, or social world. From a sociological perspective, it makes sense that perceptions of the quality or value of objects or experiences are socially constructed, something learned within the context of a particular social group (Bourdieu, 2014).

All of these approaches to the study of taste and judgment are important and all offer insight on the choices people make about media and popular culture. In this chapter, we focus on the first two (the aesthetic and psychological explorations of taste) and in Chapter 8, entitled "Who Decides What Makes Media 'Good?," we examine the third one, looking at ideas from sociology and cultural studies that study the ways in which taste is constructed by the social and cultural environment.

When it comes to music, understanding people's preferences requires attention to the ways in which people experience music in everyday life. People may listen to different types of music for a variety of personal and social reasons. In the field of music appreciation, scholars and educators generally distinguish between three types of aesthetic responses:

- **Expression**. Some people appreciate art for the personal *feelings*, emotions, and memories that connnect art to life experiences;

- **Referential**. Some people appreciate art because of the *content* and ideas that particular artworks express;

- **Formal**. Some people appreciate art in relation to its technical virtuosity or its structural integrity, focusing on the specific qualities of its *form*.

Of course, we form our musical tastes from among the available choices in our environment. You may have grown up in a household where your parents listened to rhythm and blues, hip-hop, contemporary Christian music, or classic rock and roll. Perhaps your family listened to classical music, or music from Nigeria, Pakistan, Brazil, China, or the Caribbean. For this reason, exposure to a wide variety of music during childhood is thought to be good for children in order to develop taste preferences as they grow older.

When it comes to music, children start to show particular preferences for certain types of music as young as age 2. Simple songs with clearly defined themes and chord progressions that resolve predictably are generally liked best, but as children get older, they begin to prefer more complex music. Daniel Levitin, the author of *This Is Your Brain on Music*, explains that his grandfather had a collection of old 78 rpm records, and he liked listening to old novelty songs like "Would You Like to Swing on a Star?" As he got older, Levitin developed a taste for jazz, which uses some of the same rhythms and tone qualities as the familiar songs from his childhood. If he had not been exposed to this type of music when he was young, he might not have liked it when he got older. Researchers have confirmed that musical tastes are intergenerationally shared among family members (Ter Bogt et al., 2011).

By age 14, most teenagers have a clearly defined set of favorite musicians and genres. Music becomes more important during adolescence in part because of its role in helping people cope with emotions, sexual impulses, and relationships. After all, when we are trying to make sense of new feelings, music can help manage our moods.

By age 20, most people have well-formed music preferences and tastes, having used music as part of the identity-formation process. Most people stop listening to new music well before they reach the age of 35. Although some people keep discovering new genres or music throughout their lives, most people tend to stick with the preferences they developed as young adults. That is why your grandparents easily remember their favorite songs from their teen years.

When it comes to music preferences across the life span, it turns out that we never really leave middle school. Using data from Spotify, researchers have identified important generational patterns in music preferences. Table 7.1 shows these results. For example, 35-year-old women love Janet Jackson's "That's the Way Love Goes," which was released when they were age 11. Women who are 41 seem to love the song "Just Like Heaven" by The Cure, which was released when they were 11. This trend can be found across ages and genders (Stephens-Davidowitz, 2018).

Can Something Be Made Popular through Repetition?

In short, the answer is "yes." All cultures have music, and repetition is a defining element of music around the world. Musicologists estimate that, during more than 90% of the time spent listening to music, people are actually hearing passages that they have listened to before. But most people are unaware that

---

Table 7.1

Generational Patterns in Women's Music Preferences

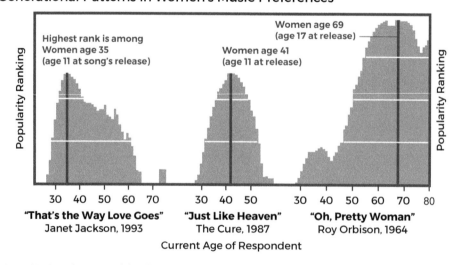

SOURCE: Stephens-Davidowitz, 2018

Consider the Question

With a partner or in a small group, share your memories of listening to music during your childhood to answer the following questions:

·   How did parents and siblings affect the development of your musical tastes?
·   What special experiences and everyday routines for music listening can you recall?

If your parents played musical instruments, perhaps they encouraged you to learn to play one too. Perhaps your parent took you to concerts. Those are special experiences. But most of the time, music socialization happens through everyday routines of daily life, including listening to music while in the car and at home.

repeated exposure affects their attitudes. This is called the *mere exposure effect*. People tend to be initially hostile to or suspicious of new experiences, then gradually come to accept and even like anything that has become familiar.

Repeated exposure actually makes anything more appealing. Repetition sets up satisfying expectations that people experience as pleasure. This is true for music, art, movies, and books—and even for food, advertising, and fashion. Elizabeth Hellmuth Margulis has conducted experiments that clearly show that people prefer music with more repetition in it. Other music scholars have demonstrated that popular music continues to get more repetitive over time. Computer programmers have developed a variety of visual tools to analyze the structure of popular music and explore the power of repetition. For example, the 2009 Lady Gaga song "Bad Romance" features an immense number of repetitive hooks squeezed into its 5-minute length. Five different hooks are repeated five or more times (Caswell, 2018). The song is incredibly popular, with more than 1.2 billion views on YouTube as of 2020.

Repetition is powerful. Musical repetition can create feelings of transcendence. When people hear a familiar musical hook, researchers have found, they are more likely to move their bodies or tap their fingers to match the beat. Musical repetitions do not just make us active participants in listening, though. Repetition actually causes our attention to shift and intensify (Margulis, 2014). When we hear a musical hook for the first time, we may pay attention to the words—the lyrics. As we hear it again and again, we notice the melody, the

Why is musical repetition so appealing ?

Lady Gaga - Bad Romance (Official Music Video) - YouTube
YouTube · LadyGagaVEVO

© Vevo LLC

beat, the hook, the bridge, and other features because repetition can intensify human perception.

Repetition also heightens attention in ways that can open up emotional pathways. Like any ritual activity, sequences of repeated actions concentrate the mind on immediate sensory details. A researcher who asked thousands of people to describe their most powerful experiences with music discovered that people reported that their peak musical experiences involved a sense of *transcendence*. People lost a sense of their personal identity, escaped the limitations of their bodies, and became one with the sounds they were hearing. These very deep and moving experiences can be partially explained by the shift in attention and the heightened sense of pleasure that repetition creates. Neuroscientists have discovered more activation in the emotional region of the brain when the music we are listening to is familiar, whether or not we actually like it (Lehrer, 2011).

People often think that repetition is a sign of a lack of creativity. But enormous creativity occurs in the skillful use of repetition. For example, Beyoncé's 2016 song "Formation" has two halves, with one set of repetitive hooks at the beginning and one set at the end, creating a satisfying mix of novelty and familiarity. Music that strikes the right balance between novelty and familiarity can be appealing.

In fact, all creative work can be balanced along the *familiarity–novelty continuum*. For example, Kirby Ferguson examined the relationship between J. J. Abrams's *The Force Awakens* and the previous films from the *Star Wars* saga, including *A New Hope*. Of course, *The Force Awakens* was designed to be familiar, because this ensures solid performance at the box office. J. J. Abrams is a filmmaker who has specialized in remakes, having copied story elements from tried-and-true plotlines and genres as he reboots familiar material, including the *Star Trek* series. Because people seek a balance of both the familiar and the novel, creative people try to balance between these two poles. Just as musical artists embed samples of older songs in their work, writers and filmmakers do too, because in general, people enjoy an optimal blend of the novel and the familiar.

Choices Matter

Consider the *levels of choice* embedded in all forms of media use. For example, you may decide whether to listen to

How do filmmakers balance familiarity and novelty?

Walt Disney Studios Motion Pictures/Photofest

audio in the car (or not). People's media choices are always embedded in a particular situation and context. If you choose to listen, you next must decide which device to use. Should you listen to your preselected music on your cell phone, use a digital streaming service like Sirius or Spotify, or select an AM or FM radio station?

Next you must make a decision regarding your purpose: Will you use media for entertainment or information? Will it be Top 40 pop music, hip-hop, contemporary Christian, or something else? Will you choose to listen to news, a podcast, or an audiobook? Your choice may be specific and granular if you decide to listen to a particular musical artist—or it may be more general if you surf the channels listening for something good. Each of these choices may be made deliberately and intentionally or without much thought, as something done automatically as part of a routine.

Sometimes, when making media choices, we may choose affirmatively or negatively. We may make a choice by turning something off, choosing not to listen, read, use, or view. The concept of *selective avoidance* was developed to explain why people make choices through avoiding unpleasant or undesirable content. Some people may avoid messages that make them angry or frustrated. Others even choose not to use news media because they do not feel that fits with their lifestyle. Becoming more aware of these choices creates opportunities to reflect on their potential unintended consequences when it comes to all forms of media.

An urban legend postulates that 15% of all Internet content consists of photos and videos of cats. While this is not true, the plentiful nature of cat-related online content does raise interesting questions about aesthetic pleasure, choice, and our relationships with animals. A special exhibition on the history of online media about cats, held at the Museum of the Moving Image in New York, traces the phenomenon back to 1995, when cat images began appearing on the Internet. In truth, cat-related media make up no more than 0.3% of the Internet, according to computer scientists (Kingson, 2016).

But scientists say there is universal appreciation for cute animals. It seems humans are biologically programmed to be attracted to visual cues of cuteness, which include a big round face, bright, forward-facing eyes, floppy arms and legs, and a side-to-side gait. These

Do you seek out or avoid animal-related content on the Internet❓

are the qualities of human babies, of course, but people seem attracted to many creatures with similar features. According to one journalist, this includes "Japanese cranes, woolly bear caterpillars, a bobbing balloon, a big round rock stacked on a smaller rock, or even a colon, a hyphen and a close parenthesis typed in succession" (Angier, 2006: 1).

Media Awareness: What Attracts Your Attention?

The term *media awareness* has been used to describe the process that begins when people take conscious notice of the media that are part of their everyday life. Indeed, the term was once a synonym for media literacy. To begin the journey of becoming media literate requires increasing your media awareness.

All learning requires attention. But you learned to speak a language as a child without consciously being aware of the fact that you were paying attention to language. Language learning occurs naturally through human social interaction. It requires attention but not awareness. Paying attention to something and being aware of it may seem like the same thing, but psychologists have demonstrated that they are distinct processes. By measuring eye movements, scholars have learned that attending to a stimulus does not inevitably lead to awareness of it.

People may take a wide variety of routine objects, events, and experiences for granted without noticing fundamental aspects. For example, can you remember what song you listened to most recently? Can you recall the billboards you saw while driving to school? When you used your cell phone today, what was the first app you used or the first activity you performed with it? Because these actions have become automatic, they are sometimes not encoded in long-term memory.

Nobel Prize–winning cognitive psychologist Daniel Kahneman calls this type of automatic processing *System 1 thinking*, which is the fast, efficient, and near-automatic processing of information from the world around us. By contrast, *System 2 thinking* is the slow, deliberate, analytical, and consciously effortful mode of reasoning. In *Thinking Fast and Slow* (2011), Kahneman emphasizes the evolutionary value of both of these forms of cognition and shows how they sometimes contribute to cognitive biases. To heighten awareness of media use in everyday life, System 2 activities like keeping a media diary or engaging in a media fast can be useful. Such activities transform automatic processing into more conscious and deliberate opportunities for reflection and analysis.

A *media fast* can help consumers deepen awareness of their dependence on media and technology. Thomas Cooper, a professor at Emerson College, recommends this practice and notes that while it helps people become more aware of media dependence, it is also a means to gain fresh insight on life. For example, three Carleton College students decided to stop using their laptops for 3 weeks during the middle of the semester. They quickly learned how to use an old-fashioned typewriter. In the process, they discovered how much of college work is dependent upon the use of email and computer databases and how much leisure time is tied to the use of the Internet.

One graduate student in Chicago avoided cell phones, email, and social media for 90 days in a project he called "Going Amish." He removed himself from the Cloud and developed workarounds for simple things like coordinating meetings with friends. Over time, he came to love the increased variety of experiences that opened up to him when he removed screen time from his life. "I looked around at the world instead of reading about it on my phone," he explained (Reilly, 2012). While fasting from media is one way to heighten awareness, simply documenting media use (without fasting) can also be useful. Keeping careful track of media use helps users see patterns. For most students, it can be a transformative experience to observe and document their use of time and in particular, to discover how multitasking affects productivity.

Binge-Watching

People all over the world watch a lot of movies, and streaming media are changing the way we watch. With 182 million Netflix subscribers watching nearly 2 hours per day, more than half of users say that, if forced to choose, they would keep Netflix over traditional television programming. This is partly because *binge-watching* (or binge-viewing) is becoming a valued style of media consumption. It is generally defined as watching three or more 1-hour episodes of a television show or six or more 30-minute episodes in a single sitting (Steiner & Xu, 2018). The word has been around only since 2013, and it is linked directly to Netflix's decision to release all episodes of a television season at one time, not spread out on a weekly basis as was the tradition inherited from broadcast television.

Because television shows have been using complexity as a means to enhance user engagement and attention, binge-watching may be a form of active viewing that results in the pleasures of *immersion* (which is sometimes called *transportation*). These feelings are associated with a type of media consumption that occurs when readers, listeners, or viewers feel so engaged that they lose all sense of time and space, feeling "in" the story. When people watch in this way, they have high attentiveness to the narrative content and form.

Which movies and TV shows have created feelings of pleasurable immersion for you?

But not all binge-watching is done with high levels of attention to the media content. It tends to be a solitary experience and not something that viewers do with family and friends. Researchers found that viewers engage in binge-watching for different reasons (Steiner & Xu, 2018).

Alamy

Some want to catch up with the story before the new season begins. Others see it as a relaxing and nostalgic diversion. Some people choose to rewatch shows they have seen before as a way to relax before bedtime. People report feelings of satisfaction from viewing a show to its conclusion, but some describe binge-watching as more of a compulsion, explaining that they feel a need to get through the whole series. Some viewers perceive binge-watching as a type of guilty pleasure, noticing that they felt bad afterward or that it interfered with sleep or work. You can learn more about the addictive qualities of media consumption in Chapter 13.

Comprehension: Putting Messages in Context

Humans fear what they do not understand. We seek meaning in the world around us. But comprehension depends greatly on context: we rely on all kinds of information that exists beyond the text in the interpretation of symbols. Indeed, texts only make sense within a particular context. When we lack context, misunderstandings occur. For example, everyone knows that the same sentence can mean vastly different things when uttered by different people in different situations. Researchers have shown that even the craziest nonsense can be comprehensible when additional context is provided (Haviland & Clark, 1974).

What is the weirdest and most incomprehensible video you have seen on YouTube ❓

When online, we may encounter messages that are out of context. Have you ever come across a weird, inexplicable YouTube video? Or one that you could not quite make sense of? Or even one that unnerved or scared you? The Reddit community hosts a group of users who like to view, discuss, and unravel weird and mysterious YouTube videos. Of course, YouTube features quite a lot of strange videos. But in general, you can identify the people, objects, and events depicted in weird videos to make some sense of what you are seeing and hearing.

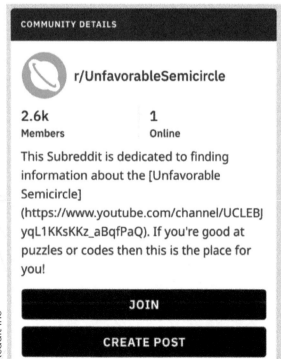

But one set of videos really captured widespread attention because they were so completely incomprehensible. When people stumbled onto a strange set of videos from Webdriver Torso in 2015, they were unnerved by the fast-changing mix of brightly colored shapes and random, high-pitched tones. These videos were simply weird. Some people thought they might be delivering coded messages. The strange nature of these videos prompted all kinds of conspiracy theories.

Another YouTube channel, Unfavorable Semicircle, soon started posting videos every 2 or 3 minutes, also beginning in 2015. Some are only a few seconds long and others are up to 11 hours in length. These videos are blurry constellations of dots in seemingly random arrangements. But it is the audio that spooks people: a male voice recites random letters. One freaky video, called "Lock," features intense flashing colors and unnerving, warped audio.

These videos have aroused people's curiosity. One Redditor explains that one video has sounds of a man whispering and kids singing. Other users have experimented with slowing down or speeding up the clip to see if they can make sense of it. Still others have set up a website, with a database of the videos, so as to enroll people in helping to find coherence in these incomprehensible videos. Is this the work of a disturbed mind or a set of coded messages? Are these videos from the CIA or part of a foreign government plot? Were they created by aliens? Because these videos did not make sense, people made up possible interpretations using the frame of conspiracy theories.

As it turns out, the weird, incomprehensible YouTube videos are merely test videos created by Google engineers as they developed the YouTube platform. By echoing 1980s pop star Rick Astley's hit song "Never Gonna Give You Up" in reference to these tests, the engineers cleverly acknowledged the phenomenon of Rickrolling, one of the Internet's most famous memes linked to the Astley music video (Wakefield, 2014). In an official statement, Google said: "We're never gonna give you uploading that's slow or loses video quality, and we're never gonna let you down by playing YouTube in poor video quality. That's why we're always running tests like Webdriver Torso." Once people could situate the videos into a context by identifying the author and purpose, the videos were no longer mysterious. To comprehend and then evaluate media messages, we need contextual information.

Context collapse is the term used to describe how the sharing of digital media can lead to the blurring of boundaries between people and groups in ways that can contribute to misinterpretations. This term has been applied to explain how Instagram and Facebook posts can be misunderstood when viewed by those who were not the target audience or intended receivers of the message (Marwick & boyd, 2010). Because the rise of Internet culture has enabled many forms of expression and communication to become detached from their original context, these slippages of meaning can also contribute to disinformation and misinformation.

Some people suggest that maintaining a single digital identity will minimize the problem of context collapse. But there may be important reasons why Facebook users have multiple Facebook accounts and create anonymous fake profiles. In some cultures and contexts, it is acceptable for people to present themselves differently to various audiences using social media. Although Mark Zuckerberg prefers that people have only one identity on Facebook, in some countries, different social pressures and cultural expectations encourage people to keep separate social contexts strictly divided (Costa, 2018).

Genres Aid Comprehensibility

Media genres are cultural categories that operate for both people, profits, and platforms. Genres help you make sense of media, and they shape your expectations as an audience member (Mittell, 2015). For authors, they help with the creative process by supplying the form, content, and even the process of creating media messages. The concept of genre emerged as the sheer volume of media increased in society. In the 18th century, as the rise of print media made new forms of expressive art available to mass audiences, the need for criticism arose as a way to make sense of the explosion of new content. During the Enlightenment, people published all manner of print content: children's picturebooks, novels, gardening advice, spiritual guidance, and more. Over time, categories and labels developed as people copied, reworked, and modified succesful works.

Media genres are categories that reflect and embody features of particular texts. Media literacy scholars and educators use the term *codes and conventions* to refer to the textual features of a particular genre. For example, modern cookbooks have a certain set of structural characteristics that are typical of the genre: they give a name to a particular recipe and include a list of ingredients followed by instructions on food preparation using standized units of measurement. When readers see these features, they recognize it as a recipe. But old cookbooks from before 1920 rarely follow these codes and conventions. You might take notice of the codes and conventions of the most popular video games, and if you play video games regularly for years, you may notice subtle shifts that occur. Codes and conventions emerge from within a creative community and they change over time.

Consider the ambiguity inherent in identifying media genres. When you see lines of phrases or words, presented in sequence but without capital letters or periods, you may interpret it as text messaging or poetry. If it seems to be two voices interacting with each other, you might recognize it as text messaging. If it makes unique use of metaphors, you may recognize it as poetry.

Text messaging and poetry have many similarities. Carol Ann Duffy, Britain's poet laureate, once explained, "The poem is a form of texting. [...] it's a way of saying more with less [...] We've got to realize that the Facebook generation is the future—and, oddly enough, poetry is the perfect form for them. It's a kind of time capsule—it allows feelings and ideas to travel big distances in a very condensed form" (Moorhead, 2011).

Although we use and adapt many genre terms from print media (such as *comedy* and *drama*), new genres are constantly being developed as creative people find novel ways of expressing themselves in order to inform, to entertain, or to persuade. In your own lifetime, you have yourself experienced the development of new terms to describe video content. Even before YouTube was created in 2006, people were experimenting with new forms of video, as the Internet made it easy for people to share digital video files. As more people uploaded original content, new genres were born.

The Birth of the Vlog

One of the most famous examples of the emergence of a new genre is the *vlog*. In 2006, when YouTube was brand-new, a woman named Bree released videos about her life under the name LonelyGirl15. These low-quality videos, posted to YouTube, had few (if any) edits and featured a young girl speaking directly to the camera.

The girl spoke intimately about her life, and her talk was sometimes raw and unfiltered. As the number of viewers increased, the stories of her life became more surreal and sensational, and more like a movie. The size of the audience grew as LonelyGirl15 became an Internet sensation. Eventually the girl was revealed to be an actor as journalists discovered that the videos were professionally produced by a Hollywood talent agency. Still, even after being discovered as scripted, the *web series* continued for 2 years. The vlog was even the first YouTube channel ever to secure a product placement deal (Cresci, 2016).

Given this history, it is ironic that vlogs have been lauded for their authenticity. Today, vlogs are so common that you have likely seen many different types of them, including makeup tutorials, media reviews, and entertaining, informational, or persuasive vlogs. The genre has even developed its own set of codes and conventions. Recognizable features of a vlog include:

- a clever username;
- a regular schedule of posting videos;
- the speaker uses direct address, looking at the camera;
- the individual uses words like "you" to refer to viewers as if speaking to a friend;
- a strong character, personality, or performance holds viewers' interest;

© Bree vlog collage

What are some benefits and drawbacks to viewing and creating vlogs?

- questions to viewers that inspire feedback and interaction through comments;
- jump-cut editing transitions remove extra words and speed up the overall pace of the video;
- requesting viewers to subscribe to the YouTube channel and share the videos with others.

Vlogging may be good for you. The confessional style of the vlog is likely to have some mental health benefits to the vloggers who create them. Psychologists have demonstrated that expressive writing about traumatic experiences can help people regain a sense of control. This has been called the *Pennebaker paradigm* in honor of the University of Texas psychology professor who first conducted research on expressive writing as a form of therapy. He asked some students to write for 20 minutes at a time over the course of several days about a neutral topic while others wrote about a traumatic experience. Those who wrote about traumatic experiences reported better psychological health months later and had made fewer visits to the campus healthcare center. The effect has been replicated by many other medical professionals who found that simply writing about health problems can improve emotional well-being (Smyth & Lepore, 2002).

Categories Shape Expectations

When you choose to watch a comedy film, for example, you naturally have some *expectations* that the experience will make you laugh. You may expect characters to be exaggerated and oversimplified. Surprises in the story and plot may be delightful. But the genre of comedy is not rigid. Categories are blurry and films can often be categorized into multiple genres. Genres are a type of label; they may be based on the content (like the war film), the size of the budget (like the indie film), or many other categories.

Because computer scientists have taken up the study of *pattern recognition* in developing the field of artificial intelligence, many of the ways we discover media have changed in just the past 10 years. For example, when you access Netflix, you are presented with a sample of you in a strip-like format. But you are not seeing the thousands of TV shows and movies available to stream because Netflix uses an algorithm that gives users options based on what it thinks viewers might like to watch. Netflix has more than 76,000 genre categories including "Action and Adventure," "Latin and Ballroom Dance," "Exciting B-Horror," and many more. The categorization even gets as precise as "Feel-Good Sports Movies for Ages 8 to 10" and "Visually Striking Movies for Ages 5 to 7" or "Fight-the-System" TV Shows."

Recommendation engines make the experience more relevant to viewers. They are information filtering systems that deal with the problem of information overload by filtering according to users' preferences, interests, and behavior. They narrow down choices in order to make decision-making less complex.

New genres are emerging all the time as people see similarities between different types of media. Among the most popular genres on YouTube are beauty, gaming, tech, family, and fashion. In the comedy/skit genre, there is work by Jenna Marbles, who first started uploading videos in 2010 and now has more than 20 million subscribers as of 2020, attracting audiences with videos like "How Guys Pack a Suitcase" and "Throwing My Dogs a Pool Party." But Jenna's videos are not always in the comedy/skit genre. She sometimes does funny makeup tutorials or reviews new apps. Blending genres in creative ways is part of why her work is so popular.

Why do genres matter for media literacy? Genres shape expectations. If viewers think they are watching a documentary, they may be confused, disturbed, or surprised when the movie turns comedic. Because genres are built upon generalizations from previous experience, they represent a kind of tacit contract between authors and audiences (Chandler, 2007). While some people may think that genres limit the creativity of the author, most say that a genre helps the author because it enables them to take advantage of the preexisting knowledge and expectations of the audience.

Algorithm-Based Playlists

You may be a fan of Spotify's Discover Weekly, a service that, each week, curates a fresh list of 30 new songs that they predict you will love. Nearly 300 million people around the world subscribe to the service. Such playlists have a long history. In the analog age of music, people shared physical copies of records and tapes with each other, creating personalized mixtapes. Back in the 2000s, humans tagged and labeled music to assemble playlists to reflect their own interpretation and judgment of the music. Today, algorithms are also used to analyze the content of music, allowing computers to perform music identification, personalized recommendations, playlist creation, and analysis. Spotify's Discover Weekly uses three recommendation strategies.

First, *collaborative filtering* uses input from users to inform its understanding of which songs to recommend to other, similar users. Akin to Netflix's recommendation engine, Spotify gathers data on exactly what consumers stream, including whether a listener saved the track to his or her own playlist or visited an artist's page after listening to a song.

What makes algorithmic playlists both thrilling and scary?

Second, *natural language processing* is also used to gather metadata, news articles, blogs, and other text from around the Internet and to analyze them to find patterns. According to software engineer Sophia Ciocca, "Spotify crawls the web constantly looking

Dave Horwitz
@Dave_Horwitz

It's scary how well @Spotify Discover Weekly playlists know me. Like former-lover-who-lived-through-a-near-death-experience-with-me well.

3:09 PM - Oct 27, 2015

♡ 261 💬 180 people are talking about this

© Twitter, Inc

for blog posts and other written text about music to figure out what people are saying about specific artists and songs—which adjectives and what particular language is frequently used in reference to those artists and songs, and which other artists and songs are also being discussed alongside them" (Ciocca, 2017: 1).

Finally, Spotify's recommendation engine also employs *raw audio models* to identify new songs. Using software that analyzes audio data utilizing neural network architecture, songs can be identified through characteristics like estimated time signature, key, mode, tempo, and loudness. By understanding fundamental similarities between songs, these models can predict which users might enjoy them based on listening history. It can be both thrilling and scary to receive recommendations that are so personalized.

5 critical questions about Instagramming your meals

Your Instagram feed is shaped by recommendation engines. In this Instagram post, we see an example of the common practice of taking photos of restaurant meals. Using five critical questions of media literacy, we can analyze this media message so as to gain insight on its meaning and value.

1. **Who is the author and what is the purpose?** Author MerkelRob reports his location as Bremen, Germany. His Instagram page contains a variety of beautiful travel photos. Because he has chosen to use more than a dozen hashtags on this image, his purpose may be to develop and find an audience for his travel photos.

2. **What techniques are used to attract and hold attention?** The photo has a number of attention-getting elements, including the medieval church, which suggests his location is a café in Bremen, Germany. The stein of beer and the gigantic quantity of food on the plate also attract attention. The use of the ellipsis (the three dots between words) invites the reader to wonder about the author's real attitudes toward the food. Using the word "special" instead of more gustatory words like "delicious" creates doubt.

3. **What lifestyles, values, and points of view are depicted?** The location of the café, the choice of food and drink, and the time of day suggest the lifestyle of an upper-middle-class person having a lunch or an early supper. The decision to frame the church in the image suggests the lifestyle of a tourist. Hashtags like #globetrotter and #wonderfulplaces communicate the stance of someone visiting a place for the first time.

4. **How might different people interpret this message?** Pierre Bourdieu would say that this author is displaying his cultural capital, as a photo of restaurant food and European travel obviously suggest a form of symbolic wealth. Germans might be more knowledgeable about the cuisine depicted here if it is a typical meal for the region. Photographers might observe that the photo is not exactly a form of food porn, a genre of photography that features a glamorized visual presentation of cooking, eating, or food. Others might simply experience feelings of envy as they imagine how fun it would be to sit at a sidewalk café in Europe in the shadow of ancient medieval churches, enjoying a cold beverage, and trying out the local cuisine.

Algorithmic decision-making about music may have complex unintended consequences. People have strong emotional responses to discovering new music: Many describe it simply as "joy." Spotify has found that its users trust the company to provide a good listening experience and to protect their personal information. But in 2019, Spotify decided the time was right to exploit that joyful trust as a source of revenue. With 200 million users, it is now selling access to users to advertisers. After Spotify began selling advertising on Discover Weekly, it patented an algorithm that selects specific ads based on the mood of songs. Ads will soon be placed in consumers' playlists in order to extend and connect to the emotions they feel as they listen to specific songs. With algorithmic persuasion like this, one writer noted, soon "the marketing of our emotions and trust will all be seamless" (Tiffany, 2019: 1).

merkelrob • Follow
Bremen, Germany

merkelrob I've always found this meal to be very.... special
merkelrob #germany #bremen #foodporn #herring #cafe #beer #instafood #igfood #instaeats #foodlove #food_lovers #food_oclock #travel #wanderlust #globetrotter #igtravel #instatravel #ig_europe #travelingthroughtheworld #helloworldpics #wonderfulplaces #travelgram #travelmor
merkelrob #2018trippp

vaculikova_betty, audreyverse, tanillz, m_a_f_f_o and polkadotinparis like this

5 MINUTES AGO

Add a comment...

© Facebook, Inc

5. What is omitted? Despite all the hashtags, the verbal content does not give details like the name of the restaurant and the name of the dish. The photo does not clearly show what kind of food is on the plate. Instagram has not informed me why it served this particular image when I searched for #foodporn, which is a popular hashtag. Perhaps it has used my own posted images (which document my frequent travel experiences) and selected images aligned with the images I have shared.

Media as Environment

Discussions of taste preferences emphasize the individual choices of the media user. But many aspects of media use, of course, do not involve choice. Much exposure to media is really determined by the social and cultural environment. For example, babies do not choose to use media: parents make choices on behalf of their children. When you enter a sports bar, you will see sporting games and advertising on multiple giant screens. You do not really have a choice—it is a part of the media environment. While you pump gas, you may have to watch the commercials for snacks and soda.

When you were growing up, your parents may have controlled the car radio and you may have had no choice but to listen to the content they selected. Think about it: in many aspects of our lives, we cannot personally control our media exposure. Because children and young people are required to attend school, they engage with books and reading through coercion. *Coercion* is a form of persuasion where people do not really have

Intellectual Grandparent:
Marshall McLuhan

Photofest

Marshall McLuhan was a Canadian professor of English at the University of Toronto who explored the nature of mass communications. In the 1960s, television was becoming the dominant medium of the culture just at a time when many things were changing as a result of the civil rights movement, the rise of feminism, and media coverage of the Vietnam War. Through a series of books, television interviews, and influential magazine interviews, McLuhan became, for a time, a guru on the new media environment. He used a highly creative and experimental style of writing and speaking that included aphorisms, puns, and wordplay and drew upon wide-ranging knowledge from across the arts, humanities, history, and the social and physical sciences. Today, his work is associated with *medium theory*, the practice of primarily examining the form and structure (not the content) of media messages. His most well-known ideas include:

We shape our tools and thereafter our tools shape us. At a time when most cultural critics were offering simplistic value judgments about television's presumed inferiority to print media, McLuhan was claiming that television was neither bad nor good. Media are extensions of human senses and engage the senses in different ways. Media symbolically enlarge our experience of the world. Like all forms of technology, media extend our "physical and nervous systems to increase power and speed" (McLuhan, 1964: 90). Media are outward expressions of human consciousness. McLuhan made a distinction between "hot" and "cool" media by reflecting on the different ways our senses experience print and visual media. Cool media are high in audience participation.

free choice. In some work settings, music may be playing for customers that you must listen to as well. You may be required to use the Internet, email, and websites as part of your job. As a form of persuasion, coercion offers no "opt-out" mechanism.

It is important to look at the carefully designed and hidden features of the media environment that are part of daily life because these features are not inevitable (Strate, 2017). They do not have to be designed the way they are. Neil Postman, coined the term *media ecology* to describe the practice of noticing how "media of communication affects human perception, understanding, feeling, and value; and how our interaction with media facilitates or impedes our chances of survival." When we think of the word *environment*, we generally associate it with things like water, air, and architecture. But Postman argued that an environment is "a complex message system which imposes on humans certain ways of thinking, feeling, and behaving" (Postman, 1970: 164). He contended that environments structure many aspects of life, affecting what we see, say,

Hot media extend a single sense in high definition. For example, a photograph is "hot" because it offers a lot of information; a cartoon is "cool" because to make sense of it, the reader must fill in the missing information. The idea of sense ratios was a way to explore how media are used in different ways in a particular society, and to observe how these practices change over time. Essentially, McLuhan believed that different media extend different features of the five human senses, and that people internalize certain mental processes associated with the dominant media in their culture.

The medium is the message. Contemporary culture is so media-saturated that people use media without much conscious awareness. Just as fish fail to notice the water in which they swim, people fail to notice the bombardment of information, entertainment, and persuasion that comes to them through print, visual, and electron-

ic media. Because it is everywhere, it is invisible (McLuhan, 1964).

Media awareness is required for full participation in society. Media environments are invisible to the people who inhabit them. McLuhan believed in heightening people's awareness of media, and much of his life's work was spent on this endeavor. How can media awareness be increased? Through art, people can refresh their perception, McLuhan believed. Some have suggested that McLuhan valorized the position of the artist in society, seeing that artists reframe culture through art and enable people to see the interrelationship among things, anticipate technological changes, and "consider their social and cultural implications before they happen" (Bobbitt, 2011: 1).

If Marshall McLuhan has influenced your thinking about media, you can share a comment on the Grandparents of Media Literacy website at www.grandparentsofmedialiteracy.com.

and do. Books, movies, TV, music, video games, the Internet, and social media are part of the environment. By looking at media as a system, Postman claimed, we can observe "what roles media force us to play, how media structure what we are seeing, why media make us feel and act as we do." Today, the media ecology perspective emphasizes the study of the history of communication and particularly the ways in which media shape time, space, and place.

Learning to analyze the features of our media environments is not easy because they seem so inevitable, so natural, and so routine. George Gerbner, the former dean of the Annenberg School for Communication at the University of Pennsylvania, also considers media from an environmental point of view. Recognizing how we learn our gender and cultural identity from the images and stories that surround us, Gerbner explains, "For the first time in human history, children are born into homes where most of the stories do not come from their parents, schools, churches, communities, and in many places even from their native countries, but from a handful of conglomerates who have something to sell." Gerbner sees media as a coalescing and increasingly integrated *cultural environment* that "constrains life's choices as the natural environment defines life's chances." By telling us what to value and how to live, media messages may contribute to "a narrowing of perspectives, homogenization of outlooks, and limitation of alternatives" (Gerbner, 1998: 118).

When media are understood as an environment or as a system, individuals can be seen as victimized by the problems in the system. Just as breathing in poisonous air or living in houses with toxic lead levels can trigger health problems, contemporary life with media may also create physical and mental health issues. Although some see people as having a rather limited ability to control how media influence them, others recognize that the choices about what people read, view, listen to, play, and use are significant.

What the future may hold: The Illusion of Choice

Long ago, people wandered the stacks of a library and asked elders about which books to read. Publishers and editors made choices of what books to create and librarians made selections that influenced readers' choices, creating indexes to help people independently find print resources, using keywords and other metadata. In the age of mass media, editors and producers made choices for people too. They selected and created content for newspapers, radio, and television. In the age of the Internet, explosive growth in content and search engines help people find what they are looking for online. Today, consumers do not need to do much searching because much of the media they view, listen to, and read comes to them. It has been selected by a machine.

This may sound cool—or scary—but *illusions of choice* are embedded in many features of our social environment. Human freedom is not unlimited. Think of a restaurant menu. Menus give people an illusion of choice, but all choices are ultimately controlled by the chef. People do not generally ask, "What is not on the menu?"

People who are media literate

are trained to notice how media content is always selective and incomplete. This is not an easy skill to learn. Tristan Harris, In describing a Google engineer and ethicist, notes how, by controlling the online menu, social media platforms control users' choices. For example, when people use recommendation engines, the software may falsely encourage them to see the list provided as a complete set of choices. In describing a group of friends using Yelp to look for a place to hang out together, Harris (2016: 1) writes, "While looking down at their phones, they do not see the park across the street with a band playing live music. They miss the pop-up gallery on the other side of the street serving crepes and coffee. Neither of those show up on Yelp's menu." Learning to recognize the biases and limitations of recommendation engines is an important media literacy competency.

Media dependence is a theory that predicts that the more a person depends on media to meet psychological and social needs, the more important media will be in that person's life, and therefore the more effects media will have on that individual (Ball-Rokeach, 1985). Some worry that recommendation engines will have a negative influence on freedom of choice when it comes to the movies, music, news, information, and media consumers use (VanEs, 2017). Are automatic content feeds truly beneficial for users, or do these techniques undermine the autonomy and limit the truly free choice of people who are increasingly exposed to online, targeted information?

On the other hand, with the explosion of media content brought about by the ability of every human to be both a consumer and creator of content, recommendation engines may be an empowering tool that enable us to sift and sort and make sense of the ever-growing variety of music, movies, information, games, entertainment, and more. Since content that is easily findable is more likely to be used, perhaps recommendation engines will improve to better support our online lives.

TIME TO REFLECT

Reflect on your media tastes. Choose one of these activities to explore features of your taste in music or movies:

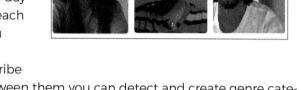

- Create a detailed timeline to chart the development of your taste in movies or music since you were a child and write about the patterns you notice over time.
- Keep track of all the music you listen to in one day by identifying the genre and noting whether each song you hear is familiar or novel. What do you learn?
- Make a list of your 10 favorite movies and describe each one. Then see how many similarities between them you can detect and create genre categories for your list.

Consider these questions: What patterns do you notice in your taste preferences? How satisfied are you with your choices? How have your taste preferences changed over time?

Then, share your ideas in the Flipgrid Inquiry by contributing a brief oral presentation. You can also view and respond to comments of other people who have offered thoughtful reflections on their own media tastes. Visit www.medialiteracyaction.com to learn more.

CREATE TO LEARN

Change One Thing about Your Media Diet

Gain awareness of your media diet by making one simple change to it and then documenting what you experience in an essay. For one day, do a personal audit of all your media use—all your reading, listening, viewing, and game play. Reflect on which of the behaviors you engaged in are typical for you in an ordinary day.

Then change one specific feature of your typical media use habits for a brief period—3 days at the most. For example, if you typically listen to music in the car, switch to a podcast or do not listen to music at all. In a personal essay (500 words or fewer) or video (two minutes or shorter), reflect on your experiences before and after your experiment. You can post and share your experience using the #MLAction hashtag.

When it comes to media, popularity and quality are socially constructed

Who Decides What Makes Media "Good"?

8

Learning Outcomes

1. Examine how forms of recognition shape the distribution of power in many different professional and creative fields

2. Understand how the public plays a role in signaling social values in ways that bring visibility to social issues, conflicts, and controversies

3. Recognize the role of ratings and reviews in defining quality and popularity

4. Reflect on how social media sharing practices can intensify and amplify social pressure and conformity, which may affect people's judgments about quality and value

Perhaps you like to watch the Oscars for the best Hollywood films or the Grammy Awards for the best popular music. A growing number of media awards are presented each year, including the Country Music Awards, the Golden Globes, and the BET Awards. Perhaps you even like to predict which musicians, films, actors, or directors will win.

Awards and honors are a form of public recognition that can increase the value of people and the things they create. Creative artists and creative work have economic value when perceived favorably by thought leaders and when the public responds by allocating their money, time, and attention. Award rituals are an important part of many social groups, including in many professional fields as well as in the media industry. They establish public expectations in response to questions about what (and who) is valued and respected.

Consider the Heisman Trophy, the highest award offered in collegiate football. Named after Ohio college football player and coach John W. Heisman, the Heisman Trophy is awarded through a voting process involving 840 people selected from different geographic regions of the country. The award honors an outstanding college football player "whose performance best exhibits the pursuit of excellence with integrity. Winners epitomize great ability combined with diligence, perseverance, and hard work."

Everywhere you look, it seems, you find award ceremonies. Well-established and broadly publicized awards in the media and culture industries include the Pulitzer Prize (journalism and book publishing) and the Oscar (motion pictures), Grammy (music), Tony (theater), and Emmy (television). These prizes have become global cultural icons signifying popular and critical success.

Certainly, there have been some particularly dramatic, unusual, or controversial moments in award ceremonies, as when Taylor Swift's 2009 acceptance speech for MTV's Video of the Year Award was interrupted by Kanye West, who grabbed the microphone from her to say, "Beyoncé had one of the best videos of all time," referring to "Single Ladies (Put a Ring on It)."

Award shows have long been sites of controversy because they can reveal cultural tensions both within the industry and within the larger society. For example, the first rap music group nominated for a Grammy Award was Run DMC, a legendary group of hip-hop artists including Jason Mizell, Darryl McDaniels, and Joseph Simmons. They also performed the first rap music ever broadcast on MTV. In fact, when the Grammys introduced a Best Rap Artist category in 1989, the award was not aired on TV. Music executives believed that mainstream audiences would not accept rap music. This bad decision led Will Smith, Jazzy Jeff, LL Cool J, Public Enemy, and Salt-N-Pepa to boycott the awards the following year (Coscarelli, 2016). This media controversy provided people with valuable opportunities to discuss racism and representation in American society.

When we evaluate the quality of media, we must also consider the role of places, platforms, social practices, and institutions, and the opinions of critics and other influential people, all of which may shape our sense of what is "good."

Perhaps you have noticed the difference between watching a movie in a crowded theater as compared with watching in a nearly empty one. Both of these practices are different from viewing movies at home in your living room in front of a big-screen TV or on the bus watching a film on a smartphone. And perhaps you have noticed the difference between watching a movie after reading reviews as compared with going in "cold" to a movie that you knew little about. Shared media experiences provide people with important information about how to feel, think, and act.

In this chapter, we explore the many factors that influence perceptions of "quality" when it comes to media by considering these questions:

- Why do so many people enjoy award ceremonies?
- What strategies do media producers use to increase the likelihood that their work will be popular?
- What makes a video or meme go viral?
- Do human-created reviews of movies, musics, and video games have a future, or will they eventually be replaced by algorithmic filtering and curation?

Tournaments of Value

Decisions about quality—whether in football, music, film, theater, or other creative pursuits—involve the collective interest of audiences and industry professionals, who are at all times aware of the relationship between quality and popularity. Awards offer a type of collective value judgment. The selectivity and exclusivity of awards are a form of *social power*, because by definition, many are excluded from receiving them. Many very fine college football players will never receive the Heisman Trophy. Many high-quality films, songs, TV shows, and Broadway plays are not honored at award ceremonies. According to some critics, award ceremonies can be an opportunity for dominant social groups to strengthen their elite position.

Award ceremonies can be thought of as *tournaments of value*, because "participation in them is likely to be both a privilege of those in power and an instrument of status contests among them." These ceremonies are not only about "status, rank, fame, or reputation of actors, but the disposition of the central tokens of value in the society in question" (Appadurai, 1988: 21). Being nominated for an Oscar can enhance the visibility of a creative individual and his or her work, increasing the artist's reputation and social standing in the field. Receiving awards does not guarantee success, but is a type of public recognition that can increase business opportunities.

Consider the Question

Working with a partner, brainstorm a list of all the value tournaments you are familiar with. Think about those that you may have experienced during childhood and adolescence. Be sure to consider those you may participate in as well as those that you experience as a spectator and as a participant. As you make your list, identify the various cultural values that the rituals reward, celebrate, and emphasize.

Award ceremonies are a type of *public ritual*, a way of communicating cultural values through highly visible actions. Anthropologists like Clifford Geertz have explained the central role of symbols in constructing shared public meaning. Public rituals enact *culture*, which is expressed as "an inherited conception expressed in symbolic forms by means of which men communicate, perpetuate, and develop their knowledge about and attitudes toward life" (Geertz, 1973: 89). As viewers of award ceremonies, we participate in the maintenance of the social order concerning how quality in media creative industries is socially defined.

Inequality in Hollywood

Controversies emerge when consensus shifts about what constitutes quality, fairness, or justice. In 2015, activist April Reign started a hashtag movement called #OscarsSoWhite, after all of the nominees for all of the acting awards were white. *Hashtag activism* happens when large numbers of posts appear on social media under a common word, phrase, or sentence using the hashtag symbol to increase the findability of a particular message. The release of these mutually connected posts in networked spaces provides *rhetorical agency* to a group of people. This concept has been defined as the capacity to "speak or write in a way that will be recognized or heeded by others in one's community" (Campbell, 2005: 3).

To address the rise of the #OscarsSoWhite movement, in 2017 the Academy invited 774 new members, including a number of African American, Latino, and Asian actors, directors, and other film professionals. This increased the proportion of nonwhite voters to 13%. One critic explained, "#OscarsSoWhite refers to all marginalized communities and is not about quotas but about asking inclusive questions when staffing films—from the actors cast to the boom operators and craft-services teams hired. It is about operating outside of the same networks that

Have you engaged in hashtag activism? Why or why not?

have been used for years and instead providing opportunities to talented craftspeople from groups not usually included" (Reign, 2018: 1).

Hollywood's concern about the diversity of movies is rooted in the *profit motive*. The film industry is finally discovering that, from a business point of view, the more inclusive a film is, the more money it can make. Research shows that nonwhite moviegoers purchased 49% of tickets sold in the United States in 2016. Given that 40% of the U.S. population is nonwhite, this means nonwhite moviegoers are a vital sector of the audience. To demonstrate the relationship between diversity and box office success, the Creative Artists Agency examined 413 theatrical films released from January 2014 to December 2016, detailing cast ethnicity for the top 10 billed actors per movie, a total of 2,800 people. The Agency found that for the top 10 grossing movies in 2016, 47% of the opening weekend audience were people of color. Moreover, 7 of the 10 highest-grossing movies from 2016 (and four from 2015's top 10) delivered opening weekend audiences that were more than 50% nonwhite (Anderson, 2017).

Hollywood understands that a more diverse cast brings a more diverse audience, which brings in more money. But, according to Spike Lee, director of *Boyz in the Hood*, "The real battle over racism in Hollywood is not with the Academy Awards but in the executive studios and TV and cable networks, where gatekeepers decide which projects get made and which don't" (Berman, 2016: 1).

Gender and racial inequality have long been part of the industry, claims the Hollywood Diversity Report. In Hollywood, women are represented in front of the camera, but behind the scenes, few women work as direc-

Why is gender and racial diversity important for people who work behind the scenes in film and media productions❓

Steve Granitz/WireImage/Getty Images

tors, writers, producers, or cinematographers. For example, of the top 250 films of 2017, 88% had no female directors, 83% had no female writers, and 96% had no female cinematographers (Lauzen, 2018). Of the 234 comedy and drama series presented across 18 broadcast, cable, and digital platforms in the 2016–2017 season, fewer than 10% were led by minority group (Hunt et al., 2018).

Although gender inequality often makes national news, it is not clear whether or how the industry will make changes. Many Americans learned about the scope of inequality when news broke that actor Michelle Williams, who was nominated for a Golden Globe Award for her performance in *All the Money in the World*, accepted $80 a day for the film's reshoots, while her costar Mark Wahlberg got $1.5 million for the same work. Because this news came at the time when producer Harvey Weinstein was criminally prosecuted for rape after 80 women had made allegations against him, it contributed to the #MeToo social media campaign that increased the visibility of men who abuse their power by demanding sex with women who work for them.

Geena Davis, the Academy Award–winning actor who starred in *The Accidental Tourist*, recognizes that gender inequality is even reproduced in entertainment media that is directed at children. She has taken steps to solve the problem through media literacy. In 2004, while watching TV with her young daughter, she observed how many TV shows lacked female characters. She has funded research demonstrating that children's TV shows have three male characters for every one female character. Partnerships with Google and Girl Scouts have enabled her to highlight the need to reform how women and girls are represented in popular culture.

By surfacing the topic through hashtag activism at the Oscars award ceremony, the issue of diversity in the film industry gradually gained visibility inside the creative community, especially among leaders in the industry. Such efforts also help viewers recognize and appreciate the importance of diverse representations in all forms of media.

Memes: Making Morality Visual

Now that social media have gone global, anthropologists and media scholars have begun to explore the many different social functions they serve around the world. When social media were new, scholars focused on specific digital platforms, including Facebook, Twitter, Instagram, Snapchat, WeChat, WhatsApp, and others. While much scholarship still concentrates on individual platforms, anthropologists have observed how content migrates easily across platforms. Increasingly, people share images across platforms in order to visualize ideas, opinions, and feelings. Free online digital tools make it easy for anyone to manipulate an image or create a *meme*. When people share memes, they can express deeply felt emotions, but they can also challenge authorities and make fun of social values.

Professor Daniel Miller and his colleagues from countries including Turkey, China, Chile, and Syria have taken a broad look at social media. In traditional societies, they discovered, social media are used differently than in urban and industrialized communities. Because people around the world use social media in different ways, insights can be gained by looking cross-nationally at particular types of social media expression.

As memes are shared as a visual form of expression, they are particularly significant as "a kind of moral police of the Internet. By using them people are able to express their values and disparage those of others in less direct and more acceptable ways than before" (Miller et al., 2016: xvi). For example, in Brazil, many low-literate adults share memes, images, and videos in order to express themselves. Through the choice of images, they can convey their opinions, values, and tastes without writing. For people with less confidence in putting their own words out into a public space, sharing memes is a way to be socially present online. In a rural Chinese factory town, researchers found that young people share images edited to include motivational or sentimental wording and picturesque imagery. In northern Chile, memes are used to take pride in ordinary life. For example, people share photos that contrast ideal lifestyles "with the 'reality' of overweight bodies, rusted-out trucks and a burned dinner" (Miller et al., 2016: 172).

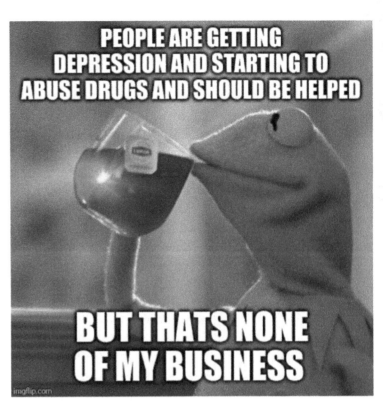

Imgflip LLC

How do memes reinforce, challenge or critique cultural norms?

Memes can also reinforce, challenge or critique social norms. Perhaps you have seen the Kermit the Frog meme, which shows him sitting in a café, sipping calmly on his cup of tea. The meme includes the phrase "But that's none of my business." Among social media users, researchers found that memes are used to offer critical commentary on the questionable behavior of others. Thus conservatives can make fun of liberals, and middle-class people can comment on the behavior of poor and working-class people.

Cultural Hierarchies in Media, Education, and Society

Every society has *status markers* to indicate the social position of individuals. Through clothing, dialect, and manners of behavior, you indicate whether your family is from the peasant class or a member of royalty. In the United

States, status markers emerged more visibly in the 19th century as part of Victorian morality. Under the influence of Queen Victoria, British people slowly shifted their values as they prohibited slavery, diminished the practice of cruelty to animals, and began the legal fight against child labor. Norms of genteel politeness spread across the British colonies and influenced the attitudes of Americans too, establishing clearly defined *cultural hierarchies* that persist to this day (Levine, 1990).

American culture grew more diverse and economically divided in the early part of the 20th century with the rise of immigration. Tensions between native and foreign-born became articulated in distinct ideas about what forms of entertainment are appropriate. Vaudeville, burlesque, the circus, and the freak show appealed to working-class audiences who had limited money and leisure time. Those with more money preferred musical concerts, dramatic performances, and shopping in department stores. The wealthy traveled abroad or took in ballet or opera as these were considered exotic performances with a refined European sensibility.

Such cultural hierarchies even inspired the history of media literacy education, which has long been tied up with efforts to build film, radio, and television appreciation into the education system. In the United States, Thomas Edison proclaimed, "The motion picture is destined to revolutionize our educational system and [...] in a few years it will supplant largely, if not entirely, the use of textbooks" (quoted in Oppenheimer, 2004). Following his inspiration, between 1900 and 1920, a large number of film projection entrepreneurs sold equipment all over the United States to schools, civic clubs, and other community organizations. But the quality of film content was slender, and a lot of it was commercial propaganda for business (Saettler, 2004). In England and the United States, beginning in the 1920s, two ideas grew in importance. First, there was widespread concern that children and youth were being harmed from watching popular films. Second, there was hope that film could be a powerful visual aid in education while raising the standard of film appreciation among the public (Bolas, 2009).

In England and the United States, radio became a big hit with educators and thought leaders. They immediately understood that it had educational, political, and religious potential, noting that "every radio listener could have the best seat in the auditorium" with access to a radio university that would educate the world, "leveling class distinctions and erasing Ivy-league elitism" (Fabos, 2004: 4). For those in rural communities, radio could end geographic isolation. States began experimenting with publicly funded educational radio. But they could not really compete with commercial stations. Unlike in England, where the government funded the BBC, American public broadcasters lacked funding. As a result, educators themselves were divided about whether to fight the commercial interests in radio or work with commercial broadcasters to improve it.

By the early 1950s, as television was just beginning, plenty of terrible radio programming was out there as well as some really outstanding work. Citizens' groups recognized the need to amplify the high-quality work in broadcasting and to diminish the influence of broadcast junk. As a form of civic activism, one such group banded together under the slogan "Radio-TV, Everyone's Responsibility." The American Council for Better Broadcasts,

with chapters in 93 cities across the United States, hosted the "Look Listen Project." The project activated people's media literacy competencies. Groups were enlisted to listen to and watch eight network programs and to give their opinion about the quality of the shows. In 1954, more than 6,800 people participated, and not surprisingly, they rated news and information programs highly and gave the lowest scores to sensational crime dramas (Better Broadcasts Newsletter, 1954).

A monthly publication helped members learn more about radio and television, including the economics of advertising and the regulatory traditions regarding media ownership rules for radio and TV stations. This organization gradually transformed into an advocacy organization for media literacy known as the National Telemedia Council. It was aligned with an early *media reform* effort designed to produce data to help the Federal Communications Communication (FCC) fulfill its obligation to ensure that broadcasting serves *the public interest, convenience, and necessity*. This important history reveals that media literacy and media reform initiatives have long been intertwined.

Popularity as a Measure of Quality

Each week, *The New York Times* publishes best-seller lists of books sold in the United States. This has been a tradition since 1931, when the newspaper compiled lists created by big-city newspapers around the country. Many people who love to read use the list as a *proxy measure* of quality and base their purchase decisions on it. Research has found that appearing on *The New York Times* best-seller list increases first-time author sales by 57%.

The list makes use of book sales data, but the exact formula for developing the list is a trade secret. The list includes sublists for advice books, children's books, nonfiction, and fiction. Some authors have found ways to get themselves on the list by buying large quantities of their own books. For example, Gannett publisher Al Neuharth, author of *Confessions of an S.O.B.*, asked the Gannett Foundation to buy 2,000 copies of his book, which advanced the book to the best-seller list for a short while. Today, marketing companies will buy books in bulk in order to get them featured on *The New York Times* best-seller list.

The *popularity–quality continuum* is complex, of course. It seems to be present in all forms of media, including books, TV shows, music, video games, apps, and more. This reflects a basic social phenomenon concerning popularity: people tend to like what other people like. For movies, the general standard of popularity is measured by opening weekend box office gross sales. These data report the amount of money taken in from Friday to Sunday night. For example, for the weekend of July 20–22, 2018, *The Equalizer 2* took in more than $36 million and *Mamma Mia! Here We Go Again* took in $34 million. These movies get the most attention from media outlets and thus attract more viewers. Figure 8.1 shows that *The Incredibles 2* seemed destined to be the big hit of the summer, as the chart reveals that it has sold $557 million in total gross sales after only 6 weeks.

Hollywood ticket sales have been declining for years. The year 2016 saw a new low, with fewer tickets sold in the United States than at any time since the 1920s. While once upon a time, Americans went to the movies every week, now the average American goes to the movies only four or five times a year. The industry relies on a small group of power viewers, as 10% of filmgoers buy half of all movie tickets. These people are likely to be between the ages of 24 and 39, because fewer people aged

Figure 8.1
Box Office Mojo, Week Ending July 22, 2018

This Week	Last Week	Title	Studio	Weekend Gross	% Change	Theater Count/Change		Average	Total Gross	Budget (in millions)	Week #
1	N	**The Equalizer 2**	Sony	**$36,011,640**	—	3,388	—	$10,629	$36,011,640	$62	1
2	N	**Mamma Mia! Here We Go Again**	Universal	**$34,952,180**	—	3,317	—	$10,537	$34,952,180	$75	1
3	1	**Hotel Transylvania 3: Summer Vacation**	Sony	**$23,765,709**	-46.1%	4,267	—	$5,570	$91,704,977	$80	2
4	2	**Ant-Man and the Wasp**	BV	**$16,507,156**	-43.3%	3,778	-428	$4,369	$165,005,448	—	3
5	4	**Incredibles 2**	BV	**$11,865,063**	-26.9%	3,164	-541	$3,760	$557,710,503	—	6
6	3	**Skyscraper**	Universal	**$11,360,030**	-54.4%	3,822	+40	$2,972	$47,149,150	$125	2
7	5	**Jurassic World: Fallen Kingdom**	Universal	**$11,263,420**	-30.5%	3,381	-314	$3,331	$384,164,925	$170	5
8	6	**The First Purge**	Universal	**$5,105,305**	-45.2%	2,331	-707	$2,190	$60,316,670	$13	3
9	N	**Unfriended: Dark Web**	BH Tilt	**$3,653,035**	—	1,546	—	$2,363	$3,653,035	$1	1
10	7	**Sorry to Bother You**	Annapurna	**$2,863,420**	-32.0%	1,050	+245	$2,727	$10,292,624		3

18–24 are going to the movies than ever before. To inspire more people to go to the movies, Hollywood studios spend 60 cents of every dollar they earn on marketing to reach domestic audiences. As a result, most films become profitable only after they reach the international market. Since international sales are so important to profitability, it should be no surprise that action films are plentiful. As Thompson (2016: 1) explains, "There is no language in the world more universal than heroes destroying bad guys with explosions."

To maximize profit, Hollywood studios have traditionally used a system of *distribution windows*, establishing a certain number of days after a movie's theatrical release that a film can be (1) sold as a DVD, (2) shown on a premium cable network, (3) shown on a broadcast or regular cable network, or (4) sold to the international market. When Disney executives announced that some of their new movies would go direct to streaming, they acknowledged that digital platforms now enable the greatest revenue stream for a studio (Amos, 2020). The demand for instantaneous access creates new opportunities and challenges for local exhibitors.

Another dimension of the popularity–quality continuum is the practice of *brand exploitation*, an approach to media production that carefully uses remakes and sequels of successful and highly familiar films, calculating economic benefits against the risks of box office failure. For example, the six *Spiderman* movies since 2002 have grossed almost $5 billion with three different starring actors and directors (Fritz, 2018). The aim of brand exploitation is to build upon success. But critics believe that in their quest for sure-fire profits, Hollywood filmmakers have overused the sequel format. In 1996, none of the top 10 films was a sequel or superhero film. In 2018, half of the top 10 films were sequels. Brand exploitation may eclipse the creative power of both stars and directors.

What are the rewards and the risks of brand exploitation ❓

Emerging Entertainment/Photofest

It is impossible to predict what media products will become a big hit, according to most people in the creative industries. No one can say for certain which books, movies, music, TV shows, or video games will become popular. Most efforts to predict hits are colossal failures. But researchers continue to try to understand the factors that make something popular. When Duncan Watts (2007: 1) found himself wondering what factors cause certain music to become popular, he wanted to document the role of social influence on people's judgments of quality. He observed:

> People almost never make decisions independently—in part because the world abounds with so many choices that we have little hope of ever finding what we want on our own; in part because we are never really sure what we want anyway; and in part because what we often want is not so much to experience the "best" of everything as it is to experience the same things as other people and thereby also experience the benefits of sharing.

Watts and his collaborators developed an ingenious way to test the relationship between quality, popularity, and social influence, testing the idea of *cumulative advantage*, or the "rich-get-richer" effect. Watts created a pop music website that reached 14,000 participants separated into eight different social "worlds" who were asked to listen to, rate, and, if they chose, download songs by bands they had never heard of. Some participants saw only the names of the songs and the bands. Other people also saw how many times the songs had been downloaded by those in the same world. When users could see the number of downloads, the most popular songs were much more popular (and the least popular songs were less popular) than when people judged the quality of songs independently. But the particular songs that became hits were different in the different worlds.

When it comes to media, what is the relationship between quality, popularity and social influence?

The intrinsic quality of a song helps to explain success, researchers found. Good songs were downloaded more frequently in all the online worlds. But overall, social influence played as large a role as quality in determining the

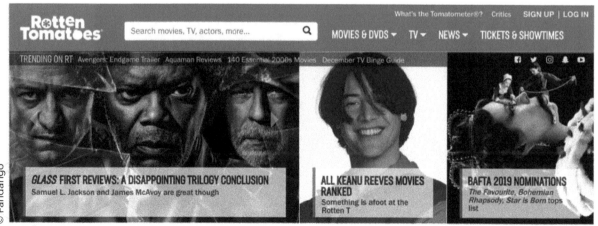

market share of successful songs. The overall popularity of a song depended on the decisions of a few individuals whose opinions "were subsequently amplified and eventually locked in by the cumulative-advantage process" (Watts, 2007: 1).

Although we like to believe that more popular works are somehow "better" in quality, the evidence suggests that what people like depends on what they think other people like. Therefore, what becomes popular at any point in time depends on consumers' perceptions of the people already using it.

Reviews and Ratings

Reviewers play an important role in the economics of media. Their writing and comments help draw public attention to products available in the media marketplace. As books became more widely available in the 19th century, book reviewers were often freelance writers like Edgar Allan Poe, whose anonymous reviews could be thrilling to read. Poe wrote scathing and entertaining reviews of other writers, which also served to call attention to his own creative work.

Do you pay attention to reviews and ratings? Why or why not?

In the early 20th century, under the influence of reviewers like H. R. Mencken, reviews emphasized the writer's own ideas as much as they offered guidance and interpretation for the potential reader (Fay, 2012). Academics first got involved in writing about the film viewing experience in 1907 when Hugo Munsterberg, the first professor to formally study film, shocked his peers by visiting the nickelodeon theaters in Boston, which generally attracted only working-class immigrants. In the 1920s, journalists merely reported on the behind-the-scenes world of Hollywood stars and studios. Modern film criticism as we understand it today began in the 1940s, when reviewers like James Agee began writing film criticism for *Time* magazine.

Some say that good media reviews are on the decline while others argue this is a golden age for reviewers, when more opportunities are available for people who want to review work to get their voices heard. A. O. Scott, a film critic for *The New York Times*, describes reviewing in a way that seems quite aligned with the practices of media literacy. He notes that today,

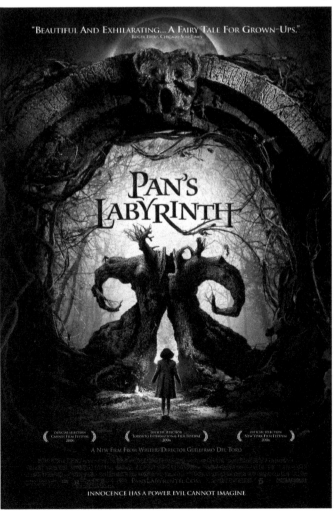

pan's labyrinth

"everyone is a critic, which means that each of us is capable of thinking against our own prejudices, balancing skepticism with open-mindedness, and sharpening our dulled and glutted senses and battling the intellectual inertia that surrounds us" (Scott, 2016: 12).

Many film, book, and media reviews use the power of comparison-contrast as reviewers think about other media in relation to the specific piece they are reviewing. They might compare a current film to previous films made by the same director. Or they may compare acting performances to prior roles or characters an actor has played. This makes sense. If you hated the 2017 romantic dark fantasy film *The Shape of Water* by Guillermo del Toro, it might be because you were unfamiliar with his distinctive body of work. If you had seen *Pan's Labyrinth* (2006), you might have noted interesting similarities between the two works, despite their differences in time period and theme.

Film critic Owen Gleiberman has been writing about movies since he was an undergraduate at the University of Michigan. Gleiberman admits that he has a vested interest in thinking that film criticism matters. He also acknowledges the *situational ethics* of film criticism, given that his work is influenced by pressures from the film industry. For example, he has had the opportunity to hang out with directors and actors, and studios have even applied pressure to place an interview with a hot actor as a way to mitigate a tepid review.

What pressures do film critics face

Owen Gleiberman @OwenGleiberman · Mar 31

#TheMatrix opened 20 years ago today. I look back in @Variety at how it was the first sci-fi movie in which the artificial intelligence lives in us.

'The Matrix' 20 Years Later: The Artificial Intelligence Lives in Us (Col...
Owen Gleiberman on how "The Matrix," 20 years later, stands as the first sci-fi movie in which the artificial intelligence lives in us.
variety.com

11   74   256

© Twitter, Inc

Even the best movie critics can feel social pressure that affects their work. In describing "the sting of the pressure to conform," Gleiberman tells a story about attending the premiere of *The Circle*, a 2017 drama about the dangers of a social media company like Facebook. He loved the film and posted an enthusiastic review, but when he looked at Rotten Tomatoes, most reviewers hated it. That is when he realized that overreliance on social ratings may contribute to conformity. The lack of diversity of opinion about movies is, as Gleiberman puts it, "a violation, rather than a fulfillment, of what film criticism should be" (2017: 1).

As Gleiberman's story reveals, sites that aggregate film reviews from both professional and amateur critics are changing the nature of the film reviewing business. For example, Rotten Tomatoes divides reviews into thumbs-up ("fresh") or thumbs-down ("rotten") ratings by crunching film reviews into a simple metric. This aggregated rating has a lot of power to shape people's decisions about which movies to view. Gleiberman notes that "a score, a rating, a number lends it a unique weight. In an age of marketing surveys and corporate quantification, 'The critics liked it' doesn't seem to be as powerful a statement as 'It got a 94% Fresh rating'" (Gleiberman, 2017: 1).

Do human-created movie, music, and video game reviews have a future? Truthfully, the future of reviews and reviewers is uncertain. The algorithms of Rotten Tomatoes may encourage critics to agree with one another so that "their voices can all add up to a single powerful voice that's greater than the sum of its parts" (Gleiberman, 2017: 1). This may help great movies get noticed and bad movies get panned, but as critics spend more time looking at the work of other critics online, their reviews become more similar because critics realize that they have stronger public influence only when they agree with each other.

Spreadability

When a work has value, people are inspired and want to share it with their peers. In the book *Convergence Culture* (2006), Jenkins shows how storytelling has shifted greatly in an age of user-generated content. For example, he documents the ways that the *Star Wars* universe has developed through fan participation in the franchise. Using available *Star Wars* media as their raw material, fans have made parodies, spoofs, and other films that demonstrate their appreciation for the characters and stories. He analyzes the fans of the *Harry Potter* series who invent new stories for the inhabitants of Hogwarts, using writing communities online to share and comment on work.

How do people decide which types of media to share with the people in their social network?

William Murphy

Intellectual Grandparent:
Pierre Bourdieu

Ulf Andersen/Hulton Archive/Gettty Images

He understood that taste is a form of social power. Pierre Bourdieu (1930–2002) was a 20th-century French intellectual who served as the chair of the sociology department at the College de France and authored seminal works examining the economy, social class privilege, literature, and art.

Bourdieu rejected the traditional view of aesthetic judgment developed by Enlightenment scholars like Emmanuel Kant, who claimed that aesthetic judgment should focus only on the form and structure of an object and not its content. In his book *Distinction: A Social Critique of the Judgment of Taste*, he developed ideas to understand how the lens of social class shapes people's preferences for music, fashion, art, and entertainment. Bourdieu's ideas include:

Language makes the world. Bourdieu believed that people use language in a self-interested way, as a form of social power to express their material interests. He used the term *habitus* to describe the way individual human action is situated and embedded in a historical and cultural context. Culture thus structures human action, so that individuals develop particular dispositions and behaviors through the way language is used to define their realities (Webb, Schiarato & Danaher, 2002).

People may possess different symbolic forms of wealth. Economic wealth is the most traditional form of capital, but people may also possess symbolic wealth in the form of *cultural capital*, which may include (1) knowledge gained through experience, (2) possessions and things people use and own, and (3) educational background. Parents who give their children music and dance lessons, travel

These activities are part of *participatory culture*, a term that can be defined as one with relatively low barriers to artistic expression and civic engagement; strong support for creating and sharing one's creations with others; informal mentorship whereby what is known by the most experienced is passed along to novices; where members believe that their contributions matter; and where members feel some degree of social connection with one another (Jenkins et al., 2009). Thus, fans may shape the values of participatory culture as the most active and responsive audience members.

How do people create media that people will want to share with others? Henry Jenkins, Sam Ford, and Joshua Green (2013) note that (a) media must be available when and where audiences want them; (b) they must be portable; (c) they should be easily reusable in a variety of ways; (d) they should be relevant to multiple audiences; and (e) they should form part

excursions, and summer camps increase their cultural capital through developing their background knowledge. Even experiences like going to concerts and plays or eating in restaurants increase a person's exposure to new things and help that individual gain knowledge about how others live. Such cultural capital makes it easier to interact with people from different cultural backgrounds.

Bourdieu also recognized "who you know" is a form of *social capital* that has value and that can be used as a form of symbolic wealth. When you enroll in Girl Scouts or Boy Scouts, for example, you begin to learn about the value of knowing other children. Fitting in and standing out in a group are both a form of symbolic wealth. Knowing people in your field and in your community is great for your LinkedIn identity, but it actually helps you advance in your career too. People with more social capital have networks of social relationships across a wider range of people, including those further up and lower down in the social hierarchy.

Taste preferences change over time as people jockey for social power. Bourdieu saw the constant changes in all fields of culture. He interpreted the changes as struggles between producers of culture over symbolic power. All creative people are drawn into the "dialectic of cultural distinction," which is not merely the search for fame and attention (Bourdieu, 1993: 117). People need to exploit their own identities. By being innovative and new, authors and artists can achieve dominant positions within any given field. Status is gained by offering something different. Through innovative expression that exploits cultural and social capital, a few can become wealthy. However, such efforts are fleeting as a result of the continual changes that occur in the marketplace due to the extreme competition for symbolic power.

If Pierre Bourdieu has influenced your thinking about media, you can share a comment on the Grandparents of Media Literacy website at www.grandparentsofmedialiteracy.com.

of a steady stream of material. Content producers must be responsive to audience needs and motivations as well as use digital platforms that are rising in popularity.

When many people are motivated to all share the same media content at the same time, it can be called *viral media*. Some people talk about virality as a type of superpower with the potential to influence elections, start social movements, and revolutionize industries. But researchers have found that the sharing of viral media, by itself, does not lead to real social or political change. For example, *Kony 2012*, a 30-minute film about Ugandan militia leader Joseph Kony, has been viewed on YouTube more than 100 million times, but it did not achieve its ultimate goal: as of 2020, Kony and his militia, the Lord's Resistance Army, remain at large. One of the reasons why the film did not accomplish its goals is that a backlash occurred when critics identified inaccuracies and biases in the production.

Although spreading viral media may not change the world, it does create considerable economic value. Instead of the quest for truth, online news is now often driven by the quest for page views, leading to a merging of commercial and editorial interests that is detrimental to democratic values (Couldry & Turow, 2014).

Today, people get their news from shared content, in an environment where many online media producers do not distinguish between quality and virality. According to one expert who calls himself the Virologist, "The ultimate barometer of quality is: if it gets shared, it's quality" (Marantz, 2015).

Although journalists were first jealous and then enamored of how fast digital media can spread, reaching millions of people within a few days, there are many critics of viral media. People are frustrated with *clickbait*, the digital content whose main purpose is to attract attention and encourage visitors to click on a link to a particular Web page. For example, by cultivating curiosity through appealing headlines, Buzzfeed lists attract interest with topics like "30 Signs You're Almost 30" or "27 Shocking and Unexpected Facts You Learn in Your 20s." These kinds of articles are not truly informative, entertaining, or persuasive. They exist only to be shared.

What factors lead people to share online content? People are more likely to share an article than actually read it. A simple comparison of all stories shared to all the clicks attached to those reveals that far more links are shared than are clicked on. People form an opinion based on a summary without making the effort to go deeper. Facebook has identified some *baiting* techniques people have been using to increase the shareability of content:

- *Vote-baiting* occurs when a post asks people to vote using a Facebook reaction icon. For example, a post may ask, "Choose the angry icon if you like the cute kitten." This is manipulation of the "like" function on Facebook;

- *Share-baiting* is when a user sees a post that says, "Share with friends to win a chance at a Chevy convertible." You are offered a reward for sharing;

- *Tag-baiting* means a post is designed to grab attention through the use of people's names. You are flattered by the use of your name, and this inspires you to share;

- *Comment-baiting* happens when people are encouraged to leave a comment and made to feel guilty if they do not. They are provoked emotionally into commenting.

Facebook now reduces the visibility of such posts. Although posts may evoke an emotional reaction from readers, they should not be designed to manipulate emotions for the sole purpose of increasing engagement (Facebook, 2017). Digital citizenship and media literacy can increase consumers' ability to spot and resist various unethical forms of user engagement.

Today, online content is carefully tested to measure its appeal to viewers using headline testing, a now-standard practice in online marketing. When a post is created, it initially appears under as many as two dozen different headlines, distributed at random. As users are exposed to the different headlines, the most popular one is easily revealed.

A/B testing is a type of statistical marketing test. Essentially, a random sample of website users sees one version of a website and other users see a different version. If the goal is to have users click a link (to read a story, view a video, or buy a product, for example), marketers can measure which headline attracted more attention and led to the desired results. Statistical tests tell whether the differences are statistically significant, or not likely to be due to random chance (Marantz, 2015).

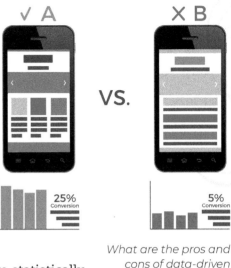

What are the pros and cons of data-driven headlines?

For example, which of these headlines are you most likely to click on?

- "You Won't Believe What This Guy Did with an Abandoned Factory"
- "At First It Looks Like an Old Empty Factory. But Go Inside and ... WHOA"

Suspense is effective in activating curiosity. Among those who specialize in digital content, the headline that generates the most clicks is, by definition, the most effective. You will want to reflect carefully and consider the implications of the claim that quality and popularity are identical.

Quality as a Form of Influence

Other metrics are available for evaluating the quality of a media work besides popularity. The quality of a work of media can be evaluated by considering how it influences the people who read, view, play, or use it. We might identify a high-quality work as one that would have a strong influence while a mediocre work would have little or no influence. It is difficult to measure *media influence*, but researchers have shown that some forms of media can affect our views of the world, of other people, and even of ourselves.

Movies can influence how people see the U.S. government. For example, researchers asked students to view two 2012 dramas, *Argo* and *Zero Dark Thirty*. Both these dramas address political themes through recounting true stories of the heroic behavior of the intelligence community. Both the CIA and the U.S. military have long maintained relationships with Hollywood producers and directors, providing them with special access to personnel in exchange for favorable treatment of their institutions (Schou, 2016). Take for example *Argo*, directed by Ben Affleck. It is the true story of how six people were rescued from the American embassy in Iran in 1979 after Iranian revolutionaries invaded it and took several Americans hostage. Or consider *Zero Dark Thirty*, a 2012 film directed by Kathryn Bigelow and starring Jessica Chastain. It tells the story of the Navy SEALS who assassinated Osama bin Laden.

In the research study, college students' attitudes about government changed dramatically after watching these two entertaining movies about the American intelligence community. After viewing, 20–25% of the participants developed a more favorable opinion on a variety of questions about

5 critical questions about the problem with

After viewing the YouTube video at www.media-literacyaction.com, use five critical questions of media literacy to analyze this review.

1. **Who is the author and what is the purpose?** Chris Stuckmann has been reviewing movies on YouTube since 2010, and he is among the most popular of film reviewers there, with more than 1.2 million subscribers. This video looks at a series of horror films from 2014 to consider larger patterns and themes in the genre. His purpose includes the goals of informing people about the features of the horror genre, entertaining by offering insight and a playful sense of humor, and persuading people to accept his position on the status of horror films in society. He believes that audience expectations limit the potential of the genre.

2. **What techniques are used to attract and hold attention?** The production technique

The Problem with Horror Movies Today
3,345,975 views • Nov 6, 2014

117K   3K   SHARE   SAVE   ...

the government. Their trust in government increased as did their general optimism about the direction of the country (Pautz, 2015). Why did this occur? "Younger people, particularly teens, are much more likely to be impacted than older adults because they are still developing and shaping their worldviews," the researcher explains. "Since they are still being socialized politically, they are more likely to absorb all sorts of influences, including influences from film" (Guida, 2015: 1). To understand the social power of shared media experiences, it is important to realize how media messages can change or reinforce values and ideologies.

horror movies

used in this video combines a strong voice-over narration of an essay with still and moving image sequences from a wide variety of horror films. Within the first minute of this video we see stills from many classic movies, including *The Shining*, *The Exorcist*, and more. To hold attention, Stuckmann also compares horror films to sex, arguing that when suspense and tension are not built well throughout the narrative, it ruins the dramatic arc of the film. To illustrate this point, he also manipulates the sound of the classic 1978 horror film *Halloween* to show how today's filmmakers would produce it. He reveals how cheap sound effects are used to scare viewers. He explains the economics of horror films, noting how most are produced on a small budget, like *The Blair Witch Project*, which cost $60,000 and earned $248 million in box office sales.

3. **What lifestyles, points of view, and values are presented?** Stuckmann criticizes users who seem to care about horror only for the thrills, commenting on a review posted to IMDB.com. He reads the comment aloud in a stilted, comical way to point out how inane it is. Stuckmann hates how audiences have come to expect cheap jump scares,

where a loud noise causes a startle effect in viewers. He is a film fan who loves psychological thrillers, and his point of view on their superiority over other types of horror films is clearly evident.

4. **How might different people interpret this message?** When Stuckmann argues that movie marketing is reshaping viewers' expectations, he uses the case of the 2004 film *The Village*, directed by M. Night Shyamalan, which he claims was marketed as a horror film but was really a historical romance. Viewers who have seen this film may agree or disagree with this analysis.

5. **What is omitted?** Stuckmann blames audiences for the decline in horror film genre, claiming that they have forgotten what real horror is all about and noting that inferior films like *Ouija* and *Annabelle* make more money than better-quality films. But he never mentions that the target audience for most horror films is people aged 15–25. The most common reason for this is that young adults and teenagers enjoy thrills. Sensation-seeking adolescents are choosing horror films not for the quality, but simply for the chance to experience the adrenaline rush of being scared.

What the future may hold: Algorithmic Content Discovery

While people once made decisions about which TV shows or movies to watch by reading movie reviews, today many people tend to use recommendation engines. You might use websites like Rotten Tomatoes or MetaCritic to decide what movies to watch. There you can find a range of both professional and amateur reviews and get a sense of what audiences liked or disliked about a film. Just like Spotify offers music discovery suggestions through the use of algorithms, Netflix recommends movies based on data that users share. These are two of many companies following Google's lead in the practice of *algorithmic content discovery*. Google pioneered the practice in 2009 when it rolled out a new version of its search engine that used a variety of data signals from individual users to determine which content to display. Such practices are enormously popular and profitable because machine learning makes use of huge volumes of user data that enable companies to anticipate, predict, and even control consumer behavior (Zuboff, 2019).

You will not be surprised to learn that Netflix manipulates its recommendations in a very intentional manner to increase the amount of time viewers watch its content. People who use Netflix watch 600 hours per year or nearly one movie per day, according to company data from 2015. When Netflix began releasing all episodes of series at once, it encouraged the phenomenon of binge-watching, when people view an entire series of television programming over a short period of time. For most people, watching at home on a high-definition television is a more appealing form of entertainment than going to a movie theater. After all, if you start watching a film and do not like it, you can just switch to another choice.

Netflix even structures users' choices in very subtle ways that are hard for users to detect. Because the thumbnail images on Netflix influence people when they are deciding which movies to watch, Netflix customizes these thumbnail images to the identity of specific users, depending on who is watching. For example, if you have watched romance films like *Seredipity*, you are highly likely to be shown an image of a scene from *Good Will Hunting* that emphasizes the romance scenes. If you have watched quirky TV series like *Arrested Development* or *Zoolander*, you will be shown a still from *Good Will Hunting* that features Robin Williams (Nelson, 2016). Algorithmic personalization like this goes unnoticed by consumers because we are largely unaware of how others experience the many ways that Netflix structures choice.

Amazon also relies on algorithmic personalization to shape consumers' choices. Amazon owns IMDb, the largest movie website in the world with more than 250 million unique monthly visitors. The IMDb database offers information on more than 3 million movies, TV shows, and entertainment programs. There, reviews from both professional critics and amateur reviewers help people decide what to watch and where to watch it.

On its e-commerce platforms, Amazon also relies on algorithms that include users' purchase history, items in their shopping cart, items they have rated and liked, and what other customers have viewed and purchased. Such algorithms are carefully fine-tuned to be effective. Algorithmic decision-making tools are so effective that 35% of all online sales are estimated to be generated by the Amazon recommendation engine. Using artificial intelligence, Amazon and other companies are developing machine learning technology to make recommendation engines even more efficient. For some critics, this level of control over human choices is potentially dangerous because of the ways in which computational certainty could "replace politics and democracy, extinguishing the felt reality and social function of an individualized existence" (Zuboff, 2019: 21).

TIME TO REFLECT

Consider the ideas presented in this chapter in relation to your own experience as a media consumer. Reflect on these questions:

- How important are reviews and reviewers to you in shaping your media choices?
- How do people judge or evaluate each other based on the quality of media choices they make? What are potential consequences of this behavior?
- How do social recommendations from peers influence what you see, watch, listen to, play, and read?
- How do algorithms structure your choices of media content?

You can share your ideas on the Flipgrid Inquiry by contributing a brief oral presentation. You can also view and respond to comments of other people who have offered thoughtful reflections on these topics. Visit www.medialiteracyaction.com to learn more.

CREATE TO LEARN

Review a YouTuber

Select a YouTube video or a YouTuber who you think offers something of value to audiences and compose a brief review, either in writing or as a spoken word performance. In the opening of your review, provide basic information about the YouTuber whose work you are examining. Then describe and evaluate the video you are focusing on, remembering that your audience has not yet seen it. Offer some description to help the audience visualize the video without giving too much away that could "spoil" the viewing experience for them. You should consider the quality of both the content and the format of the video. Give your audience an explicit rationale for why you think this YouTube video has value. You can post and share your work using the #MLAction hashtag to reach a global community of media literacy learners.

catfish

THE TV SHOW

Decisions to trust or mistrust rely on judgments about authority, expertise, and authenticity

How Do People Decide Who and What to Trust?

Learning Outcomes

1. Examine the power of trust in social relationships, personal identity, and every aspect of human well-being

2. Understand how distrust of media and growing levels of political polarization have a corrosive impact on social institutions and the democratic process

3. Evaluate the scope and limits of freedom of expression in relation to authors who disguise their purpose and goals

4. Reflect on authority, expertise and authenticity as dimensions of social trust that marketers may exploit

5. Consider the consequences of shifting patterns of social trust and mistrust for individuals and society

In 2010, Nev Schulman was a New York City–based college dropout who made a documentary about his experience in unexpectedly discovering that the beautiful dancer he fell in love with online was a middle-aged, married woman from Michigan. The resultant narrative documentary entitled *Catfish* that follows the dramatic and suspenseful search for the reality behind the online representation resonated with audiences everywhere. As film critic David Edelstein (2010: 1) put it, the documentary "dramatizes the paradox of the Internet, which has made us all so much closer to one another yet created so many more ways for us to misrepresent ourselves."

As people interact more through a screen, a lot of trust is at stake—and required—for living life online. Over the past 20 years, online dating and relationships have become more important for many. Among 18–29-year-olds, nearly 50% have used online dating apps. One in ten American adults say they have been in a committed relationship or married someone they met through a dating site or app (Vogels, 2020).

Nev Schulman has now built a career from examining people's online relationships in his long-running MTV show, *Catfish*, which skyrocketed to popularity in 2013. What makes the show fun to watch is that viewers first learn about different methods Nev uses to verify online identities. Viewers also find themselves evaluating the victims and the perpetrators. People may sympathize with the victims who are duped by *catfishing* or the individuals whose online images are used to falsely represent someone else's identity. They may even identify with the catfishers themselves.

Catfishers lie and mislead people in their search for intimate and personal relationships through text, chat rooms, email, instant messaging, and other apps. Some of the people featured on the show are downright malicious and seem to enjoy inflicting psychological distress on their victims. But the show also introduces viewers to complicated people who are catfishing in order to find true love. These people have created an *avatar* of sorts, an alternate or idealized version of themselves. An avatar is a representation of the self that helps people become comfortable interacting with strangers online. You may have created an avatar so as to interact with people in the virtual world of a video game. In *Catfish*, viewers see the range of different reasons that led people to mask their identities online, including embarrassment about their appearance or their weight, discomfort with sexual identity, or difficulties in face-to-face communication.

Although most people do not intentionally fake their online identities as catfishers, many people do seek to project an identity that is much better than how they really feel about themselves. As *The New York Times* critic Jenna Wortham points out, in a world "where people are so pressed into being 'themselves' all the time online and projecting a personal brand that they can compare and contrast to their peers, they need a reprieve, because for whatever reason they don't feel good enough" (Caramanica, 2013).

This chapter addresses the questions "What should I believe? Who can I trust? Why should others trust me?" These are epistemological questions about how the nature of knowledge is being reshaped as a result of changes in media and technology. This chapter explores how authority expertise, and authenticity serve to justify people's reasoning processes in choosing who and what to trust. We will also look at bloggers and influencers who enter into people's everyday social interactions in ways that may affect trust.

To reflect upon and analyze these issues, this chapter considers these questions:

- How does trust develop?
- Why do comedians sometimes seem more trustworthy than experts and political leaders?
- Why do some people mistrust climate science experts?

Why Trust Matters

Trust is a rare commodity, one that is vital to human functioning. Consider your personal response to this question:

> **"** Generally speaking, would you say that most people can be trusted or that you can't be too careful in dealing with people? **"**

Back in 1972, nearly 50% of American adults who participated in a national survey thought that most people can be trusted. But trust has been on the decline since 1984, according to researchers who have documented the downward trend, noting that in 2012, only 32% agreed that people can be trusted. Figure 9.1 shows changes tht hve occurred between 1972 and 2012 in how people respond to the statement, "Most people can be trusted." Most people who agree with this statement rate themselves as "very happy" or "pretty happy." The figure shows that, in 2012, only 20% of people who identify as "not happy" believe that most people can be trusted.

Studies also show that, compared to older people, young people are the least trusting, with only 19% of Millennials (people born between 1981 and 1996) saying they feel other people can be trusted (Morgan, 2014).

As it turns out, happiness and trust go hand in hand. Researchers have shown that declining trust among Americans over time is correlated with a decrease in their happiness. But because trust is also linked to social power, people with higher incomes and levels of education, and those who identify as white, have higher levels of trust compared with low-income people and minorities without a college education (Morgan, 2014).

Mistrust is a learned behavior. Certain polarizing habits of mind and heart contribute to mistrustfulness. People who engage in either/or thinking (or who view uncertainty and ambiguity as a weakness) can be more mistrustful. Mistrust can be exacerbated by a natural and common form of

Figure 9.1
Happiness and Trust are Related

SOURCE: Morgan, 2014

What is the relationship between social trust and happiness ❓

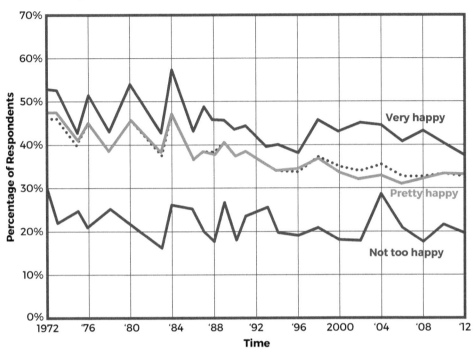

cognitive bias called *confirmation bias*, which refers to the tendency to search for and believe evidence that supports existing beliefs and attitudes. You may have noticed how you tend to trust sources that confirm your existing beliefs and you try to knock down or oppose views that do not fit your world view (Blankenhorn, 2018).

Confirmation bias occurs because humans seek cognitive consistency. With so much information and stimuli around us, the mind works to find shortcuts for information processing. Being aware of confirmation bias good, but confirmation bias is highly functional and it cannot be eliminated or cured (Kahneman, 2011). In general, to avoid problems caused by confirmation bias, it is important to hold your beliefs and opinions lightly, being willing to change your mind in response to new evidence. People can also avoid confirmation bias by understanding that disagreements are productive for learning: people learn much more from exposure to multiple points of view.

Why are respectful disagreements useful in building trust ❓

Deagreez/iStock

Respect for diverse experiences and perspectives is essential for learning. When we respect, we accept differences of opinion because we understand that we are all limited by bias. We come to value *multiperspectival thinking* and gain curiosity about differences of interpretation when we realize we do not have to fear people or ideas that are different from ours.

When people can respect their fellow citizens and leaders, they are more likely to participate in voting and elections and less likely to engage in corruption. Respect even makes us more resilient in the face of disasters—it improves human experience and is a key factor in our survival in the face of adversity.

Consider this quote commonly attributed to American writer Ernest Hemingway: "The best way to find out if you can trust somebody is to trust them." Developing respectful and trusting relationships takes a significant amount of courage and self-awareness. What behaviors and habits of mind build respect and trust? In the book *Rising Strong* (2015), Brene Brown notes seven qualities that are part of developing trustworthy relationships:

B = Boundaries. In trustworthy relationships, people communicate what is okay and not okay in their relationship. They say "no" when they need to and know their boundaries will be respected.

R = Reliability. In trustworthy relationships, people consistently follow through on their promises. They do not make promises they cannot keep.

A = Accountability. When people make mistakes, they apologize and make amends. They admit their failings and do not blame others.

V = Vault. In trustworthy relationships, people can be confident in sharing personal and private information and rely on others to hold that information in a symbolic lockbox, a vault.

I = Integrity. People do what is right even when it takes courage and involves personal or professional risk.

N = Nonjudgment. People ask for help when they need it. When people share their tribulations, they are offered empathy, not judgment or evaluation.

G = Generosity. In trustworthy relationships, people assume positive intent. They assume that people are doing their best and they demonstrate a spirit of trust.

If you want to be trusted, these essential qualities will be useful to you, both in your personal relationships and as a professional communicator.

Truth Decay

Whether we like it or not, lying is a natural part of human life—everyone does it, to a greater or lesser extent. It is an evolutionary adaptation to life in groups. As researchers have noted, "The ability to manipulate others without using physical force likely conferred an advantage in the competition for resources and mates, akin to the evolution of deceptive strategies in the animal kingdom, such as camouflage" (Bhattacharjee, 2015). At the same time, from an evolutionary standpoint, *social trust* also developed, making it possible for people to live in groups, engage in division of labor, and seek out life, liberty, and the pursuit of happiness. Social trust thus gave giving groups of humans an advantage. Lying is a form of social power that takes advantage of people's natural willingness to trust.

Sissela Bok (2015), a philosopher and ethicist, notes that voters and politicians alike need to distinguish between:

- a lie and an honest mistake;
- a lie that has been proved and lies that are only suspected;
- deception through half-truths and silence;
- foolish promises (or predictions) and knowingly false ones;
- slipping into a lie, undertaking a policy of deceit, and choosing to be someone who deals with others through deceit.

The great American writer Samuel Clemens, known as Mark Twain, is credited with the famous remark that "A lie can fly halfway around the world while truth is putting on its shoes." Journalists have long struggled with how to handle authoritative untruths, the lies and false information provided by politicians, government officials, experts, and others with positions of authority and influence in society. Unfortunately, journalists and other media communicators, under pressure to report information in a timely way, find themselves reporting content they know to be false simply because an important person has stated it. This is a dangerous phenomenon that can erode public trust in both journalism and the political process. Substantial effort is needed to correct a lie uttered by a person with political, moral, or academic authority.

After the election of President Donald Trump, the RAND Corporation, a Calfornia-based think tank, began to explore the diminishing role of facts and data in American public life. RAND researchers observed how aspects of contemporary life are leading to the erosion of civil discourse, political paralysis, alienation and disengagement of individuals from political and civic institutions, and uncertainty over national policy (Kavanagh & Rich, 2018). Their concerns, as explained in a report entitled "Truth Decay: An Initial Exploration of the Diminishing Role of Facts and Analysis in American Public Life," include these ideas:

- People disagree more about facts and interpretations of facts and data;
- The distinction between opinion and fact is eroding;
- Sources of information that used to be trusted are no longer automatically considered trustworthy;
- People are relying on opinion and personal experience instead of facts.

Why is this occurring now? Contrary to what some people assume, it is not a recent phenomenon. The changes resulting from increased competition in the news and information system have played a role in the public's declining trust in news media for many years. Back in the 1980s, when cable television rose to prominence and challenged the dominance of the broadcast

Figure 9.2
The American Public Has Become More Distrustful of News Organizations over Time

Evaluations of the News Media 2011

*Responses that equal or surpass record highs in **bold***

Positive	OR	Negative
Pretty independent 15	80	Often influenced by powerful people and organizations
Deal fairly with all sides 16	**77**	**Tend to favor one side**
Willing to admit their mistakes 18	**72**	**Try to cover up their mistakes**
Gets the facts straight 25	**66**	**Stories are often inaccurate**
Careful to not be politically biased 25	**63**	**Politically biased in their reporting**
Care about the people they report on 26	63	Don't care about the people they report on
Moral 38	**42**	**Immoral**
Protect democracy 42	**42**	**Hurt democracy**
Stand up for America 41	39	Too critical of America
Highly professional 57	**32**	**Not professional**
Care about how good a job they do 62	**31**	**Don't care about how good a job they do**
Keep leaders from doing things that shouldn't be done 58	25	Keep leaders from doing their job

PEW RESEARCH CENTER July 20–24, 2011.

television networks, a decline in trust of the news media was beginning. Figure 9.1 shows that by 2011, the American public's judgment about the news media included increasing negative evelation, with 80% agreeing that news coverage is often influenced by powerful people and organizations.

Free Speech and the Paradox of Tolerance

People need to make decisions about who and what they can trust because, in a democracy, individuals have widely respected rights to *freedom of expression*. All that freedom means a lot of wrongheaded, bad, and even dangerous ideas and information spread throughout the cultural environment. Everywhere you look, it seems, you can find racism, sexism, homophobia, Islamophobia, neo-Nazism, and many more forms of expression that cause harm to others. When violent conflicts occurred in Charlottesville, Virginia, in 2017, people wondered about the limits of tolerance. Are there any ideas that should not be tolerated in a free society?

Philosophers have long noted that intolerance can wipe out tolerance. Writing immediately at the end of World War II, Karl Popper, a philosopher of science, showed how unlimited tolerance would inevitably lead to the disappearance of tolerance. He called it *the paradox of tolerance*, noting that "if we are not prepared to defend a tolerant society against the onslaught of the intolerant, then the tolerant will be destroyed, and tolerance with them" (Popper, 1945: 581). Of course, intolerance can be countered with reason or simply ignored. But Popper believed that force may be needed when the intolerant "forbid their followers to listen to rational argument, because it is deceptive, and teach them to answer arguments by the use of their fists or pistols" (p. 581). Thus, to preserve tolerance, we cannot tolerate the intolerant.

Working with a partner, make a list of 10 specific individuals, businesses, and political, social, and cultural institutions that you are both familiar with. Think about all the people, groups, and institutions that have been a part of your entire life. Then, working individually, each person should rank the list, putting the most trustworthy at the top and the least trustworthy at the bottom. Discuss the similarities and differences that exist between you and your partner to articulate why you find some individuals, businesses, and institutions more or less trustworthy.

Other scholars have described tolerance as a ladder, noting that at the lowest level, we can more easily tolerate intolerant private speech that does not interfere with the choices of others. A quote attributed to the French philosopher Voltaire captures this idea: "I disapprove of what you say, but defend to the death your right to say it."

With the rise of haters and trolls online, it can be a struggle to know how to respond to hateful speech. The general mantra is "Don't feed the trolls," which means people should not respond or give attention to those whose behavior is hateful and intolerant. By ignoring intolerance, it can be marginalized. But should we also defend the rights of trolls and haters to be intolerant? Speech and expression can have powerful negative impacts on individuals and society. The paradox of tolerance acknowledges that "to protect free speech, we will have to oppose some kinds of speech" (Godfrey-Smith & Kerr, 2017: 1). According to the paradox of tolerance, speech that prevents others making their own choices or speech that incites violence should not be tolerated. To preserve freedom of expression, it must be protected.

Mistrust and Polarization

Many people distrust news media because they have the perception that news coverage serves the needs of powerful political and corporate interests. And these beliefs are not confined to the United States. In nations around the world, polarization has emerged over topics like LGBTQ civil rights, immigration and migration, crime and law enforcement, the election process, the environment and climate change, and more. *Political polarization* varies from country to country and is influenced by dynamic situational factors. For example, after the election of Donald Trump, general trust in news media became even more polarized, with 49% of Americans who identify with the left as generally trusting the news media and only 17% of those on the right trusting them (Newman, 2018).

Around the world, concern about what is real and fake on the Internet can be found among approximately half of the population. It is highest in countries like Brazil (85%), Spain (69%), and the United States (64%), where polarized political situations are combined with high social media use, and it is lower in countries like Germany and the Netherlands (Newman, 2018).

In some parts of the world, news media are still a highly trusted source of information. In democratic and relatively homogenous countries like Finland and Portugal, as much as two-thirds of the public agrees that "I think you can trust most news most of the time." However, in the United States, only one-third of the public agrees with this statement. In fact, these researchers found that trust in news media and journalism is lower in the United States than in almost all other countries (Newman, 2018).

In general, people trust news coverage they find from familiar brands more than they trust sources shared on social media and found through search engines. The rise of social media has not only increased the volume and speed of information flow but it has also increased the visibility of opinions, amplified by newspapers and TV companies in their hypercompetitive quest to maximize profits.

Intellectual Grandparent:
George Herbert Mead

The History Collection/Alamy Stock Photo

George Herbert Mead was an American sociologist who was part of what we now call the Chicago School, a group of scholars including John Dewey and Charles Cooley. They communication, education, human development, and democracy at the turn of the 20th century. They were pioneers in the academic study of communication and media. The Chicago School scholars "gave voice to the idea that media and communication have a central role to play in shaping individual and collective lives, and in cementing identities and communities." To understand society, we must first understand "how we communicate with each other and how the media shape our social bonds and social worlds" (Wahl-Jorgensen, 2012: 1).

In communication scholarship, Mead is considered the founder of the theory of *symbolic interactionism*, which positions communication as the sharing of meaning through language and symbols. This theory positions people as actively shaping the social world, in effect "creating their reality" through social interactions. Mead's ideas include:

People's sense of personal identity emerges from their social interactions. During childhood and throughout life, how people treat you gradually shapes how you see yourself. In his book *Mind, Self and Society* (1934), Mead describes how the individual mind and self arise out of the social process of interacting with others. Through first gestures and then language, humans gain a sense of self as they engage socially. Instead of approaching human experience in terms of individual psychology, Mead analyzes human identity and experience from the standpoint of "communication as essential to the social order" (Mead, 1934). By claiming that individual identity is socially constructed, he views the development of self-awareness as also driven by social processes. During adolescence, people come to care about the perceptions of others, including parents, teachers, and peers. Mead's colleague Charles Cooley called this identity process "the looking glass self" (Wahl-Jorgensen, 2012:

People mistrust what they do not understand. Researchers have found that people's basic knowledge of how news and journalism is constructed is very low. In one study, researchers measured "news literacy knowledge" using three multiple-choice questions: (1) Did people recognize that public broadcasting does not rely on ad funding? (2) Did people understand that corporations write press releases so as to influence journalists and shape public opinion? (3) Did people recognize that algorithms (not human curation) are how news content is delivered through Facebook and other social media? In a study of more than 90,000 individuals from 45 countries, only 10% answered all three questions correctly, thus demonstrating that few people around the world have sufficient knowledge about how news and journalism is constructed (Newman, 2018).

1). We learn about ourselves through our interpretation of how others react to us.

By understanding and manipulating symbols that circulate within a culture, individuals come to understand and empathize with others. In examining human development, Mead noticed that children are self-centered and cannot take the perspective of another. Gradually, through imitation and play, they take on the attitudes of the people around them, especially parents, caregivers, and siblings. Through play, children practice using symbols and communication and then experience situations that create a sense of belonging. Pretend play enables children to mentally assume the perspectives of another person. Over time, children acquire a deeper sense of being part of a group, and by adolescence, they become "capable of holding membership in different groups, both simultaneously and serially" (Cronk, 2015). Young adults gradually come to view themselves as members of a nation, a profession, or an occupational group and for each group they participate in, they develop a sense of identity in relation to the generalized others. This is how children acquire a sense of themselves as a member of a community.

Human relationships are fundamentally situational and multiperspectival. Mead believes that an individual's perspective is shaped in relation to a particular situation or environment, but he does not see different human perspectives as imperfect representations of some absolute reality. He does not believe that some people's interpretations are flawed, distorted, or inadequate. On the contrary, "these situations are the reality" that is the world (Cronk, 2015). Because the self is socially constructed, Mead sees social interaction as enabling the full potential of human freedom. Mead believes that there is "no absolute limit to the individual's capacity to encompass new others within the dynamic structure of the self" (Cronk, 2015). Fundamentally, human freedom is enabled through the choices we make in our social relationships and interactions with others.

If George Herbert Mead has influenced your thinking about media, you can share a comment on the Grandparents of Media Literacy website at www.grandparentsofmedialiteracy.com.

What Fact Checkers Do

Given the wide range of news and informational content available to people today, identifying the author and purpose of a particular message is an essential first step in determining whether it can be trusted. Mike Caulfield frames this as *reading laterally*, a process he uses to analyze an author's expertise and qualifications or the overall trustworthiness of an informational website. Just clicking the About page is unlikely to provide the information needed to make a discerning judgment, because these are generally written as a form of self-promotion. When initially evaluating a website, fact-checkers actually don't spend much time on the site itself. As Caulfield (2017) explains, "Instead, they get off the page and see what other authoritative sources have said about the site. They open up many tabs in their browser, piecing together different bits of information from across the web to get a better picture of the site they're investigating."

Good readers also look at pages linking to the site, not just pages coming from it (Caulfield, 2017). Once they understand how the website is understood from within a particular knowledge community, they focus on the content now that they are in a better position to trust the author and the facts and analysis presented to them. Obviously, *context* is essential to make sense of any particular work of nonfiction. Knowledge is constructed within communities of practice; since scholarship is a conversation, it is important to listen and read widely to see who is saying what.

You are more likely to trust an information resource if you recognize and understand the author's purpose for communicating. Sometimes, it is easy to infer the purpose of a media message by looking at clues in the text or the context. Sometimes, when you gain information about the author, you can better understand the purpose of his or her work. At other times, you cannot figure out who the author is and why particular content has been created. For example, *ghostwriters* are used in political and business communication to write speeches, articles, and books on behalf of a client. In these works, it may be hard to fully understand the author's purpose.

In making inferences about the author's purpose, we can consider how people create messages for at least six different reasons:

- to inform;
- to persuade;
- to entertain;
- to teach;
- to make money;
- for self-expression.

Making inferences about an author's purpose helps people to gain critical distance, to step back and evaluate and analyze media messages. A skillful reader can recognize clues in the text to establish which conventions a text is deploying. To find clues about the author's purpose, people can examine the content, format, and genre of the work, its target audience, and the context in which the message occurs. Identifying authorship and making inferences about its purpose is the most important initial step media-literate individuals take to determine whether content can be trusted.

Of course, at some level, *authorial intent* is fundamentally unknowable. To be clear: the reader's *impression* of the author's intent shapes interpretations, but the author's actual intent cannot fully be known (Rourke, 2014).

Sometimes, companies seek to actively prevent the public from recognizing authorship by intentionally disguising it. In public relations, a technique called *astroturfing* is sometimes used when an artificial support group is created that appears to be a group of grassroots activists. The term refers to the idea of "fake" grassroots. Such groups are actually sponsored, managed, and created by a company or business (Monbiot, 2011). Astroturfing is used to create the false impression that a particular action, belief, or policy has widespread public support.

On the Internet, it is easy to create and manage support groups that fight for one or another cause in great numbers. The term *sockpuppet* is used to refer to fake online identities, each supporting the puppeteer's views in an argument. Generally, a sockpuppet will support ideas purportedly representing majority opinion and aim to sideline other voices. Marketers may create a number of fake personas, each one claiming to be a different enthusiastic supporter of the sponsor's product, book, or ideology. In reality, they are all from one individual who is paid to send messages that distort the public's perception of what others think or feel. Companies even use special software that allows them to create multiple Internet-based identities that have a complete history with all necessary background details attached.

Understanding Authority

Authority is an important dimension of the formal systems of institutional power. Human survival has depended on our trust of others, including authorities, those officially sanctioned experts and leaders who guide public knowledge, beliefs, and attitudes. From a very early age, we are conditioned to obey institutional authority. In the home, we learn to obey parents and in the school, we learn to obey teachers. In the community, we learn to obey police officials. At work, we learn to obey employment supervisors.

Respect for authority is cultivated through a variety of different mechanisms including routines, expectations for behavior, and assessment. Authority can be expressed through symbols like job titles, the display of wealth or status, the use of weapons, and even physical size and strength. Political officials are authorities, of course. But so are celebrities like Oprah and media personalities like Kanye West, who have authority because of their visibility and wealth.

Expertise is another type of authority where, through specialized knowledge, some people can assert what is true in their respective occupations or areas of practice. We trust experts because society has become more complex. People with specialized knowledge enable us to bypass the impossible job of knowing everything ourselves. We all benefit from *collective intelligence* (Weinberger, 2012). As one scholar put it, "It is generally more rational to defer to the authority of the relevant expert than it is to think for oneself" (Pierson et al, 1994: 399). Trust in authority is thus reciprocal, because although we give up control to authorities, in exchange we expect to gain a sense of safety and security.

But what do we do when experts disagree? How can a layperson accurately and rationally distinguish between experts and frauds? During the coronavirus crisis in 2020, many people faced this challenge. Because you are not a medical professional, you lack the means for determining the truth or falsity of expert claims about health, so you must place your trust in experts. For example, when experts recommended that people not gather in face-to-face groups, they were offering information based on scientific evidence about the transmission of the virus. Most people cannot perform the scientific tests that could provide evidence determining whether social distancing is beneficial or harmful. You cannot easily evaluate the quality of the evidence provided by any particular expert's inquiry. Scientific studies are generally written by experts for other experts. For some of the studies that include microbiological concepts, the expert knowledge discovered through a Google search on the coronavirus may be incomprehensible to you. Even when you can understand this primary source material, you should not automatically feel confident that you can really understand it. You probably know the limits of your knowledge. To gain expertise on the science of the coronavirus, you would need regular social contact with experts in epidemiology and infectious diseases, which is a particular knowledge community that specializes in the study of epidemics (Collins & Evans, 2008). For these reasons, trusting experts is a vital part of being well informed.

But does asking critical questions about media lead people to be suspicious about everything? Through asking critical questions about what we know and how we know it, scholars have wondered, are media literacy

Why is trust in experts important? What are the limits of this trust **?**

Harley Schwadron/CartoonStock

educators creating a crisis of trust? (boyd, 2018). Some see skepticism of expertise and authority as dangerous or destabilizing for society, while others see such skepticism as a productive and positive virtue.

These are issues of *epistemology*, the study of the nature of knowledge. Perhaps skepticism is a way of relating to the world. Over the past 20 years, the trust once reserved for experts has diminished as experts are increasingly perceived as elites with vested interests and political agendas. For example, as income inequality has become more pronounced, social class divides have also intensified public awareness of who is treated as an expert. When wealthy white elites write about rural poverty, it is easy to recognize the limits of some traditional forms of expertise and authority (Yarrow, 2018).

Skepticism is itself a form of epistemic knowledge. In the dialogues between Socrates and Plato, the ancient Greeks remind us that the good life must be understood in terms of *epistemic autonomy*, the process of valuing and trusting one's own reasoning so that you do not let just any expert tell you about your own happiness (Quast & Seidel, 2018). Why is this so important? As it turns out, while many people value authority and expertise, they value authenticity even more.

Authenticity Rules

According to philosophers, authenticity connects experience, feelings, and knowledge, which can be objects of reflection and reasoning. Sociologists, psychologists, and philosophers have studied the term *authenticity* for more than 100 years (Bourdieu, 1987).

Building upon the work of George Herbert Mead, some 20th-century scholars see authenticity as performative and deeply connected to consumer culture. Sociologist Erving Goffman, for example, views everyday life as a series of performances. Little of human experience is really authentic, he says. People display a series of masks to others, constantly trying to set ourselves in the best light. Depending on who we are interacting with, we might have to juggle different performances. For example, to be identified as an authentic bro, you may play sports, listen to EDM, wear an inside-out T shirt, rest your sunglasses on the back of your neck, and misspell every other work in your text messages. Of course, you reference friends as "bruh," "bro," or "dawg" and say "aight" instead of "yes." While an individual acting and dressing this way may feel it is a genuine expression of authentic identity, this performance is constructed to manage other people's impressions (Taylor, 1991).

Other ideas about authenticity are more individualistic, rooted in the idea that we can stay true "to our inner selves rather than accepting the social position into which we are born" (Sanchez-Arce, 2007: 140). According to researchers, authenticity is a quality that can be cultivated, and it includes four interrelated processes: self-awareness, balanced information processing, relational transparency, and an internalized moral perspective. In this

Which media professionals do you find most trustworthy❓

view, authenticity is all about human possibility, creativity, expression, and freedom.

Being authentic does not mean you will never lie. But people who are authentic are less likely to tell self-centered lies, where an untruth is designed to make themselves look good. They may be likely to tell other-centered lies, where an untruth is designed to protect the feelings of someone else (Thacker, 2016).

In a sense, authenticity is a type of legitimacy rooted in the Aristotelian concept of *ethos*, the character of a speaker. It emphasizes the sincerity of self-expression. In an age of Instagram influencers, such sincerity has become a symbolic marker of status and distinction. An authentic individual expresses a set of values that convey the originality and uniqueness of the individual. In an important way, authenticity can be understood as a form of social power distinct from traditional forms of authority (Bourdieu, 1993).

Let us explore the case of Jon Stewart in order to understand the relationship between authenticity and trust. When Jon Stewart retired from *The Daily Show* in 2015, many people lost a thought leader whose perspectives on news and current events they valued. Jon Stewart is a comedian. Back in 2007, the number of people who named him as "an admired journalist" was high enough to make Jon Stewart tie with other professional news anchors Brian Williams and Tom Brokaw at NBC, Dan Rather at CBS, and Anderson Cooper at CNN. In examining news and public opinion, the Project for Excellence in Journalism concluded that, as more young people turn to alternative sources of news and information on the Internet, *The Daily Show* is "getting people to think critically about the public square" (Kakutani, 2008: 1).

Jon Stewart is never playing a role: he is always being himself. When the incongruity of the juxtaposition is particularly hypocritical or absurd, Stewart's facial expressions communicate volumes about his feelings. Stewart is equally skilled at skewering Democrats and Republicans. Viewers watching the show over time got a sense of Stewart's genuine reactions to the news, sensing his deep patriotism, his social justice values, and his authentic civic engagement. Viewers also got a sense of how privileged he knows he is as an American. He regularly displays humility and gratitude in being able to live in a country where comedy serves as a kind of catharsis for the upsetting issues of the day.

Trust is advanced when people say and do the things they actually believe. People will put up with your failures, limitations, and weaknesses, when they perceive that your communication and actions match your beliefs. What made *The Daily Show* so appealing to a large audience was not only its wickedly funny sense of humor. It was not only the marvelous juxtapositions of video clips and sound bites that offered a critical perspective on the inanities of political discourse. It was also appealing because Stewart himself authentically shared his personal reaction to the absurdities of the current events of the day. His frequent exclamation, "Are you insane?!" reflected a post-9/11 world where news events seemed increasingly surreal and outrageous (Kakutani, 2008). In a world of unreal realities, Stewart's authentic performance of personal identity resonated to make his hilarious and insightful messages highly trustworthy.

Public Relations in the Digital Arena

Because of their visibility in movies and television, most people understand the job of the print or broadcast journalist. Movies like *Spotlight* show us the work of investigative journalists who uncover uncomfortable truths about powerful people and institutions. But far fewer people understand the job of public relations professionals. Yet they are an important source of information about news and current events, and their work raises important questions about what and who can be trusted.

Publicity is one of the "news neighborhoods," as Howard Schneider of Stony Book University likes to put it. It is a gigantic neighborhood, actually. There are five public relations professionals for every working journalist. Most estimates suggest that 50–70% of all journalism content has been influenced by a public relations initiative (MacNamara, 2016).

Public relations professionals aim to communicate with the public, telling stories that resonate with target audiences on behalf of their client in order to accomplish business goals. As we learned in Chapter 5, public relations is a *strategic communication process* that builds mutually beneficial relationships between organizations and their publics. Public relations involves understanding how public opinion and public policy affect a company's business operations and creating content to engage selected target audiences in order to accomplish business goals and protect the reputation of the firm.

Today bloggers and influencers have personalized and democratized the work of public relations, which has traditionally been available only to corporations, large institutions, and other businesses. Some bloggers are part of a world of marketing known as *influence marketing*. This form of marketing relies on identifying and mobilizing people who have influence over potential customers. Much blog content is designed to look like news and information when in fact it is *sponsored content* (also called content marketing), hidden efforts to persuade or influence audiences designed around the needs of a particular client.

Sponsored content is becoming a major force in journalism. For example, when *The New York Times* launched T Brand Studio in 2014, it aimed squarely to develop "stories to influence the influential"—*brand stories* that capture the facts and feelings embodied by a business. Companies pay

The New York Times T Brand Studio

*Why do companies create sponsored content***?**

The New York Times to develop sponsored content that creates an emotional reaction in the hearts of their audience, which tends to be affluent and influential. Meredith Kopiet Levin, the chief operating officer of *The New York Times*, works with companies including Delta Airlines and Stella Artois beer to create sponsored content that helps companies accomplish their strategic communications goals. Some projects are spectacular, as when *The New York Times* mailed all its customers a Google Cardboard player and encouraged readers to download an app to play specially designed news stories shot with a virtual reality camera (Robertson, 2016).

On a smaller scale, bloggers also work for companies to promote their products and services. We do not have good data on how many millions of blogs are in existence and we do not know what proportion of them are used for public relations purposes. Tumblr alone hosts 360 million blogs. In 2015, 28.3 million Internet users updated a blog at least once per month. The number of bloggers in the United States is set to reach 31.7 million in 2020. The most popular topics include entrepreneurship, personal development, small business, online business, marketing, and lifestyle design. But there are also parenting blogs, fashion blogs, fitness blogs, and blogs about food, beer, wine, and more (Convertkit, 2017). Bloggers with a network of readers or followers are important for the launch of a new product or service. Of course, blog content may or may not be accurate, and it may or may not be something consumers can trust and believe. People need to make individual judgments about which bloggers and social media influencers they trust.

Public relations professionals often try to get influential bloggers to write about their clients, knowing that placement of a key story can eventually lead to coverage from a major news media organization in a process known as "trading up the chain." This phrase was developed by Ryan

Holiday, whose 2013 book *Trust Me, I'm Lying* offers a behind-the-scenes look at digital marketing and public relations. In describing the process, he tells the story of how he manipulates the media for a good cause. In one case, a client was trying to raise money for a community art project using Kickstarter, a crowdsourced fundraising platform. He created a YouTube video for the Kickstarter page about the charity, using exotic locations and other visually appealing content. He wrote a short article for a Brooklyn-based blog and embedded the video there. It caught the attention of the *Huffington Post*, which featured the story. Then, he sent email from a fake address with these links to a reporter at CBS in Los Angeles, who produced a television piece on it—using mostly clips from the YouTube video. At the same time, he was promoting the project on Reddit (where users vote on stories and topics they like) so that when the TV news segment aired, Reddit users upvoted it.

Then, other bloggers who rely on Reddit for story ideas wrote about the charity as well. As Holiday explains, "With no advertising budget, no publicist, and no experience, his little video did nearly a half million views, and funded his project for the next two years. It went from nothing to something." By exploiting people's tendency to trust what they see and read on social media posts and blogs, Holiday was able to create an elaborate illusion that tricked a journalist into promoting his campaign.

New forms of marketing enable people to exploit the power of social media, news media, informational media, and the blogosphere for profit. Because media-literate individuals recognize that all media messages are constructed in an economic and political context, they ask, "Who's making money from this message?" in responding to all the forms of content they view, read, and listen to.

Beauty Bloggers as Influencers

As beauty blogging has become a big business, questions of situational ethics have arisen. Some bloggers pride themselves on not accepting marketing money, preferring to feature their own makeup line. Others accept *swag*, in the form of free products and gifts from the beauty industry. Still others receive fees for promoting certain products.

On Instagram, Huda Kattan has been called the most influential beauty blogger in the world (Shapiro, 2017). With 26 million followers, she has her own makeup line and emoji collection, and her net worth is estimated at $500 million. Although

How do truth-in-advertising laws apply to beauty bloggers?

Hanna Kuprevich / Alamy Stock Photo

5 critical questions about a global warming cartoon

After viewing this cartoon at www.medialiteracy-action.com, analyze this political cartoon about climate change using five critical questions of media literacy.

1. **Who is the author and what is the purpose?** This is a political cartoon, which is a distinctive genre of editorial typically found in the opinion pages of a newspaper. Now these cartoons can be found on blogs and websites too. It was created by Steve Breen, a Pulitzer Prize–winning political cartoonist who works at the *San Diego Union-Tribune* and is syndicated in more than 150 newspapers around the country. The purpose of this cartoon is to entertain and persuade, as it expresses the idea that climate change skeptics are merely criticizing some of the small details of the scientific evidence.

2. **What techniques are used to attract and hold attention?** The skeptics are fat and

Steve Breen/Creators Syndicate

she never felt comfortable on YouTube, she's been on Instagram since 2012. Her strategy involves sharing other users' posts to gain a community and being active in conversations with both followers and customers. She rarely accepts paid posts in order to appear more credible to her followers. But when she does feature a product that is not her own, Huda's followers take notice. For example, Alterna Haircare saw its Instagram following jump up by 5,000 after Ms. Kattan featured its products in a post. Why has she become so successful? People trust Huda Kattan because she communicates with authenticity.

But the large majority of beauty bloggers actively seek *sponsorships*, which have become such a big part of the marketing business that in 2017, the Federal Trade Commission updated its rules about *influencers* in relation to the fundamental principle of truth in advertising. It notes that because "an endorsement must reflect the honest opinion of the endorser," if there is a connection between an endorser and the marketer that would affect how

round, which contrasts with the thin, tall stature of the scientist, easily recognizable by his white lab coat. The blackboard is filled with equations, which communicates the idea that climate science is complex. The underlined word "fraud" stands out, and this creates humor from incongruity: the small grammatical errors they are pointing out do not seem to fit with the term, which is generally used to describe falsified data or other intentional distortion of evidence.

3. **What lifestyles, values, and points of view are represented?** This cartoon highlights the gap between the knowledge of the expert and the ignorance of the nonspecialist. Because the nonexperts lack contextual understanding of the scientific principles described on the blackboard, they cannot comprehend the ideas. But they do not even know what they do not know. They can only engage with the scientist's argument at the most superficial level, by critiquing the grammar. As depicted here, the cartoonist believes that the quality of the science cannot be judged by the quality of the grammar. This cartoon seems to imply that the skeptics are trivial-

izing scientific knowledge and expertise by judging it by the wrong criteria.

4. **How might different people interpret this message?** Scientists would probably appreciate this cartoon because they may experience situations like this, where nonexperts evaluate their work without understanding the ideas and context of the scientific contribution. Climate change deniers might feel that this cartoon insults their genuine scientific and cultural interests in questioning evidence and reasoning.

5. **What is omitted?** This cartoon suggests that climate science evidence is a matter of one scientist. But real insight on climate change occurred only after a large number of scientists, working in fields including meteorology, geophysics, geography, mathematics, botany, ecology, atmospheric science, oceanography, and computer science all began to share knowledge across the disciplines. The cartoon also omits the perspective of climate change activists, who work to communicate with politicians and the business community about the need to make policy changes in energy use.

consumers evaluate the endorsement, that connection should be disclosed. Clearly, "knowing about the connection is important information for anyone evaluating the endorsement." The multipage document lists dozens of different kinds of *conflicts of interest* that are becoming more common with the rise of digital marketing (Federal Trade Commission, 2017).

From a business point of view, many companies find online influencers difficult to resist. For example, Nikkie De Jager is a 24-year-old Dutch make-up artist with more than 9 million followers. She uses expensive make-up and lots of it. To buy these products, subscribers can click *affiliate links* that pay her commission for each sale. As one journalist puts it, "Having your product's features read aloud by someone with a dedicated audience who perceives him or her as being 'down to earth' is a more direct and cost-effective way of reaching customers than recruiting a Hollywood star to wear a new shade at the Oscars" (Lancaster, 2018: 1).

What the future may hold: Mistrust of Expertise

Mistrust is increasing political polarization and intensifying political and cultural divisions. Economists know that countries with low levels of trust rely more on business and government regulation, which then leads to lower economic growth. As one reporter put it, "In distrustful societies, people are more likely to craft public policy and do business in ways that benefit their own family, social class, tribe, religion or other group" (Swanson, 2016: 1).

Mistrust of all institutions—not just government and media—is growing. In higher education, public mistrust is also growing. While in 2006, 41% of the American public had a lot of trust in higher education, less than 10 years later, only 14% had a lot of trust in academia (Johnson & Peifer, 2017). Once mistrust becomes normative, it can be difficult to reverse it. In his book *The Death of Expertise*, Tom Nichols worries that rising levels of mistrust can threaten democracy itself. High levels of mistrust seem to be a revolt against elites, and honestly, it makes sense for elites to be blamed. After all, the expertise of military and political leaders and policy-making experts has contributed to two wars in Iraq and Afghanistan and the economic collapse of 2008. Eyewitness videos of police brutality have caused us to lose faith in local police, and the #MeToo movement has revealed the enormous scale of widespread sexual harassment in many business sectors. Reports of Donald Trump's payoffs to porn stars and evidence demonstrating Russian interference in the election process have contributed to growing public mistrust.

Media literacy alone will not solve a trust problem of this scale. But it can help. Through simple actions, you can be part of the solution. If you share only media content that you believe is truthful, that is a good start. If you choose to read, listen to, and view only media content that you believe is truthful, that can help. If, as communicators, you avoid attacks that create "us-versus-them" discourses, and if you can show respect for perspectives that differ from your own by valuing diversity and multiperspectival reasoning, that can make a difference. But perhaps the most important solutions are in regards to matters of the heart and the spirit. To rebuild a world of broken trust, we all must commit to a embrace a spirit of optimism, despite all the unpredictability of the present time. As both consumers and communicators, we can choose to honor the power of hope, courage, forgiveness, empathy, and love in all our relationships and social interactions.

CREATE T▶ LEARN

Compose a Memoir on the Experience of Trust

Decisions about trust and mistrust are among the most profound decisions we make in life. Write a short personal *memoir* to reflect on a time when you made a decision to trust certain information or a certain person. A memoir is a highly personal essay that uses a combination of memory and imagination to tell a brief story that offers insight or value to readers. Consider these questions:

- What situation or memory represents a time when you had to make a decision to trust or mistrust?
- What factors influenced your decision? Was it a good decision? Why or why not?
- What role did communication or media play in your experience with trust or mistrust?
- In general, how have your life experiences and relationships shaped your perspectives on trust and mistrust?

You can post and share your work to a global community of media literacy learners using the hashtag #MLAction.

TIME T◉ REFLECT

Offer a brief summary of the insights you gained after writing your memoir, reflecting on media literacy in relationship to cyncisim, skepticism, and trust. Use the Flipgrid Inquiry at www.medialiteracyaction.com to contribute your ideas in a brief oral presentation. You can also view and respond to comments of other people who have offered their insights as well.

Renee Hobbs

PART III

MEDIA ECONOMICS

The value of creative labor is shaped by business practices and government regulation

How Do Media Companies Make Money?

10

Learning Outcomes

1. Examine the changing nature of the workplace for freelancers and professionals who work in media industries

2. Appreciate how consumers support media industries through the purchase of goods and services

3. Consider how global media systems are shaped by regulatory and business practices that include both freedom of information and censorship

4. Reflect on the social value of media regulations as they influence workers, consumers, and society

Have you ever wondered about how you could make money from the photos you create? Many people put their photos on Instagram and enjoy the likes and shares they receive from people in their social network. But James Wheeler found a way for his photo hobby to bring in a revenue stream—and one photo earned $4,000!

As Wheeler began to develop from a casual photographer into a hobbyist, he started buying higher-quality camera equipment and looking for a way to sell his work online. He uploaded his work to a variety of microstock websites, which sell photos to Web designers and other small businesses that create media content. It can be a tedious process to upload photos to such websites, because each submission needs to include keywords, categories, and other details about authorship, date of creation, and location. After Wheeler uploaded 300 of his best travel photos to five different websites, his sales were generating about $100 monthly. Most of his photos made no money at all.

But one stunning photo of a mountain range in Alberta, Canada, generated a lot of income, partly due to cumulative advantage, a concept discussed in a previous chapter. On one site, this particular photo was purchased early on by one or two buyers, which then sent it to the top of the list whenever someone searched for the word "Canada." Thus, the photo reached even more potential buyers, increasing sales.

In the social media universe, many more people view content than create and share it. Even though no money is involved for the large majority of digital creators, those contributing their work generally perceive it as a private good, in which payment for their efforts is not in money, but in attention. Because attention is such a valued resource, some people are often willing to forsake financial gain in order to obtain it. This has been called *the cult of the amateur*. Some critics believe that professional media organizations (including newspapers, magazines, music, and movies) are being overtaken by user-generated free (or nearly free) content (Keen, 2007). Other see how social media has democratized the business of media, enabling anyone to provide from their creative labor. How the work of amateur creators is affecting the professional media industries is a fascinating, complex, and ever-changing story.

Clearly, the work of both professionals and amateurs shapes the media content users receive each day. The media and technology sector is an important part of the global economy with enormous influence around the world. As the saying goes, "Follow the money." By understanding the economic and basic legal concepts that underpin American film, television, video games, music, and publishing, consumers can advance their media literacy competencies. To reflect upon these ideas, we consider questions such as:

- What are professional careers in media actually like?
- Which laws and policies affect the media marketplace?
- How does censorship affect media industries?

- How do media companies actually make money?

- Why is fair competition important for the future of media companies?

Entrepreneurship and Media Careers

What does it take to be a media entrepreneur? Today, creative individuals find it easier than ever to create media, given the easy access to low-cost or free media production tools. It is also easier to get their work in front of audiences through the strategic use of social media promotion. Such efforts are a form of entrepreneurship, the discovery of business opportunities by starting a new business or carrying out new initiatives within existing businesses.

Gradually, people are beginning to pay for quality content that they appreciate. Some media entrepreneurs choose to start a *for-profit* business, where the owners receive the profits. They may also choose to be a *nonprofit* business, where a clear social benefit to the public is conceptualized and any money left after the organization has paid its bills gets put back into the organization.

Subscription-based business models like Patreon enable people to support the work of podcasters, journalists, comedians, YouTubers, novelists, comic book artists, and other creative collaborators. Crowdfunding connects audiences with creative authors and "gives users the chance to participate in the creative process through voting, comments, sharing, twittering or a direct connection to creators" (Carvajal et al., 2012: 4). Crowdfunding may allow for a better adjustment between supply and demand because creators attempt to generate value for the people who support them (*The Economist*, 2010). These kinds of funding models could lead to a wider variety of artists

What are the pros and cons of freelancing **?**

and creative practices by forging closer connections between the people who make media and those who enjoy it.

Many people are employed in media industries as freelancers. A *freelancer* is someone who does not work for one company, but who sells his or her labor and services independently. The United States has 53 million freelancers—35% of the U.S. workforce (World Economic Forum, 2016). These people may drive cars for Uber, offer Web design services for local businesses,

paint houses, plan wedding events, create jewelry, or bake cookies. They may develop newsletter copy for specialized manufacturing, banking, or real estate firms or pitch articles to *Slate* or *Wired*. Freelancers have flexibility in their work arrangements, which may be valuable for parents of young children or those nearing retirement. Some people even freelance while holding a full-time job, seeing it as a source of extra income or as a creative outlet. Freelancers often have several clients at one time, report their earnings to the government, and withhold their own taxes. They do not receive health insurance or get retirement benefits from an employer.

In the fields of art, design, media, and communications, many specialists offer their services as freelancers, moving from project to project. Many of the people listed in movie credits—from hair and makeup stylists to location scouts to sound and lighting engineers—are not employed by a single company. In Hollywood, unions protect some of these workers and ensure they receive a decent income, with health insurance and other benefits.

However, some freelance jobs engage in repetitive tasks that do not require much expertise or creativity. Workers on Amazon's Mechanical Turk, for example, may edit and transcribe audio content, translate work, or verify information about restaurants and local businesses. They may tag images in order to identify objects or choose which product images are visually most attractive for inclusion in a company's social media campaign.

The rise of the freelance economy stands in stark contrast to the growing levels of *income inequality* in Hollywood and in corporate America more generally. A small number of movie stars, celebrities, and athletes earn truly gigantic sums for their work. In 2019, Daniel Craig was paid $25 million for his work in the film *Bond 25* and Jennifer Lawrence received $15 million for *Red Sparrow*. Considered by some to be the greatest basketball player, LeBron James earned nearly $150 million from the Los Angeles Lakers in 2019. Think that sounds like a good job? The odds of becoming a professional athlete or movie star are greater than one in a million, according to professional analysts.

Given these data, it is reasonable to wonder: why do famous athletes, celebrities, and actors make so much more money than nurses, teachers, police officers, and firefighters, the people in our communities who provide such vital services to our society? Malcolm Gladwell (2008) has argued that, sometime in the 1970s, changes occurred to shift the relationship between those who controlled capital and those whom they employed. Before 1970, income inequality was not as severe as it is now. Back then, celebrities, CEOs, finance leaders, and corporate lawyers did not make the enormous sums of money they do now. Prior to the 1980s, taxes on the wealthy were much higher than they are now. In 1980, the tax rate was 70%. In 1945, it was 95%. Under the Reagan administration, taxes on the wealthy were dramatically reduced. Athletes, actors, lawyers, and other people with scarce forms of talent began to ask for more money. Business leaders recognized that talent is tied to profitability. This led to a rapid increase in the incomes of the top performers in many fields, including medicine, finance, sports, and other industries. But gender and racial disparities in income persist, with women and minorities paid substantially below men (Gladwell, 2008). Clearly, the marketplace for talent is not a level playing field by any means.

Although many media entrepreneurs use media production as a sideline to their ordinary jobs, millions of other people work in media industries in the United States and around the world. As a proportion of the economy, however, full-time media jobs are actually a very small percentage of the overall workforce. In 2016, jobs in the information sector amounted to 1.8% of all jobs, according to the U.S. Bureau of Labor Statistics. The U.S. Census reports that media and information jobs (including in the fields of publishing and telecommunications) peaked in the year 2000 and have been declining ever since. The Internet publishing industry has seen increases in both the number of people employed and the number of companies, but employment in television broadcasting has declined substantially since 2010.

However, film and video production industries have seen increased employment over the past 10 years. Employment in other information industries has decreased, including motion pictures and video, radio broadcasting, sound recording, and newspapers and book publishing. Several hundred thousand people work in the media sector, and their positions are often well-paid jobs with substantial benefits. The U.S. Census reports the largest number of media-related positions are editors (98,990 employees), producers and directors (82,880 employees), photographers (54,410 employees), and audio and video equipment technicians (49,180 employees).

Producers and directors have the highest annual wages among these occupations, $70,660 at the median, followed by technical writers ($64,610) and multimedia artists and animators ($60,830). Photographers, producers and directors, writers and authors, and editors are expected to be the largest media-related occupations in 2020. Based on historical projections, the U.S. Census expects the number of photographers, producers, directors, writers,

Daniel Dempster Photography/Alamy Stock Photo

How are professional careers in media depicted in movies and TV programs?

Consider the **Question**

With a partner or in a small group, discuss the advantages and disadvantages of being a media entrepreneur or having a full-time media job.

- What are the advantages and disadvantages of having a full-time media job?
- What are some of the benefits of "working for yourself" as a freelancer? What are some of the disadvantages?
- What competencies, skills, and habits of mind are important to develop in order to succeed as a media entrepreneur?

and authors to grow while fewer reporters and correspondents will be employed in 2020 than in 2010 (U.S. Census, 2013).

At the same time, however, jobs in advertising, promotions, and marketing have significantly increased, and these have been growing faster than other occupations. Advertising and promotions managers plan, direct, and coordinate advertising and promotional campaigns, introducing new products into the marketplace. For most of these new jobs, the ability to manage digital media campaigns through the use of websites, social media, or live chats is an important skill set. Marketing managers have the highest salaries ($132,230), with those in professional or technical fields earning even more.

The Media Marketplace

To really understand the question "How do media companies make money?" it is important to understand the U.S. economy as a whole as well as the regulatory environment that shapes and controls it. *Capitalism* is a market-based economy that relies on the largely unregulated exchange of goods and services. Because it relies on the relationship between buyers and sellers and uses the principle of supply and demand to regulate prices, a market economy has certain advantages over economies that rely on a large amount of central planning by governments.

A market economy is responsive to changes in the environment and encourages innovation as new products and services can easily be brought to potential buyers. While some sectors of the media marketplace have high *barriers to entry* (for example, the up-front equipment and personnel expenses in launching a cable television network), other sectors are relatively low in cost for new competitors. With a robust flow of information, entertainment, and persuasion, people can choose freely from among the large supply of media messages available to them. Capitalism assumes that people are rational actors who select messages that are in their best interest.

But the market model has some important limitations. For a market to be truly fair for consumers, it needs to be a *level playing field* where every entrepreneur has an equal chance of success. But differential access to money, personal connections, education, and talent gives some people big advantages over others, even when the quality of their ideas is the same. Also, markets may not work effectively when people choose inferior products and services because they have been heavily marketed using deceptive or misleading advertising techniques.

At the most basic level, businesses serve the interests of those who own them. When investors purchase stock in a company, they become a part owner of the company. The firm they invest in is obliged to put their financial interests over the welfare of customers, employees, and management. Businesses can choose to serve *the public interest*; but they are not required to do so. In fact, companies can sometimes face challenges when they aim to serve the public interest or when they favor the needs of customers, employees, or managers.

Forbes

Do consumers make rational choices in the marketplace? Why or why not?

Under U.S. law, public companies are obligated to serve *shareholders*, not customers or employees, and must maximize shareholder value. To do this, some companies maximize profits at all costs by firing employees or selling shoddy products. In a market economy, businesses are free to make decisions about what is best for the company. For example, in 2014, Time, Inc. laid off many journalists who worked for *Entertainment Weekly* as part of a broader reorganization that involved staff reductions across the whole company. Since labor costs are the largest part of business expenses, reducing the number of employees created more profit for the company's owners.

Still, some business leaders see the dangers of an exclusive focus on maximizing shareholder value. In 2019, a large group of business leaders (including those from Apple, Pepsi, and Walmart) spoke out about the need to redefine the role of business in society. They argued that companies should no longer advance only the interests of shareholders. Instead, businesses must also invest in their employees, protect the environment, and deal fairly and ethically with their suppliers (Gelles & Yaffe-Bellany, 2019). Only time will tell whether this new approach will help address the growing economic inequality in the United States and around the world.

Who Pays for Media?

Media companies use one or more of these three economic models to make money:

Direct Revenue Stream. For books, movies, and video games, consumers pay directly for media they choose. When you buy a book on Amazon, they forward some of the money to the publisher, who has spent money in the creation of the paper copy. Based on the number of books sold, the publisher then returns a small portion of the revenue (usually 8–15%) to the author in the form of a *royalty* payment.

If you are buying video games, you might visit the GameStop at the local mall or go online to Steam. In any case, the middleman distributor gets a part of the payment, but a big chunk is returned to the game company. If you purchase music, you may pay a middleman like iTunes, Pandora, or Spotify to download files or stream music, but part of that revenue is returned to the musician. Film box office revenues work the same way. The *exhibitor* who owns the venue where the film is screened takes a portion (usually about 40%) and returns the rest to the film studio. When a filmmaker licenses a film to air on a digital streaming service, they receive 80% of the revenue. During the 2020 coronavirus pandemic, the movie sequel Trolls World Tour was released as a digital rental for $19.95, earning over $100 million, a record for streaming. Critics believe that local exhibition companies like AMC and Cinemark may not be able to financially compete in an era where people prefer to watch movies at home (Stewart, 2020).

Indirect Revenue Stream. Some media companies provide their products as a free service, using an *indirect revenue stream* as their business strategy. Terrestrial radio and television do not require payment from consumers. Instagram, Facebook, and Google do not charge fees either. In this business model, the advertiser is charged a fee so as to gain access to the consumer. In effect, for these media companies, the attention of the viewer, reader, or listener is the "product" sold to advertisers.

Under this business model, media companies establish prices for the cost to reach certain consumers, based on their gender, age, income, and geographic location. Typically, advertisers purchase consumers who live in a *designated marketing area*, which is a geographic region. The media company charges a fee based on the *cost per thousand*. So a potential advertiser seeking to promote his or her company will approach a local radio station, which will offer a price list in the form of a rate card. In New York City, clients can buy 15 ads that will air Monday through Friday and four that air on the weekend for just under $4,000. In Denver, the same number of ads will cost just a little more than $1,000. The prices depend on the size of the city and the number of listeners.

To place an ad on Instagram, clients can expect to pay nearly $7.00 per thousand viewers, but they can target the type of people they want to reach with great precision. Do they want to reach people who have purchased a car in the past year? Or people who watch reality TV? Or people interested in media literacy? The ability to target audiences means that the price to reach some audiences is higher (or lower). Among those who search for the keyword "media literacy," for example, I can expect to pay $2.16 every time someone sees an ad (perhaps for this book) and clicks on the link.

Mixed Revenue Stream. The third major way media are funded is the *mixed revenue stream*, where consumers pay for media, advertisers pay to reach audiences, or other third parties, including foundations, think tanks, or governments, pay for media. Table 10.1 shows the sources of funding for many types of media, and it reveals that cable and satellite television and telecommunication services use this model. In the United States, public broadcasting relies on the mixed revenue stream model as it includes four sources of funding: (1) donations from audiences through annual fundraising, (2) advertising (called underwriting), (3) financial support from philanthropies and charitable organizations, and (4) money from the federal government. In

Table 10.1
Sources of Funding for Media Industries

MEDIA TYPE	DIRECT REVENUE	INDIRECT REVENUE	MIXED REVENUE
Book Publishing	X		
Music			X
Movies	X		
Video Games	X		
Magazine and Newspapers			X
Broadcast Radio and Television		X	
Cable and Satellite Television			X
Internet			X
Public Broadcasting			X
Search Engines		X	
Social Media		X	
Streaming Media	X		

How may ESPN change in the years ahead?

2021, the federal government will spend $465 million on public TV and radio broadcasting or about 75 cents annually per American citizen. By contrast, in Great Britain, government spending on public broadcasting was £3.7 billion in 2019 (or about $4.8 billion). Each year, British homeowners pay an annual TV tax of about £200 per TV set for public television. In many countries, government spending on media is considered a public service obligation that enables consumers to have noncommercial programming that includes news, documentaries, and educational programming. Public broadcasting in most countries uses a mixed revenue stream. For example, British TV networks sell advertising in addition to receiving tax revenue.

In the United States, the mixed revenue stream has been very profitable for media companies like ESPN, which receives revenue from both cable companies and advertisers. To watch the ESPN sports network, viewers pay a cable or telecommunications company for monthly service. They might pay $130 or more per month for cable and Internet access. Nine dollars of that monthly charge goes directly to ESPN, owned by Disney. Thus, American cable TV consumers pay for access to ESPN, whether they watch it or not.

Many households do watch ESPN; it is ranked as the highest-rated cable network among men and adults between ages 18 and 54, and second among total viewers in prime time. Viewers of ESPN see plenty of advertising for restaurants, cars, technology, and financial and insurance services. In 2014, ESPN made $10.8 billion, with 60% of that coming from consumers who paid their cable bills and 40% coming from advertisers (Thompson, 2017).

Although ESPN is one of the most profitable cable television networks, analysts are concerned about its future. ESPN was hugely profitable during the boom years of cable television, but its profitability led to a massive increase in the cost of *licensing rights* to broadcast sporting events. Now the cable TV model is declining even as the annual cost of rights contracts with professional leagues are continuing to grow.

In 2018, ESPN spent $1.1 billion for the rights to the Monday Night Football franchise. All together, the National Football League takes in $3.7 billion annually from cable and broadcast networks. ESPN spends a lot of money to purchase the right to air those games. With about 150 production employees at each game, it spends $2 million per hour. That works out to about $65 million per game. This is 10 times the normal cost of prime-time programming (Easterbrook, 2018).

No one knows how the future of ESPN will develop. More people now engage in *cord-cutting*, moving away from cable television and replacing it with digital media services; ESPN has lost 13 million subscribers in 6 years. The network had 88 million U.S. subscribers at the end of September 2017, but that is down from a peak of 100 million in 2010 (Thompson, 2017). Despite its current leading role, ESPN's parent company, Disney, has to explore the potential long-term future of the cable television network.

The Shape of Media Institutions

Media companies cannot be examined apart from the legal context in which they operate. Business and law are inextricably linked. Of course, it may seem obvious that the media organizations in any society will take on the particular characteristics of that society (Lotz, 2014). Newspapers in the United States have different content and form than newspapers in Belgium, Croatia, or Jordan, due to the nature of media regulation. In Jordan, when King Abdullah gives a speech or visits a hospital, it is page one news, because the news media are required to report on their monarch. In Belgium, local business leaders and politicians own the newspapers, so readers can easily detect how the news is shaped to align with their interests.

How do governments around the world regulate different types of media?

Maen Zayyad/Alamy Stock Photo

Intellectual Grandparent:
Dallas Smythe

He understood that audiences are the product of mass media industries driven by advertising revenues. Dallas W. Smythe was a professor, activist, and economist who explored the field of communications and mass media. He served as the economist for the FCC during and after World War II, at a time when the agency was trying to ensure broad public access to television and telephone service. Before moving to Canada in 1963, when his political activism was under scrutiny by J. Edgar Hoover's FBI during the Cuban missile crisis, he taught communication research at the University of Illinois's Institute of Communication Research (ICR), which Wilbur Schramm established in 1948. He worked with Herbert Schiller, whose work explored the rise of cultural imperialism as the United States exported its mass media entertainment abroad. His key ideas include:

The audience is the product. Smythe developed the idea that audiences are a type of commodity that is produced, sold, distributed, and consumed. Applying Marxist analysis to daily life, he observed that even when workers are not working, their leisure activity is commodified through advertising. By using media and viewing advertising, workers end up participating in capitalism even when they are relaxing at home (Smythe, 1977).

People pay for media indirectly. Smythe once commented on critic A. J. Liebling's famous aphorism "There's no free lunch" by applying the concept to mass media.

> As with the hors d'oeuvres or potato chips and peanuts given to the customers of the pub, bar, or cocktail lounge, the function of the free lunch is to whet the appetite. In this case, to whet the prospective audience members' appetites and thus (1) attract and keep them attending to the program, newspaper, or magazine; (2) cultivate a mood conducive to favor-

Around the world, only a few countries rely completely on a market-based system for mass media and communications. Many countries utilize a mix of strong state-controlled or state-owned media and private commercial media companies. In Europe and parts of Asia and Latin America, media companies are subsidized by political parties or directly owned by the state. Many of these countries, such as Germany and Britain and nations in Scandinavia, have strong democratic traditions that rely on well-funded and carefully regulated public broadcasting systems.

Globally, *media systems* fall into three major types: (1) the liberal model, which relies on free market capitalism and little regulation; (2) the democratic corporatist model, where media are tied to organized social and political groups; and (3) the polarized pluralist model, where state control of media is dominant and commercial media is relatively weak (Hallin & Mancini, 2004). All three of these models may coexist within one country. For example, England has a robust newspaper business that relies on the

able reaction to the advertisers' explicit and implicit messages. In the policy of the mass media, the characteristics of the free lunch must always be subordinated to those of the formal advertisements, because the purpose of the mass media is to produce audiences to sell to the advertisers. (Smythe, 1981: 242)

Smythe demonstrated how, even though consumers may experience newspapers, magazines, television, and radio as "free," they ultimately pay for media indirectly through the purchase of goods and services.

As an economist studying mass media, Smythe contributed to the emergence of critical cultural studies research in North America by unpacking the political and economic consequences of a media system built upon "selling eyeballs to advertisers." In this system advertisers control the content, limiting consumers' freedom of choice. He points out that this system supports capitalism by enrolling the communications industry in maintaining the political and economic status quo.

Advertisers support business interests because government rewards it. As Smythe predicted, advertising-supported media systems have been very robust over a long period of time, fueling the development and rise of newspapers, magazines, radio, and television and digital platforms like Facebook and Google. Expenditures on marketing are considered a business expense. Spending money on advertising can reduce the amount of tax a business may pay. Today, marketing companies find new ways to saturate every public and private space with advertising and use data supplied by consumers to deliver micro-targeted messages that can be hard to resist. Smythe and other scholars of the *political economy* of mass media emphasize the importance of examining the relationship between business, government, and the public interest.

If Dallas Smythe has influenced your thinking about media, you can share a comment on the Grandparents of Media Literacy website at www.grandparentsofmediliteracy.com.

liberal model. But their book publishing industry is tied to major British universities, reflecting the democratic corporatist model. The polarized pluralist model is evident in the role of the public broadcaster, the BBC, which is paid for through an annual TV license tax.

In countries like Saudi Arabia, Turkey, Russia, Iraq, and China, the government controls media content through a variety of mechanisms. Laws on extremism grant the authorities great discretion to punish any individual, organization, or activity that lacks official support. National television networks and many radio and print outlets are controlled by state-owned companies and state-friendly business magnates. Being a media entrepreneur in these countries can be challenging, risky or even dangerous.

When governments or political parties control media companies, they can produce content they believe is in the public interest. They may not report news if it could damage the reputation of the political leadership.

Why does CCTV produce content for English-speaking audiences ❓

For example, China Central Television (CCTV) is a government-owned network of 50 television channels that broadcast to the more than 1 billion people in China. All the major media, including radio, newspapers, and the Internet, in China are controlled by the Chinese Communist Party. The Chinese government strictly regulates the creation and distribution of materials regarding Chinese history. People are not allowed to publish stories about their lived experience during the Cultural Revolution, which subjected ordinary people to terrible privation, torture, and other punishments for 10 years beginning in 1966. Today, only 34 foreign films may be shown in China each year, and books cannot be published before China's General Administration of Press and Publication has screened them. It is illegal to use Facebook, Snapchat, Pinterest, and thousands of other websites, including the website of *The New York Times*. Laws also give competitive advantages to Chinese media and Internet services, including Baidu, Tencent, and Alibaba.

The concept of freedom of expression exists in China, but it is conceptualized differently than in Western democracies. Chinese people have freedom of thought, of course, and they can express critical ideas in face-to-face conversation and in some online contexts. Because people in China do not elect their leaders or vote on government policies, government authorities recognize a certain value to self-expression as a useful way to monitor potentially problematic social issues. For some, the Internet is an important outlet for the average person to express dissatisfaction with local government. This also enables the government to monitor the mood of the people and to track citizens inclined to express discontent (U.S. Congress, n.d.). The Chinese government encourages CCTV broadcasters to engage in targeted reporting on local forms of political corruption. Some people in the society (sometimes called the "free-speech elite") can criticize the government with less fear of punishment than the average Chinese citizen.

Media Regulation: Freedom of Expression

In the United States, media companies are regulated by the legislative, judicial, and executive branches of government. Understanding the First Amendment and the role of regulatory agencies including the Federal Communications Commission (FCC) in media ownership rules can provide a good starting point for appreciating the relationship between economics and public policy. Economic and legal issues are fundamentally linked since the protection of property is important to keeping domestic peace and promoting social justice. To understand media economics, an understanding of media regulation is essential.

One major component of media regulation in the United States centers on the idea of *freedom of expression*. Ratified in 1791, the First Amendment to the U.S. Constitution protects five freedoms: (1) religion, (2) speech, (3) press, (4) assembly, and (5) the right to petition the government for a redress of grievances. The First Amendment has been an important regulatory tradition that has advanced both the freedom and financial power of media industries. It is well understood that the First Amendment is essential to self-governance in democratic societies.

But over time, scholars and legal experts have had different interpretations of the First Amendment. Some libertarians emphasize the phrase "Congress shall make no law," which explicitly calls attention to the negative concept of "no law." Libertarians see this as ruling out any type of government actions in relation to the press (Coll, 2018). Others see press freedom as a positive concept that uses law as a form of protection to limit the inevitable harms done by unrestrained market forces (Picard, 1985). In this view, media regulation is needed to ensure that the press can be truly free. Media regulation tries to balance unrestrained freedom of expression with the need to ensure open competition and robust economic activity.

Duncan Hill/CartoonStock

How has the American legal tradition of freedom of expression shaped the business of media? In Paul Starr's 2004 book *The Creation of Mass Media*, he demonstrates how the U.S. government advanced the public sphere by using political action to increase the scope and influence of the media industry. For example, the establishment of the post office enabled publishers to radically expand the dissemination of information. Anyone who could print something could send it anywhere,

Which forms of censorship are most dangerous to democracy **?**

using low-cost subsidies provided for the shipping of books, newspapers, and magazines.

When you think about the First Amendment, you might interpret it as meaning that people can choose freely what to say, read, and view without interference from the government. But freedom of the press is not just about limiting government power. It is also built upon the assumption that information from diverse and antagonistic sources is essential to the welfare of the public. Undoubtedly, press freedom can be diminished by corporate interests that privilege the voices of the powerful, turn journalism into entertainment, publish lies, and fail to uphold the essential checks and balances on power that keep democracy strong. As McChesney (2006: 445) argues, the state has "not only the right, but the duty, to see that a viable press system exists, for if such a media system does not exist the entire constitutional project will fail."

Understanding Censorship

All types of media systems are vulnerable to censorship. Scholars explain that people restrict speech and expression for all kinds of reasons, both good and bad. *Censorship* is defined as a disruption of the chain of communication from author to audience that occurs when (1) the work threatens the political, social, or moral order; (2) the content might reveal information that elites want hidden; or (3) somebody believes the author does not deserve to be heard (Fellion & Inglis, 2017: 17). While some people think that only a government can censor, censorship also involves editors, publishers, TV producers, teachers, prison officials, and many others.

When corporations control and limit media content so as to prevent the dissemination of certain ideas and information, it is called *corporate censorship.* One recent example comes from the United States with a practice called "catch and kill." It happens when someone makes a payment to a source that prevents them from talking to other news media, keeping a news story out of the public eye. This type of corporate censorship is legal and it is protected under the First Amendment, except for political candidates, where it may be a violation of campaign contribution rules. For example, just before the 2016 presidential election, the *National Enquirer* paid $150,000 to Karen McDougal, who says she had a lengthy adulterous affair with Donald Trump 10 years earlier. The paper paid for "exclusive rights" to Karen McDougal's story but intentionally never published it to protect Donald Trump (Sullivan, 2016).

State censorship takes many forms. All around the world, media organizations can also be controlled or co-opted by political leaders using a number of political techniques. In 2019, the World Press Freedom index downgraded the rating of the United States, noting that the harassment of journalists and the rise of disinformation from the U.S. government under President Trump made press freedom "problematic" in this country. For example, U.S. Customs and Border Patrol agents have hounded and intimidated journalists who have travelled abroad, accusing them of spreading propaganda (Tracy, 2019).

Other forms of censorship can be more subtle. In the United States, a law restricts federal funding to libraries unless they install content filters on the Internet that limit access to pornography. In China, laws against foreign organizations have been used to justify restrictions on religious expression, including the removal or destruction of Christian churches.

Repressive strategies to control and manage information may include state censorship that occurs when journalists and activists are harassed, threatened, or imprisoned for criticizing political leaders. Since his election in 2014, Egyptian President Abdel Fattah el-Sisi has waged war against media companies, silenced critics, and weakened political opposition, convinced

Why do governments threaten, pressure or punish journalists?

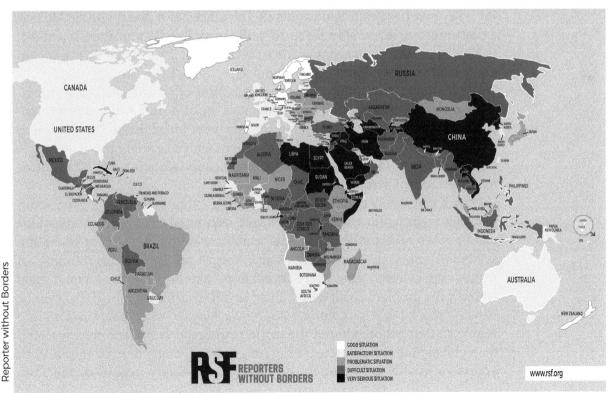

Reporter without Borders

that freedom of information is dangerous in a time of crisis, Journalists are arrested for reporting on political protests. el-Sisi has blocked websites, arrested writers, and even "turned something as simple as reading into a dangerous act" (Farid, 2017: 1). Among the 40,000 political activists now in Egyptian jails, one was sentenced to 5 years in prison for the crime of possessing a book authored by Karl Marx.

Governments might also justify censoring the Internet by saying it is necessary to suppress hate speech or to fight terrorism, which is a type of censorship called *masked political control*. In Turkey, President Recep Tayyip Erdoğan exercises control over both government and private media, using direct pressure and regulatory authority to stifle independent journalism. After an attempted coup in 2016, Erdoğan went after supposed critics, firing 160,000 people from their jobs and arresting more than 70,000. This form of censorship is especially pernicious because of the way that it promotes a *culture of fear* that can damage all aspects of public life. Dissent can also be controlled through a form of censorship called *technology capture*, including monitoring and surveillance of critics, blocking websites, and "using trolling to shout down critical voices, or by sowing confusion through propaganda and false news" (Simon, 2017: 1).

The most extreme form of censorship is controlling journalists through violence. In 2019, the number of journalists killed in the line of duty fell to the lowest level in 17 years, as dangerous regional conflicts stabilized in some countries. For many years, being a journalist in Mexico and Syria has been especially dangerous. In December 2018, drug lords left a box containing a severed head and hands outside the offices of a newspaper in Mexico, a warning that inevitably leads to self-censorship (Committee to Protect Journalists, 2020). In many countries, the killing of a journalist does not generally lead to a successful prosecution.

While some may think of the phenomenon of journalists being threatened or killed as something that happens in other countries, it can happen close to home. In 2018, five journalists were killed in the *Capital Gazette* newsroom in Annapolis, Maryland, by a man who was angry about an article published about his harassment of a high school acquaintance (Committee to Protect Journalists, 2020).

Only a few weeks before his brutal murder, Jamal Kashoggi, a Saudi-born journalist writing for the *Washington Post*, explained that, in the Middle East and in other parts of the world, the combination of poverty, poor education systems, and state-controlled media warps people's understanding of reality. He believed that transnational media organizations could help address the problem so citizens can be better informed about global events. He was grateful that his columns for the *Washington Post* were translated into Arabic so that people around the world could read them, and he advocated for a global platform to increase the range and diversity of Arab voices. With access to quality information, he believed, "ordinary people in the Arab world [will] be able to address the structural problems their societies face" (Kashoggi, 2018: 1).

Despite the risks, in-depth reporting projects survive thanks to the courage and independence of journalists, the existence of new business models, and the ability to disseminate information through social media, blogs, and mainstream media as well. Robust, fact-based reporting *without fear or favor* is the best way to fight back against the many forms of censorship that exist today.

Content Moderation

While users might think that they can say whatever they like on their Facebook, Instagram, or Snap pages, social media platforms are not a *public forum*. A public forum has traditionally been designated a place for free expression. Parks, streets, and sidewalks are typically understood as part of the public forum. Unlike a public place, the managers of social media sites can choose to shape or limit user participation in any way they like. They are not bound by the First Amendment. Indeed, Facebook's mission statement makes a commitment to "remove bad actors and their content quickly to keep a positive and safe environment."

Content moderation is used to limit and control people's expression on social media platforms. Facebook actually monitors online content using both human raters and programming algorithms. Monitors are paid $15 per hour to remove beheadings, bestiality, and child pornography, reviewing an average of about 8,000 posts per day, roughly about 1,000 posts per hour (Solon, 2017). In 2017, a document was leaked to the press with the details of some of Facebook's moderation policies. For example, Facebook permits images of animal abuse, but will remove the imagery if a user shows sadism, defined as the enjoyment of suffering. According to the rulebook, videos of violent deaths are not deleted (Hopkins, 2017). Photos and videos of nonsexual physical abuse and bullying of children are not deleted unless there is a sadistic or celebratory element. Videos of abortions are allowed, as long as there is no nudity. Facebook will even also allow people to livestream attempts to self-harm because it "doesn't want to censor or punish people in distress." Only in 2019 did Instagram, which is owned by Facebook, prohibit depictions of self-harm, including cutting.

When it comes to other forms of violence, celebrities and regular users are treated differently. Facebook will remove posts that contain credible threats of violence against a celebrity or head of state. For example, the post "Someone shoot Trump" will be deleted. In the rulebook, public figures are described as "vulnerable persons." For example, according to the Facebook rulebook, it is okay to post "I hope someone kills you" directed at an ordinary user, because this is not regarded as a credible threat (Kaminski & Klonick, 2017).

Content moderation is a form of control over information and it can have significant consequences for public knowledge. When a Norwegian writer posted on Facebook an iconic Vietnam War image featuring naked children fleeing a napalm attack as part of a discussion on pictures that changed the history of warfare, he was stunned to find that the image was removed and he was subsequently blocked from Facebook. When a Norwegian newspaper reported on the issue and included the image in its story, it was also blocked by Facebook. Facebook has a policy of barring images of nude children as it makes an effort to prevent the platform being used to promote child pornography. Given that 40% of people get all their news from Facebook, this case drew considerable concern.

When Facebook algorithms are used to shape access to news and information, some may see it as a new kind of editorial decision-making, akin to how *The New York Times* makes decisions about what to feature on page one. Is Facebook a publisher or a platform? We explore this question more deeply in Chapter 11.

The Fairness Doctrine and Deregulation

In the United States, while the legislative and judicial branches of government protect freedom of expression and intellectual property, the executive branch of government regulates media industries. When radio broadcasting was first developed in the 1900s, the need for government regulation became obvious. The Radio Act of 1912 was the first legislation that addressed the growing competition between broadcasters, assigning parts of the electromagnetic spectrum for different purposes. Over time, competition became so extreme that listeners experienced disruption of services due to interference of radio signals. In 1934, Congress created the Federal Communications Commission (FCC) as a federal agency to regulate the wire and radio communication businesses. Because radio uses the airwaves, which are deemed to belong to the American public, the mission of the FCC is "to make available so far as possible, to all the people of the United States, without discrimination on the basis of race, color, religion, national origin, or sex, rapid, efficient, nationwide, and worldwide wire and radio communication services with adequate facilities at reasonable charges."

As the radio and television industry became increasingly centralized, with only two big companies controlling what most people heard, the FCC created the *Fairness Doctrine* in 1949. The ruling, an extension of the public interest clause of the 1934 Communications Act, mandated that broadcasters give adequate coverage to significant public issues and ensure that such coverage is fair in that it presents conflicting views. Later, the FCC added *personal attack rules* that granted those personally attacked during a presentation of controversial issues a right to reply to the broadcast. These rules aimed to extend traditional journalistic ethics from the world of print journalism into the world of broadcasting.

The Fairness Doctrine empowered citizens to monitor broadcasters to ensure that they gave adequate coverage to significant local issues and provided a balanced range of perspectives on controversial issues. For example, in 1976, when Congress was debating laws to regulate strip mining, WHAR in Clarksburg, West Virginia, refused to carry any coverage of the issue. The TV station said the issue was too controversial. Citizens complained to the FCC and it asked the station to discuss the controversy from different points of view. When a gas company launched a promotional campaign on Oklahoma

Should journalistic ethics be strengthened through regulation? Why or why not?

radio and TV stations to get a rate increase approved, citizens approached radio and TV stations asking for a balanced presentation as required by the Fairness Doctrine. One station then scheduled two half-hour public affairs programs on the rate hike, and other stations aired spot announcements opposing the hike (Meadows, 1987).

In the eyes of critics, the Fairness Doctrine limited freedom of expression. By imposing fairness, the law inadvertently discouraged the coverage of controversial issues. After all, critics argued, no law mandates that journalists present fair and balanced news. It is a professional norm, not a legal requirement. First, the law was challenged as unconstitutional. But the Supreme Court ruled on the Fairness Doctrine, acknowledging it was constitutional. In 1969, in *Red Lion Broadcasting* v. *Federal Communications Commission*, a unanimous Court held the personal attack rules did not violate the First Amendment because the information needs of viewers and listeners supercede the rights of media owners (Klein, 2020).

For many years, the Fairness Doctrine enjoyed support from both liberals and conservatives. It was seen as a way for citizens to check the potentially significant power of increasingly centralized media companies. With the Fairness Doctrine in place, the mere suggestion that the FCC might become involved in an issue would encourage broadcasters to balance news coverage or avoid controversial topics altogether. This practice was called *regulation by raised eyebrow*, the idea that the mere threat of potential sanction or regulation could be a powerful deterrent to control the abuse of power (Clogston, 2016).

But after the election of President Ronald Reagan. In 1980, many laws and policies were perceived to interfere with business innovation. Media companies argued that the Fairness Doctrine was no longer needed. With the rise of cable television, the government no longer needed to intervene in the broad-

Should a new type of Fairness Doctrine be developed? Why or why not ❓

cast marketplace to ensure balance among the few "scarce" voices. At the heart of this argument was a belief in the value of smaller government and less regulation, the core platform of the Reagan presidency. Even more important, the Fairness Doctrine had seemed to create two different free speech standards. Under the law, print newspapers and magazines did not have to adhere to the Fairness Doctrine. Cable TV companies did not have to adhere to the Fairness Doctrine. The law only applied to TV and radio stations. With the rise of cable television, the law was anticompetitive by restricting one group of media companies but not others.

As media systems change, the law gradually follows suit. The leaders of administrative agencies like the FCC are appointed by the nation's president. When Ronald Reagan appointed Mark Fowler the FCC chairman in 1981, Fowler was a lawyer in private practice who represented many media industry clients subject to FCC regulations. He immediately initiated a rulemaking process that questioned the efficacy of the Fairness Doctrine. Within a very short time the FCC published a report that said the doctrine was no longer in the public interest, was probably unconstitutional, and had *a chilling effect* that limited broadcasters' freedom of expression. The FCC repealed the Fairness Doctrine in 1987, even though most members of Congress supported it.

The repeal of the Fairness Doctrine became an important catalyst for the rise of conservative talk radio and the growing dominance of partisan news and opinion. Rush Limbaugh began his national broadcasts in New York City in 1988 and since then, his favorite topics have been abortion, immigration, feminism, and government regulation. Other conservative talk radio hosts are Michael Savage, Glenn Beck, and Dr. Laura Schlessinger. Thanks to the demise of the Fairness Doctrine, talk radio flourished and Fox News became one of the most influential forms of political media in the United States.

Some people believe that a new version of the Fairness Doctrine could address the problems caused by the weaponization of information and the rise of political propaganda. Because the Supreme Court established that the rights of viewers and listeners to access information supercede the free speech rights of broadcast proprietors, such a law would likely be constitutional. If applied to social media, a new law could establish that "the right of voters to factual information is superior to any right of media companies to profit from fake news clickbait" (Tyler, 2018: 1).

Net Neutrality

The FCC's regulation goes beyond industries such as television and radio. It also regulates telecommunications, cable television, and broadband services. The term *broadband* is used to describe all forms of data transmission where signals are sent and received through wire or wireless media. High-speed Internet access into homes and businesses occurs through broadband services. Regulating competition is needed for services that are so-called natural monopolies, where it is economically inefficient for companies to build parallel systems. Telephone service, which relied on copper wires strung across streets and into homes, was deemed to be a natural monopoly, for example.

The FCC uses *common carrier regulation* for telecommunication services, which requires companies offering their services to the general public to provide services to all customers, without discriminating based on the identity of the customer or the content of the communication.

In 2015, after a long process of public discussion and debate, the FCC reclassified Internet service providers (ISPs) as common carriers, which enabled the official creation of *net neutrality* rules. These rules restricted broadband companies from speeding up or slowing down service or discriminating against some consumers and favoring others.

But only 2 years after its passage, during the Trump administration, the FCC repealed this rule and the Republican-dominated Congress ratified the decision. It is now legal for ISPs to offer "fast lane" service to customers who pay more money for special priority service.

In 2018, California legislators restored net neutrality by passing a law that bans Internet providers from blocking and throttling content or prioritizing some sites and services over others. More than 30 states have introduced similar legislation that would override the FCC decision. This opens up the possibility for Congress to pass legislation that explicitly protects net neutrality in the future.

What are some consequences of offering "fast lane" Internet service to some customers?

Paul Fell/CartoonStock

Do media mergers benefit or harm the public❓

Who now benefits from the repeal of net neutrality? Telecommunications companies like Verizon, AT&T, and Comcast are the obvious winners. They now have the ability to charge websites and digital platforms more for using their network. They can offer enhanced services for those who have the ability to pay more. Even if they do not offer high-speed lanes, these companies might also buy up other media companies that provide content and then deliver those websites at faster speeds while slowing down others.

Media Regulation: Ownership Rules

Issues of media ownership have long been a concern for the American public. Many consumers are frustrated with the costs of broadband, cable, and mobile services. Americans spend about $2,800 per year on entertainment, which adds up to about $840 billion per year. The FCC is responsible for regulating mergers and acquisitions as part of its mission to ensure quality and low-cost services. Under the Trump administration, 2018 was the year of two gigantic media mergers:

- AT&T bought Time Warner, which includes companies like HBO, Turner, and Warner Brothers, in a deal worth $85 billion;

- The Walt Disney Company agreed to a $71.3 billion purchase that gives it the bulk of 21st Century Fox, the largest portion of the Rupert Murdoch media empire. This is the second biggest media merger of all time, after the AOL–Time Warner merger in 2001 for $103 billion.

Proponents of the plan say these mergers are needed in order to address the growing dominance of Facebook, Amazon, Apple, Netflix, and Google (the so-called *FAANG companies*), which have pushed into the entertainment business by attracting ever-larger audiences. The older Hollywood companies feel the need to expand in order to compete with the newer Silicon Valley firms. With the new assets from the merger, Disney now competes with Netflix by offering Disney+, a subscription video-on-demand streaming service.

Should we be concerned about media monopolies? Critics of such mergers warn that decreased competition among film studios will affect the quality of filmmaking overall in the United States. Now that Disney owns 21st Century Fox, it controls more than 40% of all the films distributed in the United States. About 4,000 Fox and Disney employees lost their jobs as a result of the merger.

Platform companies have had amazing profits and have benefited greatly from the absence of government regulation of the Internet. Allowing media companies to merge may help create real competition. But it also may have negative consequences for the diversity and quality of media products and services.

Since the 1990s, Silicon Valley executives have argued that the Internet's growth and development was possible only because it was nearly completely unregulated. But as Google and Facebook have become some of the largest companies in the world, there is a concern that their power has become anticompetitive. In 2019, several states began antitrust investigations on Facebook. *Antitrust laws* emerged 100 years ago after John D. Rockefeller used his railroad monopoly to control and manipulate business markets across the United States. His abuse of power led to the development of laws that "protect liberty and democracy from concentrated economic power, or what Franklin Roosevelt called 'industrial dictatorship'" (Mitchell, 2018: 1).

Many big tech companies now face the threat of antitrust regulation as a result of their anti-competitive business practices. For example, Amazon is being investigated for favoring its own products in algorithmic search results, taking unfair advantage of the data it collects on users. Apple has been accused of prioritizing its own apps at its App Store, abusing its power to harm competitors. Facebook has been accused of buying up its competitors, as when it acquired Instagram for $1 billion in 2012. And Google has been accused of abusing its power by selectively featuring its own products and services. As we learned in Chapter 3, nearly half of all searches begin and end on Google, without users going to another website. Because it handles more than 90% of all searches worldwide, Google's ability to steer users away from some businesses could be considered anticompetitive. In Europe, regulation has already limited the power of these companies through rulings that enforce substantial fines for antitrust and privacy violations (Nicas et al., 2019).

In the current political climate, people may not trust the big tech companies, but they trust Congress even less. Is Congress capable of making laws that are truly responsive to the public interest? Or will its laws offer special protections to big tech firms and help them grow even more powerful? The increasing public distrust of government may actually work to the advantage of platform companies in their quest to avoid regulation.

5 critical questions about taxes paid by tech firms

In this infographic, viewers are invited to consider differences between tech companies and other companies in how they pay taxes. Use five critical questions to analyze this media message and gain insight on its meaning and value.

1. **Who is the author and what is the purpose?**
   This infographic was created by *Esquire* magazine to accompany the article "Silicon Valley's Tax-Avoiding, Job-Killing, Soul-Sucking Machine" by Scott Galloway, published on February 8, 2018. The purpose of this infographic is both informative and persuasive. Because the source of the data is identified as the S&P Global Market Intelligence, we tend to trust the accuracy of the information presented. But the visual design suggests a persuasive goal—the author clearly

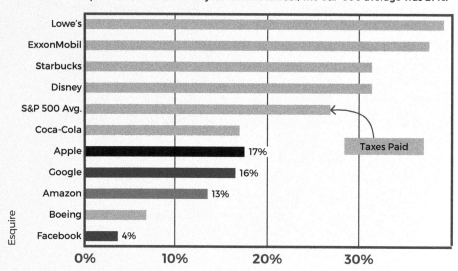

BIG PROFITS, SMALL PAYBACKS

For economies to thrive, companies need to hand over about a quarter of their profits, but the Four are treated differently. Between 2007 and 2015, Amazon paid only 13% in corporate income tax, Apple paid 17%, Google paid 16%, and Facebook just 4%. In contrast, the S&P 500 average was 27%.

SOURCE: S&P Market Intelligence.

wants readers to believe that FAANG companies are not paying their fair share of taxes.

2. **What techniques are used to attract and hold attention?** The headline "Big Profits, Small Paybacks" also features a sentence that calls attention to the percentage of corporate income tax paid by Amazon, Apple, Google, and Facebook, creating a high level of redundancy between the chart and the headline. These companies are even featured visually with the distinctive colors of their logos in the line graph. The highly familiar nontechnology companies (Lowe's, Starbucks, Disney, and others) are presented with the use of white lines, a color traditionally associated with goodness.

3. **What lifestyles, points of view, and values are represented?** The chart quantifies the idea that tech companies are somehow different (and worse) than traditional American businesses. But the inclusion of Boeing, the aerospace company, suggests that tax avoidance may be a larger problem among American corporations.

4. **How might different people interpret this message?** Most people understand that taxes pay for shared services essential for modern society. Some will see the technology companies as "cheating" by not paying their fair share. Other people may not believe that paying federal taxes is a good thing. For example, when President Trump refused to release his tax returns when running for president, he said, "That makes me smart." Because some people have warm and fuzzy positive feelings about Apple, Google, Amazon, and Facebook, they may experience confirmation bias in viewing this chart, resisting new information that contradicts their existing beliefs.

5. **What is omitted?** The chart does not explain why big differences exist between these companies in the amount of taxes they pay. The strategic decision to include mostly companies that pay around 25% creates a bias that makes it seem like tech companies are outliers by paying less. Although the headline reads "Big Profits," this chart omits information about the actual profitability of these companies. However, in the article accompanying the graphic, the author points out that Apple uses an accounting trick to avoid paying corporate taxes on its profits: it moves its profits to Ireland, holding billions of dollars overseas. The author also notes that General Electric pays little in corporate taxes. By exploiting complex tax loopholes to pay less in U.S. corporate taxes, American corporations make more profit for global shareholders.

What the future may hold: The Amazon Monopoly

Amazon sells virtually everything under the sun, but it also produces hit television shows and movies, publishes books, designs digital devices, and operates the world's largest streaming video game platform. The company also dominates the online services business, controlling one-third of all cloud-computing services through Amazon Web Services.

Amazon has become so important that it can set terms that other companies must adhere to and charge fees to be included on its platform. According to one critic, the world is "moving us away from a democratic political economy, in which commerce takes place in open markets governed by public rules, and toward a future in which the exchange of goods occurs in a private arena governed by Amazon" (Mitchell, 2018: 1).

Jeff Bezos, the founder of Amazon, is the richest person in the world. Because he owns Amazon, Twitter, Alexa, Twitch, Audible, and the *Washington Post*, he is a media mogul, but the scope of his enterprises goes far beyond media. In fact, when he bought the *Washington Post* for $250 million, it seemed like an unlikely business deal. In 2014, the business model for journalism looked on the verge of collapse. But since then, thanks to the very newsworthy election of President Donald Trump, the *Washington Post* has doubled the number of digital subscriptions and increased online traffic and advertising revenue. But the employees who contributed to the company's success have not seen improvement in wages, benefits or retirement, family leave, or health care. Billionaires like Jeff Bezos are not buying newspapers as an act of charity. Rather, they want to influence political discourse and public policy (Gelles, 2018).

As demonstrated in this chapter, a media-literate citizen will need to have a strong understanding of the political economy of this rapidly changing media and technology environment in order to participate in public discussion about the best approach to balancing private and public interests.

TIME T🧠 REFLECT

With a discussion partner, consider the advantages and disadvantages of the three different revenue models explored in this chapter.

As you analyze these different economic models, be sure to consider the different points of view of the media creator, the consumer, and the society as a whole.

After discussion and analysis, reflect on what you have learned about media economics by considering these questions as you plan a Flipgrid response:

- What are the advantages and disadvantages of the different ways of paying for mass and digital media?
- Which approaches are best and worst for creators, consumers, and society as a whole?
- If you could change something about how you pay for media, what would it be?

Use the Flipgrid Inquiry to contribute your ideas in a brief oral presentation. You can also view and respond to comments of other people who have offered thoughtful reflections on the topic of media economics. Visit www.medialiteracyaction.com to learn more.

CREATE T⊙ LEARN

Compare and Contrast Information Sources about a Media Company

Select a media or technology company of interest to you. It might be a company whose products and services you use every day or a company that you have acquired an interest in as a result of reading this book. Use the Internet to find two different types of sources:

- The company's annual report, which is how the company describes its successes to its stockholders
- At least three independent news stories about the company over the same 12-month period as the annual report

Construct a Venn diagram using PowerPoint or another digital tool to compare and contrast the information sources by considering these questions:

- What key ideas and information are presented in both the annual report and news coverage?
- What information and stories were presented in news media that were not highly visible in the annual report?
- What information was presented in the annual report that was not in news coverage?

You can post using the #MLAction hashtag to share your published work with a global community of media literacy learners.

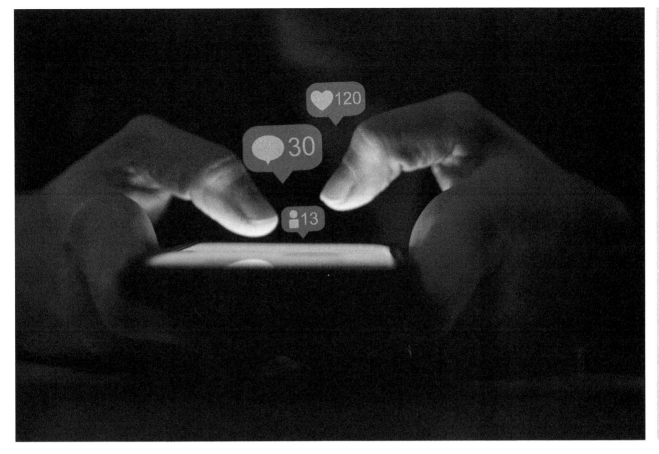

Social media platforms profit from users who create and share content

Are Social Media Free?

11

Learning Outcomes

1. Gain knowledge about why and how people freely share photos, information, and aspects of their personal identity using a variety of social media platforms

2. Consider the negotiated balance of power between social media platforms and their users

3. Examine how social media companies harvest, use, and profit from monitoring the behavior of users

4. Understand the legal frameworks that protect social media and reflect on potential changes to social networks that might affect how people use them.

IT IS OFFICIAL. IT WAS EVEN ON THE NEWS. FACEBOOK WILL START CHARGING DUE TO THE NEW PROFILE CHANGES. IF YOU COPY THIS ON YOUR WALL YOUR ICON WILL TURN BLUE AND ... ... FACEBOOK WILL BE FREE FOR YOU. PLEASE PASS THIS MESSAGE ON, IF NOT YOUR ACCOUNT WILL BE DELETED IF YOU DO NOT PAY

Share · 2 minutes ago via BlackBerry · 🌐

Sarah saw the post sometime in 2011. It read: "What are the advantages of a Facebook Gold Account?" She wondered, because as a frequent flyer, she had once or twice received an upgrade to a business-class seat, with free drinks and more legroom. During this time, Facebook had been making changes to the design of its navigation bar, the display of profiles and notifications, so Sarah thought this could be something she needed to check out. As an active Facebook user with more than 600 friends, she felt it might be worthwhile to get a Facebook Gold Account. After all, was she not hearing on the news that Facebook was going public and selling shares on Wall Street?

More of Sarah's Facebook friends also began wondering when Facebook would begin to charge a fee to use the service. But the Facebook Gold Account was a *hoax*—and only one of many. In 2018, some WhatsApp users were offered WhatsApp Gold, with a range of extra features for the platform. But when users tried to claim the service, they were directed to malicious websites that would take over, disable, or deliver viruses to their mobile phones. In responding to the hoax, Facebook simply said, "We have no plans to charge for Facebook. It's free and always will be."

Facebook is one of the top five companies in the world, according to the Fortune 500 list of the most valuable companies. It had 2.4 billion monthly active users as of 2020, 85% of them from outside the United States. More than 1.5 billion log in to Facebook every day, and the most common demographic is female users between the ages of 25 and 34. The company was valued at $630 billion in December 2019. Others on the list include Apple (valued at $1 trillion), Amazon (valued at $930 billion), Google/Alphabet (valued at $ trillion), and Microsoft (valued at $1 trillion). As we learned in Chapter 10, advertisers and other companies pay to gain access to Facebook users because they value the ability to use online behavioral data to predict people's future actions.

In this chapter, you will lern about important issues related to social media and human freedom:

- How do your feelings about privacy affect your social media sharing?

- Are your information and photos, once you have posted them on Facebook, free for others to use?

- Is Facebook free, as a company, to sell your information to anyone it wants?

As you explore these questions, you face key issues regarding the future of social media. You will consider whether social media platforms are (or are not) publishers and how they should (or should not) be regulated. You will discover how much freedom people actually have when using other people's information and creative work they find online, especially considering copyright and other intellectual property regulations. Finally, we examine the changing regulatory environment for social media in response to concerns about surveillance and social control.

How do you express your identity through social media?

Digital Identity in Social Context

People share content online as an expression of self and identity. As social beings, we care about what others think and feel about us. Even the word *identity* has its roots in the dialectic between standing out and fitting in: the Latin root *idem* means "the same."

Identity is a very personal issue. As David Buckingham has noted, identity can be a struggle for self-determination that requires individuals to be self-reflexive in making decisions about "what they should do and who they should be" (2008: 9).

Social media platforms offer many *affordances* when it comes to expressing your identity in social relationships. When you share content that others like or value, you gain status as members of a group. For people of all ages but especially during the teen and young adult years, online communication can increase their sense of belonging by supporting the ability to engage in *self-disclosure*, which is the ability to reveal aspects of personal identity to others.

The typical Internet user spends nearly 1 hour per day with Facebook, Instagram, and Snap, as Figure 11.1 shows. Most research on adolescent online communication shows that casual exchanges between friends have a positive effect on the quality of the friendship. Sharing a joke, commenting on a photo, or asking a question can activate feelings of emotional connectedness. Researchers have found that sharing YouTube videos and playfully commenting on them is another activity used to cement friendship bonds. For many, "Facebook has expanded their sphere of connections, providing them with new opportunities to experience a sense of belonging and validation from their peers" (Davis, 2012: 1534).

Figure 11.1
Social Media Use by Android Users, in Minutes Per Day

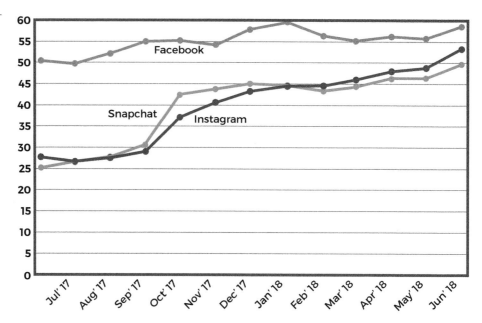

SOURCE: Recode / Similar Web

The strong feelings of peer group loyalty that emerge online may also explain why some people share false and inaccurate content, even defending such content against critics. Notes Siva Vaidhyanathan, "When we post and share demonstrably false stories and claims, we do so to declare our affiliation, to assert that our social bonds mean more to us than the question of truth" (2018: 51). The *social validation* people experience when using social media is powerfully compelling, providing them with a thrilling combination of social power and pleasure.

Today, anyone can create and share any content online, and this brings a fascinating tension between the private and the public into people's daily lives. If you publish content to your Twitter account, you can see how many people actually find and read it. Data analytics allows the precise measurement of *impressions*, the number of people who have seen a digital message.

Some users are unaware of their actual audience when they use social media while other users are hyperaware of how many likes and clicks they receive. Some people use social media as a personal diary, recording their funny experiences or fleeting feelings. Others make strategic choices, posting content for an audience that may include friends but also acquaintances and other people they do not know. For these reasons, many social media users face the *visibility–obscurity continuum*, the relative position of one's personal identity on a spectrum from public to private. On social media, many people want both visibility and obscurity. They want to be seen—but they also like the feeling of being unknown. As Baym and boyd (2012: 325) explain it, "As people communicate publically through social media, they become more aware of themselves relative to visible and imagined audiences and more aware of the larger publics to which they belong and which they seek to create."

In their shift away from the risks of a public online life, some young people rely on text messaging or use *peer-to-peer platforms* like Snap, WeChat, or WhatsApp. In these types of social media, users share text messages, photos, or other digital content with individuals or a small group. Other people may prefer to interact with like-minded people using Facebook's closed and secret groups. Closed groups are searchable online; secret groups are invisible to all except those who receive an invitation from another member.

Privacy decisions occur in a variety of contexts and can have a range of beneficial and harmful functions. Across the lifespan, people make decisions about privacy. Young parents make privacy decisions on behalf of their babies when they decide what images and stories are appropriate to share online. As a form of *privacy stewardship*, parents may create private groups for sharing baby milestones, photos, and other content with family and friends. Older parents experiencing deaths in the family or other trauma may find it valuable to share feelings with others using a private or closed group. For example, a grieving mother may belong to a Facebook group like After the Storm—Grief Recovery after Addiction Loss. When people can express themselves with others who have had similiar life experiences, bonds of trust and respect may emerge (Kumar & Schoenebeck, 2015).

While private groups can be used to protect privacy, they can also be used to promote unhealthy behavior. When Instagram banned hashtags like #thinspiration and #loseweight from its social networks, it did not stop the sharing of images, recipes, and strategies for reducing food intake in unhealthy ways. The medical community has recognized the dangers of exposure to online content that glorifies eating disorders like anorexia or bulimia. In one study, researchers found that that girls with no history of eating disorders decreased their caloric intake after being exposed to pro-eating disorder sites for just 90 minutes (Jett & LaPorte, 2010).

Have you experienced how peer-to-peer platforms be used to promote unhealthy or dangerous behavior?

Private groups also enable the spread of misogny, racism, and hate. Consider the case of the private group of 30,000 male Marines who created a private Facebook page to share revenge porn that included 2,500 photos of women taken without their knowledge along with lewd comments about female Marine colleagues. After this private Facebook page was discovered, more than 100 Marines were investigated and seven were court-martialed (Roose, 2018).

Help Us Understand What's Happening   ✕

What's wrong with this group?

- It's harassing me
- It's harassing a friend
- Sexually explicit content
- Spam or a scam
- Violence or harmful behavior
- Hate speech
- It's for selling drugs, guns or other regulated goods
- I think it's an unauthorized use of my intellectual property

Continue

After conspiracy theorist Alex Jones was suspended from Facebook, a private group with more than 100,000 followers continued to discuss conspiracy theories and engage in hate speech. Such online groups can be an incubator for hateful behavior.

It turns out that the quality of online social connections can have implications for offline relationships. Sociologist Robert Putnam distinguishes between two types of social capital that affect both individuals and society. *Bonding* social capital is when people make social connections within a homogenous group, a practice that supports feelings of support and solidarity. *Bridging* social capital is created when people make connections with more diverse groups. Bridging is important because it helps people expand their horizons and creates trust. As Rangappa (2017) notes, "When people connect on Facebook, they are mostly connecting with others who have similar political beliefs, educational backgrounds, and religious outlooks." If most of your positive social interactions are occurring more with people you already agree with, you may not get much practice to develop the skills required to interact with people whose worldviews and life experiences are different from your own.

Feeling Free

People feel free to express themselves online because the perceived anonymity and invisibility of the medium combines with feelings of social power and pleasure. Perhaps you have experienced intimate, intense, or unusual experiences online—or perhaps you have read about stuff that has happened to others. Perhaps you have encountered online content that you wish you had not seen. This is because people can say and do the strangest things online. No doubt about it: truly depraved ideas, photos, videos, and weird stuff appear online. There are users and channels devoted to finding the creepiest stuff you could ever imagine.

What makes people feel so free to post and share this stuff? The *online disinhibition effect* (ODE) is the lack of restraint one feels when communicating online in comparison to communicating in person. These distorted beliefs can shape a person's behavior:

- **Anonymity**: My actions cannot be directly linked to me;
- **Invisibility**: Nobody can see or judge me;
- **Asynchronicity**: My actions are recordings and do not occur in real time;
- **Solipsistic introjection**: These interactions with other people are all in my head;
- **Dissociative imagination**: These are not real people. It is the Internet, not real life;
- **Minimizing authority**: I cannot get in trouble from my online activities.

If you have ever been the victim of cyberbullying, you know that real harms can come from behavior enacted through text messages, videos, or social media. Fortunately, in most states, people can be held criminally liable for their online speech and actions including stalking, harassment, and bullying.

For most people, the sense of feeling free can be both positive and negative. Many people have actually experienced important positive outcomes from the online disinhibition effect. They have had meaningful, open, and honest conversations about complex and often taboo topics, like self-harm, alcohol or drug use, suicide, or sexual identity. When some people report they can truly be themselves online, it can lead to meaningful relationships that add value to human experience. As the cyberpsychologist John Suler puts it, "If the online disinhibition effect tells us anything, it's that personal identity is complex, expressing itself in different ways under different conditions. No one part of the self is more true than another" (Suler, 2016: 1).

Creating and Sharing Content

People have been creating media content since time immemorial. For thousands of years, writers, poets, novelists, essayists, photographers, and filmmakers have engaged in creative expression—but their work was once largely unseen by any outside a small group. Only a minuscule proportion of people ever saw their work distributed to large audiences. During the 20th century, the rise of mass media led many forms of creative media production to become professionalized. This resulted in increased interest in careers in publishing, film, and media. As soon as the Internet was invented, people started sharing their writing, photos, and other creative work online.

Economists knew that the Internet would affect the economic value of creative work, and they predicted that more easy access to information and creative expression would lead to the democratization of knowledge.

What is the value of the content that you share using social media?

The rise of digital platforms like Facebook, Google, Instagram, and YouTube has enabled the supply of content and its distribution to the end user to be located in one place. But as we learned in Chapter 10, this also monopolizes advertising money, giving platforms enormous political and cultural power. For example, Google and Facebook now receive 50% of all of the world's advertising spending. But digital platforms may also provide new opportunities on which entrepreneurs can build (World Economic Forum, 2016).

iStock

By the early 2000s, the term *user-generated content* (UGC) was employed to describe the works created and shared by people uploading images, videos, text, and audio, using platforms and services to store this content. Social media platforms like YouTube and Facebook also made this content more findable and easy to share.

User-generated content shifts power away from traditional editorial gatekeepers like book publishers, broadcast journalists, and newspaper editors, who carefully reviewed and approved content before it was aired or published. Companies quickly discovered that user-generated content is more effective for advertising than their own branded content. For example, the British ice cream company Magnum reviews thousands of Instagram posts of its products and studies *social media metrics*. This is the term used for patterns of data that reveal how content is used. This helps marketers to decide which images will best increase the visibility of the brand (Hudson, 2017).

Social media has led to many important changes in how people communicate with each other. Writer Helena Fitzgerald recalls her experience using LiveJournal, a blogging site popular in the early 2000s.

> When I made my own humiliatingly verbose and confessional posts, I never imagined the audience to be the few real-life friends who also used the website. I was often embarrassed or even annoyed when these friends referenced those posts in offline conversations. What I loved about LiveJournal, in my early online days, was that it felt like a public space in which I got to talk to no one, a place where I could yell into the void. Putting any part of one's self online is always a cry for attention to some degree, but sometimes, against all logic, the desire is just as much for the opposite. I want to confess things out loud and be ignored. I want to say the things I can only say if I believe that I am nowhere.

When *Time* magazine named "You" as its Person of the Year in 2006, it emphasized the radical shift in *digital authorship* taking place as ordinary people produced entertainment, information, and persuasion for themselves, each other, and no one.

Remix, Copyright, and Fair Use

Today, the products of our culture are available at the click of a mouse or the swipe of a finger. We can easily copy, cut, paste, and combine images, videos, sounds, and texts to create various new forms of expression and communication. Remix genres have long been practiced in forms including music sampling, film remakes, magazine image collages, and music mashups. Figure 11.2 shows a sample of remix art created by the Illegal Art collective. It is a group of artists who create participatory-based public art to inspire self-reflection, thought, and human connection. Each piece is presented or distributed in a method in which public participation is simple and encouraged.

Figure 11.2
Illegal Art Collective

Why do people use, combine, and remix the creative works of others?

The term *remix* has been used in different ways in just the past 50 years. Back in the 1980s, the term was associated with fixing music through electronic manipulation. Then DJs began creatively combining sounds from different musical and sound sources as dance music and hip-hop moved into mainstream contemporary music. In the early 1990s, people used the term remix in relation to music sampling, and this is the first time that the legality of remix was brought into question (Borschke, 2011). By the late 1990s, the term *remix culture* was applied to the dance club or rave, where popular culture images and music were creatively combined as art, entertainment, and social commentary.

Media literacy activists pioneered the use of remix as early as 1991 when San Francisco video editor Phil Patiris created *The Iraq Campaign*. This 18-minute video weaves together clips from *Star Trek*, the science fiction film *Dune*, sports coverage, and news coverage of Project Desert Storm, the name given to the First Gulf War, into a devastating critique of the *media-industrial complex*. Expressing ideas using skillful juxtaposition and no narration, Patiris offers a

The Iraq Campaign 1991: A Television History - by Phil Patiris (1991)

3,430 views • Sep 7, 2011   👍 49 👎 1 ➤ SHARE ≡+ SAVE ...

Why is creative work that comments or critiques culture so important for individuals and society?

compelling critique of media culture through remix. Media literacy educators made active use of this video and others like it to teach about media culture.

Well before the origins of YouTube, film and video makers were creating works that appropriated mass media audiovisual source material without permission from copyright holders. These works were generally distributed by VHS tape, underground screenings, and, eventually, self-hosted websites. By explicitly commenting on, deconstructing, or challenging "media narratives, dominant myths, social norms, and traditional power structures," these videos helped to model the critical analysis of media, sometimes in ways that could be "either sympathetic to or antagonistic to their pop culture sources, sometimes both at the same time" (McIntosh, 2012: 1).

Thus, remix developed into an art form that often had a critical and even subversive edge. By 2005, the term began to be used to describe the work of video editors who remade movie trailers in humorous or bizarre reconfigurations. One example, called *Scary Mary*, re-edits scenes from the 1964 Disney fantasy musical *Mary Poppins* as a horror story, complete with terrifying music and jump scares. Such works create alternative meanings with purposes very different than the original work (Dusi, 2017).

The practice of remix reflects a deep appreciation of how reliant creative individuals are upon the preexisting works of culture available to them. Thus, it is likely that remix will continue to be an important part of the creative process even as the media and cultural environment changes.

Copyright law offers strong protections to creative people, users, and platforms. Platforms have the legal right to decide what content to show and what content to hide. Their editorial decisions, informed by algorithms, are protected under the First Amendment.

As a creative person, you are a direct beneficiary of copyright law because your course notes, your music lyrics, doodles, and drawings, your academic papers, your poems, your photos and text messages are all copyrighted automatically at the point of creation. You do not have to fill out any forms or pay any fees. As soon as you create content in a fixed and tangible form, you are entitled to the long and strong protections of copyright. *Copyright law* grants you the right to copy, display, perform, distribute, and make derivative works of your creative work. You can charge license fees to give others permission to use your work in limited ways. American copyright law offers the strongest intellectual property protections in the world. Your own creative work is protected by copyright, which gives you control over how the work is shared and copied. This means that you can choose to give your poems away for free, publish them in a book that people pay to access, or make them available to musical composers for a license fee.

Copyright Law Balances Rights of Owners and Users

OWNERS   USERS

Why is the balance of rights between copyright owners and users so important for individuals and society?

Even when you put your photos online, they are still protected by copyright. This protection—the ability to control the distribution of creative work—ensures that copyright fulfills its constitutional purpose: to support the growth of knowledge, creativity, and innovation.

To facilitate sharing, creative people can use a *Creative Commons license* to indicate their willingness to have other people share, repurpose, or use their work without payment. Other licensing schemes can also allow copyright holders to make money from their creative work (Aufderheide & Jaszi, 2018).

Copyright law does not just project owners. Users of copyrighted content are also protected by copyright law. Copyright law balances the rights of owners and users. After all, if owners could control access to all content, they could lock up information and ideas in ways that would violate the First Amendment. Copyright law cannot interfere with freedom of expression. To make this possible, the law gives users a number of important protections, but the most important one is Section 107, the *doctrine of fair use*. This part of copyright law specifies that, under some conditions, users can use copyrighted materials without payment or permission, when the social benefit that results is greater than the harm to the copyright owner.

Digital platforms like Facebook, Twitter, and YouTube are also protected by copyright law. When Congress passed the *1998 Digital Millennium Copyright Act* (DMCA), no one could fully appreciate how the law would affect the development of the Internet and the explosion of the blogs, search engines, video sharing, social media platforms, and apps we take for granted today. The DMCA was originally designed to ensure that U.S. law complied with aspects of an international copyright treaty. Internet companies asked Congress for protection from the possible intellectual property violations of their users (Band, Butler & Morris, 2018). For example, if someone uploaded a digitized episode of the TV series *Star Trek* to YouTube, YouTube wanted to be free from liability in case the owners of the intellectual property decided to sue.

Section 512 of the DMCA says that digital platforms cannot be sued for the intellectual property violations of their users if they use a *notice-and-take-down provision*. Platforms get immunity for any copyright infringement by their users if they agree to promptly remove material if the copyright holder sends a takedown notice. The company can restore the content if the user certifies that it is a non-infringing fair use and the copyright claimant fails to sue. By protecting platform companies from lawsuits, the U.S. government has provided them with a tremendous business advantage that traditional media companies (like publishers) do not have.

How much freedom do you have to use other people's creative materials that you find on Facebook or another social media platform? Users have many rights to access copyrighted content without permission or payment. When a library buys a book, it can legally loan it to you and you can legally make a photocopy of portions of it for your own research and study purposes. The 1976 Copyright Law carves out an exemption to the long and strong protections of copyright law. It says: "the fair use of a copyrighted work, including such use by reproduction in copies [...], for purposes such as criticism, comment, news reporting, teaching [...], scholarship, or research" is not considered an infringement. Fair use provides the balance between the rights of creative people (copyright owners) and those who use and build upon their work (users) to develop new expressions, ideas, and information (Aufderheide & Jaszi, 2018).

Courts examine the facts of each particular case and weigh and balance the following four factors to determine whether the particular challenged activities constitute fair use or infringement:

1. the purpose and character of the use, including whether such use is of a commercial nature or is for nonprofit educational purposes;
2. the nature of the copyrighted work;
3. the amount and substantiality of the portion used in relation to the copyrighted work as a whole; and
4. the effect of the use upon the potential market for or value of the copyrighted work.

Each factor is analyzed individually and then balanced with the others. If someone's use of your copyrighted work merely retransmits the work, it may affect the potential market and limit your ability to profit from your creative work (Hobbs, 2010b). This is a copyright violation, and creative people who find others using their work this way can file a *cease-and-desist letter* and initiate a copyright lawsuit. If you make an amateur music video by using a whole pop song from Beyoncé without buying a license, you may be violating copyright and face substantial legal and financial risk.

But many times when a creative person uses other people's work to create a new work, it may lead to the development of a wholly new form of media.

The new work may then be called *transformative*. Transformative work is not merely retransmitting the original copyrighted content. Instead, the use of copyrighted materials in a creative way has altered the original copyrighted material with new expression, meaning, or message (Tushnet, 2018b).

Courts have recognized that transformative use of copyrighted materials contributes to the spread of knowledge and innovation. The more transformative the new work, the more likely it is that fair use will apply. Today, you can confidently use copyrighted content in your own creative work. To make a fair use determination, simply ask yourself:

- Was your use of the copyrighted material for a different purpose than that of the original? Did you add value?
- Are you primarily retransmitting the original for the same purpose and for the same audience? If you are, this is probably not a fair use.
- Was the amount of material taken appropriate to the purpose of the use? Did you use only the amount you absolutely need to accomplish your purpose?

In their book *Reclaiming Fair Use*, Pat Aufderheide and Peter Jaszi note that the vast majority of fair uses are never challenged. But when they are, "juries have overwhelmingly rejected claims of infringement and supported fair users when they carefully employed this reasoning to make their decisions" (2018: 25)

Algorithms of Emotion for Surveillance Capitalism

Social media use can affect people's emotional health: it can help people feel supported and loved by family and friends. But it can also make them feel worse about themselves. You are not alone if you have noticed that sometimes social media platforms leave you feeling bitter and resentful. Seeing all those positive, beautiful images and relationships and stories about the great things happening in other people's lives may leave people feeling even more unsatisfied with their own lives. This is part of *social comparison theory*, which suggests that individuals determine their self-worth by comparing themselves to others.

When you compare yourself downward, you might end up feeling superior to others. When you compare yourself upward, you might end up feeling inferior. People who regularly compare themselves upward often experience negative feelings of dissatisfaction and may engage in self-destructive behaviors, including disordered eating (Gerber, Wheeler & Suls, 2018).

In their quest to get people to spend more time on Facebook and Instagram, company researchers explored the question of whether seeing friends' positive content makes other users sad or depressed. This is an effect called *emotional contagion*, and the term refers to the idea that emotional states can be transferred from person to person. Facebook researchers manipulated the positive and negative content of nearly 700,000 users' News

© Danah Boyd

Intellectual Grandparent:
danah boyd

She is determined to both empower and protect people living their lives online.

With expertise in computer science, media, and communications, danah boyd (she uses lower case to spell her first and last name) is a principal researcher at Microsoft Research and a fellow at Harvard's Berkman Center for Internet and Society. She founded the Data & Society Research Institute in New York City. Boyd has two decades studying how teens use social media. Her most well known article, entitled "Why Youth (Heart) Social Network Sites" (2008), examines how social media platforms like MySpace serve as places to gather and see and be seen by peers. Some key ideas include:

Teens use social media to explore issues of identity. During adolescence, risk-taking is a part of natural human development—through it, teens build cultural knowledge about people (and the world outside their family). In dana boyd's book *It's Complicated* (2016), she describes a practice she calls *social steganography,* the act of hiding information in plain sight. Teens sometimes create messages that can be understood differently by different target audiences. Teens learn to communicate through exploiting people's familiarity with cultural referents, as when they post a fragment of a music lyric, a meme, or a line of dialogue from a film or TV show. Only people who possess specific cultural knowledge will understand the meaning. Boyd has observed that teens whose parents use social media have even developed new techniques to speak with friends knowing that their parents are overhearing. By using social media, teens experiment with communication and action as a form of social power.

Social media amplifies marginal voices. In turning her attention to so-called fake news, big data,

Feeds for 1 week in January 2012 to see what effect the changes had on the tone of the recipients' posts. When people use Facebook, they typically see more than 1,500 posts, but Facebook selects only about 300 for people to view using an algorithm that includes a number of variables. Facebook found that when people see negative, sad, or depressing content from their Facebook friends, the words in their own posts become more negative. When they see positive and happy posts from friends, the words they use in their own posts become more positive (Goel, 2014).

Concerns about Facebook's growing power and influence led members of Congress to want to learn more about Facebook's business model. Is Facebook free, as a company, to sell user information to anyone who wants it? At a House judiciary hearing in 2018, Mark Zuckerberg was asked this question dozens of times. Over and over, he emphasized the point that Facebook does not sell data to third-party vendors like advertisers or other businesses. "We don't sell data to anyone," he said.

While this is technically correct, it is also quite misleading. Facebook is not selling users' private data on an open market. Instead, it is selling its ability

privacy, and misinformation, boyd demonstrates that manipulating the information ecosystem turns out to be surprisingly easy to do. She identifies how a network of people, working together, can create fake accounts that they use to subtly influence journalists and other powerful actors to pay attention to certain ideas and content. This is a coordinated effort to amplify certain ideas and, in the process, make them seem more acceptable and normal, shifting the *Overton window* to increase the range of topics that are acceptable to discuss in public (boyd, 2017). The technique can be used for a variety of purposes. For example, topics like gay marriage, white supremacy, and racial hatred were all once considered unacceptable but now are part of mainstream public discourse.

The public can hold social media providers accountable. Because the general public treats the Internet as something magical, and Internet entrepreneurs keep delivering free services that keep users ever more attached to their screens, it has been difficult to figure out how to critically analyze platforms, apps, and services. But people can learn to think more about their social, legal, and economic responsibilities in creating, developing and using digital technologies. She was among the earliest media literacy advocates to emphasize that people need to understand how platforms are designed to collect, aggregate and use data by shaping human behavior in particular ways. She notes, "The more that people can understand how data operates in a networked society, the more that we can have a meaningful conversation about trust. And the more that people can start asking questions of the services they are using in order to hold those services accountable" (HASTAC, 2014).

If danah boyd has influenced your thinking about media, you can share a comment on the Grandparents of Media Literacy website at www.grandparentsofmedialiteracy.com.

to predict your behavior based on the data it collects from you. This concept has been called *surveillance capitalism*. The data users provide to Facebook when using the platform is the primary source of its extreme wealth. As we learned in Chapter 10, user attention is sold to advertisers based on specific characteristics that go far beyond demographic variables like age, race, occupation, and geographic location. Now advertisers may target you if you like classical music, have bought a new car, or just got married. Facebook can even use the data it collects to identify your personality and emotional moods, enabling advertisers to target you with messages that align with your inner mental state.

The dynamic, real-time data that Facebook collects from you is key to the company's profitability (Rogers, 2018). For years, no one really knew what kind of data Facebook collected or how it used those data to sell audiences to advertisers. Then, in 2014, Facebook opened up access to the data it had been collecting about individual users. The company expected that giving users a bit more control over their data would make people less likely to be afraid or even shocked. They hope that Facebook ads will be perceived as valuable and useful since they are so closely targeted to people's lifestyles and values.

iStock

What are the pros and cons of data surveillance for individuals and society ?

Here is a small sample of the data that both Google and Facebook collect and store about you to predict your future behavior:

- Physical location, now and at any point in the past;
- Travel habits;
- Political leanings;
- The content of every YouTube video that you have ever viewed;
- The URL of every website that you have ever visited;
- All the apps that you have ever used;
- Documents, files, and other information that you have deleted from Google Drive;
- Every ad that you have ever clicked on;
- Any content that you have liked or shared with your social network;
- The content of every photo that you have ever uploaded;
- If a you wear a Fitbit tracker, details of your exercise routine, heart rate, and other biodata.

Europeans worry most about the loss of personal autonomy that may result when Google, Amazon, and Apple "use their wealth of data and control over cutting-edge technology" to control users' attention. Given the history of Nazi and Communist regimes and their abuse of data and surveillance to control people during the 20th century, European concerns about data privacy are high. As Dutch researchers Moeller and Helberger (2015) point out, Europeans are most concerned about "the creation of new digital inequalities as a result of the different ways in which users use, and are used by the Internet" (p. 26).

Data surveillance gives social media companies the power to shape people's information and knowledge in ways that influence public opinion. Where this gets especially problematic is when such data are used to sell political candidates to the public. Many people are concerned about the impact of social media data on the political process. During the Obama reelection campaign of 2012, media reporters described it in glowing terms (Vaidhyanathan, 2018). But immediately after the presidential election of 2016, journalists uncovered the work of a political campaign company,

Cambridge Analytica. This company was granted access to large volumes of Facebook data from more than 85 million users, creating psychographic profiles in order to target people with customized digital ads and other information to try to influence their decision to vote in the 2016 election.

After the Trump election, critics have compared the use of big data in politics to a form of mind control, with social media manipulating the unconscious mind through microtargeted ads, *autoplay plugins*, and other strategies designed to induce addictive behavior (Ienca & Vayena, 2018). It now seems possible to manipulate social media in ways that reduce the space for authentic debate and the robust interchange of ideas.

To solve this problem, some have called for social media companies to be treated as *information fiduciaries*, a term that would legally mandate these corporations to act in the best interest of the people whose data they have collected. As Vaidhyanathan explains, "If Facebook were required by law to consider us clients instead of (or in addition to) products to be sold, it would have to generate clear, public, enforceable protections against political and other sorts of manipulation" (2018: 67).

Carole Cadwalladr @carolecadwalla

If you are watching the Cambridge Analytica story unfold, please please support our journalism. We've fought off 3 legal threats from CA & 1 from Facebook. It's a whole year's work & we gave it to @Channel4News & @nytimes for the greater good. We need you!support.theguardian.com

♡ 54.4K   10:30 PM - Mar 19, 2018

© Twitter, Inc

How should tech companies be regulated?

Consider the Question

Working with a partner, discuss these two claims and then express your position using reasoning and evidence.

- Facebook emotional contagion experiments are unethical, manipulative, and potentially dangerous to the public.
- Facebook uses emotional contagion experiments for good purposes to improve its products through research and development.

mr.jahko
Jahkori

karmachibana
カルマ・チバナ

the.marchie
Madison Archibald

mvpuniversity
MVPCC

mediawise ✓
MediaWise

thinkfirstnews
ThinkFirst News

txwatson
T.X. Watson

dav1dhatesyou
david

vishuddhadass
Vishuddha Das

How could European data privacy laws affect Americans ❓

Terms of Service

We have all done it: when downloading a new app, you are presented with an online privacy policy or other legal-type agreement. You immediately scroll down to the bottom and click "I agree" without ever reading it.

Accepting *terms of service* and privacy policies is a prerequisite for using most online services. These are sometimes called end-user license agreements (EULAs). These are based on a *notice-and-choice* model, where websites, apps, or online services provide users with disclosure about their data collection, sharing, and security practices. Such information is designed to empower individuals to make choices with respect to whether and how they will use the service.

But do you really have choice? Some policies are written in legalese, a jargon-filled document that ordinary users cannot understand. Other policies are written so vaguely that users cannot identify specific data-harvesting practices that might be in use.

Are such policies legally enforceable when most people do not actually read them? Some judges have viewed privacy policies as general statements of policy rather than enforceable contracts. But when users are presented with an "I agree" statement to click on. These policies are considered enforceable, even when users have not read the terms (Norton, 2016).

In Europe, substantial efforts to educate the public about their privacy rights and responsibilities are under way. Beginning in the fall of 2018, anyone residing in the 28 states of the European Union began seeing this notice (or something like it) on every website they visited:

> We and our partners use cookies on this site to improve our service, perform analytics, personalize advertising, measure advertising performance, and remember website preferences. By using the site, you consent to these cookies. For more information on cookies including how to manage your consent visit our cookie policy

What are *cookies?* They are small text files that a website stores on your computer or mobile device to make websites work more efficiently by saving your preferences. They are also used to follow your Internet use as you browse. This enables the creation of user profiles that permit the display of targeted online advertising.

In Europe, the *General Data Protection Regulation* (GDPR) guarantees the protection of personal data for all who reside in the member countries of the European Union. The rules apply to any individual or organization that offers goods or services in the European Union, including Facebook and Amazon. These rules also apply to the information you supply when filling out a job application, establishing a bank account, or surfing the Internet. The law mandates that you sign a consent form or select "yes" from a clear yes/no option on a Web page. This is called *opt-in* decision-making, and it has the advantage of continually reminding users that they are sharing data when they use the Internet.

One unique feature of the GDPR is the *right to be forgotten*. In the European Union, you can request access to the personal data a company or organization has about you, and you have the right to get a copy of your data, free of charge, in an accessible format. If you choose, you can ask for your data to be erased. With Google, for example, European users can ask for links to Web pages including their name to be removed from search engine results.

European laws have an impact on Google users around the world. Before the GDPR was passed, Google used the content of people's emails to make decisions about what types of ads to show them. Google has now stopped that practice, perhaps as a result of this new law (Tiku, 2018). Time will tell whether this and other laws will help change the economics of the industry in ways that alter the financial incentives that encourage companies to collect and monetize data from users.

Platform or Publisher?

The question of whether Facebook, Twitter, and Google are publishers or platforms has become a more important issue since the summer of 2018, when Congress got involved in examining the so-called fake news problem through hearings held by the House Judiciary Committee, where Mark Zuckerberg was asked to testify.

Most people know that, just as the government cannot tell a broadcaster like Fox News what content to air, they cannot tell Facebook what content to filter. They understand that publishers are entitled to make editorial decisions and that this right is well protected by the First Amendment.

What are the pros and cons of government regulation of digital platforms❓

If Facebook is a publisher, then it is 100% free to choose what to display and what to delete. It can suppress content or make it more visible. The company has First Amendment rights just as individuals do.

But because Facebook is also a platform, it also gets special benefits from a little-known law, *Section 230 of the Communications Decency Act* (CDA). Part of the 1996 Telecommunication Act, this law protects Internet service providers who publish content provided by others; platform companies cannot be sued for libelous or fraudulent con-

Mr. Mark Zuckerberg

Alamy

285

tent on their websites. Some have claimed the law is the single most important piece of regulation that has enabled the growth of the Internet (Kosseff, 2019). It has protected platform companies from lawsuits sought by people harmed by fake profile sites, sexually explicit content directed to minors, false information, and more.

This special protection was granted because Congress wanted the public to have access to diverse ideas that advance public discourse and wanted to avoid platform companies engaging in *collateral censorship*, which occurs "when A censors B out of fear that the government will hold A liable for the effects of B's speech" (Harvard Law Review, 2018). Courts have observed that a powerful chilling effect would occur to freedom of expression if a bookseller could be held liable for the contents of every book sold in the store.

5 critical questions about Facebook for Creators

In this Instagram post from Facebook, creators are invited to use the Facebook for Creators platform for sharing video and other creative work. View the video at www.medialiteracyaction.com and then use five critical questions to analyze this media message to gain insight on its meaning and value.

1. Who is the author and what is the purpose?
This is a post from Facebook on Instagram. It is a type of promotional advertising for a set of resources to encourage more people to use Facebook for sharing their videos. With this initiative, Facebook is trying to compete

facebook ● Follow

icecoldcombos Hello Facebook. My account was permanently disabled this past January for repeated offenses of posting videos with music in the background. I was wondering if there was a way for me to prove that I have learned from my mistakes, and be allowed back on Facebook. While the "rebel-status" is a cool conversation starter at parties, I have lost valuable contacts, photos of friends, and documentation of massive life events. I am hoping to appeal to your forgiving side, as I don't think that I am a bad person, and I would like to use my account to spread love, joy and good vibes. Please allow me to rejoin. Thank you for your consideration, Adam

nonnyworldwidestar ♥
mrsmoothb @beyourowndad 😊

117,004 views
NOVEMBER 17, 2017

© Facebook, Inc

Critics say that the CDA creates an uneven playing field, providing more protection for Internet speech than for other forms of expression in journalism, book publishing, or broadcasting, where laws for defamation and libel apply. Others note that the law disproportionally harms the powerless, as was the case when, in 2007, the LiveJournal blogging system removed thousands of digital drawings and art and suspended the accounts of amateur artists who had no recourse to the loss of their creative work (Tushnet, 2007). Because the CDA does not exempt Internet providers from child pornography laws, they are more likely to take down creative work that involves images and drawings of girls and boys in order to avoid the threat of legal action. At the same time, other potentially harmful speech (including racism, terrorism, depictions of gun violence, and self-harm) is plentiful on many social media platforms.

---

with Google's YouTube in social media video sharing. A user named "ice cold combos" has commented on the post in an effort to speak directly to the company.

2. **What techniques are used to attract and hold attention?** Clicking the play icon plays a short video with attractive images of Latino, African American, and Muslim young people having fun and making media. The tag line reads, "Discover how to make your thing a thing."

3. **What lifestyles, value, and points of view are represented?** The overall message suggests that playful use of video is a part of a creative person's lifestyle. But the comments from Instagram users on the right-hand side of the post suggest that some users have not had positive experiences with Facebook. One user describes how he was kicked off Facebook for copyright violations. He used unauthorized music and his content was taken down and his account suspended. In the comment, this user asks to have his account restored so he can "spread love, joy and good vibes." His message seems to contradict the welcoming promotional message.

4. **How might different people interpret this message?** Some people will be happy that Facebook is inspiring the potential contributions of minority youth. Others will see it as a mere competitive move on the part of Facebook to reach younger minorities. People of all races use social media networks about equally, but Latinos and African Americans are more likely to use Instagram than whites. Teen boys are more likely to use YouTube and teen girls are more likely to use Snap or Instagram. So this ad may be a way to flatter the intended target audience.

5. **What is omitted?** This message contains nothing about the purpose for sharing videos online beyond the ambiguous "make your thing a thing." The message does not appeal to youth as citizens, change agents, or even creative artists. It is not particularly inspiring. Data from 2018 reveal that low-income teens are more likely to use Facebook than teens from higher-income groups. When it comes to their business goals, it may not matter much to Facebook whether video sharing is an art form, a form of community engagement, or just another form of playful goofing around.

In general, Internet companies now get both free speech benefits and protection from liability from harms caused by the speech on their platforms. Legally, this gives them a lot of power with a very little responsibility. Although legal scholars have considered various remedies for the way in which the First Amendment has become detached from key threats to freedom of speech, some legal scholars have suggested that the federal government examine the value of media literacy education as a First Amendment issue. As Harvard Law School professor Rebecca Tushnet (2018a, 29) notes, "Understanding the new information environment may be the most important tool citizens have to participate in democracy."

What the future may hold: A Dislike Button

Would social media be better or worse with a "dislike" button? Facebook has been experimenting with a feature that members of the Reddit community have had for years: the ability to upvote or downvote user-generated content. Reddit is an entertainment and news website, owned by Advance Publications, which owns Conde Nast, a global mass media company. On Reddit, users can share content, which includes links to articles elsewhere on the Web or posts in the form of texts. Reddit uses an upvote/downvote system where users can increase the visibility of a particular post by voting and commenting. A user collects "karma" according to how many upvotes his or her posts and comments get upvoted.

Other social media platforms have been experimenting with the "dislike" button. In a Facebook trial conducted in Australia and New Zealand in 2018, some users saw little gray arrows underneath comments on posts from public pages. Users were encouraged to "Stop bad comments. Press the down arrow if a comment has bad intentions or is disrespectful." Your input is anonymous, a pop-up adds (Withers, 2018).

Could such a feature help minimize the visibility of hateful comments? Or could this new feature be too easily gamed, motivating people to engage in downvoting wars and increasing polarization? When discussion platforms like Discus made downvoting visible to users, they saw an increase in retaliation and vindictive trolling from users who were angry that their comments received a downvote. While positive feedback did not seem to affect what people post, downvotes made users even more likely to post antisocial content. So they solved the problem by hiding the downvoting statistics even as they used them as algorithmic data to display content to users (Ho, 2015).

TIME T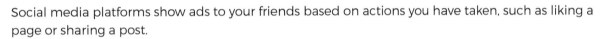 REFLECT

Take a look at one of the social media platforms that you use most and "go under the hood" to see what it knows about you.

On Instagram, this can be found under Privacy and Security, View Account Data. On Facebook, this can be found under General Account Settings.

Consider these questions as you explore:

- What does the platform think your interests are? How accurate is it?
- How does the platform profile you based on the content you have clicked on?
- How accurate is the platform's profile?

Social media platforms show ads to your friends based on actions you have taken, such as liking a page or sharing a post.

- Which ads did your friends see because of your actions?
- What are some potential long-term benefits and limitations of digital platforms personalizing content for you?

Use the Flipgrid Inquiry to contribute your ideas in a brief oral presentation. You can also view and respond to comments of other people who have offered thoughtful reflections on media literacy. Visit www.medialiteracyaction.com to learn more.

CREATE T LEARN

Make the Familiar Strange

In this creative writing activity, try to offer a brief description of one form of social media that you use. But write your description as if you were explaining it to a space alien. Assume your reader knows nothing about social media and even less about human beings and our strange ways of interacting and communicating. This kind of playful creative writing enables *defamiliarization*, which is a way to heighten awareness by taking something familiar and making it seem strange. You can post using the #MLAction hashtag to share your work with a global community of media literacy learners.

PART IV

MEDIA EFFECTS

People construct identity by consuming and creating media

Why Do People Worry about Stereotypes?

12

Learning Outcomes

1. Examine how stereotypes function in storytelling to create social consensus

2. Consider how exposure to media during childhood may shape people's expectations about identity and human behavior

3. Understand how race, class, and social power are represented in entertainment media

4. Recognize how self-representation in social media enables people to perform identities in order to gain attention and approval

W hen the MTV show *16 and Pregnant* launched in 2009, it depicted the lives of real teenage mothers, their partners, and their parents. The unscripted show followed the conversations and actions of Maci, Amber, Farrah, and Catelynn, who were the first of 47 pregnant teenagers on the show. Viewers have since followed these and other characters in spin-off shows, including the *Teen Mom OG* franchise. On these shows, viewers see young women struggle with adoption, medical problems, alcoholism and drug abuse, domestic violence, poverty, the challenges of parenting, custody disputes, involvement in the porn industry, and other family and relationship drama.

Some people worry that these shows normalize teenage pregnancy. Others observe that the shows themselves rarely ever feature discussions about abortion. But the shows offer a variety of representations of young mothers and fathers so as to present different incarnations of "good" and "bad" parenting, especially in relation to traditional conceptualizations of masculinity and femininity. You might perceive these shows to be realistic or unrealistic in their depiction of teen parents. Given the significant attention some of the parents on the shows have received, pregnancy and motherhood might even look a bit glamorous, given the showcasing of *Teen Mom* reality TV stars in magazines and on TV.

This chapter explores the issue of media *representation*, asking questions such as:

- Why are people so sensitive about stereotypes in entertainment media?
- How do people evaluate the realism of a media message?
- How do media representations affect people's sense of personal and social identity?
- How do media stereotypes change over time?

Stereotypes have considerable power because they shape the depiction of people, events, and ideas. Media depictions of gender, race, social class, sexuality, occupations, and events can impact how we understand ourselves and the world around us.

The Problem with Apu

Launched in 1989, *The Simpsons* is the longest-running American scripted narrative prime-time series. The family adventures of Homer, Marge, Bart, Lisa, and Maggie have had a significant effect on American culture. The show combines comedy with social commentary about the life of a dysfunctional American family. When Hari Kondabolu, a comedian and the first-generation American son of Indian immigrants, was growing up, he loved the show and it helped to inspire his interest in comedy. As a teen, he had experienced *cultural exclusion* and felt the sting of negative stereotypes, which he reflected upon in a 2017 documentary film entitled *The Problem with Apu*.

Apu is the name of the cartoon convenience store owner in *The Simpsons*. As an Indian immigrant who owns the Springfield Kwik-E-Mart, he is best known for his catchphrase, "Thank you, come again." The documentary features several celebrities and newsmakers, including comedian Aparna Nancherla and actor Kal Penn, who recall how Apu's popularity affected their own identities. Other South Asian actors have reflected on Apu's outsized role in their childhood. In the first season of the popular comedy-drama television series *Master of None*, Aziz Ansari's character, Dev, an aspiring actor, loses out on a role for refusing to perform in an Apu-like South Indian accent. This is a familiar tale because racial stereotypes are embedded in Hollywood entertainment, and actors must make complicated decisions to negotiate roles that perpetuate and reproduce negative stereotypes.

What kinds of portrayals of rich, working class, and poor characters are presented in The Simpsons?

Of course, all races and ethnicities are stereotyped on *The Simpsons* as part of its humor, but Hari Kondabolu claims that because so few Indian or Pakistani characters appeared in film and on television, these stereotypes have had a disproportionately negative influence. Since Apu was virtually the only South Asian character on television during the 1980s and 1990s, he influenced how many Americans understood immigrants from the region.

For many, Apu was their first introduction to South Indian immigrant culture. The documentary demonstrates how racial and ethnic stereotypes are perceived by some members of a particular group—in this case, South Asian actors and celebrities. This is a valuable contribution to public discussion. The documentary helps to raise consciousness as viewers are invited to consider how creative choices shape the representation of people and groups in ways that have social significance and impact.

Reflecting back to his childhood, Hari Kondabolu remembers how the Apu character was used as a tool for bullying. During middle school, bullies used Apu's catchphrases in catcalls that made fun of Kondabolu's heritage, as older boys pulled up to him in a car, rolled down the windows and shouted, "Thank you very much, come again!" Of course, bullies have always used whatever social or cultural resources they can to hurt others, but in this particular case they weaponized the character of Apu as a means to demean, exclude, and humiliate Kondabolu.

The documentary also points out that the character of Apu is performed by Hank Azaria, a white *voice actor*; the accent is an exaggerated representation of Hindi-inflected English. Viewers of the film watch as Kondabolu tries and fails to make face-to-face contact with Azaria. But because voice acting is perhaps the only part of the media industry where appearance has no bearing on the ability to play a role, Kondabolu's critique of the performer's

THE WHOLE WORLD IS BINGE WATCHING BUT NONE OF THE CHARACTERS ARE EVER SHOWN BINGE WATCHING.

Andrew Weldon

What types of media activities are frequently depicted in movies and TV shows and what activities are rarely shown ❓

racial identity seems misplaced. For example, did you know that the character of Bart is performed by a woman?

While the documentary has its fans, some were openly scornful of Kondabolu's claims, seeing the film as oversimplifying the multifaceted character of Apu and ignoring the complex context of *The Simpsons* and its approach to comedy and social criticism. One critic, cartoonist Max Gilardi, has compiled a 45-minute remix commentary, depicting scenes from the 30-year history of the show and offering a critique of Kondabolu's documentary. We see numerous representations of Apu that show him to be kind, romantic, spiritual, smart, and hard-working. We learn that he has a doctorate in computer science and that Apu also "likes building furniture and then having a discussion about where it could be placed in a room." Such unique qualities are hardly stereotypical.

Of course, when you think about it, Apu is actually a far more flattering depiction of an adult man than Homer Simpson, the leading character. Early in the series, some of the humor concerning Apu's character is based on the fish-out-of-water theme—he is new to America and is confused by aspects of American culture that he encounters. Since people think he is a mere convenience store owner, some humor comes as the viewers' expectations about Apu are circumvented as they learn about Apu's complex and humorous life history, bowling skills, fast car, love life, and spiritual personality.

The idea that immigrants are more complicated and interesting than people give them credit for is another common trope for how immigrants and immigration are depicted in film and television. Critics note that Indian Americans are the richest and most educated minority in America.

The Simpsons producers have not decided to eliminate Apu as a result of the backlash, but the character has not been featured on the show in a speaking role since 2018. Perhaps *The Simpsons* producers agreed with the premise of the documentary and realized that comedy that was acceptable in the past may not be acceptable now. Or perhaps they would rather eliminate the character than capitulate to critics. One critic worried about the potential long-term consequences of this controversy, wondering, "How will Hollywood execs *greenlight* any future comedies concerning South Asians? How exactly does Hollywood ever create a comedy around any Indian character going forward, without being theoretically insulting to Indians in the same manner for which Apu was criticized?" Since many comedies are built around stereotypes, some even wonder whether the future of comedy may be at risk in a culture sensitive to issues of bias and misrepresentation (Shanker, 2018b).

Understanding Stereotypes

The word *stereotype* is used in different ways across the humanities and social sciences, including psychology, sociology, philosophy, literature and the arts, and communication and media studies. Each of these fields can help you understand this complex and important topic. In social psychology, a stereotype is typically understood as "a set of characteristics of a group of people based on generalizations about appearance and behavior."

As discussed in Chapter 10, the term originated with Walter Lippmann, who described a stereotype as "a picture of the world on which we can act." Think about how many ideas you have in your head based on media (not direct) experiences. Long before you ever set foot on a college campus you acquired stereotypes about what college would be like. Perhaps these stereotypes came from TV shows like *Community*, which depicts the students and faculty at a community college. Or perhaps your stereotypes about law school came from films like *Legally Blonde*, a 2001 comedy featuring Reese Witherspoon as a Harvard law student. In this film, the character is a *counter-stereotype* because she appears to be a dumb blonde, but she is actually smart, tough, and deeply committed to justice.

Stereotypes are actively formed subjective constructs that are dependent on the attitudes and worldviews of the interpreter. But stereotypes don't develop in a vacuum: they rely on intersubjective systems of consensus and social orientation. Lippmann (1922) explains it like this: "In the great blooming, buzzing confusion of the outer world we pick out what our culture has already defined for us, and we tend to perceive [...] the form stereotyped for us by our culture."

As much as stereotypes can be problematic, Lippmann recognizes they are an essential part of social life and that through becoming aware of stereotypes, people can learn to "hold them lightly and modify them gladly" (Lippmann, 1922: 50).

Stereotypes may be an essential part of making sense of the world. As psychologists studied perception and cognition, they discovered that

How have stereotypes affected your life **?**

MGM/Photofest

people use structural features in their environment for organizing and categorizing experiences. These are sometimes called *schema*. Schema are the elements of human experience that serve as recognizable features and become defining traits. Schema are a bit like cognitive stereotypes (Potter, 2004). For example, based on your experience, going to a restaurant involves familiar elements: being escorted to a table and given a menu, with a waiter writing down your request for food. Because human lived experience has so much complexity, we use stereotypes to filter out and simplify experience.

Stereotypes have always been part of media culture. As we learned in Chapter 6, character archetypes have long been part of storytelling. When movies were rising in influence during the 1920s, people had high hopes for its transformative potential. Filmmakers were exploring how to inspire and enlighten through narrative fiction, documentary, and propaganda. But by the 1930s, filmmaking had become a business—a big business—and film studios cranked out ever more fiction—mostly light comedies—at a furious pace. The industry produced many films that all seemed much the same. Studios hired actors and actresses who were conventionally attractive and hired writers to create stories based on themes like good-trumps-evil, lovers-love-to-love, and bad-people-get-what-they-deserve.

Why did audiences seem to flock to the most conventional stories while more artful, offbeat, and distinctive films had lower box office returns? Critics like Walter Benjamin believed that the nature of art was changing in an age of mechanical reproduction. Films and popular culture in general were a part of the political economy of capitalism. Critics like Theodor Adorno believed that popular culture conditioned people to accept the easy pleasures of the cheap comedy, instead of inspiring them to explore the more difficult and challenging pleasures of literature and the traditional art forms (Cappello, 2016).

In his work in *semiotics*, a term used for the study of signs and sign systems, Roland Barthes viewed photographic images, magazines, and films as "repeating machines." He used terms like *denotation* and *connotation* to describe the ways in which photographs had both literal and symbolic meanings, but over time, he rejected the idea of literal, denotative meaning, recognizing that "all meanings, all human acts, are social and contextual. There is no pre-social meaning that would be literal and free of connotation" (Polan, 2016: 75). Barthes recognized that people derive some comfort from the familiarity of stereotypes. He identified how ideologies are expressed through signs in appealing ways that are difficult to resist.

In the fields of humanities, literature, and the arts, the term stereotype is applied to conventional patterns of expression that are repeated frequently. Why do writers, poets, and playwrights repeat certain verbal formulas and familiar phrases? Classical scholars have pointed out that ever since the first written literature, authors have used conventional expressions that are repeated for emphasis. For example, in the *Iliad*, sailors cross the "wine-dark sea." Whenever the sea is referenced, it is always "wine-dark." Why is this phrase used? Literary theorists imagined that such familiar phrases represent a nod to the oral language tradition, where repetition helps people remember ideas and information. Other critics see repetition as a type of negotiation between authors and audiences, a way for their expectations to meet. As one scholar puts it:

> The perception of an artistic text is always a struggle between audience and author [...] the audience takes in part of the text and then "finishes" or "constructs" the rest. (Schweinitz, 2011: 19)

Thus, stereotypes are embedded in all forms of storytelling because the real pleasure and value of stereotyped characters, phrases, or forms of expression is in their *familiarity*. Authors, filmmakers and storytellers set up patterns of fulfilling and disrupting the expectations of the reader or viewer in ways that create engagement and pleasure.

Gender Matters

Gender stereotypes are part of culture and thus they are transmitted generationally, from parents to children. Gender stereotypes even influence what parents are concerned about and how they interact with their children. Is there gender equity in the United States? A study of anonymous, aggregate data from

What were the most common gender stereotypes you encountered when you were growing up?

Common Sense Media

Is my son overweight?

For every **10** U.S. Google queries about
boys being overweight . . .

Is my daughter overweight?

. . . there are **17** queries about girls.

(In reality boys are about 9 percent
more likely to be overweight than girls.)

Is my daughter gifted?

For every **10** U.S. Google queries about
girls being gifted . . .

Is my son gifted?

. . . there are **25** queries about boys.

(In reality girls are about 11 percent
more likely to be in a gifted program.)

SOURCE: *The New York
Times* (2014)

*How did your parents
express social norms
about attractiveness
and intelligence in your
family*❓

Google searches suggests that "contemporary American parents are far more likely to want their boys smart and their girls skinny. It's not that parents don't want their daughters to be bright or their sons to be in shape, but they are much more focused on the braininess of their sons and the waistlines of their daughters" (Stephens-Davidowitz, 2014: SR6).

In a study of aggregate data from Google queries, researchers noticed that for every 10 Google queries about boys being overweight, there were 17 queries about girls being overweight, even though in reality, boys are more likely to be overweight than girls. Similarly, for every 10 Google searches about a daughter's intelligence, there were 26 about a son's intelligence.

Survey research with parents shows that many parents are concerned about how media messages about gender affects their daughters, who are perceived as more vulnerable to media. The media literacy organization, Common Sense Media, surveyed more than 1,000 parents about their perceptions of how stereotypes influence their children. Many parents believe media have great influence on children, particularly girls. About 75% say girls are "very" or "extremely" influenced by TV shows and movies when it comes to "how they look." When it comes to "how to act in a romantic relationship," 56% of parents say TV shows and movies are "very" or "extremely" influential for girls. Far fewer parents are concerned about the influence of gender stereotypes on their male children, however (Ward & Aubrey, 2017).

But boys are significantly influenced by gender stereotypes, too. Social scientific research in human development reveals that television programming influences boys by reinforcing the idea that masculine traits include aggression, power, dominance, status seeking, emotional restraint, heterosexuality, and risk taking. Preschool boys who are heavy viewers of superhero television programs tend to engage in more male-stereotyped toy and weapon play (Coyne et al., 2016).

Social learning theory posits that people learn through observation and strategic imitation. Developed by Albert Bandura, this theory notes how human knowledge and behavior can be learned vicariously through observation of media models. People are more likely to learn behavior that is reinforced through the display of positive outcomes, but viewers can also learn from observing others' mistakes and can alter their own actions to avoid negative consequences (Jeffries, 1997).

Play is a form of learning where children practice the social relationships they observe from the role models in the world around them. Role models come both from real life and from media sources. Thus, early exposure to television that features gender stereotypes may influence people's behavior as they grow older. Early in childhood, girls are exposed to stereotypes about appearance, beauty, and sexuality. Women are depicted as eye candy even in G-rated movies. Female characters are far more likely to be shown in sexualized attire (i.e., tight or revealing clothing). They are more likely to appear with exposed skin between the chest and upper thigh regions and more likely than males to be referenced as physically attractive (Smith et al., 2010).

Exposure to gender stereotypes may contribute to the formation of a *gender hierarchy*, where children may develop attitudes of gender superiority. Researchers found that preschool children who watch more TV are more likely to believe that other people think boys and men are better than girls and women. In a study of 4-year-olds, researchers found that those who watched more television were more likely to answer "boys" when asked "Who do most people think are better? Boys or girls?" Figure 12.1 shows the relationship between children's ideas about the superiority of boys and the amount of television they watch (Halim, Ruble & Tamis-LeMonda, 2013).

Between the ages of 9 and 14, as children enter puberty, attitudes about gender and appearance begin to play a more important role in their lives, affecting their peer relationships and academic choices. During these years, appearance ideals are *internalized*, and this mechanism is thought to account for the influence of media exposure on body image. In one study of a large sample of Belgian boys and girls, researchers found that watching shows on Nickelodeon was associated with higher levels of agreement about the benefits of attractiveness and beauty, including beliefs that attractiveness makes people happier, more self-confident, and do better in school. One year later, when they surveyed children again, those who had positive beliefs about the benefits of attractiveness were more likely to agree with statements reflecting the internalization of media beauty standards, like "I compare my

How did the media you used as a child represent social norms about attractiveness and intelligence❓

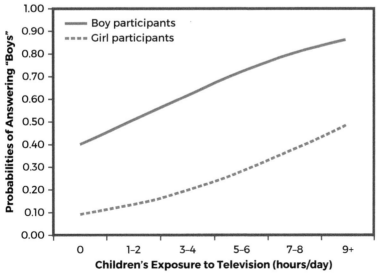

Figure 12.1

Correlation Between Preschool Children's Beliefs about Gender Hierarchy and Their Exposure to Television

SOURCE: Halim, Ruble & Tamis-LeMonda, 2013

Consider the Question

With a partner or in a small group, discuss these questions:

- How may have gender stereotypes affected the lives of your parents? How have gender stereotypes affected you?
- Some people say that, with so many forms of media available today, gender stereotypes are no longer as important as they once were. Would you agree or disagree? Why?

body to the bodies of TV and movie stars" and "I would like my body to look like the people who are on TV" (Trekels & Eggermont, 2017).

During the teenage years, gender stereotypes can intensify. Researchers have found that boys who watch more sports and reality TV are more likely

Donald Maclellan/Hulton Archive/Gettty Images

Intellectual Grandparent:
Stuart Hall

Stuart Hall is an intellectual grandfather of media literacy whose work influenced a whole generation of teachers and scholars. He was a Jamaican-born British cultural studies scholar who was the director of the Birmingham Centre for Contemporary Cultural Studies and a professor of sociology at the Open University. He explored the relationship between media, representation, communication, and social power by looking at the everyday work of images, advertising, and popular culture. His key ideas include:

People construct meaning through interpretation. In 1980, Stuart Hall developed the communication model of encoding and decoding, sometimes called *reception theory*. It examines how authors encode meaning through the choices they make in constructing messages and how readers decode meaning through their interpretations. The idea of the *active audience* was part of this work, because Hall recognized that the audience interprets media messages in relationship to their own social contexts. In examining the concept of representation, he argued that meanings are not fixed and static. He understood that "the meaning of an event does not exist outside of representation or before representation" (Jhally, 1997). Hall examined how, through analysis, people make choices in the act of interpretation and can reject messages that they disagree with. When a reader resists the dominant cultural norms embedded in a media text, he or she can use an alternative ideological code to interpret a media message, an approach that has been called reading against the grain. Making a *resistant reading* involves analysis of the text and engaging in alternative interpretations that scrutinize the beliefs and attitudes that typically go unexamined, noticing the gaps, silences, and contradictions. For example, a feminist resistant reading of the Disney princess may observe how in *The Little Mermaid*, Ariel literally gives up her voice for a man she barely knows, validating the theme that women must sacrifice their whole selves to have relationships with men.

than other boys to agree with statements depicting stereotypical masculine beliefs like: "I hate it when people ask me to talk about my feelings," "If I could, I would frequently change sexual partners," and "I would be furious if someone thought I was gay." Agreement with these attitudes is also associated with risk-taking behaviors in young men, including sexual risk taking, alcohol and drug use, and speeding while driving (Giaccardi et al., 2016).

Representation, Realism, and Diversity in Video Games

Many scholars study representation in popular culture, looking at patterns of how race, class, and gender are constructed in news, entertainment, music, and video games, and on social media (Fiske, 2010). When it comes to video games, however, scholars have performed fewer studies of representation. In some video games, white, English-speaking, heterosexual males are the default

Media and popular culture socially construct identity. Hall's numerous publications examined racial prejudice, media, and social and cultural theories. Growing up in a Caribbean country under British colonial rule, he wrote about *hegemony*, a Marxist concept that describes all the ways that one political group controls another through manipulating the value system of a society and the individuals in it. Through hegemony, the powerless consent to be controlled. Hall also explored how media and popular culture construct an identity position for people, noting that "images construct us" as we project ourselves into the image in some way in order to make meaning.

Instead of treating meaning as something that happens inside the heads of individual interpreters, Hall believed that meaning is socially constructed through culture. Culture offers "maps of meaning" that allow us to make sense of the world, and people capture meaning through language, images, gestures, sound, music, and more. In cultural studies scholarship, researchers examine discourses and texts and trace these texts' meanings to larger ideological forces, power interests, and social groups. This makes it possible to identify social and ideological forces including capitalism, nationalism, patriarchy, whiteness, and heterosexism, to name just a few.

An act of interpretation can be a form of social power. Because meaning is not a fixed property of representations, it can be changed through interpretation. This idea positions the act of interpretation as a potentially radical and transformative act. Stuart Hall helped people to recognize and challenge stereotypes as a means of increasing the diversity of images in the media, but he did not believe that "good" representations are superior to "bad" representations—and he did not believe that "bad" representations can be fixed. Hall recognized that when people interrogate media messages through critical questions, those ideas lose their social power because people understand them as constructed and are free to interpret them in relation to their own culture and values.

If Stuart Hall has influenced your thinking about media, you can share a comment on the Grandparents of Media Literacy website at www.grandparentsofmedialiteracy. com.

This billboard ad states, "A website makes it real." How do you interpret this message? Do you agree or disagree? Why❓

characters. In other games, players can customize their avatars and change their skin color, body type, gender, hair, and clothing. The representation of characters in video games is always a strategic choice made by the game makers.

Some people argue that in the context of video game play, differential patterns of representation of race and gender do not really matter. According to this point of view, games are fantasy worlds unencumbered by reality. People say, "Of course *Grand Theft Auto* is violent, misogynistic, and racist. It is a gangster fantasy!" But this argument holds a paradox: it "curiously combines realism and fantasy as justifications for misogynist and racialized violence. The game is just a fantasy, so the violence does not count. It is realistic because violence exists in these worlds, so it is not offensive" (Shaw, 2015: 162).

Entertainment media cannot be expected to mirror reality, according to some critics. Calling attention to media representations is primarily a way of making media producers responsible for the choices they make. Whether a particular video game is realistic or unrealistic is a judgment made by users themselves. When assessing the realism of a first-person shooter game, you will come to a different conclusion based on your own background, life experience, and beliefs. Military veterans will likely make different judgments than teen boys. For many game players, "good" representations are believable representations, and believable representations draw on the diversity people see and experience in everyday life (Shaw, 2015).

Middle-class white people may be less aware of the importance of representation because they are surrounded by familiar representations of people who look like them in advertising, news, and entertainment. People of color and those who identify as LGBTQ care about representation because they are more aware of how it may marginalize them as "other." When researcher Adrienne Shaw studied video game players, she noted that people of color are found only in sports, urban crime, and war games. It is not common to find people of color in fantasy games or other genres. For example, African American characters are present in games like *Madden NFL*, one of the only video games with large numbers of depictions of African American men. Shaw explains, "Racial diversity is present, it seems, only when game content makes it 'matter'" (2015: 160).

Representations Influence Attitudes and Behavior

Perhaps the most important reason why stereotypes make people worry is that researchers have discovered how media representations can influence knowledge, attitudes, and behavior. In studying the role of media in the lives of adolescents, researchers have found that teens encounter plenty of depictions of sexuality in movies, TV shows, and music. Magazines offer advice about sexuality, and pornography is readily available on the Internet.

During puberty and early adolescence, teens seek out media that depict sexuality, and their perceptions of the *perceived reality* of this content can make a difference in what young people take away from these representations (Brown, el-Toukhy & Ortiz, 2014). For some young people, the representations of sexuality seen in mass media and through social media may shape perceptions about how frequently young men and young women are having sexual experiences. Media messages may affect gender norms regarding the initiation of sexual behavior and the use of contraception.

The study of *social norms* has also demonstrated the process by which people look to others, consciously or unconsciously, as guides for how to act and think. Norms are standards of behavior based on widely shared beliefs about how people ought to act in particular situations. Because humans have a fundamental need to belong, we prefer to have attitudes and engage in behaviors that are similar to the behaviors of others. A number of public health initiatives have aimed to dispel myths and inaccurate information held by the public in an effort to shift social norms in ways that encourage more realistic and accurate perceptions of social reality.

What information have you learned about public health, law, or politics from watching entertainment movies and TV shows?

One approach to social norms research has been developed through an *entertainment-education strategy*, where informative or educational messages are embedded in entertainment media in hopes of increasing knowledge, raising awareness, and encouraging audiences to make responsible health decisions. One organization, Power to Decide, works with Hollywood producers, writers, and media professionals to help them develop media characters that accurately and responsibly depict teen sexuality and pregnancy. Media representations of teen pregnancy can spark conversations that help young people's decision-making. Media strategist Marisa Nightingale points out that if a young person sees a favorite TV character handle a situation, it can help him or her make a decision. If a parent sees a media depiction of adolescent sexuality, there is an opportunity for conversation and dialogue. In coordination with Power to Decide, Nightingale helped the producers of *Jane the Virgin*, a 2014 *telenovela* that aired on the CW network. They depicted how unplanned pregnancy affects the lives of community college students in a way that aligned with evidence from survey research on completion rates for pregnant students. She also provided consulting services to the producers of *Glee*, a 2009 comedy, helping them depict the details of Quinn's unplanned pregnancy and her decision to give the baby up for adoption (Nightingale, 2014).

The start of this chapter featured *16 and Pregnant* and the *Teen Mom* franchise, the long-running MTV series that showcases the lives of young mothers who are pregnant and raising young children. In representing the young women as empowered to make individual choices, the show depicts the transitions young women experience as they move from "at risk" pregnant teens to capable and adaptive young moms. Viewers are invited to compare themselves to the characters in order to manage the stresses of teen pregnancy.

In fact, the show's immense national popularity created a unique research opportunity. Could *16 and Pregnant* influence teen pregnancy rates? Researchers measured the show's influence in different parts of the country, since there is geographic variation in the popularity of the show. Using statistical analysis, they tested whether differential exposure to the show led to differential changes in teen birth rates. They used Nielsen ratings data provided regionally along with data about the frequency of live births provided by the federal government. They found that, in regions where the show was most popular, there was a 4.3% reduction in teen births over 18 months. They also found that the show influenced viewers' interest in the topics of birth control and abortion, as measured by Internet searches and social media activity. In the days immediately following a new episode of *16 and Pregnant*, users conducted more frequent searches for terms like "how to get birth control," "birth control," or "abortion" (Kearney & Levine, 2015).

Because people interpret messages differently, you understand that not all viewers interpret *16 and Pregnant* the same way. In one study, those who perceive themselves as similar to the young women depicted in the show (as well as those engaged in fan activities through social media) had lower perceptions of the risks of pregnancy and more favorable attitudes about teen pregnancy. These viewers perceived the show as sending positive messages about teen pregnancy, showing that teen pregnancy is not a risky endeavor. Researchers note, "For viewers who think that the show encourages teen pregnancy, it was easier to perceive themselves to be similar to the teen moms" (Aubrey, Behm-Morawitz & Kim, 2014: 1157). Despite the intentions of the show to discourage teen pregnancy and despite the actual frequencies of the depictions of positive and negative consequences of teen pregnancy, viewers freely construct interpretations that align with their beliefs and worldviews.

You may not be aware of how implicit bias shapes your perception and memory. *Implicit bias* is defined as the attitudes or stereotypes that affect our understanding, actions, and decisions in an unconscious manner (Banaji & Greenwald, 2013). These biases can be favorable or unfavorable and they are activated in the subconscious. These positive or negative feelings and attitudes about other people can be based on characteristics such as race, ethnicity, age, and appearance, and they develop beginning at a very early age through exposure to life experiences, entertainment media, and news programming.

Stereotypical associations about gender, race, body size, attractiveness, intelligence, and age are evident in how people connect these characteristics to positive and negative feelings. Through measuring people's reaction to computerized time tasks, researchers have found that people more quickly and ef-

How do real-life interactions with people who are different from you help disrupt stereotypes?

fortlessly connect names and faces of women to various aspects of family life, whereas names and faces of men come more easily to mind when thinking about professional careers (Ellemers, 2018).

Even as they depict stereotypes, some media companies are trying to diminish their impact on our lives. In 2016, MTV developed an interactive set of activities it called "Look Different: Bias Cleanse." Viewers received an email each day with information and activities designed to increase their recognition of perceptual biases and reflect on the forms of unconscious bias we experience in daily life. For example, consider the value of this task for Day 7 of the MTV Bias Cleanse:

Day 7: Can I sit at your lunch table?

Today, we've got a pretty simple request for you: sit with someone who's a different race than you at lunch (or just hang out with someone you usually don't hang out with). Try speaking to someone you're in class with, or someone who shares some of the same interests as you. It's really important to actually get to know people from different racial groups—it lets you understand who they are as a person, what they like and don't like, and helps you to avoid thinking of them as a stereotype.

This is such a basic act, but simple practices like this can be powerful in helping young people become comfortable with difference. Why does it work? Personal experience with people from different racial, ethnic, and social class backgrounds generally displaces and disrupts media stereotypes. But it is also worth reflecting on why MTV presents stereotypes in its TV programming but aims to disrupt stereotypes in its public service initiatives. It is possible that the company, owned by the media giant Viacom, recognizes the complex nature of the love–hate relationship its viewers have with stereotypes in mass media.

Loyalty, Identity, and Representation

When the Marvel action film *Black Panther* was released in 2018, it was a milestone, offering a superhero action film about what it means to be Black in the world today. Directed by Ryan Coogler, it was the first big-budget action movie to have an African American director and a predominantly Black cast. Viewers of the film see how the people of Wakanda are divided as to how to interact with the rest of the world. Is isolationism in the face of *colonialism* a solution, or does it equal complicity-by-silence? How should people respond to the growing economic inequalities occurring globally?

For some African Americans, the film was a refreshing depiction of the possibilities and potentials of identity. In a *Time* magazine essay, Jamil Smith explains, "If you are reading this and you are white, seeing people who look like you in mass media probably isn't something you think about often. Every day, the culture reflects not only you but nearly infinite versions of you—executives, poets, garbage collectors, soldiers, nurses and so on. The world shows you that your possibilities are boundless" (Smith, 2018: 1). But for people of color, there are far fewer depictions out there.

Although the movie depicts plenty of fast-paced action and violence, this superhero action film also takes on the complex politics of loyalty in relation to personal and social identity. *Black Panther* revolves around a series of important tensions: Should you be loyal to your lover? Your family? Your nation? Your race? The protagonist, T'Challa, played by Chadwick Boseman, is a man of restraint who balances his loyalties, which is why his father astutely observes, "You are a good man, with a good heart, and it is hard for a good man to be king." As we discover through the narrative storytelling arc, T'Challa is loyal to the truth, "and it is this loyalty to truth that differentiates him from the kind of fickle person who has no loyalties" (Ayomide, 2018: 1).

The film tackles themes of anticolonialism through the depiction of characters who are themselves creators of advanced technology. Unlike other films that feature pain, suffering, and poverty, "the usual topics of acclaimed movies about the Black experience," *Black Panther* ponders the relationship between Africans and African Americans and honors an attempt to reconnect with cultural heritage. In the eyes of one critic, the film offers viewers "the envisioning of a free self" where freedom is defined as the absence of fear. "This is why it doesn't matter that Wakanda was an idea from a comic book, created by two Jewish artists" (Wallace, 2018: 1). Diverse representations of identity can help people negotiate the structures of power that maintain inequality.

Objectification and Self-Representation

Today, we represent ourselves through selfies, avatars, images, posts, texts, and tweets. For active users of social media, online identity can be cluttered with a voluminous amount of information. For example, in using Twitter for 10 years, I have composed more than 15,000 tweets about my personal and professional identity—that is nearly 1,500 tweets per year! Because I sometimes use social media as a vehicle for private expression, I sometimes express thoughts and feelings indiscriminately, without regard for my public audience.

What are some examples of media that has activated your feelings of loyalty and belonging?

Other times, I treat my identity like a product, being careful to advance only those messages and images that are consistent with my brand. Deciding what and how to share involves new challenges when living life online.

Online identity construction brings the issue of self-representation to the foreground. *Self-representation* includes all the practices people use to express and share their identity and life experiences. Many young people first experience the pleasures of self-representation on TikTok, Snap or Tumblr, which enables users to create text, photo, quote, link, chat, audio, and video posts. People can be anonymous and yet public, creating a unique digital community through sharing and commenting on content.

For some youth, self-representation on social media grants individuals a kind of *micro-celebrity* (Marwick & boyd, 2010). Online, we communicate with imagined audiences and build desired images, even though we cannot assume that people actually view and read what we share. Success is measured through the number of likes, shares, retweets, followers, and comments, so that quantitatively, at least, the bigger the audience, the stronger the brand. The phenomenon occurs because in a consumer society, everything and everyone is framed as a brand. Audiences, hungry for reality, are beginning to prefer "ordinary" people in the spotlight (Khamis, Ang & Weliing 2017). Perhaps this is why so many children want to be YouTube celebrities when they grow up!

In social media, you may vary your self-presentation based on the audience you imagine will read or see your post. People's online identity can be perceived as inauthentic and fake by some people and as sincere and real by others. This can create a challenge for the communicator: "since authenticity is constituted by the audience, context collapse problematizes the individual's ability to shift between these selves and come off as authentic or fake" (Marwick & boyd, 2010: 124).

Speaking to an imaginary and real audience may open up possibility for self-reflection. In examining how LGBQT youth use Tumblr for self-representation, scholars have noted that participation in social networks through the circulation of images helps young people articulate their *subjectivity* in ways difficult to express in other contexts. Subjectivity involves taking the perspective of the individual self, rather than some neutral perspective, from outside the self's experience. In feminist scholarship, the concept of subjectivity is contrasted with the concept of *performance*. In order to be masculine or feminine, you perform an identity in socially recognized ways, through the way you dress, talk, and behave. Your gender is not just biological, but a set of correctly performed gestures that link an individual to what is socially perceived as a standard identity type (Rosalind & Kanai, 2018).

Self-representation through media can help people develop their identity in new ways that are not restricted by expectations of family and local culture. According to one researcher, "LGBTQ youth are creating new spaces not only to express their thoughts and identities but also to be known differently," using visual representation to write a self that feels most real to them (Wargo, 2017: 575). Given the significant amount of oppression and violence LGBTQ young people may experience in their face-to-face relationships with family and peers, such forms of expression and community connections can literally be life-saving. The #ItGetsBetter campaign was designed to address this problem by demonstrating how LGBTQ adults managed through the stresses of adolescence and young adulthood to develop personally meaningful relationships, careers, and lifestyles.

But self-representation carries some risk, and it may also foreshorten and narrow identity development, not just during adolescence but at any stage of life. You may remember the Facebook exhibitionism that occurred in the early years of social media, when people posted extreme photos and updates, with images of nearly naked and highly sexualized bodies engaged in drunken revelry. Through being outrageous, it seemed, you could gain followers. But who could be surprised that so many people turned toward self-sexualization? After all, consider the widespread objectification of female bodies in advertising and mass media. *Self-objectification* refers to the

How do the selfies created by other people affect your expectations of them?

tendency to treat an individual not as a person with emotions and thoughts, but as an object, there to provide pleasure to others. Growing up in a world full of semi-clothed female models in movies, TV shows, magazines,

advertising, and video games may lead girls and young women to believe that showing more skin is the expected norm.

When you engage in self-representation through sexualizing yourself, it can decrease your self-esteem, making you feel dependent on how you look, and not on your knowledge, character, values, or behavior. Researchers have found that even brief exposure to sexualized images can inspire people to select more sexual messages about themselves, researchers have shown. In one experiment, 221 young woman aged 18 to 25 in the Netherlands participated in a study that they thought was about women's product choices. They were randomly assigned to look at one of four ads, two of which contained a nearly naked women in a sexualized depiction and two of which featured a blue or pink perfume bottle. Then they completed a questionnaire, designed an avatar, and wrote five sentences describing themselves.

Half of the participants were told their avatars and sentences would be visible to an online audience and half were told that the information would be private. Self-objectification was measured by the frequency of written references to physical attractiveness. Statements like "I am beautiful" or references to working out or an interest in cosmetics and fashion were counted. Researchers measured how exposure to sexualized representations might explain their choice to create objectifying self-representations. Findings show that participants who saw the sexualized perfume ads and thought they were describing themselves for an online audience wrote more statements emphasizing their physical attractiveness as compared with participants who did not think their self-representations would be public, as Figure 12.2 shows (De Vries & Peter, 2013). Increased awareness of the dangers of objectification in social media may help people make more strategic choices in how they represent themselves.

How you adjust your self-expression when addressing a public audience ❓

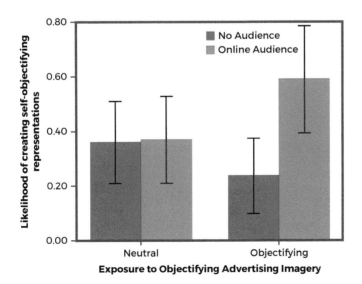

SOURCE: De Vries & Peter, 2013

Figure 12.2
Correlation Between Young Women's Exposure to Objectifying Advertising Imagery and Self-Objectifying Personal Descriptions

5 critical questions about "Not Your Exotic Fantasy"

After viewing this YouTube video at www.medialiteracyaction.com, use five critical questions of media literacy to gain insight on its meaning and value.

Not Your Exotic Fantasy - Tropes vs. Women in Video Games
209,002 views

© Feminist Frequency

1. **Who is the author and what is the purpose?** "Not Your Exotic Fantasy" is a video Anita Sarkeesian created as part of the Feminist Frequency series "Tropes vs. Women in Video Games," a series of 18 videos that examines the representation of gender in video games. In this episode, Sarkeesian reviews a number of video games and makes visual connections to Hollywood films from throughout the 20th century. Her purpose is to illustrate and common on how racism and sexism intersect in the depiction of women of color. She may also be directly addressing game makers to encourage them to become more aware of how harmful stereotypes can limit creativity.

2. **What techniques are used to attract and hold attention?** Sarkeesian visually weaves together action sequences from a variety of video games along with excerpts from Hollywood films and her spoken word commentary, which is presented in direct address to the viewer. For people who do not play video games, the sheer diversity of genres shown in this video grabs their attention. In the opening of the video, Sarkeesian shows segments of game play from *Far Cry 3*, a game Ubisoft produced in 2012. Viewers experience the narrative arc of the game, which involves a group of white people who find themselves captured by dark-skinned pirates while vacationing in Bangkok. Her precise description of the fantasy game emphasizes its absurdity. For example, in the game, the player must choose to leave the island or stay and kill his vacation friends. If the player kills his friends, he is first rewarded by having sex with a dark-skinned female and then killed in a bloody, violent stabbing. The representation of various female characters of color, with their stylized sexuality, clothing, and body paint, is the most attention-getting element of this video.

3. **What lifestyles, values, and points of view are represented?** Female sexuality is presented as a reward for the white game player,

as sexism and racism intersect. We see how video games emphasize women of color as mystical, primitive, and savage. By using a montage of American Hollywood films, we see how *exotification* of women occurs in movies and how these images are tied to values. Sarkeesian also shows how in the *Zelda* franchise of fantasy video games, virtuous female characters are fair-skinned and evil female characters are dark-skinned. The characters of lighter-skinned Black women are presented as more virtuous than women with darker skin color because they come closer to matching the culturally dominant ideal of whiteness.

4. **How might different people interpret this message?** Some people, after watching this video, will fear that Sarkeesian's work might inspire efforts to censor video games. Video game fans might notice that she offers examples of positive representation of women of color in videos, including one video game called *Never Alone*, which delves deeply into the traditional lore of the Iñupiat people. Others will respect the deep reading and study involved in the production of this video. Sarkeesian's credibility is enhanced through her use of strategic quotes from scholars who have studied stereotypes in historical context. For example, we learn

how, in the 19th century, whites perpetuated myths about Black women's sexuality through media as a way of rationalizing their cruel treatment of female slaves. Some viewers might object to her examination of *cultural appropriation*, where Sarkeesian critiques people who dress up in sombreros for Halloween. The term refers to the disrespectful use and repurposing of symbols of minority cultural heritage by people from the majority culture.

5. **What is omitted?** On the YouTube page, comments are disabled for this and other videos in the series. Some viewers may not be aware of the backlash that developed over the "Tropes vs. Women in Video Games" series beginning in 2012, when Sarkeesian raised money to support the series on Kickstarter. She received numerous death and rape threats from critics who hacked her Web pages and social media, vandalized her article on Wikipedia, and posted disparaging comments online. The events generated by the #GamerGate controversy received substantial press coverage, and while the scandal increased the visibility of sexism in video games, it also fueled the rise of online hate speech.

What the future may hold: Racist and Sexist AI

Gender stereotypes are likely to be part of our future for some time. It is worth noticing that most of the artificial intelligence (AI) systems now entering our homes and lives, including Google's Siri and Amazon's Alexa, feature a female voice. After all, the term *robot* comes from the Czech word for slave. As artificial intelligence becomes an ever larger part of everyday life, will it disrupt or reproduce sexism, racism, and other forms of prejudice and discrimination?

When researchers at Amazon designed an artificial intelligence tool to help employment recruiters identify talented applicants in 2015, they used a large set of résumés gathered over a 10-year period. The goal was to create a machine learning optimization algorithm that would enable the computer to review 100 résumés and sort out the top 20% of candidates by automatically scoring applicants on a scale of 5 to 1. But because 90% of the engineering résumés used to "teach" the computer were from men, the machine learning software began to automatically favor male candidates over female candidates, offering lower scores to résumés with the word "women" in them, including phrases like "women's chess club champion" (Baccarin, 2017).

One tech expert explained, "As the tech industry begins to create artificial intelligence, it risks inserting racism and other prejudices into code that will make decisions for years to come" (Garcia, 2017: 1). Consider the experience of an Italian biomedical engineer who asked members of the audience to search for images of a CEO using their cell phones. Participants found no images of women, Black women, or disabled people, thus revealing how dependent AI systems are on the diversity of information used to "teach" them (Baccarin, 2017). Like machines, of course, children learn from the data available to them. Media literacy education is a strategic effort to try to make sure that the discriminatory attitude and prejudices learned in childhood through parents, family, and the mass media can be questioned, analyzed, and resisted.

TIME T◉ REFLECT

Choose one of the short films from the curated list of short documentaries on race, bias, and identity provided by the New York Times Learning Network's Film Club. After viewing, record a brief reflection on Flipgrid using these questions as a guide to your response:

- What moments in this film stood out for you?
- What messages, emotions, or ideas will you take away from this film?
- What questions did this film raise for you?

After you contribute your ideas in a brief oral presentation, you can view and respond to comments of other people who have offered thoughtful reflections on race, representation, and the media. Visit www.medialiteracyaction.com to learn more.

CREATE T▶ LEARN

Spot the Stereotypes Image Slideshow

Choose any form of media that interests you and use it for 1 hour, strategically documenting all the examples of stereotypes that you find. For example, while playing a video game, watching a film, or using Instagram, you can capture image screenshots of gender, racial, or occupational stereotypes. While listening to music, you can write down lyrics in order to document stereotypes about sexuality and attractiveness, for example.

After you have collected examples, consider the patterns in the examples you found and then compose a media literacy *image slideshow* to document your findings. An image slideshow uses a combination of five or more images, language, and sound to identify patterns in the representation of race, gender, ethnicity, age, or occupation. You may want to refer to one or more concepts from this chapter so as to deepen your image slideshow's value to potential viewers. Your slideshow should aim to create an "aha!" experience for your viewers. After publishing, share your creative work with others using the #MLAction hashtag.

Movies, video games, and apps tap into people's fascination with aggression and sexuality

Cagkansayin/iStock

13 Is My Brother Addicted to Media?

Learning Outcomes

1. Understand why children are thought to be vulnerable to media influence and why most people think that others are more likely to be influenced by media than they are themselves

2. Consider how public attitudes about the potential benefits, risks, and harms of media and technology have changed over time

3. Examine how pleasure is activated from carefully designed immersive forms of media, including film, video games, and apps

4. Consider how media use affects the development of adolescent sexuality in relation to personal and social identity

Karen was worried. Around the age of 5, her youngest brother was beginning to show signs of screen addiction. If given unlimited access to a mobile device, he would watch videos or play games for hours at a time. He became more introverted and sometimes more impulsive and aggressive. Her parents did not know what to do. As Karen's brother got older, the problem seemed to get worse. She once wrote a social post describing the situation. "The more he games, the less he laughs, the less he engages with family members, the less willing he is to participate in household chores."

Maria responded to Karen's post with a description of her son, who has played video games since he was 6 and is now a well-adjusted 14-year-old. She allows him to play as much as he wants, and he aspires to be a professional gamer. Through gaming, he has become interested in Japanese culture and music, and he has enrolled in Japanese language classes while also learning violin and piano. He may play for 4 hours or longer per day because video games are an important part of his young life, but they do not seem to be interfering with healthy development.

Maria's cousin, Michael, also struggled with life and relationships. In high school, he had participated in sports like soccer and basketball and played video games with friends. During his sophomore year in college, he played *League of Legends* for hours every day. It seemed that the game had taken over his life. *League of Legends* involves teams of players who are systematically paired with each other before a match begins. The game is very social and immerses players in continuous challenge. As an avid player, Michael rarely left his dorm room. He did not take care of his hygiene or his health. He stopped attending classes and avoided social interaction with peers. His friends and his life were now all in the game. While playing, Michael met many others who were also deeply immersed in *League of Legends*. Some were struggling to balance their relationships, their jobs, and their gaming. One gamer even told Michael, "Quit this game. It's awesome, but it can also take over your life."

These three stories are familiar to most people. You probably have experienced some of the benefits, risks, and harms that are associated with exposure to film and television as well as the use of cell phones, music, video games, social media, and pornography. As media consumers, people can experience violent, gory, aggressive or sexually explicit content in many different forms. They can encounter racist speech or depictions of hate. They may stumble upon financial scams, conspiracy theories, manipulative advertising content, or misinformation. In using social media, people can be victims or perpetrators of harassment, stalking, and cyberbullying. People's social media data can also be exploited and misused in ways that create personal, social, financial, and even physical risk.

Chapter **13** | Is My Brother Addicted to Media?

This chapter explores the following questions:

- Why are children thought to be more at risk to media influence?
- Does watching film and TV violence make people aggressive?
- Why does media use sometimes become a compulsion that can interfere with work and social relationships?
- Can pornography help or hurt the quality of people's sex life?

Media Do Not Affect Me

Almost everyone recognizes both the benefits and harms of media as we encounter them in daily life. But you probably tend to think that others are more likely to be harmed by media than you are. This concept has been called the *third-person effect*: the perception that other people are more influenced by media communications than oneself.

It does not seem to matter whether the harms focus on misogynistic rap lyrics, depictions of violence and aggressive behavior, sensational advertising, extreme political views, or Internet porn. People imagine that other people are highly influenced by those messages while at the same time perceiving themselves as generally immune from influence.

And while most Americans tend to see the Internet as having a positive influence in their own life, they are more ambivalent about how society as a whole has benefited. According to survey research conducted by the Pew Research Center, people value how the Internet has increased the ease of access to information and the ability to connect with other people.

But when asked about the potentially harmful features of the Internet, one in four mentioned how it isolates people from each other or how it encourages them to spend too much time with their devices. Others mention the prevalence of fake news or misinformation. Still others are concerned about its effect on children, and some even note how it encourages illegal activity. Only 5% expressed concerns about privacy (Smith, 2018).

Similar survey evidence exists about the perceived benefits and risks of news media, television, film, and video games. Some scholars believe that the third-person effect is a universal perceptual tendency, a kind of cognitive bias (Peiser & Peter, 2000). For example, when asked about hate speech or other forms of content widely understood to be problematic, people unsurprisingly tend to perceive negative messages as having more effect on others than on themselves.

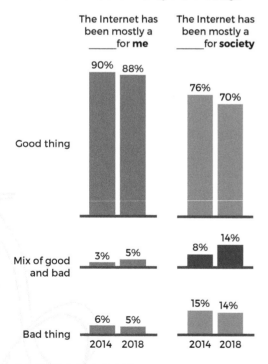

Growing share of online adults say the Internet has been a mixed blessing for society
% of online U.S. adults who say the following...

SOURCE: Smith (2018)

But when media influence is considered a "good" thing, people can flip, rating themselves as superior to others in being influenced positively by media. For example, in an experiment involving public service announcements about organ donation, researchers found that people rated themselves as more likely to be influenced than others. So perhaps, when you are asked to compare yourself to others, it's simply natural to try to put yourself in a positive light (Perloff, 2002).

Parent Attitudes about Media

As we have learned, children and young people watch a lot of television and spend a lot of time with video games, apps, and digital media. Since 2000, concerns about media influence on children have declined and in general have been less visible outside a narrow circle of advocates and academics. A survey of parents in 2006 found that 72% were "not too worried" or "not worried at all" about the types of programs their children watch. Research from the Kaiser Family Foundation found that the majority of children and teens do not have any rules about the type of media content they can use or the amount of time they can spend with television, video games, or music (Rideout, Foehr & Roberts 2010).

In many families, *screen time* centers on the use of tablets, mobile devices, and gaming devices, which are far more difficult for parents to monitor than TV or movie viewing. In Britain, one in three parents use technology tools, like ISP content filters, that limit usage (OFCOM, 2016). But in general, most parents are satisfied with their children's media use. Two out of three parents agree that their child has a good balance between screen time and doing other things. Adults use a variety of strategies for *parental mediation*, or managing media use in the home, including:

- Developing rules about time spent using media;
- Implementing rules about media content or activity;
- Engaging in co-viewing, co-use, or direct supervision;
- Talking with children about media use and content;
- Using technology tools that monitor or limit usage.

Public concern about media and technology and its potential harms goes in cycles that may be affected by media coverage. For example, news stories about media violence shifted in tone after 2000, as concerns about video games began to rise, displacing older concerns about depictions of violence in film and television. In one study, researchers reviewed 368 news stories and 172 opinion pieces about media violence research. About half of the articles suggested that media violence can increase aggressive behavior while half were more ambivalent. Overall, most news reports described the evidence as inconclusive. Some researchers perceive that media outlets create a *moral panic* about media violence. The term refers to the activation of fear and anxiety as a means to influence public opinion. But other research has found that the news media instead suggests that significant ambiguity exists within the research. It could be that journalists are "reluctant to report the negative effects of something that so many people enjoy" (Martins et al., 2013: 1082).

Some critics consider the impact of people spending so much time with machines. For example, Sherry Turkle has written extensively on the psychology of human–technology relationships; she laments the loss of social connectivity and affective relations caused by the Internet. Today, many people seem to prefer virtual and mediated relationships over face-to-face ones. In her 2015 book *Reclaiming Conversation*, she describes the vicious circle that happens as children see their parents glued to their cell phones. Children cannot compete for attention with the cell phone, so they want one of their own. Once the child has a cell phone, family members feel free to use digital devices while interacting with their children. Parental love is demonstrated by posting pictures on Facebook. According to Turkle, less face-to-face communication occurs than ever before in American families and, as a result, people are feeling more isolated and disconnected than ever.

On the other hand, being digitally connected is part of being a functional, productive member of society. For most people, disconnecting from media and technology is simply not an option. And who would want to? Most people appreciate the range of information and entertainment choices available and value the ease of connecting with family and friends.

But like any other sociocultural practice, people generally adhere to certain rules in order to ensure that their online lives are considered normal. One researcher notes, "Refusing to embrace new technologies makes one a luddite; too much enthusiasm could prompt accusations of wanton technophilia" (Zekany, 2014: 1). Most people balance their attitudes along a *luddite–technophilia continuum*. Luddites hate technology, while technophilia is the love of technology. I have called this phenomenon our "love-hate" relationship with media and technology (Hobbs, 2010a). Much of our media participation is a matter of delicate negotiation between these two poles. Public attitudes about media and technology may sometimes swing from an embrace of all things digital to fears about media manipulation, in part from our lived experience with media and in part from how media organizations report on media influence.

Consider the Question

How did your parents manage media use in the family when you were growing up? Did they set rules for how you used the computer, video game system, TV, or cell phone? Conduct a brief interview with one or more parents and family members about their memories by exploring these questions:

- Did your parents have any concerns about the use of media during your growing-up years? Why or why not?
- What specifically were they concerned about?
- Were any rules or guidelines used to manage your media use at home? What were they?
- How effective were these rules? How did they change over time?
- Are rules about media use still important for families today? Why or why not?

Empowerment and Protection in Video Games

The content of video games that can be enthralling: warriors, wizards, soldiers, villains, heroes, and adventurers populate virtual worlds enjoyed by game players. But the context of their use can be important too. The structure of the game world and how we move and behave in it can be fascinating.

One of the great sources of pleasure in video game play is the feeling of *mastery*. Through practice, you can control your destiny. In the real world, so much of our experience seems controlled. There is school and work and family, and everyone has expectations for how you should fulfill your obligations. Some video games feature worlds worth escaping to, worlds like *Uncharted* 4, a fantasy-adventure game where the protagonist and his colleagues search for lost treasure. Players have the freedom to explore the world and fight against enemies, and these experiences can be emotionally satisfying, too.

Game play can also connect the player to the narrative story in ways that create a sense of wonder that may offer insight on real life. For example, in the adventure video game *Journey*, the player is moving through a vast desert, traveling toward a mountain in the distance. When two players meet, the only form of communication between them is a musical chime, communicating the experience of the journey. The game suggests how we use our limited communication skills to forge emotional connections with people we meet during our journey through life. No language is used in the entire video game, only music and sounds. Each level is essentially a stage of life, notes critic Brandon Jacobs (2017). The game offers a series of adventures where you must navigate risks and dangers, battling weakness and incapacity, with a culminating experience that offers a thrilling conclusion.

At the Smithsonian American Art Museum, a special exhibition on "The Art of Video Games," funded by the videogame industry, introduced visitors to the people who design and create video games and their strategy for engaging players. Through *game mechanics*, you become an essential ingredient in video games. Within its constructed world, you shape the experience yourself. Thus, video games may be "the only form of media that allows for personalizing the artistic experience while still retaining the authority of the artist" (Mellissinos, 2015: 1).

Video games are a major component of contemporary media and can offer much that is beneficial and empowering for individuals and society. As noted in Chapter 1, the dialectic of *empowerment and protection* is important for media literacy even as the pendulum swings to emphasize one or the other of these two poles at any particular point in time.

Historically, shifting beliefs about the benefits and harms of media, technology, and

Are video game ratings useful to players? Are they useful to game companies? Why or why not?

Entertainment Software Rating Board

Are individuals solely responsible for the content of the media they see, watch, read, listen to, and play❓

popular culture have occurred over time. When new communications technologies arrive, a predictable pattern occurs, starting with delight and appreciation, followed by public concerns, followed by research inquiry and attention from government officials, which leads to increasing public attention. Then a new media arrives, and the cycle starts again (Wartella & Jennings, 2001). When each medium is new, people appreciate all of its glorious possibilities for learning, democracy, and social justice. When the medium is maturing as a commercial business and becoming more a part of everyday life, people notice how it changes existing structures of social power. Inevitably, the disadvantages and downsides of the medium become more evident, creating *resistance and reform*. Activists emerge to challenge media power when it is perceived to be damaging public welfare.

One example of resistance and reform occurred in response to the rise of violent video games in 1993, when the public became concerned that the game industry was irresponsibly marketing violent video games to children and teens. During this period, 16-bit home video game systems including Sega Genesis and Super Nintendo adapted arcade games like *Mortal Kombat*, where players decapitate their opponents or rip people's hearts out in a game that includes great pools of blood. This game became a sensation for the intense emotional shock it delivered to players.

Members of Congress held a hearing in Washington, D.C. in 1993, and the Parent Teacher Association even brought in Captain Kangaroo, who emphasized the need to help parents understand the value of adult supervision and monitoring. In response, the industry created the Entertainment Software Rating Board (ESRB), an organization that assigns age and content ratings to video games (Kohler, 2009). Concerns about video game violence abated as a result of the use of ratings, which position consumers as solely responsible for the content of the media they consume.

Gaming Addiction

Worldwide, 2.3 billion people play video games, and that number is expected to rise in the years ahead. Most people who play games do so in moderation, but some struggle with addiction. Public health experts have recognized that, for some people, video game play can become a compulsion that interferes with work, leisure, and social relationships. But is it an addiction?

Of course, the term *addiction* itself is complicated. Some people mistakenly see addiction as a moral failure or as a term limited to the use of a substance that causes physical dependence and withdrawal symptoms. But experts say that addiction is not just the physical or physiological need for a drug. Addiction occurs when a person compulsively does something even as it leads to negative outcomes, physical dependence, or not. In 2018, the World Health Organization (WHO) recognized *gaming disorder* in the latest version of the International Classification of Diseases (Lopez, 2018). It is defined this way:

- a person prioritizes gaming so that it takes precedence over other life interests and daily activities;

- gaming activity that escalates in frequency despite the occurrence of negative consequences;

- a person experiences significant impairment in personal, family, social, educational, occupational, or other important areas of functioning.

How do people overcome compulsive use of media❓

Note that the description mentions no physical symptoms, like loss of sleep. Similarly, the description offers no mention of the number of hours played for addiction to occur.

People experience pleasure from the *designed immersion* that video games provide. In *World of Warcraft*, you *are* the character. Role-playing games engage people in challenges in concert with others, as a social activity. There may be intermittent rewards, including a random chance at a desirable reward that can entice a person to keep playing for far longer than he or she would otherwise. Indeed, game developers consult with psychologists in order to make games as addictive as possible. For example, most games offer rewards that include advancing to higher levels or collecting new tokens or treasures.

Consider the power of *Candy Crush*, a mobile game created by Activision Blizzard. Players try to arrange a grid of brightly colored candies into rows and columns. When they are aligned in the right pattern, they disappear with a visual poof, a chime, and a cascade of new candies to take their places. These elements serve as rewards that provide little bursts of pleasure. In 2013, the game was so popular that it brought in $1 million in sales per day. One survey of *Candy Crush* players found that one in three users ignored their own friends or family in order to play the game. One in 10 got into arguments with significant others over how long they played (Dockterman, 2013).

Game play can affect people's perceptions of the real world. As game manufacturers and developers create games with high-resolution graphics, the immersive experience becomes more intense, leading players to experience the *game transfer* phenomenon, when activity in a virtual world bleeds over into real life. For example, in one study of gamers, a player reported seeing floating health bars above their opponents while playing soccer. Other players have experienced the illusion of objects moving upward on the screen after playing games such as *Guitar Hero* and *Rock Band* (Ortiz De Gortari & Griffiths, 2016).

The 90-Day Gaming Detox

It is part of a *digital wellness* movement. A variety of self-help communities are developing to help people control their addiction to social media, video games, and other digital media. There are many different types. One example is the 90-Day Detox developed by Cam Adair, a recovering video game addict. He has created a series of short videos and activities that help people regain control over their use of video games.

Adair explains that gaming gives people a rapid release of dopamine, the brain chemical that makes people feel good. Over time, people get adjusted to high levels of dopamine and they can experience cravings when they try to stop. Gaming also fulfills a lot of psychological needs. For many, it is a temporary escape from the pressures of everyday life. It also offers social connections that build people's need for identities as members of a team. The constant measurable growth people experience in mastering a video game gives people a sense of accomplishment and pride. Video games also provide challenges linked to a structured sense of purpose. In gaming: there is always a mission. You always know what to do next. Games give people a set of clear goals. They can be an effective way of escaping reality.

Real life can be as stimulating as video games, of course, but gamers can miss out on it as a result of desensitization, where real life seems dull and boring compared to the thrills of gaming. By taking a 3-month break from the activity, people can develop their social skills and find new sources of structure and challenge in their lives. Cam Adair says, "If you can't go 90 days without gaming, you probably shouldn't be gaming."

90 Years of Media Violence

Consider how the long history of public concern about media violence is enacted through research, self-regulation, media, government, and advocacy.

MEDIA AND RESEARCH	GOVERNMENT POLICY AND INDUSTRY SELF REGULATION
1927: **Research.** A series of research reports, called the Payne Fund Studies, examines the effects of film and radio on children's learning, attitudes, emotions, sleep, and other behavior. This research creates awareness among parents and educators that film and radio can have negative effects on children and youth.	1930: **Self-Regulation.** In response to public concern about the content of movies, the film industry self-regulates through the Hayes Code, a set of moral guidelines suggested to film writers that limit the depiction of children's sexuality, prostitution, profanity, brutality, and sympathy for criminals.
1967: **Media.** Viewers are shocked by the ending of Arthur Penn's film *Bonnie and Clyde*, which features the characters being ambushed by lawmen, their bodies jolted repeatedly by rifle fire. Slow-motion filming and rapid editing intensifies the graphic violence.	1968: **Self-Regulation.** The film ratings system developed by the Motion Picture Association of America (MPAA) replaces the Hayes Code. Film companies use labels that include: general audiences (G), parental guidance (PG), restricted (R), and X.

Continued...

1972: Research. A blue-ribbon committee reviews research evidence on media violence and the U.S. Surgeon General publishes the report, noting that experimental and survey research shows a modest relationship between exposure to media violence and aggressive behavior, leading some children to become more aggressive after exposure.	**1974: Self-Regulation.** Television broadcasters institute the Family Viewing Hour, agreeing to schedule the first hour of prime-time TV with programming suitable for all audiences.
1982: Research. The U.S. National Institutes of Mental Health (NIMH) releases a report that identifies television as a source of informal learning for children, noting that TV violence increases children's aggressive behavior. Exposure to television also harms the development of cognitive and attention skills that contribute to academic achievement. The report recommends teaching children critical TV viewing skills.	**1984: Self-Regulation.** Broadcasters eliminate the Family Viewing Hour as a result of challenges to its legal status from the FCC and the courts. After complaints about violence and gore in *Indiana Jones and the Temple of Doom*, the film industry adds PG-13 to its film ratings system.
1995: Media. PBS *Frontline*'s documentary "Can TV Kill?" draws national attention to television violence as a public health issue and increases public concern about the risk of media violence.	**1993. Government.** The U.S. House of Representatives holds 3 days of hearings on television violence and 10 bills and resolutions are introduced for consideration to the House and Senate.
1998: Research. In the most sophisticated content analysis of American television programming ever conducted, the National Television Violence Study surveys the prevalence of violence on network television, revealing that 40% of violent incidents are perpetrated by "good" characters and 71% of violent scenes include no remorse, criticism, or penalty for violence at the time it occurs.	**1996: Government.** The Telecommunication Act of 1996 is passed into law, which mandates the installation of the V-Chip in TV monitors, enabling parents to block programming they do not want their children to watch. The TV industry self-regulates by establishing a voluntary rating system in order to provide information about the content of entertainment programming.
2005: Research. The American Psychological Association releases a statement noting that exposure to violent media increases feelings of hostility, encourages thoughts about aggression and suspicions about the motives of others, and demonstrates violence as a method to deal with potential conflict situations.	**2001: Government.** The U.S. Surgeon General says media violence is associated with aggressive behavior but the size of the impact is small compared to other influences.
2015: Research. The American Psychological Association conducts a comprehensive analysis of research and finds that exposure to violent video games increases aggressive behavior, thoughts, angry feelings, and physiological arousal, and decreases helpful behavior. Exposure to sexualized violence in the media is linked to increases in violence toward women, rape myth acceptance, and anti-women attitudes.	**2018: Government.** Immediately after a school shooting, President Donald Trump meets with members of Congress and representatives of the video game industry and shows a clip reel of violent sequences from *Call of Duty*, *Modern Warfare 2*, *Wolfenstein*, *Dead by Daylight*, *Sniper Elite*, and *Fallout 4*.

Intellectual Grandparent:
Albert Bandura

Albert Bandura was one of the most important psychologists of the 20th century. A professor at Stanford University, he pioneered the concept of social learning theory, now often called *social cognition*. Several generations of social scientists in psychology, media studies and communication, and education have been influenced by his ideas. Media literacy scholars with interests in media effects value these key insights generated by his many decades of research and scholarship:

People learn through observation. Bandura studied how people learn from vicarious experience. He is well known for his early research on media and aggressive behavior, which demonstrated the conditions under which children will imitate actions they see on television. In the Bobo Doll experiments, he found that when children see actions rewarded, they are more likely to imitate them than if they see actions by perpetrators who are punished. His research proved that while people of all ages learn from observation, many moderating factors are present in an individual's decision to imitate an action.

People's behavior is influenced by the models available to them. Bandura's work enabled a generation of researchers to understand how media representations influence individuals and society by transforming, challenging, or reproducing cultural values and social norms. Some girls are exposed to thousands of images

Understanding Media Effects

Media definitely affect our emotions. The emotional enjoyment we get from media is probably why we use them so much. But repeated exposure to emotionally stimulating media content can lead to habituation, a process called *desensitization*. Desensitization refers to the decline in intensity of emotions experienced in response to media exposure. When you are physiologically aroused by an exciting scene in an action movie or a video game, you experience increased heart rate, skin perspiration, and emotional response. However, with repeated exposure, you no longer experience these same kinds of feelings. Researchers have discovered that desensitization may be associated with an increase in aggressive behavior, a reduction in physiological arousal to real-world violence, and even a reduction in the likelihood of helping a violence victim.

But desensitization can be valuable too. It is commonly used as a therapy for people with phobias. If you carefully expose people to images of snakes, they will gradually be less fearful of snakes. For medical students, becoming desensitized to surgery is necessary in order to perform surgery. But, as

of women who are tall, thin, and fair skinned, and they come to see their behaviors and characteristics as desirable. Other girls see images of female activists and politicians and come to see their behaviors and characteristics as desirable. Others who see violence depicted as a solution to difficult problems come to view violence as justified and heroic. When politicians and other figures in authority act as bullies, this may inspire others to copy and imitate their behavior.

People's behavior is reciprocally influenced by their technological and cultural environment as well as personal factors. Bandura proved that people do not merely copy or imitate the models around them. He recognized how human behavior is situational and contextual. It is influenced by the economic and structural components of societies and by individual will and volition. Ban-

dura understood that individuals are proactive, self-reflective, and self-regulating, interacting with the people, events, and processes all around them. He demonstrated how people's *self-efficacy* can affect the process of learning. People have different levels of confidence and feelings of control over different parts of their life. Parents, teachers, and peers can all influence how a person comes to feel capable of acting in the world. He also emphasized that individuals influence social structures, in a type of mutual influence called *reciprocal influence.* He admitted that such mutual influence may be both positive and negative at the same time.

If Albert Bandura has influenced your thinking about media, you can share a comment on the Grandparents of Media Literacy website at www.grandparentsofmedialiteracy.com.

researchers point out, the main public health concern with desensitization to violence is that viewing media violence "lowers responsiveness to real world violence" (Carnagey, Anderson & Bushman, 2007: 490).

You may have experienced this yourself in relation to the problem of school shootings. By the time a gunman fired on students at Parkland High School in Florida on February 14, 2018, 23 school shootings had already occurred in just the previous 2 months. In Parkland, 17 people were killed and a dozen more were seriously injured, more than the Columbine massacre in 1999. The shooting captured national attention—for a few days. Desensitization can be harmful to society as a whole when it creates a sense of helplessness, resignation, emotional withdrawal, or a tendency to blame the victims.

In the United States, children are thought to be more vulnerable to harms of all kinds as a result of their dependence upon adults. For example, nearly half of all deaths of children under age 5 are due to malnutrition. In the United States, child poverty rates are higher than in other developed countries (World Health Organization, 2019). Children are also thought to be more susceptible to media influence than adults because of the developmental characteristics inherent to childhood. Children are concrete, not abstract, in their thinking, and they lack world knowledge with which to evaluate the authenticity of media messages.

Do you think children need special types of media? Why or why not❓

The idea that children are a special audience with special needs predates television and is rooted in the development of children's literature in the 18th century, when books were first designed especially for children's use. By the turn of the 20th century, a well-developed market for children's books emerged thanks to the professionalization of children's librarians, who ensured that public libraries had well-stocked collections of literature for preschoolers, young children, and young adult readers. Radio programs for children were broadcast right from the start of radio broadcasting in the 1920s.

While many parents believe that children need special television programs, music, or movies, others do not see the need for special content. They see children as members of a family whose learning occurs from full participation in the ordinary practices of life in the home. For example, in some families, children watch horror movies right alongside parent or other family members enjoy the horror genre.

Over several generations, exposure to depictions of violence in entertainment media has emerged as an issue of special concern. People's vulnerability to media violence has been conceptualized in multiple ways. In an effort to synthesize the thousands of research studies conducted on television violence, violence in video games, and aggressive behavior, Anderson et al (2003) distinguished between four different *violent media effects* as shown in Table 13.1.

You may want to take some time to reflect on how the concepts in this table apply to your own childhood and early life experiences. Many college students and young adults can easily remember particularly scary or frightening media they experienced when younger. These four concepts are also be useful to illustrate different ways that other forms of media may influence human behavior.

With the rise of the Internet and social media, parental concerns about children's exposure to inappropriate content has also grown. In England, the British government is mandated to measure the media literacy of citizens, which it does through an annual survey. Children themselves report exposure to online risks that increase their fearfulness about the world. For example, in 2016, around 10% of children ages 8 to 11 who use the Internet said they encountered something online that they found worrying or nasty. Among 12–15-year-olds, nearly 20% reported such exposure. When asked to describe their experiences, kids share stories of encountering pornography or seeing footage of murders and executions. They describe seeing images of people being tortured. They notice how other people's pain and suffering can be treated as funny or humorous (OFCOM, 2016).

Table 13.1
Four Types of Violent Media Effects

NAME	DESCRIPTION	BEHAVIORAL PROCESS
Aggressor Effect	After exposure to media violence, some people become more mean, aggressive, and even violent toward others.	Imitation
Victim Effect	Exposure to violence leads some people to become more fearful, mistrusting, or self-protective. Over time, people perceive risks and dangers in the real world as similar to their exposure to media depictions of violence in entertainment and news coverage.	Social Learning
Bystander Effect	Exposure to violence contributes to callousness and apathy toward victims of violence.	Desensitization
Appetite Effect	Exposure to violence leads people to prefer increasingly violent, shocking, and emotionally stimulating forms of entertainment.	Arousal

Bullying is a topic of special concern. *Cyberbullying* is the most common type of online harassment children and teens encounter. Cyberbullying can take many forms, including name-calling, spreading false rumors, or constantly asking someone where they are, who they are with, or what they are doing. Some people have experienced cyberbullying in the form of physical threats to their safety or well-being or through the transmission of sexually explicit images. In 2018, a Pew Research Center survey found that nearly 60% of people aged 13–17 have experienced one or more of these problems. One in four teens has been sent sexually explicit images they did not ask for, and 7% say someone has shared explicit images of them without their consent (Anderson, 2018).

But when most people think about media risks and harms to children and teens, they think about *online predators*, not about risks and harms from known individuals within a child or teen's own peer group. Public interest in this issue rose between 2004 and 2006 as a result of the TV show *To Catch a Predator*, a reality show which featured a sting operation on men attempting to make contact with teens. The show attracted more than 7 million viewers. The public learned that pedophiles lurk on the Internet, enticing children into chat rooms, developing relationships, and then meeting up with them in person.

And for about 1 in 10 American children, such contact occurs. When an adult interacts with a child or young person, sometimes it is for the purpose of sexual abuse. Other times it is not. When adults encourage a child to talk about sex or share personal sexual information, it is called *grooming*. This can have negative effects on children's self-esteem and mental health. In a large U.S. survey, about 9% of youth ages 10 to 17 reported unwanted sexual solicitation (Jones, Mitchell & Finkelhor, 2012), and a British study found that 7% of adult participants in a national survey had communicated about a sexual topic with unknown others (Bergen et al., 2014).

Researchers who have studied grooming have discovered that it includes the stages of access and approach, when trust is cultivated, followed by entrapment, when children are requested to perform activities designed to test their dependence, social isolation, and neediness. It can occur in face-to-face situations or in online chat rooms or multiplayer games. Girls ages 13–15 are the most common target; at this age, talking to someone older can seem exciting. Some girls are attracted to opportunities to interact with older men. Teen boys questioning their sexuality are the second-most targeted group because they often feel talking about sex online is safer than sharing in real life. Grooming can be a form of sexual abuse when an adult takes advantage of an imbalance in power to coerce, manipulate, or deceive (Elgersma, 2017).

Unfortunately, teens themselves may treat contact with strangers as a type of risky game. Normal sexual development includes growth in curiosity, knowledge, and experimentation with sex. By the time youths reach age 13, they usually understand the risks of the Internet. As they get older and gain more experience online, their greater use creates greater risk. For example, older teens are the most likely to intentionally take risks involving privacy and contact with unknown people (Wolak, el-Toukhy & Ortiz, 2008).

On *To Catch a Predator*, the formula was always the same: young adults pretended to be teens, interacting with men online and then agreeing to meet for sexual encounters. When the men showed up at the house of the

Did you take risks in interacting with strangers online when you were younger? Why or why not **?**

Google and the Google logo are registered trademarks of Google LLC. used with permission.

presumed teen, a *gotcha moment* took place on camera, when men were humiliated before being arrested (Stelter, 2007). The show's focus on public humiliation demonstrates the appeal of law-and-order formulas that use a "riches-to-rags" narrative theme that allows the display of strong emotions like guilt and shame.

During the show's run, questions emerged about the possible entrapment of the child molesters and the role of the nonprofit organization that supported the work. Journalists also examined the role of local police who benefited financially from these sting operations. But the show's popularity remained until 2006, when one of the men featured on the show committed suicide and the network was sued for $105 million. The case with the grieving family was eventually settled out of court and the TV show was cancelled (Woodman, 2015).

Sexual Media

Many young people use film, TV, and the Internet as sources of information about sexuality, beginning in puberty. Researchers have found that attitudes about casual sex can be influenced by media representations, but less is known about how media's depictions of sexuality affect the development of adolescents' ideas about romantic love (Brown et al., 2014).

Indirect talk about sex in movies and TV shows, in the form of the double entendre, has long been used to keep audiences amused and entertained, and we see evidence of it even back to the time of Shakespeare (Hass, 1997). Today, you can find these kinds of references in sitcoms, reality TV shows, and late-night comedy. You can find them in pop music lyrics and in video games. Media depict sex as just something that people like to do; in real life, however, talk about sex is relatively rare and uncommon.

How are the vicarious pleasures of sexual media interpreted by people differently?

Sexual media are a significant part of media culture, and depictions of sexuality are as old as recorded history. But while depictions of sex can be entertaining, *pornography* is not designed for entertainment but for the purpose of sexual arousal. Pornography has also been part of culture since before the printed book was invented; examples of sexually explicit artwork have been found from ancient India and Greece. Pornography is defined as printed or visual material containing the explicit description or display of sexual organs or activity intended to stimulate erotic feelings (Tarrant, 2016).

When you think of it, pornography is actually a form of educational media. Children and young people are exposed to pornography usually at the onset of puberty. The average age of first exposure to pornography is 11.

5 critical questions about game addiction

After viewing this YouTube video at www. medialiteracyaction.com, use five critical questions of media literacy to gain insight on its meaning and value.

1. **Who is the author and what is the purpose?** James Portnow and Daniel Floyd created this video as part of the Extra Credits YouTube channel, which discusses subjects including freedom of speech, religion, politics, security, unethical business practices, education, history, and other topics. This weekly video lesson series has more than 2 million YouTube subscribers. Portnow sees his own videos about the video game industry as a type of media literacy. He said, "Nobody's going to let me make better games if the consumer doesn't demand better games" (Treece, 2013).

2. **What techniques are used to attract and hold attention?** The typical Extra Credits video is an informative, entertaining, and simply–illustrated lecture. In this video, however, the show's writers explain that they will use a different format for this topic because it is impossible for them to be objective. Then James Portnow faces the camera and reads aloud a stunningly lyrical first-person narrative. As he describes his teen years, his face and body language convey high levels of authenticity and his stories are rooted in the familiar and universal themes of adolescence. His stories about his own gaming practices illustrate the ways in which compulsive behavior develops.

3. **What lifestyles, values, and points of view are represented?** James conveys the idea that people turn to games when the challenges of life become overwhelming. People find that games and electronic worlds

For most children, their first exposure to sexual media was inadvertent and accidental. Researchers who studied people's memories of pornography asked college students to write about their experiences. Most describe feelings of disgust, shock or surprise, embarrassment, anger, fear, and sadness. If children experienced sexual media under the age of 12, guilt and confusion are the dominant emotions they recall. If they were 13 or older, disgust, anger, and sadness were more common. Positive feelings were more common for males because "responses to sexual media, including pornography, have different meanings and impacts for girls and boys" (Greenfield, 2004: 742). For some boys, watching porn may signal entrance into masculine identity.

It is important to reflect and ask critical questions about the messages pornography offers and how those messages influence personal, social, and sexual identity. In 1987, when the U.S. Surgeon General brought together an expert group to discuss pornography and public health, experts emphasized the risks associated with the various depictions of sexual violence. There was broad consensus that adolescents who see depictions of sexual violence

engage their curiosity more than school and work. "I was an *EverQuest* junkie," he admits. He describes the intense feelings of friendship and bonding that occur and explains how gaming became more important than schoolwork, sleep, nutrition, friendships, and health. James explains that after he reached out to a girl, he was able to step away from EverQuest for a time. We also learn how games create opportunities for male friendships. He describes the shame he felt during the deepest phase of his own addiction and uses a personal story to explain how his own gaming addiction competed with meaningful relationships. The dramatic moment when "reality comes crashing down" is a very powerful part of the story.

4. **How might different people interpret this message?** James displays so much au-

thenticity and empathy that most viewers are emotionally moved by his powerful personal story. The insights James offers on the feeling of redemption that he experienced after conquering his addiction may be appreciated by people who have struggled with addictive behaviors of all sorts. People who played *EverQuest* may find the story moving or insightful, but they may be annoyed at his description of the game.

5. **What is omitted?** James explains all that he has accomplished after overcoming his addiction and sees life as a series of challenges to conquer. James believes that the real world rewards the gamer mindset. But he does not offer specific concrete and practical strategies for how to break free of compulsive behavior.

get the impression that women like to be hurt, humiliated, or forced into sexual activity. Many porn films contain physical aggression, and spanking, gagging, choking, slapping, or verbal aggression occurs in 50% of scenes (Dines, 2016). Concluding that pornography stimulates "attitudes and behavior that lead to gravely negative consequences for individuals and for society," the Surgeon General argued that it has a negative impact on the mental, emotional, and physical health of both children and adults (Koop & Goodstein, 1987: 945).

Pornography is a major media industry, but it was legalized only 50 years ago, and those in the business can be secretive about their earnings; estimates of the industry size range widely, from $6 billion to $97 billion in annual revenues. The website Pornhub draws 80 million visitors a day (Van Syckle, 2018).

Over time, the porn industry has made considerable efforts to normalize porn. When you watch movies and TV shows, you may see examples of how pornography is embedded in many aspects of entertainment culture. The producers of pornography even formed a lobbying group, the Free

Speech Coalition, to oppose obscenity and censorship laws that could restrict access to pornography. Its first successful action was to oppose a California bill intended to tax pornography differently from other forms of media content.

Porn use has been associated with relationship dissatisfaction. Do people in unhappy relationships turn to pornography? Or is pornography itself contributing to the relationship's decline? Could pornography create unrealistic expectations about sexuality? Researchers examined a group of 2,000 married couples, asking them questions over several years in order to determine when they used porn and when they stopped. They found that married people who began using porn were roughly twice as likely to get divorced as those who did not (Perry & Schleifer, 2018). The use of pornography has also been associated with more open sexual values, greater propensity toward infidelity, the objectification of women, and diminished sexual satisfaction with partners (Peter & Valkenburg, 2009). People's attitudes about pornography may be influenced by their religious and ethical belief systems. (Grubbs et al, 2017). For some, the use of pornography is a violation of deeply held beliefs. This can lead to feelings of shame and distress. In 2014, a search of the term "pornography addiction" on Amazon.com revealed nearly 2,000 results, with more than 900 books located in the category of Religion and Spirituality.

The rise of smartphones and social media has broadened the sexual media landscape considerably. New forms of sexual expression have emerged, and ordinary people have become pornographers themselves, either in front of or behind the camera.

Sexting is now generally understood as a normative behavior among consenting parties. Some experts see sexting as a safe form of sexual experimentation. Many young adults see sexting as a positive activity, fun, flirty, and relatively harmless. However, some who send or receive sexts experience negative emotional consequences, including feelings of a loss of self-respect or embarrassment.

What the the potential benefits and harms of sexting ❓

> Well you know how to turn me on

> that makes me want to even more

> then i want to kiss all the way down the inside of your thighs

> all the way down

> I can feel your kisses

The benefits and risks of sexting may depend on the characteristics of the sexual relationship. When college students were asked to evaluate how sexting affects the quality of their relationship with a partner, researchers found that women are more likely to engage in sexting with a committed partner, while men are more likely to engage in sexting with a casual partner. Men, who experience more emotional benefits and fewer emotional costs from casual sex, are more likely than women to engage in sexting. Women are more likely to send sexually explicit pictures to advance relational closeness. They may require a higher level of trust in the relationship in order to feel comfortable sexting (Drouin, Coupe & Temple, 2017)

But sexting can sometimes raise emotional, social, and legal concerns because it can be used for harmful purposes. Legally, people under the age of 18 may face charges of child pornography for sending or receiving sexually explicit images of a minor. Each state regulates sexting differently, however. In the state of Illinois, sexting between minors is illegal, but the crime is considered a misdemeanor. In Nebraska, it is a crime to send sexually explicit photos of a minor via text message, but juvenile offenders are not prosecuted for receiving such images if the image was taken voluntarily and the recipient does not distribute the image to anyone else.

Sexting can be exploited as a form of online harassment that can lead to problems that affect people's careers. When sexts are distributed beyond the initial recipient, or when sexting is coercive or nonconsensual, it has been described as *revenge pornography* (Clancy, Klettke & Halford, 2019). Roughly 1 in 25 people have been victims of revenge porn: 3% people say that someone has threatened to post nude or nearly nude photos or videos of them online to hurt or embarrass them, and 2% have had someone actually post a photo of them online without their permission (Lenhart, Ybarra & Price-Feeney, 2016). The #MeToo movement has helped raise the visibility of the role of sexual harassment in the lives of ordinary people.

James Blinn/Alamy Stock Photo

How may porn media literacy help people make informed choices about the media they see, watch and read?

What the future may hold: Porn Media Literacy

Educators are making an effort to introduce students to critical thinking activities about pornography, a practice called *porn media literacy*. For example, at the Start Strong program, developed by the Boston Public Health Commission, the five-session after-school course was called The Truth about Pornography: A Pornography-Literacy Curriculum for High School Students Designed to Reduce Sexual and Dating Violence (Jones, 2018). As part of a broader approach to sex education, porn media literacy is not common in American schools. One large-scale study of teens in The Netherlands found that those who had exposure to porn and had received porn literacy in high school were less likely to view women as sex objects (Vandenbosch & Van Oosten, 2017).

Porn literacy curriculum is not designed to scare students or tell them that using porn will ruin their lives. Because most adolescents do see porn, analyzing its messages is more likely to empower them to make informed choices. Notes Emily Rothman of Boston University School of Public Health, "Just as we teach them to review song lyrics critically, or advertisements, we felt they could also be encouraged to analyze sexually explicit media and make informed choices about whether or not they would ever want to see pornography, with whom, when, and why" (Finucane, 2018).

In the program, teens do not talk about their own sexual experiences or even whether they have seen pornography or not. They do not view examples of pornography in class. Instead, students learn about the history of pornography and the regulation of obscenity. Instructors deglamorize the idea of becoming a celebrity porn star by debunking the myth that it is a quick and easy way to get rich and famous (Finucane, 2018). Topics emphasize helping teens understand their own values and beliefs about sexually explicit media. The course offers a creative and engaging way to have meaningful conversations about pleasure, desire, consent, respect, safety, and health.

Porn media literacy can help people gain greater awareness of the pervasiveness of sexual media in film, TV, and video games, and online. Porn media literacy may help people adopt safer attitudes and practices regarding the expression of sexuality. Educators may emphasize unrealistic portrayals of sexuality or call out the absence of the depiction of safe sex practices in porn. For example, depictions of condomless sex in pornography can contribute to the perception that this practice is a social norm (Nelson, Eaton & Gamarel, 2016). Porn media literacy may simply increase people's awareness of how sexuality is represented in all forms of media, enabling people to be more aware and metacognitive in making decisions about what they read, view, use, listen to, and watch.

TIME T◉ REFLECT

Visit the Flipgrid Inquiry for Chapter 13 and consider one or more of these questions from Adele Hasinoff, author of *Sexting Panic: Rethinking Criminalization, Privacy, and Consent* (2015). Reflect on these questions and compose a response:

- Is there such a thing as safe sexting? Why or why not?
- How do you know if an image you receive is intended to be private or if it is ok to pass on to your friends?
- If you want an image to be private, what is the best way to make sure your recipient knows?
- What kind of images are the most and least likely to cause problems if someone distributes them?
- What practices could make sexting more safe?
- Do you think sexting among minors should be illegal? Why or why not?

After you identify the question you are addressing, share your thoughts in a brief oral presentation. On the website, you can view and respond to comments of other people who have offered thoughtful reflections on sexting, privacy, and relationships. Visit www.medialiteracyaction.com to learn more.

CREATE T▶ LEARN

Analyze Dating Apps

The world of dating apps continues to grow and differentiate, offering a variety of strategies for finding a partner. Surely you have heard of Match and Tinder. But have you used Hinge? Happn? How About We?

Working individually or with a partner, research the many different online hookup apps and websites. Choose two dating apps or websites to compare and contrast and then explore these tools in order to understand how they work. Considering the unique traits of the dating apps and websites, create a comparison-contrast chart that identifies their key features. Consider the clues provided to compare two dating apps or websites based on at least five criteria. Be sure to identify the target audience, the features of the app that make it fun to use, and the assumptions the app makes about the type and nature of the relationships that matter most. Be sure to consider possible unanticipated outcomes of the dating apps or websites you examine. Share your comparison-contrast chart with others using the #MLAction hashtag.

People develop intellectual curiosity by asking critical questions and creating media, in and out of school

14 How Do People Become Media Literate?

Learning Outcomes

1. Consider how people use the process of asking critical questions about media to deepen their active participation in society and culture

2. Understand why media literacy is an expanded conceptualization of literacy that involves many types of reading and writing practices with print, visual, audio and digital texts, tools, and technologies

3. Examine how media literacy changes in response to changes in technology, culture, and society

4. Appreciate how media literacy education supports public health and global citizenship

People of all ages may learn about the media through watching YouTube celebrities. Perhaps you are a fan of Captain Disillusion, also known as Alan Melikdjanian, who creates intriguing and hilarious videos in which he deconstructs and debunks the most popular viral videos on the Internet. If you have ever seen the video on the Chinese invisibility cloak or the slapping penguins, you might have wondered how these videos are made. Captain Disillusion calls himself a "pixel justice crusader supported by an army of skeptical fans." As an expert on computer-aided effects, motion graphics, and post-processing, Captain Disillusion pulls back the curtain to show how video trickery is created through production and post-production techniques. In his YouTube videos, he even reproduces special effects on his own to show viewers how it is done. After viewers watch one of his videos, they become hyperaware of how special effects are carefully constructed using software, hardware, and plenty of creativity.

Google and the Google logo are registered trademarks of Google LLC. used with permission.

© Youtube. Inc

What have you learned about media from the work of media makers themselves?

Or perhaps you are a fan of Chris Stuckmann, introduced in Chapter 8. Stuckmann reviews horror films, but he also reviews classic films like Frank Capra's *It's a Wonderful Life* and action films like *Quantum of Solace* and *The Mandalorian*. Stuckmann has even attempted to educate his fans about his copyright disputes with Universal Studios. Stuckmann knows that he has a right under copyright law to comment on films and videos and to use short clips from films to develop his ideas as a film critic.

Maybe you watch John Oliver's *This Week Tonight* on HBO, which routinely offers insanely brilliant media literacy insights for viewers. For example, in one episode, Oliver introduces viewers to astroturfing, discussed in Chapter 5, a deceptive form of propaganda in which a group appears to be a grassroots organization of citizens, but it is really funded and sponsored by a business or an industry. For example, Americans Against Food Taxes is sponsored by the food and beverage industry, and the National Wetlands Coalition is funded by oil companies. By highlighting these carefully-designed public relations efforts, Oliver invites viewers to be critical, but he does not want people to become cynical. He wants people to know that many advocacy groups do not take payments from big corporations and special interests (Greenwood, 2018).

Or perhaps you have read the work of the many fine reporters at *The New York Times* and other publications who review films, report on media industries and production practices, or examine media-related trends in culture. Every week, readers can learn about the changes in this dynamic business and cultural sector. While knowledge of the media industry alone will not automatically make consumers media literate, knowledge can support the development of critical thinking skills.

While many people are introduced to media literacy through the work of media makers, it is also possible that you have experienced media literacy education in a more formal context as part of elementary or secondary schooling. And since you are reading this book, you are probably developing media literacy competencies as part of your own formal education. But media literacy education can start in the early grades. For example, at the Brooklyn School of Inquiry, a New York City public school, Michael Novick offers a media literacy class to children in grades 4–8 and collaborates with classroom teachers to integrate media literacy across the subject areas. These activities include:

- Grade 5 features a year-long focus on human rights, where children debate whether access to the Internet is a human right and learn how to critically analyze documentaries in order to identify their purpose and point of view;

- They consider whether cyberbullying is a human rights issue and create comic book pages to demonstrate their learning;

- At the end of the year, students work in teams to research a human rights issue that interests them and create their own short documentaries using iMovie.

Because media literacy is integrated into the existing curriculum, students see key connections between media literacy and issues like human rights. Students gain confidence as independent learners and build habits of critically analyzing and evaluating all kinds of messages, aware that they are actively interpreting everything they read, view, and use. They also see themselves as media creators who share what they are learning through images, video, and interactive media. Many times, teachers learn to create such learning environments with support from experts. In this case, Rhys Daunic and his colleagues at The Media Spot offered consulting services to the Brooklyn School of Inquiry so as to support the work of classroom teachers (Media Spot, 2016).

Media literacy education comes in many forms, depending on the competencies and interests of teachers, the needs of learners, and the cultural context and learning environment. After the so-called fake news crisis of 2018, Google and Facebook both supported media literacy initiatives focused on the topic. Google's project is called MediaWise and Facebook's initiative is the News Literacy Project. When Google and Facebook gave money to news organizations to initiate media literacy education projects, it was a relatively small but important investment. After all, they wanted to demonstrate to the public that they are part of the solution in combating so-called fake news. Some of their activities include:

- Special events in schools and communities during which participants learn to be fact-checkers, using Instagram polling and Snapchat filters to share their ideas;

- Students move through a series of online lessons where they watch videos and take quizzes in order to learn about the First Amendment and understand how journalists decide what is newsworthy.

As you can see, media literacy varies greatly depending on the values of the instructors as well as the needs of learners and the community context. In informal learning settings, media literacy educators may use humor and play to engage learners. In higher education, students may participate in a community project, working to analyze and create media that are relevant to their neighborhoods, cities, or region.

This chapter examines how media literacy competencies are acquired through learning experiences, exploring these questions:

- How is media literacy education connected to educational technology?
- Why is creative media making so important to media literacy?
- How can media literacy be learned outside the classroom?
- How is media literacy developing around the world?
- Why is media literacy education not already part of every student's experience in school?

As Michael RobbGrieco notes in chronicling the history of media literacy in the United States, the practice of media literacy education has been "continuously contested and employed in very different ways by scholars and practitioners with different disciplinary and institutional interests" (2019: 5).

Media Literacy as a Literacy Practice

As discussed in Chapter 1, the most widely used definition of *media literacy* emerged from the Aspen Institute, which brought together a group of media literacy experts in 1993 who defined it as "the ability to access, analyze, evaluate and create media in a variety of forms" (Aufderheide, 1993). This definition has been used in most scholarly and practitioner discourse on media education in the United States. Globally, the term *media education* is also used to refer to the habits of mind, knowledge, and competencies that empower consumers to function as autonomous and rational citizens (Tyner, 2004).

Literacy scholars contend that literacy is a social practice, not merely a learned skill or a set of competencies. Literacy is contextual and situational in relation to people's needs for self-expression and communication in daily life. For those who see media literacy as an expanded conceptualization of literacy, it has long been embedded in English language arts education, aligned with the practice of reading, writing and creative expression, interpretation, and meaning-making. As shown throughout this book, terms like *author*, *text*, *audience*, *message*, *meaning*, and *representation* have also expanded from their earlier formulation focused on writers and writing

How did you learn about media when you were in elementary or secondary school❓

Bonnie Nishihara

toward a more *multimodal* perspective, where visual, audiovisual, sound, interactive, and digital modes of expression are recognized as essential to the practice of literacy.

For these reasons, literacy is no longer confined to the domain of printed language and paper books. Multimodality, according to Kress and van Leeuwen (1996) builds upon semiotics to consider media form and content from the position of the maker, identifying how meaning is constructed through modes that may include:

- **Materials**: the tools and resources used to create media;
- **Framing and design**: considering how particular elements could be assembled, selected, and arranged;
- **Production**: the process of developing the actual creative work.

Whether a media consumer is looking at infographics, podcasts, remixes, essays, poems, TV shows, video games, business memos, or text messages, a critical analysis of a maker's choices reveals evidence of how decisions about materials, design and production are embedded in all the works people compose and create.

Through creative work, people do not merely represent ideas and information: they reveal themselves as individuals and as members of families and communities. Because digital media platforms enable people to create media without professional training or expensive materials, media users have a dual identity: readers are writers, listeners are speakers, and audiences are media producers.

Teachers may have different motivations for including attention to media and popular culture as part of education in elementary, middle, or high school. English educators generally focus on literature because they value the heritage and traditions of literature as a genre and want to pass it on to the next generation. They may want to cultivate in learners the ability to discriminate between quality information and fake news. Other teachers may want to use media and popular culture to motivate learners for the purposes of *engagement*. These teachers may feel a deep sense of urgency about preventing students from dropping out of school. More than 7,000 teenagers drop out of school every day—that is 1.2 million American students each year (NCES, 2016).

High school English teacher Melissa Page combines everyday popular culture and current issues with traditional print literature. Her students use rhetorical strategies to analyze Arthur Miller's *The Crucible* and film clips from *Star Wars* and *American Beauty* (Page, 2012). She sees literacy practices as shifting from a concentration on individual reading and writing behavior to a focus on more collaborative, social activity. By adding film, television, radio, newspapers, video games, advertisements, music, and popular culture in addition to learning about media industries, student engagement is heightened. In these discussions, students have well-informed and sometimes skeptical perspectives. Students are more eager and able to share their ideas when popular culture texts are brought into the classroom because they can make a connection between the classroom and the culture. Applying student insight and knowledge to the analysis of familiar texts, the teacher helps students recognize connections between media and the more unfamiliar texts of classic and contemporary literature. In this way, media literacy education can be used to stimulate the students' participation in the complexities of interpretation and meaning-making (Hobbs, 2006).

Media literacy educators are responsive to changes in culture that shape how consumers use media, technology, and popular culture. By exploring important connections between creative media production and reading and writing, teachers encourage critical analysis, promote creativity and invention, consider the relationship between image and word, and destabilize concepts of linearity and originality through the application of concepts like assemblage and remix (Palmeri, 2012).

In the United States, the decentralized nature of the education system grants teachers the freedom to use media literacy pedagogies as part of existing instruction. In France and Finland, media literacy education is formally established in the national curricula and teachers receive support from governmental organizations. But in most European countries, where education is more formally centralized by national governments, integrating

What reading strategies do you use most often **?**

media literacy may not be possible in school (Frau-Meigs & Torrent, 2009). That is why media literacy education has developed in after-school and informal learning contexts, due to the absence of media literacy *education frameworks* in national curricula.

In most countries around the world, media literacy education generally happens as a result of the initiative of individual enthusiast teachers or school leaders or local activists. (Hobbs, 2011). College and university faculty members may advance media literacy by embedding it into their coursework or adopting *school-university partnership* models, which bring undergraduate and graduate students into elementary and secondary schools in order to support the integration of media literacy into the curriculum (Scharrer, 2006). Educators develop media literacy programs based on their own particular interests and motivations in relationship to the unique needs of their students and communities. This results in highly varied practices that may include a concentration on issues of gender discrimination, consumer culture, and materialism, a focus on personal and cultural identity or practices of evaluating the veracity of Internet content, or even an emphasis on understanding and analyzing advertising, news, entertainment media, and digital culture, which are the topics that you have encountered throughout this book.

Reading in a Digital World

When people encounter the term *literacy*, they initially think of reading. Today, the nature of reading itself is changing as we do more of it on screens. Consider these eight different *types of reading* that are now becoming more common as reading on cell phones and digital devices displaces the reading of paper books:

- **Simple sharing**: reading encounters with digital content, where users read only the headline and photo, instantly sharing with others;

- **Skimming**: reading a text quickly in order to get the general meaning or the overall gist of the argument;

- **Scanning**: searching through a text, looking for specific details and information without reading the whole work;

- **Pleasure seeking**: reading primarily for surprise, novelty, and excitement;

- **Community reading**: reading primarily as a social practice so as to fit in with members of a particular group;
- **Deep reading**: reading in search of knowledge by evaluating content for accuracy, relevance, and quality;
- **Literary reading**: reading with special attention to the style, grace, and execution of the prose or the design of the work itself;
- **Empathic reading**: reading as a means to feel emotionally connected to the author, ideas, or content.

Which of these practices are familiar to you? Which are associated with your reading on your cell phone and which are associated with your use of print books?

Some worry that the increasing centrality of screen reading will diminish or erode deep reading, literary reading, and empathic reading. As one reading scholar points out, the devices consumers use for reading have an impact on their purposes for reading, potentially contributing to the "subtle atrophy of critical analysis and empathy" as they "navigate a constant bombardment of information" where they retreat to "familiar silos" that leave them susceptible to false information and demagoguery (Wolf, 2018: 1).

Actually, as a result of mobile devices, people are reading more than ever. An enormous amount of basic reading activity is now essential for ordinary life online. For example, you are probably reading and writing text messages and retrieving other types of information multiple times every day. But as Kovac and Van der Weel (2018) point out, because Internet users prefer shorter texts, online reading may reduce the ability to engage with complexity in argument, syntax, grammar, and vocabulary. With less experience reading long-form works, people are more inclined to turn to videos instead of books, magazine articles, or serious journalism. As a result, today more than 50% of all learners ages 15–23 say they prefer learning from short-form videos over any other form of activity, including print reading, games or apps, or even classroom activities (Pearson, 2018).

Whether media consumers read on a screen, use a paper book, or listen to audiobooks, reading for pleasure is on the decline in the United States, according to recent statistics. The U.S. government conducts periodic time-use surveys with a large sample of 26,000 Americans, with respondents asked to fill out detailed surveys of what they do in a 24-hour period. Because the sample size is so large and the data are so granular, these studies are considered highly reliable. Back in 2004, people read about 23 minutes per day, while in 2017, the average time spent reading was 17 minutes. Most of the decline is attributed to men's decline in reading, which fell by 40% between 2004 and 2017. People ages 35–44 read less than both younger and older people (Ingraham, 2018).

It turns out that reading and many other forms of leisure simply cannot compete with video and TV viewing. Surveys show that reading, computer

With a partner or in a small group, discuss one or more of these questions:

- Which of the eight types of reading are most important to you? Which are least important?
- Which types of reading would you like to do more often?
- Should people be concerned about the decline of reading? Why or why not?
- What are some potential long-term consequences of the changes that are now occurring in how people read?

use, thinking, playing games, socializing, and communicating are all minor leisure activities compared to TV viewing. TV viewing far outpaces reading as a leisure activity. In 2017, the average American spent more than 2 hours and 45 minutes per day watching TV, every day of the year, or nearly 10 times the amount of time they devoted to reading for pleasure (Ingraham, 2018).

Creating Media

Not long ago, media production activities were considered part of a specialist subject for students enrolled in vocational classes or for those intending to pursue careers in media and communication. But today, *create to learn* pedagogies are occurring across the curriculum in elementary schools, middle schools, high schools, colleges, and universities (Hobbs & Moore, 2013). As early as first grade, children are using cell phone cameras to represent their understanding of the world. Early on, children learn that writing and visual media are ways to express ideas. As a result, many schools help students learn to use new digital tools and platforms in order to create media to represent their learning (Burn & Durran, 2007). Throughout this book, of course,

What is your earliest memory of creating media?

you have been invited to create infographics, podcasts, memes, videos, screencasts, and remixes as a way to demonstrate your learning.

In schools, this work is happening with students of all ages. At Narragansett Elementary School in Rhode Island, grade 1 students create a daily weather report using an iPad and simple software. Children learn how to create media that helps others make practical daily decisions. At Lenfest Middle School in Philadelphia, teams of students produce an informal talk show so as to explain

RosalreneBetancourt 9/Alamy Stock Photo

their understanding of media's purposes to inform, to entertain, and to persuade. They showcase their carefully designed public service announcement that aims to discourage violence in their school. At Palo Alto High School in California, students learn media literacy through participation in a school journalism program where they study journalism's norms, codes, and conventions while comparing and contrasting different news stories about the same event in order to identify media's constructed nature (Madison, 2015).

In some classes, media creation activities combine with *inquiry learning*, a method of instruction that promotes self-directed learning through a process of questioning and exploration. For example, at Roosevelt High School in Minneapolis, students create short films in their English class, using community-based research to examine a topic or issue with relevance to their community. At the beginning of the project, students view and discuss examples of community documentaries. Then they analyze videos to understand how "technical elements positioned viewers to believe, feel, or think in certain ways. Often, these discussions engage students around controversial topics such as corporate ethics or racial representations" (Dockter, Haug & Lewis, 2010: 419). As part of their project, students interview community members. Finally, students create, share, and reflect on their own media projects.

By sharing their creative products with their classmates, students deepen a sense of emotional connection to the people they represent in their media productions. One student notes that as her peers listened to her podcast memoir about being in Mexico after her mother had left for the United States, she felt her classmates telling her, "We're a part of your life." Because the course culminates in a film festival attended by parents, administrators, students, and community members, many students put in extra hours to ensure that they could be proud of their work. One learner explained, "My family is coming and I want to feel proud of it. I did a mov-

Why is collaboration so important to the creative process❓

ie with my group, right? I tried to work as hard as I could and make the best movie so my mom will be proud of me" (Dockter et al., 2010, 418–419).

Creative media production brings issues of *ethos* into sharper focus, as learners and teachers consider their identities as media makers, which include consideration of the ethical and social impact of their communication on others. For this reason, *reflection* has long been recognized as a central pedagogical

Fizkes/iStock

element of media literacy education. You have undoubtedly noticed that each chapter of this textbook concludes with opportunities for both reflection and creative work. If you have completed these activities, you already recognize the power of reflection in deepening learning to better understand the complexities, paradoxes, and contradictions of life in a media saturated-society.

Digital Literacy

Among educators, the increasingly easy access to digital technologies in education has provided an impetus for media literacy pedagogy to thrive. For more than 80 years, educators have used many different types of *educational technology* to promote learning. Depending on your age and the school you attended, you may remember getting a Chromebook in school or playing educational computer games like *Oregon Trail*. Your instructor may have presented information using an overhead projector, an interactive digital whiteboard, a DVD, or even a VHS videotape. As a student, you are familiar with educators' reliance on PowerPoint slides to transmit information through an illustrated lecture.

But teaching *with* media is not the same as teaching *about* media. The use of educational technology is quite different than the practice of media literacy education. Media literacy educators carefully differentiate between the use of media to engage learners, as a content delivery system, or as a teaching aid. When media are used in these functional or instrumental ways, critical questions about cultural, political, and economic issues may be marginalized or ignored.

For these reasons, the dominant pedagogical practice of media literacy education is rooted in *discussion and dialogue*, where the process of asking critical questions about what consumers watch, see, and read. Still, the increased use of the Internet for teaching and learning is bringing new opportunities for media creation activities as part of media literacy education. This is one reason why media literacy and educational technology are beginning to combine in interesting ways.

Media literacy competencies also change as media and technology change. Since 2011, the term *digital literacy* has represented the technical, cognitive, and social competencies, knowledge, and skills needed to communicate effectively and participate in the contemporary knowledge economy. The American Library Association has defined digital literacy as "the ability to use information and communication technologies to find, understand, evaluate, create and communicate digital information. Basic reading and writing skills are foundational; and true digital literacy requires both cognitive and technical skills" (American Library Association, 2013). The term digital literacy includes many of the issues explored in this book: issues of identity in a networked world; multimodality, hypertexts, mashups, and remixing; video games and learning; and collaboration and peer-to-peer media production (Jones & Hafner, 2012).

Another approach to digital literacy is called *digital citizenship*, and this educational practice is rooted in concern about social responsibility and Internet safety. Digital citizenship, as a concept, is embraced by educators who know that students must understand the social and legal dimensions of using the Internet (Ohler, 2011). For students, exploring the legal dimensions of the Internet may focus on cyberbullying, copyright and intellectual property, or privacy. The social dimensions of digital citizenship may include lessons on *netiquette*, the informal norms of online social communication. In these lessons, younger students are often surprised to learn that it is considered inappropriate to include emojis in an email!

For educators, digital citizenship generally includes some emphasis on laws that directly affect students, schools and libraries. As early as 1993, federal law enforcement officials became aware of the use of the Internet as a tool for child abuse and prosecuted more than 10,000 individuals through the discovery of online child pornography. This led Congress to pass the Children's Internet Protection Act (CIPA), a law designed to protect children from harmful Internet content.

Justhavealook/iStock

Were you aware of Internet blocking or filtering in schools when you were younger? Why or why not?

In the United States, the strong historical tradition of decentralized education means that the federal government can control the content of public education in only a very limited number of ways. For this reason, the federal government legally cannot require the teaching of media literacy or digital citizenship. But CIPA tied special discounts for educational technology (called *e-rate funding*) to two mandated activities: (1) filtering Internet content so as to protect students from harmful material online and (2) educating students about Internet safety during the school year. The e-rate funding discount has become an essential way that schools pay for technology infrastructure maintenance, routers, switches, and fiber-optic cable, because, depending on the community, it can reduce costs by as much as 90% (Menuey, 2009). As a result, most American schools filter the Internet in order to prevent students from accessing inappropriate content. Because it tied funding to a specific set of required actions, CIPA has actually ensured that digital citizenship is taught in every American school. Educators may offer a single learning experience in digital citizenship at the beginning of the school year, or they may integrate these lessons into existing curricula all year long.

With substantial support from charitable foundations and technology companies, another research and practice area known as *digital media and learning* has developed. This group of scholars, educators and advocates emphasized that "learning that is socially embedded, interest-driven, and oriented toward educational, economic, or political opportunity" (Ito et al., 2013: 1). For example, a young person who can pursue a personal interest or passion with the support of friends and caring adults may link this learning and interest to academic achievement, career success, or civic engagement. Such learning is conceptualized as resilient, adaptive, and effective because it is built on a foundation of the individual's interests, where social support from others helps overcome adversity and provide recognition. Such learning taps into the opportunities digital media provide to more easily link home, school, community, and peer contexts of learning. It may support peer and intergenerational connections based on shared interests; and create more connections with nondominant youth (Ito et al., 2013). Some see this approach as an alternative to the limitations and flaws of the public school system.

In one digital media and learning project, researchers developed a 3-year longitudinal study to examine a learning environment intentionally designed to provide urban youth with tools that allow them to create, collaborate, and communicate with media production technologies. The program offered a series of after-school clubs in graphic design, digital broadcasting, movie making, music recording and remixing, and video game development. Results showed that, with effective mentoring, students can shift their sense of identity to position themselves as authors (Barron et al., 2014). Scholarly inquiry on the practices that contribute to youth empowerment are a vital part of research in digital and media literacy education.

Lies My Teacher Told Me

You may have enjoyed learning about history or you may have found it not so interesting. History teachers believe that factual knowledge about history can prevent us from repeating the mistakes of previous generations. But when history is presented merely as a series of facts and information to be memorized, students may not develop the critical thinking skills needed to analyze and evaluate information.

Twenty-five years ago, historian James W. Loewen offered a critique of history education that resonated deeply with media literacy educators. In his book *Lies My Teacher Told Me,* Loewen analyzed a dozen high school textbooks, finding that Thanksgiving, the Civil War, and Native Americans were presented in inaccurate and distorted ways. Loewen revealed how history textbooks contain selective and incomplete information and reflect cultural myths and values History textbooks reflect the biases of the authors and the demands of the educational publishing marketplace.

In many schools, students are asked to read textbooks and remember key facts. "Textbooks don't teach us to challenge, to read critically—they are just supposed to provide exercises in stuff to learn," notes Loewen (1995/2008).

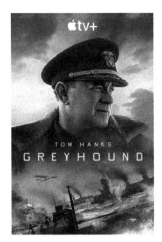   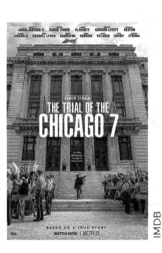

How can movies be used to activate critical thinking about media, history and culture?.

If textbook authors could admit uncertainty, students would get the idea that knowledge is constructed and that it is not fixed and static: knowledge changes over time (Wong, 2018).

Some history teachers use media literacy activities to help students understand the constructed nature of history itself. For example, in Ithaca College's media literacy program, Project Look Sharp, Chris Sperry teaches educators how to incorporate media literacy into history and civics education. As an experienced history teacher, he explores the U.S. wars in Vietnam, the Persian Gulf War, and the war in Afghanistan in three class periods, using a creative approach to analyzing old covers of *Newsweek* magazine. Students read about the histories of each conflict and then they critically analyze a dozen *Newsweek* covers from each war. In analyzing the *Newsweek* story, "How to Save the Arab World" from December 24, 2001, students learn that Afghanistan is not an Arab state. They get a brief history of Bin Laden's relationship to the Taliban, and they gain a better understanding of the Arab connection to September 11. This approach to teaching and learning includes no lectures. Historical information from the readings becomes more salient as students use this knowledge to interpret the visual messages that are presented in the compelling magazine covers. Students get a sense of how images and language both offer a point of view as they represent reality.

When media literacy is embedded into the study of history, students are challenged to ask critical questions as they gradually develop a more accurate view of how both journalism and history represent the past. Sperry encourages students to interpret the cover imagery, but he also demands that students provide reasoning and evidence to justify their interpretations. One student explains how the learning experience actually made her less cynical, forcing her "to reject the simplistic notion that everything is screwed up and manipulated" as she learned that through "informed and reasoned thought" she can "identify better and worse decisions" (Sperry, 2006: 43).

In teaching history at the college level, history professors have discovered that their students arrive to college having learned numerous online shortcuts for gathering and accessing information that do not involve critical analysis of the content. As you have already learned by reading this book, in order to embody the practice of critical analysis, it is important to ask questions about what you watch, see, and read. In his book *Teaching History in a Digital Age* (2013), T. Mills Kelly helps students engage in historical research, beginning by critically analyzing history websites. Students explore questions like these:

- Who owns the website?
- What metadata does the website use to attract visitors?
- What is the history of the website?
- What reviews are available about the website?
- What biases are evident in your personalized search history, and how do they affect the information a search engine presents to you?
- Who can you talk to about your search process who might offer insight or valuable advice?

In order to examine the value of having students create history as a way to learn history, Kelly created a special course called Lying about the Past, in which college students studied fake documentaries and historical hoaxes. He invited students to create their own historical hoaxes, working collaboratively over 6 weeks to build a website that would trick people. For example, one group of students created The Beer of 1812, a website about Harris Thompson's discovery of a special recipe for beer brewed in Baltimore. All the facts and information presented on the website are true, except for the central claim of the discovery of a vintage recipe.

How can media literacy competencies be embedded in courses and assignments?

In completing this project, students had to wrestle with difficult ethical issues about how truth is understood and who has the authority to claim it, engaging in *historiography* from the point of view of intentional fabrication (Kelly, 2013). Historiography is the study of how history is constructed. Every class included dialogue about ethical issues, as students confronted their perceptions and attitudes about hoaxes, satires, and parodies like *The Onion*, the parody news website whose contents are frequently mistaken as news. Students agreed to remove their hoax websites at the end of the semester. They became aware of how information and data can be intentionally misrepresented and made to "look" credible. For students enrolled in this unique course, they certainly will never look at a website the same way after a powerful learning experience like this.

But you will probably not be surprised to learn that this pedagogical strategy was controversial. Traditional historians do not engage students in wrestling with epistemological questions through direct experience in constructing history. In an age of so-called fake news, not every educator will agree that Kelly's approach to teaching history is a wise move. But media literacy teachers have discovered that continual innovation in pedagogy requires strategic risk-taking (Hobbs, 2013). Such risk-taking is part of the pedagogy of media literacy education because of the fast-changing nature of media, technology, and popular culture. To be responsive to contemporary culture, media literacy educators must engage in developing new lessons and learning activities that connect the classroom to the culture (Hobbs, Deslauriers & Steager, 2019).

Critical questions are relevant to all forms of knowledge, including that which is presented in textbooks, academic scholarship, and news media as well as many other forms of media like websites, podcasts, YouTube videos, novels, and movies (Rheingold, 2012). Given the nature of the information landscape today, asking questions and creating media are pedagogical strategies that can enhance the development of *intellectual curiosity*, which may be the most important competency needed as a lifelong learner. Media literacy educators aim to help learners of all ages internalize the process of asking questions through all of their encounters with information, entertainment, and persuasion.

Media Literacy as a Public Health Issue

Public health professionals, concerned about media's deleterious effects on violence, body image, sexual behavior, and nutrition have developed educational programs using media literacy as an *intervention*. Many of these initiatives have demonstrated meaningful effects on targeted attitudes and behavior (Jeong et al., 2012). These interventions may address issues including media violence, stereotypes in the representation of gender and race, materialism and consumer culture, the glamorization of unhealthy behavior such as drinking and smoking, the practices of sexting and cyberbullying, and more.

Media literacy in public health aims to increase the *resilience* of children and youth, which is a key factor in health and human development. Media literacy has proven itself to be effective in a wide variety of contexts and

Milestones of Global Media Literacy

DATE	MILESTONE
1915	The Cleveland Cinema Club is founded to promote community discussions about film.
1915	Columbia University offers a critical analysis of film class (Photoplay Composition).
1937	The Institute for Propaganda Analysis distributes curriculum resources for high school educators and librarians on how to analyze propaganda.
1938	The book *How to Appreciate Motion Pictures* by Edgar Dale provides insight on strategies for critically analyzing film.
1952	The American Council for Better Broadcasts involves community residents in analyzing radio and television broadcasts for quality.
1955	The British Film Institute publishes an article about engaging children in film production as a learning experience.
1960	Marshall McLuhan is commissioned to write a curriculum on understanding media in a report that later becomes the book *Understanding Media*.
1969	The National Education Association recommends critical viewing skills training as a strategy to address the problem of media violence.
1970	The Television Viewing Skills project begins in Eugene, Oregon.
1977	Elizabeth Thoman launches the first media literacy magazine, *Media & Values*.
1978	The first federal funding for media literacy provides support to four curriculum development projects.
1979	Jean Kilbourne creates the film *Killing Us Softly* in order to critically analyze representation of women in advertising.
1981	At Yale University, Jerome and Dorothy Singer develop and test a media literacy curriculum for elementary school children.
1989	The first North American conference on media literacy is held in Guelph, Ontario, Canada.
1990	UNESCO convenes the first international conference on media literacy in Toulouse, France.
1992	The National Leadership Conference on Media Literacy is hosted by the Aspen Institute; experts agree on a definition of media literacy.
1993	The Harvard Institute on Media Education offers the first summer professional development program for teachers in the United Ststes.
1998	The Partnership for Media Education builds a national coalition of U.S. media literacy educators.

Continued...

Continued...

1999	Andrew Hart develops the first comparative study of media literacy in 12 European countries.
1999	With support from Discovery Communications, Inc, the Maryland State Department of Education releases *Assignment: Media Literacy*, a curriculum designed to help educators integrate media literacy in grades K–12.
2008	UNESCO releases the Media and Information Literacy (MIL) curriculum and competencies for teachers in multiple languages.
2009	The *Journal of Media Literacy Education* is launched as an open-access, peer-reviewed journal.
2012	The National Association for Media Literacy Education (NAMLE) hires its first executive director.
2014	A report on media education is released assessing the quality of formal education in 27 European countries.
2018	Legislation is passed in the states of Washington, Rhode Island, and California to advance media literacy education.
2019	Legislation is introduced in Congress to fund digital citizenship and media literacy education initiatives.

learning environments. Some programs consist of only one or two short sessions and other programs are a semester in length or longer. Some focus on one issue (violence, advertising, alcohol) while others address a wide variety of topics (Martens, 2010). Researchers have found that adolescents with higher levels of media literacy education (as measured on the 18-item Smoking Media Literacy scale) show lower levels of smoking behavior and intent to smoke (Primack et al., 2006). They have discovered that preschoolers' fears can be mitigated with the use of a three-session media literacy program targeting their mothers. By learning about how news is constructed, parents can help calm children who might witness violence on television news (Comer et al., 2008).

Not all media literacy interventions are created equal, however. Some media literacy interventions might even be considered a form of educational coercion. In one project, researchers explored how to reduce children's exposure to television and television violence. They implemented a 28-lesson classroom-based media literacy intervention with 496 children ages 6–10. In the classroom, the children were essentially persuaded to dislike television violence. The educational experience offered rewards for adopting the desired attitudes and opinions. The program was effective in decreasing the amount of time children watched media violence (Rosenkoetter, Rosenkoetter & Acock, 2009),

Intellectual Grandparent:
Len Masterman

Len Masterman, a British education scholar, wrote the first serious book on the pedagogy of media literacy education in English, and his ideas influenced a generation of scholars and educators across the English-speaking world. In his book *Teaching the Media* (1985), he articulates both the theory and the practice of media literacy education. His ideas include:

Understanding the power of media requires analysis of institutions, rhetoric, audience, and ideology. Masterman is very direct in his understanding that media are constructed representations that need to be actively interpreted. He recognizes that media are not "windows on the world" or "mirrors of reality." Masterman emphasizes that values are implicit within media representations, and that "ideological questions permeate every aspect of media production, distribution and consumption" (1993: 12). Unlike many of his contemporaries, Masterman does not see ideology as a monolithic entity; he created a four-part model that includes *institutions* (which he calls determinants), *rhetoric,*

ideology, and *audience.* He helps students grasp the interrelated web of influences at play within any media text, including determinants, which comprise owners and controlling companies, media institutions and personnel, self-regulating bodies, the law, the state, advertisers, audiences, and media sources. He wants students to understand the tensions within and between these stakeholders (Masterman, 1985).

Teachers skillfully sharpen and deepen student learning through group inquiry rooted in dialogue and discussion. In writing about his teaching methods, Masterman mentions the need to "liberate students from the 'expertise' of the teacher" (1986: 99). His ideas about nonhierarchical teaching are based in the goal of developing student confidence through discussions that enable students to form judgments, reflect on them, and ultimately take responsibility for their own learning.

Although he does not use the term *collective intelligence,* Masterman points out that a group of people, regardless of their age or experience, will inevitably have a wider range of perceptions and cultural reference points than the teacher alone.

but it cannot be understood as truly educational. Such approaches to media literacy, do not embody the core principles of media literacy education, which respects the autonomy of the individual learner to make independent and well-informed choices. When education is intentionally designed to shift or change attitudes and beliefs about an issue of public concern, it can become a form of indoctrination or propaganda.

Media Literacy and Global Citizenship

Media literacy education can be an important tool for strengthening young people's participation in cultural, economic, and political life. The global

This is why he rejects the lecture as a pedagogical method. Tapping into a group's collective intelligence through a process of *shared inquiry* is mutually illuminating for students and teachers alike. He describes how teachers who have developed sensitivity to the differences among learners "can predict with some accuracy the range of responses which a particular text is likely to elicit" (1985: 220). Masterman believes that students themselves can also gain sensitivity about their own judgments and interpretations through the practice of listening and introspection. Media literacy teachers do not need to be dependent on curricula and teaching materials. Armed with an internalized set of big ideas, educators can artfully shape the quality of classroom dialogue through well-selected topics, the interrogation of assumptions, the insertion of relevant syntheses, and other methods.

Media literacy education focuses more on the process of learning than on delivering informational content. Masterman contends that learning about media should be contextual and rooted in inquiry. He opposes content-based approaches to teaching that attempt to "cover" or "deliver" as many different content areas as possible. Freed of the "oppressive load of content," students are empowered to apply critical inquiry to the media texts that are most salient to them. Masterman writes, "Content, in particular, needs to be thought of, not as an end in itself but as a means to developing *critical autonomy* and not submerging it" (1985: 25). When a teacher chooses what students read, view, and learn, their control can lead to conformity. Students need time for independent learning in school. But Masterman also recognizes that practical work that involves creating media does not automatically cultivate media literacy competencies. He recommends making an explicit connection between the analysis of information and creative media making. Classroom media-making activities should not be designed for students to merely emulate professional practice, but to subject media itself to critical scrutiny. Without a critical and analytical perspective, Masterman acknowledges, student creative work can produce cultural conformity, reinscribing media power and perpetuating the status quo.

If Len Masterman has influenced your thinking about media literacy, you can share a comment on the Grandparents of Media Literacy website at www.grandparentsofmedialiteracy.com.

approach to media literacy has emerged as a result of increased contact between scholars as well as cross-national studies of media literacy in Europe, Asia, and around the world (Wilson et al., 2011). As a form of civic education, it may help young people to seek out information on relevant issues, evaluate the quality of the available information, and engage in dialogue with others to form coalitions. Media literacy education may help young people use their powerful voices to advocate for social change. Media literacy education can also help students and teachers respond to globalization in contemporary society (Mihailidis, 2014). Media literacy may help address the rise of populism, xenophobia, and extreme right- and left-wing nationalisms (Ranieri, 2016). Examples of global programs include:

How does media literacy education advance democratic citizenship **?**

- The Salzburg Academy on Media and Global Change offers summer learning opportunities to students and faculty members from multiple countries (Mihailidis, 2018);

- UNESCO has developed a global teacher education program, the Media and Information Literacy Curriculum for Teachers, a resource designed for teachers;

- The Media Education for Equity and Tolerance program provides learning scenarios that support socially disadvantaged youth from five European countries to use media literacy to develop skills and knowledge about living in a multicultural society (MEET Tolerance, 2018);

- Mind Over Media: Analyzing Contemporary Propaganda is a digital learning platform for media literacy education that offers thousands of examples from more than 50 countries.

Research has shown media literacy education to be effective in supporting *habits of citizenship* in democratic societies. One study found that nearly half of high school students from 21 high schools in California engaged in various classroom activities designed to support media literacy competencies, including critically analyzing the trustworthiness of websites, using the Internet to get information about political or social issues, and creating content for the Web. These activities are associated with higher rates of politically driven online participation (Kahne, Lee & Feezel, 2012). Other research has shown that students who receive media literacy education are better at critically analyzing media messages aligned with their existing beliefs, thus countering natural tendencies toward confirmation bias. In a quasi-experimental design study with a large sample of California youth, those with greater levels of exposure to media literacy education outperformed others in their ability to recognize the bias embedded in a political media message that aligned with their preexisting beliefs (Kahne & Bowyer, 2017).

Both media industry and government have been stakeholders for media literacy. Some governments have approached media literacy largely in relation to issues of deregulation, economic development, and cultural preservation (Bulger & Davison, 2018). For example, as part of the Communications Act of 2003, the British broadcast regulatory agency OFCOM builds public awareness of media literacy so as to promote the interests of all citizens and to protect them from harm. When the agency was established, its focus was on media industry deregulation; it removed obstacles to cross-media ownership and supported global media companies operating in the UK market. For OFCOM, media literacy is more important in a deregulated, market-driven economy where people need to be responsible for their own behavior as media consumers. Some scholars are concerned about governments that position media literacy as an alternative to regulation, however (Buckingham, 2019).

The role of media companies in the development of media literacy has been a controversial topic among media literacy educators in the United States. Public broadcasting's involvement in media literacy has been welcomed, of course, and a number of broadcast stations like KQED in San Francisco offer programs for teachers, curriculum resources, and even certification programs (KQED, 2018). The U.S. media sector has supported some forms of media literacy but not others. Companies including Time Warner, Google, and other large corporations provide financial support to Common Sense Media, a San Francisco-based media literacy organization that caters to the needs of parents of young children. The New York Times Learning Network has embedded media literacy into the curriculum materials it produces for teachers and students (New York Times Learning Network, 2018). Adobe has sponsored youth media initiatives in the United States and around the world.

Some people think that media industry involvement in media literacy education is harmful and dangerous. In 2002, a splinter group developed for educators who firmly believe that Big Media is the problem and that media literacy educators must remain financially independent in order to challenge it (Action Coalition for Media Education, 2018).

Media literacy can be understood as a type of advocacy or *social movement* aimed particularly at young adults, children, and parents. Social movements arise in response to changing social norms and values as a form of political

The Learning Network

Teach and Learn With The Times: Resources for Bringing the World Into Your Classroom

LESSON OF THE DAY	WHAT'S GOING ON IN THIS GRAPH?	CONTESTS	WRITING CURRICULUM
	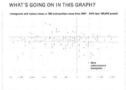		
We Are Family: 50-Plus Times Articles, Photos, Maps and More About Families of All Kinds	What's Going On in This Graph? | Dec. 4, 2019	Our Fifth Annual Student Review Contest Is Open to Middle and High School Students.	Teach Writing With The New York Times: A Free School-Year Curriculum in 7 Units

Activities for Students

More in Activities for Students »

WRITING PROMPTS	ARTICLES & QUESTIONS	QUIZZES & CROSSWORDS	MULTIMEDIA	CONTESTS

© The New York Times Company

Should media companies support media literacy education? Why or why not?

participation in which people engage in a sustained public effort to make social change, using communicative action to raise awareness, build strategic alliances, and, ultimately, to challenge and reform some aspects of contemporary culture. Those who see media literacy as a social movement are generally motivated by their awareness that changes in audience behavior can bring about changes in the media industry. This is sometimes conceptualized as *demand-focused media reform*. A wide variety of small groups, nonprofit organizations, and individuals advocate for media literacy at the local and community levels. While this approach has been criticized as a form of moral, cultural, or political defensiveness (Buckingham, 2019), it is a response to the perceived power of contemporary digital technology, mass media, and popular culture.

Obstacles and Pathways

Many distinct factors are needed for media literacy education to thrive, and obstacles and pathways stand in the way of enlarging the scope of media literacy in the United States and around the world. In an innovative study that relied on document analysis and interviews with Italian media literacy education experts and practitioners, 35 criteria were identified as essential "best practices" in the field. These included: (1) materials and resources for teaching and learning; (2) educational practices and activities; (3) educators, including their training and education and their (4) access to professional networks and continuing education opportunities; (5) the practices of formative and summative assessment and evaluation; (6) involvement and support from media professionals as well as (7) a supportive climate in the school and community (Felini, 2014).

Because the United States has a *decentralized* educational system, support for media literacy education must be cultivated locally in more than 15,000 school districts. This is why organizations like the Media Education Lab place a substantial focus on teacher education and informal professional learning networks. Although it is not known exactly how many students receive media literacy education, one study with a representative sample of California young adults found that nearly one-third of participants claimed to have had some media literacy education in school (Kahne & Bowyer, 2017). Sadly, an annual formal survey of students' exposure to media literacy pedagogy has not yet been developed in the United States.

Nearly all states include some acknowledgement of media literacy learning outcomes in their *state standards*. For example, in Florida, students are expected to distinguish between propaganda and ethical reasoning strategies in print and non-print media, "ethically use mass media and digital technology in assignments and presentations, citing sources according to standardized citation styles [, and] demonstrate the ability to select print and non-print media appropriate for the purpose, occasion, and audience to develop into a formal presentation" (Ritchie, 2011). In Maryland, students need to be able to explain the connection between reading, listening, and viewing; recognize bias in information sources; and make connections and inferences using prior knowledge (Maryland State Department of Education, 2010). School districts must decide whether and how media literacy education is implemented in alignment with state standards.

American teachers who have had *professional development* learning experiences are well prepared to integrate media literacy into existing courses. Such learning experiences, while not normative in public education, can be found in the professional networks of teachers in social studies, English, health, and technology education. Researchers have examined the many different motivations that may inspire their interest in media literacy, including an interest in demystifying media, a need to address the socio-emotional needs of learners, or as part of an effort towards social justice (Hobbs & Tuzel, 2017).

WILLSIE/iStock

What are some of the gaps between students and teachers when it comes to media, technology and popular culture?

As you have probably already experienced, serious talk about digital media, entertainment, and popular culture can be fun. Students value the opportunity to contribute to discussions that they perceive as relevant to their interests. But sometimes, younger students are so eager to share their ideas about media and popular culture that the class can get a little noisy and even chaotic. Students may vehemently disagree or argue with their peers, and there may be vigorous discussions on the nuances of issues and topics in which the teacher has little relevant knowledge or authority. Some teachers, not used to high levels of engagement, may struggle with the *messy engagement* that occurs when students use both their popular culture knowledge and creative media production skills (Hobbs & Moore, 2013). Because teachers generally know less about the immediacies of contemporary popular culture than their students, they get a chance to treat students as cultural informants. When they view the learning process as one based on shared inquiry, teachers can be co-learners and offer valuable perspective that students appreciate. For meaningful dialogue and discussion to occur, creating a learning climate of trust and respect is essential.

Unfortunately, on some occasions, talk about digital media, entertainment, and popular culture in the classroom may be perceived suspiciously by the students themselves. Some students have learned that school is not a safe space, and they hesitate to reveal their thoughts and feelings about the media they enjoy and consume at home. Some students who are active YouTubers have never told their teachers about their creative pursuits. Other students have internalized the values of school achievement rooted in test-taking, grades, and scores. These students may ask, "Will this be on the test?" or "What does this have to do with school?" A traditional content-focused framing of knowledge may lead students to accept "school knowledge" as within the logical space of the school world. Such students do not expect or want school activities to have any relevance to life outside school (Pérez Tornero & Varis, 2011).

In other schools and communities, the norms and routines of school may interfere with the effective implementation of media literacy pedagogy. Analyzing and creating media in the classroom takes time. Popular culture, including advertising, movies, TV shows, and the Internet, may be viewed with suspicion by some teachers (and parents) who view popular culture as the enemy of education. In other schools, teachers are loath to include substantial time for discussion and dialogue because teaching is still defined as lecturing.

Perhaps the biggest obstacle facing the future of media literacy concerns beliefs that the formal study of media is not a "serious" subject. Among the *academic hierarchies* of college and university majors, for example, engineering and the sciences may be considered more important than the liberal arts and humanities. And even lower are the professional programs in communication and education. For example, in the United Kingdom, a recent empirical analysis of British newspaper coverage found that courses in media studies are represented and framed as "soft" or "Mickey Mouse" subjects, with 61% of news stories depicting the academic program as having little educational value (Bennett & Kidd, 2017). The book you are holding in your hands (or reading on a screen) has aimed to address these negative attitudes. For media literacy education to thrive, it must be seen as both intellectually rigorous and responsive to the growing public interest in mass media, technology, digital and social media, education, and popular culture.

The Epistemology of "Fake News"

While some people believe that visibility of media literacy increased dramatically in recent years, a Google Trend analysis reveals that public interest in media literacy has long been cyclical. When President Donald Trump started using the term *fake news* to refer to mainstream media and other news outlets, media literacy education was commonly described as the solution to the lack of trust in news media and the rise of disinformation and propaganda.

But some are concerned that efforts like fact-checking and media literacy education are perpetuating the "fake news" crisis rather than resolving it. Researcher and activist danah boyd (she chooses not to capitalize her name) shared her concerns about the framing of media literacy as a panacea to the wider problems in society associated with the Internet and digital culture. Her essay "Did Media Literacy Backfire?" points out that some educators and librarians teach students that Wikipedia cannot be trusted because they believe that crowdsourced editing is inferior to that of expert reviewers. Perhaps encouraging students to ask questions about the media they use might create a generation of suspicious, cynical, and distrustful people.

People begin to trust authencity over authority, when faced with the self-interested and often conflicting views of experts. Other people suspect that a powerful media elite has taken control over shaping reality and the nature of knowledge. For some people, honest YouTubers seem more trustworthy than experts with their data, their charts, and their endless spin on the talk show circuit. As American culture has become more polarized, media literacy has fueled a "culture of doubt and critique" (boyd, 2017: 1).

In some important ways, the crisis over so-called fake news is really an *epistemological crisis*. It has been brought on not just by an onslaught of polarized information from an inconceivable array of sources. The power to shape knowledge (and therefore people's understanding of social reality) needs to be critically examined. For most of human history, kings shaped social reality through the use of military power. After the Enlightenment, scientists, writers, journalists, and those with access to information and data gained the power to shape social reality through the presentation of facts and evidence. Only through protests and demonstrations have those without power, money, and resources gradually acquired a form of power to shape social reality.

After the financial crisis of 2007, many Americans began to distrust those in power. They realized the need to trust their gut, their intuition, and their life experience and not rely on facts and information from experts. In some fundamentalist communities, the practice of trusting in a powerful leader is a primary social value, and questioning them is considered disrespectful or unpatriotic. "In many Native communities, experience trumps Western science as the key to knowledge. These communities have a different way of understanding topics like weather or climate or medicine. Experience is also used in activist circles as a way of seeking truth and challenging the status quo. Experience-based epistemologies also rely on evidence, but not the kind of evidence that would be recognized or accepted by those in Western scientific communities" (boyd, 2017: 1).

Questioning media may contribute to a generalized mistrust of authority. Many young people have experienced the oppression of school-sanctioned knowledge, being "force-fed information for someone else's agenda" (boyd, 2018: 1). Some people see the institutions of education, journalism, science, and mass media as corrupt, powerful, and dangerous. They believe that people need to "wake up" to how education and media are "designed to deceive you into progressive propaganda" (p. 1).

False and intentionally misleading information has become a weapon for destabilizing societies. For example, consider the controversy over school shootings. In 2018, the term *crisis actors* began to be used after the school shooting massacres at Sandy Hook and Parkland, referring to the claim that these events did not actually happen and that eyewitnesses were paid actors, not students. As the mainstream media reported on this phenomenon, they amplified a conspiracy theory. They inadvertently spread a falsehood in their search to capture and monetize audience attention.

We learn more by being curious and willing and able to appreciate differences in interpretation without feeling threatened or fearful of them. In struggling to imagine a way forward, boyd herself emphasizes the value of multiperspectival thinking and empathy by asking a key media literacy question, "Why do people from different worldviews interpret the same piece of content differently?" As demonstrated throughout this book, through media literacy education, people build the capacity to truly hear and embrace the perspectives of diverse others.

How can asking critical questions disrupt institutional power?

Richard Levine/Alamy Live News/Alamy Stock Photo

What the future may hold: Media literacy for all

Through general education courses and specialized advanced courses for students in a number of disciplines, media literacy is reaching more colleges and university students. College faculty members are integrating media literacy into existing courses, but data show that students may be more likely to encounter media literacy in high school than in college. In a survey of students at a single mid-sized American college, survey data showed that students reported using video and Web-based media in high school classes more than in college. Although they were more likely to create video and Web-based media in high school, they were more likely to analyze media in college courses (Schmidt, 2012).

Librarians have also taken real leadership in developing film screening and discussion programs, creating media production spaces, and implementing other digital learning programs for school, public, and academic libraries (Hobbs, Deslauriers, and Steager 2019).

Numerous media literacy entrepreneurs offer consulting and support services for communities, helping provide *elbow-to-elbow support* for transforming classroom practice using a combination of critical analysis of media and creative media production. YouTube video creators, comedians, and professional media makers are also providing an influx of educational resources to support media literacy learning. For example, comedian Adam Conover's TV series, *Adams Ruins Everything*, uses the genre of educational comedy to tackle big topics, like pharmaceutical marketing, the airline industry, pregnancy, and the Internet, using a process of debunking myths and misinformation through a series of hilarious skits and sketches. When Adam shares surprising facts, on-screen references appear to back up his claims with evidence. Conover made available five of his most interesting shows for the media literacy community in 2018 in honor of Media Literacy Week, an annual event sponsored by the National Association for Media Literacy Education (NAMLE, 2018). We can only hope that more musicians, athletes, celebrities, and influencers begin to help people all over the world to develop their media literacy competencies.

You can be an advocate for media literacy too. As you interact with family, friends, and co-workers, you can ask critical questions in responding to all the media messages in your envirionment. You can support legislation that brings media literacy initiatives into communities, and you can find ways to build connections between media literacy and other pressing social and political issues, including climate change and the environment, the global economy, migration and immigration, racism and economic inequalities, health and wellness, and technology and science. You can use your effective communication skills to make a difference in your community and in the wider world.

Adam Conover
@adamconover

Following

Very proud to celebrate Media Literacy Week with @MediaLiteracyEd, and to have Adam Ruins Everything be shown in so many classrooms around the country. Media literacy and critical thinking are literally critical!

3:25 PM - 9 Nov 2018

25 Retweets 218 Likes

6   25   218

© Twitter, Inc

TIME T◉ REFLECT

What is your opinion on the "great debates" of media literacy education? Consider one or more of the great debates of media literacy below and provide an using reasoning and evidence.

1. Should media literacy be designed to protect students from negative media influence? Why or why not?

2. Should media production be an essential element of media literacy education? Why or why not?

3. Should media literacy focus on popular culture texts? Why or why not?

4. Should media literacy have a more explicit political and ideological agenda? Why or why not?

5. Should media literacy concentrate on reaching students in formal public educational environments or work instead with people outside of school?

6. Should media literacy be a specialist subject or integrated into existing curriculum?

7. Should media literacy be supported financially by media and technology businesses?

After you identify the question you are addressing, share your thoughts in a brief oral presentation. You can also view and respond to comments of other people who have offered thoughtful reflections on the great debates in media literacy education. You can even pose new questions needed to advance the future of media literacy education. Visit www.medialiteracyaction.com to learn more.

CREATE T▶ LEARN

Conduct an Interview

How do educators and learners in your community understand the value of media literacy education? Working individually or with a partner, interview someone who has experience in either media or education: this might be a former teacher, a librarian, a local journalist, graphic designer, YouTuber, musician, or someone else.

Create a list of five questions to ask before you conduct the interview, using some of the concepts from this chapter to guide your inquiry. Listen carefully to each answer and ask a follow-up question that deepens the quality of the information you receive. Use your cell phone voice recorder to make a simple recording and if you like, add an opening introduction with music, transitions in between the questions, and a thoughtful conclusion. Upload your audio or video recording and use the #MLAction hashtag to share your work with a global community of media literacy learners.

Acknowledgments

I would like to thank all my current and former students at the University of Rhode Island, Temple University and Babson College. Your creativity and insights have been an inspiration to me. I acknowledge the outstanding teachers at the University of Michigan who woke me up to the essential dimensions of media literacy (even before the term was invented), including writing teacher Barbra Morris, film scholars Herbert Eagle and Hugh Cohen, journalism scholar Peter Clarke, and Israeli education scholar Gavriel Salomon. Since then, I have continued to learn from the diverse array of scholars and educators who have contributed their ideas to the *Journal of Media Literacy Education* and the National Association for Media Literacy Education. Media literacy education is not limited by disciplinary boundaries and this a source of great strength!

I would like to acknowledge the following individuals who offered valuable feedback on the book during the writing process:

Debashis "Deb" Aikat, *University of North Carolina*
Ralph Beliveau, *University of Oklahoma*
Peter Bryan, *Pennsylvania State University*
Natasha Casey, *Blackburn College*
Margaret M. Cassidy, *Adelphi University*
Gladys L. Cleland, *University of Florida*
Sherri Hope Culver, *Temple University*
Lillie Fears, *Arkansas State University*
Caroline Fitzpatrick, *Alvernia University*
Elizaveta Friesem, *Media Education Lab*
Yonty Friesem, *Columbia College Chicago*
Katherine Fry, *Brooklyn College of the City University of New York*
Stephanie Gomez, *Western Washington University*
Pamela Hill Nettleton, *University of St. Thomas*
Brian Howard, *Brigham Young University, Idaho*
Terre Layng Rosner, *University of St. Francis*
Katherine Lockwood, *University of Tampa*
Michelle Meade, *Brigham Young University, Idaho*
Pamela Morris, *Loyola University Chicago*
Elizabeth R. Ortiz, *Cedar Crest College*
James Paasche, *Indiana University Bloomington*
William Payton, *Brigham Young University*
Rob Rector, *Delaware Technical Community College*
Colin Rhinesmith, *Simmons College*
Michael RobbGrieco, *Media Education Lab*
Hans Schmidt, *Pennsylvania State University Brandywine*
Bridget Sheffer, *Brigham Young University*
Jason Shrontz, *Gogebic Community College*
Scott Sochay, *Bethel University*
Jon Torn, *Northern Arizona University*
Theresa Villeneuve, *Citrus College*
Sarah Vos, *University of Kentucky*

I am most grateful to Elizabeth Swayze, an extraordinary editor with unparalleled expertise in the field of media and communications, who helped me visualize the possibilities for what this book could be. I thank Natalie Mandziuk and the production and marketing team at Rowman & Littlefield for their strong support. I also would like to thank my colleagues at the Media Education Lab, especially Julie Coiro, Yonty Friesem, Elizaveta Friesem, and Frank Romanelli, whose ideas and insights have fertilized my thinking, research and teaching. I am grateful to international colleagues Igor Kanižaj, Bert Pieters, Maria Ranieri, and Silke Grafe, who have enlarged my understanding of media literacy pedagogy and advocacy. It is indeed a great honor be part of the interdisciplinary confederation of media literacy educators and scholars. If this book inspires you to join this vibrant global community and help it to grow, my work will have accomplished its purpose.

Glossary

A

A/B testing: a type of statistical marketing test that compares two versions of Web content in order to see which one leads to a particular desired outcome

aca-fan: the academic study of fandom, generally by academics who themselves identify as fans

academic hierarchies: the perception that some disciplines and academic fields are better than others

accuracy: in journalism, the practice of verifying facts

active audience: a theory of audiences as actively engaged in the creation of meaning through interpretation

advergames: the use of branded products, logos, and other advertising content in video games

affordances: the characteristics of an object, tool, or resource that shape what a user can do with it

agency: full control over one's actions

agenda setting: how the topics that the press identifies as important become important in the minds of the general public

agent: someone who represents a creative individual and helps them get work by serving as an intermediary

algorithmic personalization: computer programs that use data that users provide in order to make recommendations about content

alt tags: the descriptive words a producer attaches to an image or article to increase findability

American cultural studies: a theoretical approach to studying media and popular culture that examines how pleasure and power intersect through both media consumption and media production

amplification: in social media, the increase in visibility that results as people share content with others

analysis and interpretation: in journalism, an effort to explain the meaning of news and current events

animatic: a simple animation used in the preproduction process

anonymity: intentionally disguising or masking identity

antitrust laws: statutes the U.S. government has developed in order to protect consumers from predatory business practices by ensuring that fair competition exists in an open-market economy; laws that prevent monopolies from having too much power

archetypes: characters with fixed traits and functions that can be found across many different narratives

astroturf: a public relations technique whereby a business creates a fake grassroots group in order to give the illusion of public support for an idea or policy that serves that company's business goals

attribution: in journalism, the practice of naming individuals who have been interviewed in the news-gathering process

audience: the receivers of a media message

authenticity: in psychology, the state of being true to one's own self and not putting on a performance for others, or the characteristics of a media message that make it seem "real" and believable

author: the term used for an individual or team of people who create any type of media message

authorial intent: the set of inferences that readers or viewers make about the author's purpose or goals as a strategy through which to critically analyze a message

authority: a person with social power rooted in their title, role, visibility, knowledge, expertise, or other qualities, or the characteristics of a media message that make it trustworthy and credible

autocomplete: algorithmic predictions made by a search engine to assist the search process

autonomy: the ability to think and act independently

autoplay plugins: software that automatically causes videos to start playing when a user lands on a website

avatar: an icon or a figure representing a person in a video game or another type of online media

B

baiting: social media posts that promote user engagement in superficial or misleading ways

balance: a characteristic of news that involves the inclusion of multiple points of view

barriers to entry: the costs of starting a business

bias cleanse: activities that help people gain more awareness of their biases; experiences that disrupt stereotypical attitudes

binge-watching: watching multiple episodes of a television series in a single viewing session

bonding and bridging social capital: bonding relationships deepen feelings of solidarity among people with similar backgrounds; bridging relationships connect people from different backgrounds

brand exploitation: using familiar brands to create new forms of media in order to maximize profit and minimize financial risk

brand impression: a way of measuring exposure to advertising messages

broadband: forms of data transmission that use signals sent through wire or wireless media—i.e., cable television, Internet access, and cell phones

browser: a software application that displays websites

C

capitalism: a market economy based on the largely unregulated exchange of goods and services

catfishing: luring someone into an online relationship through a fictional persona

catharsis: the release of tension that occurs when we read, view, or listen to a tragedy

censorship: a disruption in the chain of communication between author and audience that is the result of power imbalances; when government engages in the suppression or prohibition of books, films, news, or other media considered obscene, politically unacceptable, or a threat to security

charisma: the personal characteristics and style of a communicator that make him or her attractive to an audience

chilling effect: the impact of a policy, practice, or regulation on limiting free expression

citation metrics: in academic scholarship, evidence about the size of the readership of a particular work

citizen journalism: the term used to describe when eyewitnesses, activists, or ordinary people report news and current events

civic imagination: the capacity of people to envision alternatives to current social and political conditions

clickbait: attention-getting but low-quality content whose main purpose is to attract attention and encourage users to click on a link

close analysis: the practice of analyzing or deconstructing a media message

codes and conventions: the shared features and patterns of a particular media genre that create expectations for audiences

coercion: a manipulative form of persuasion where people are compelled to accept a particular belief, action or attitude

collaborative filtering: using input from other users to filter content

collateral censorship: a form of censorship that arises when a bookseller (or any third party) is held liable for the contents of the books sold

collective consciousness: the idea that social norms influence people's individual behavior

collective intelligence: the sharing of specialized knowledge and expertise that makes social organization possible

colonialism: the political process of acquiring full or partial control over another country, occupying it with settlers, and exploiting it economically

common carrier regulation: regulations for companies that hold a "natural" monopoly

competitive individualism: believing that effort and ability are defining features of success and seeing competition as an acceptable means of distributing limited resources and rewards

comprehensibility: the ease of understanding a media message

comprehension: the practice of understanding a symbolic text in any form

confirmation bias: the tendency to evaluate new evidence based on whether it confirms one's existing beliefs

conflicts of interest: in journalism, when a company or individual is in a position to derive personal benefit from actions or decisions made as part of their job

consumer culture: a society where people earn money through selling their labor for wages and spend that money on a lifestyle centered around the purchase of goods and services

content curation: a way of filtering information that provides people in a knowledge community with content that has been created by others and collected to reflect the curator's particular point of view

content marketing (or sponsored content): disguised forms of advertising that match the form and content of the platform or medium in which it appears

content: the ideas, information, and emotions that are conveyed in a media message

context: the environment and background factors that influence both authors and audiences

context collapse: when the sharing of digital media blurs boundaries between different groups or contributes to miscommunication

convergence: the close relationship between media technologies, industries, markets, genres, and audiences

cookies: small text files that a website stored on an individual's computer that make websites work more efficiently by saving user preferences

copyright: laws that grant rights to owners and users of intellectual property

cord-cutting: the practice of stopping paying for cable television and using digital streaming services instead

corporate lobbying: efforts a company makes to influence political decisions

corporate or state censorship: disruption initiated by companies or governments that may include masked political control, technology capture, or violence

cost per thousand: the pricing model used in advertising to buy access to media audiences

counter-publics: social groups that situate themselves outside of mainstream public discourse

counterfactual thinking: the ability to imagine hypothetical situations and use reasoning based on "what if" scenarios

counterstereotype: in storytelling, a character who behaves in ways that explicitly disrupt audience expectations

create to learn: a pedagogical practice that involves creating media as a way to demonstrate learning

Creative Commons license: a type of license that enables authors to share their work with users for them to copy or use freely

crisis actors: a term used by conspiracy theorists who claim that paid actors were used in public disasters

critical autonomy: the ability to think for oneself and not be dependent on others' ideas

critical cultural studies: a theoretical approach to studying media and popular culture that examines how institutional power structures shape information and ideas

critical questions: a set of questions that support the process of close analysis of media

crowdsourcing: a process of collecting information and ideas by allowing Internet users to freely contribute

cult of the amateur: the growth of the number of people who create media as a hobby, not as a business

cultural capital: a form of symbolic wealth based on knowledge

cultural environment: a term used to describe how media become embedded in culture and society

cultural exclusion: the practice of marginalizing some people based on their group identity, refusing them opportunities to participate in activities equally with others

cultural hierarchies: differences in expectations, opportunities, and behavior between working-class, middle-class, and wealthy people

cultural studies: field of inquiry that explores the political dynamics of contemporary culture, its historical foundations, defining traits, and conflicts

culture industry: a term used to describe how popular culture is a form of ideological manipulation

culture jamming: the practice of subverting the symbols and values of consumer culture through hoax, parody, and satire

culture of fear: self-censorship that develops when people are afraid to speak freely

cumulative advantage: the "rich get richer" effect

cyberbullying: a form of online harassment that may include verbal aggression, threats, or hurtful behavior

D

data centers: interconnected computer servers that store information and communicate with each other

data privacy: the ability of an organization or individual to determine what data in a computer system can be shared with third parties

decentralization: in U.S. education, each school district establishes curricula and learning outcomes

demand-focused media literacy: the idea that developing media literacy competences will change the expectations that consumers have for media products

demand-focused media reform: the idea that changes in people's media uses and preferences will lead to changes in the media marketplace

denotation and connotation: in semiotics, the literal and figurative meanings of a symbol

deregulation: in media industries, the process of removing laws formerly created by the Federal Communications Commission (FCC) and the Federal Trade Commission (FTC)

desensitization: a media effect that occurs when exposure lessens the emotional intensity of reader or viewer response; or the decreased levels of emotion that occurs after repeated exposure to events, ideas, images, or information

digital authorship: the practice of producing online content as part of leisure, work, and citizenship

digital citizenship: a term used for understanding the legal and social dimensions of the Internet and social media

digital literacy: a term used for the cognitive, social, and ethical competencies required for using the Internet and participating in social networks

digital media and learning: a term used to describe learning that is socially embedded, interest driven, and oriented toward educational, economic, or political opportunity

Digital Millennium Copyright Act (DMCA): a law that protects platform companies and Internet service providers from being sued for copyright violation

digital wellness: approaches that aim to minimize the negative impact of media and technology use, generally by limiting media use

direct discovery: getting the news through intentionally selecting news content

direct revenue: in media companies, where consumers pay media creators or media companies directly for media products and services

discussion and dialogue: a pedagogical practice involving people sharing their interpretations on a topic, generally in response to some form of media

distributed discovery: finding news unintentionally through friends, family, the Internet, or social media

distribution windows: a pricing and distribution strategy used for film and television that maximizes profit by distributing media through different channels over time

DMCA counter-notification: a user's request that removed content be reinstated on a social media platform if the content is not infringing

domain name: a name that identifies the location of computer servers

double entendre: a form of sexual wordplay where a particular phrase's meaning can be understood as either innocent or sexual

dramatic conflict: an essential feature of narrative that includes the struggles of a protagonist

E

e-rate funding: federal money used to support the implementation of technology in local government, public schools, and libraries

editorial control: when media companies engage in the selection of any parts of books, films, news, or other media for business or political purposes

editorial process: the practice of decision-making that filters out content before publication

education frameworks: the set of written documents that specifies what learners should know and be able to do after completing their education

educational coercion: programs that aim to change the behavior of learners using various rewards, threats, or punishments

educational technology: pedagogical practices that involve the use of machines and software

effects: in media studies, the term for how media messages influence individuals, groups, and society

elbow-to-elbow support: a form of co-learning or mentoring in which a mentor and a learner work side by side

emotional contagion: the transference of emotional states through both interpersonal and mass communication

emotional intelligence: being aware of, controlling, and expressing emotions judiciously and empathetically

emotional truth: the power of fiction to capture people's real feelings, emotions, relationships, and experiences

empowerment: an approach to media literacy rooted in the belief that people can actively engage with and create media so as to meet their social and cultural needs

engagement: in education, the term used to describe a learner's high level of interest in a topic, issue, or activity

entertainment–education strategy: the practice of embedding useful information and educational ideas into popular narrative stories in radio, television, and film

entrepreneurship: the practice of starting or running a new business

epistemic autonomy: the process of valuing and trusting one's own reasoning process

epistemological crisis: conflict and tension that results when two or more ways of knowing raise questions about what counts as truthful, valid, and reliable information

epistemology: in philosophy, a branch of scholarship devoted to the study of the nature of knowledge

ethic of objectivity: an effort to construct news by a focus on the provision of accurate information substantiated by experts, with avoidance of interpretation and independent of political parties and advertising pressures

ethos: a term used in rhetoric to refer to the character of the speaker

exhibitor: in film, the company that owns the building where films are screened

expectancy theory: the idea that individuals will behave or act in a certain way because they are motivated to engage in a particular behavior based on their expectations

expectations: a state of mental anticipation; in media theory, how prior experiences with media messages may influence consumers' thoughts and feelings about future experiences

expertise: a type of authority rooted in the possession of specialized knowledge

F

FAANG: an acronym used for Silicon Valley companies Facebook, Apple, Amazon, Netflix, and Google

fact-checking: to confirm the truth of a statement through research and verification

Fairness Doctrine: a broadcast regulation that required media companies to present opposing views on controversial issues and to address public issues in a balanced way; it was declared unconstitutional in 1987

fair use: the part of the Copyright Act of 1976 that protects users of copyrighted content and enables them to use content without payment or permission under some circumstances

false advertising laws: laws that enable punishment of companies for deceptive advertising

false consciousness: a concept that refers to the systematic misrepresentation of beliefs, ideas, and information among a subordinate group of people that leads them to ignore the way they are oppressed by a ruling class

familiarity: in media, a pattern that viewers and readers can easily recognize and generally like

familiarity–novelty continuum: the idea that creative work includes a mix of the old and new

fandom: the social community of fans of media and popular culture

fanfic: short for fan fiction, a type of writing where authors create new stories using characters and tales from existing texts

femvertising: the use of advertising to empower women by counteracting negative stereotypes

filter bubble: the idea that digital media algorithms and recommendation engines limit people's exposure to information and ideas by offering results that the search engine considers relevant

filter forward: a type of post-publication editorial process that occurs through curation

flow: the pleasurable psychological state that exists when people are completely absorbed in an activity

for-profit vs. nonprofit: two separate economic models for business that provide different options for how profit returns to company owners or to society

form: the structure of a media message

frame shifting: a strategy for sustaining attention on a news event by selecting different facets of a social issue to emphasize

frames and framing: the idea that media focus attention on certain events and provide a way for people to understand social reality

freedom of expression: the legal protection the First Amendment provides in the United States to speech, religion, press, and assembly

G

game mechanics: the rules or methods that structure how users interact with a game

game transfer: when people experience visual or other aspects of video games in their real life

gaming disorder: in psychology, the term used to describe video game addiction

gatekeeping: the editorial process of deciding what to publish or share with audiences

gender hierarchy: in psychology, a set of attitudes rooted in the belief that males are superior to females

General Data Protection Regulation (GDPR): the European Union law that protects the personal data of all who reside in the 27 member countries

ghostwriter: a person who writes on behalf of a client, generally without getting acknowledgment as an author

goodwill: in public relations, the term used to refer to positive feelings between a company and its publics

gotcha moment: in sting operations, when an online predator is confronted on camera with a public report of his or her behavior

grassroots lobbying: the work of activists or volunteers who aim to promote certain policy goals for the public interest

great firewall: the system of Internet censorship the Chinese government uses to block information, news, entertainment, and many forms of academic scholarship

green light: in television and film production, when a proposed project is approved and a budget is allocated for production

H

habits of citizenship: the sense of personal civic responsibility and care for others that helps people engage in responsible self-governance

habitus: how individual human action is situated and embedded in a historical and cultural context

hashtag activism: when people share opinions about a political or social issue on social media by using a common phrase

hegemony: the ways that language is used to structure experience and to manipulate the cultural value system so that people with little power accept their condition as "normal"

hermeneutic code: the unanswered questions or mysteries in a story

heuristics: mental shortcuts that people use in information processing

historiography: the study of how history is constructed through historical research methods

hit-and-run reporting: a practice of gathering news that involves journalists going to a location, quickly gathering information to report, and then leaving without fully understanding the complex situation at hand

hoax: a humorous or malicious deception

host selling: when characters in ads are used to sell products during a program where the character is featured

I

ideology: beliefs and values that form a worldview

illusion of choice: the observation that humans prefer to have options that maintain a sense of free will even when their decisions are ultimately controlled by others

immersion (or transportation): when a user is so engaged in media use that he or she loses all sense of time and space

implicit bias: attitudes or stereotypes about race, gender, occupation, and other human characteristics that affect one's understanding of others in a nonconscious way

impressions: the number of times that audiences have been exposed to digital messages

independent sources: in journalism, people with expertise on a topic who are believed to have no personal stake in the outcome of a news event or issue

indirect revenue: in media companies, when advertisers pay media companies directly for access to audiences in order to persuade them to purchase products and services

influence marketing: using bloggers who have access to a large audience to promote products or services online

information cascades: a transmission process that occurs when Internet users make decisions to share content based on what they think others are doing

information fiduciaries: the idea that platform and information companies should legally be required to act in the best interest of the people whose data they have collected

information overload: the experience of too much information or too many media choices

infotainment society: the theory that cultural values are built upon a blend of information and entertainment

inquiry approach to media: asking critical questions about what one sees, plays, reads, watches, and listens to

inquiry learning: a pedagogical practice that involves asking questions, searching for information, evaluating it, and representing what is learned in some tangible form

intellectual curiosity: a lifelong learning competency that comes from being alert to novelty and complexity

intellectual property: a legal term that refers to the economic value of the tangible creative products that people produce to express and share knowledge; the term used to describe all the different forms of creative expression in fixed and tangible form that are protected by copyright

interdiction: the role of a helper character in a narrative, which can intensify dramatic conflict and help hold the attention of a reader or viewer

internalization: in psychology, the process by which attitudes are formed through repeated exposure to depictions of behaviors or attitudes that create perceived social norms

Internet of Things: the rise in products connected to the Internet

Internet service provider (ISP): a company that provides subscribers with access to the Internet

interpersonal communication: communication designed to initiate and maintain social relationships between individuals

interpretation: the process people use to construct meaning as they use media

intervention: in social sciences and public health, programs or action taken to improve a situation

IP address: a unique set of numbers that identifies each device connected to the Internet

J

journalistic routines: practices used to construct accurate, fair, and balanced news under time pressure

K

knowledge networks: the process of developing, collaborating, and sharing data and information, and knowledge with groups of people

L

learning community: a group of people who come together to share ideas and build knowledge

level playing field: the idea that business competitors have an equal chance of success

levels of choice: the structuring of choice that occurs when using media technologies, channels, formats, and genres

licensing rights: the legal mechanism for selling intellectual property

literacy: the sharing of meaning through symbols, including the practices of reading, writing, speaking, listening, critical viewing, and media production

luddite–technophilia continuum: the wide range of opinions about people's love-hate relationship with media and technology

M

machine learning: a type of artificial intelligence (AI) that provides systems with the ability to automatically learn and improve from experience without being explicitly programmed

market economy: a system that relies on supply and demand to regulate the price of goods and services

marketing: everything a company does to facilitate mutually beneficial exchange with its clients

marketplace of ideas: a term used to describe the rationale for freedom of expression

mass media: media that reach a large audience

mastery: the pleasurable feelings of control that people have when they become expert

media: the forms, formats, structures, and interfaces used for disseminating symbolic content

media awareness: the process of paying close attention to the patterns of media use in everyday life

media culture: the works and practices of intellectual and artistic activity (music, literature, painting, theater, film, and technology, among many others)

media dependence: a theory that predicts that the more a person depends on media to meet psychological and social needs, the more important media will be in that person's life, and therefore the more effects media will have on that individual

media ecology: the study of media environments and the idea that forms and codes of communication play a vital role in human affairs

media education: a term used synonymously with media literacy education in parts of the English-speaking world

media fast: the practice of intentionally abstaining from media use

media freedom: a term used to describe the independence of journalism from government or political control

media genre: a type of pattern recognition that provides names to identify the similarities between media texts

media influence research: studies that measure how particular media messages influence audience behavior, attitudes, or values

media life: a term used to describe the intertwining of media use into everyday life

media literacy: the set of knowledge, skills, and habits of mind required for full participation in a contemporary media-saturated society

media literacy inquiry process: the ability to access, analyze, and create media in variety of forms, using reflection to consider the impact of media messages and to take action, which means using the power of communication and information to share knowledge and solve problems

media ownership rules: regulation of mergers and acquisitions in order to prevent one media company from having too much power and influence

media reform: efforts to improve the media developed through coalitions of citizens and consumers

media systems: how media companies are organized in relation to other institutions in society

mediatization: the way that everyday life is contingent upon media use

medium theory: the theoretical examination of media forms and structures

meme: a digital media image with text that circulates on social media; often serves as a form of online propaganda

merchandising: all the practices involved in facilitating the sale of products and services

mere exposure effect: the idea that repeated exposure affects taste preferences

messy engagement: in education, the noisy chaos that can occur when students engage in create-to-learn pedagogies

meta-reference: when a media author explicitly comments on his or her own choices in constructing media in the context of the message itself

metadata: data used to describe the characteristics of media content

micro-celebrity: an individual who carefully crafts his or her online identity in a way that attracts a widespread audience

mixed revenue: when both advertising and payments from consumers are used to fund media companies

monopoly of knowledge: the idea that the ruling class maintains political power through control of key communications technologies

moral contagion: the idea that language and ideas with moral and emotional content can spread rapidly across communities

moral judgments: the ethical values people activate in interpreting media messages

moral panic: a term used to describe fears about the negative influence of media and technology

multi-perspectival thinking: the ability to imagine and consider many different points of view about an issue

multimodal theory: a theory of education developed from semiotics that focuses on the materials, design, and production of expressive content that uses language, images, interactivity, and design

music bed: in television news or documentary genres, the use of music to activate emotions

N

narrative analysis: a theory and a method of inquiry that examines how stories structure lived experience, culture, and personal identity

narrative arc: the structure of a story where characters are introduced, conflict increases, and resolution or climax occurs

natural language processing: using online information to filter content

net neutrality: rules that restrict Internet providers from offering "fast lane" levels of high-speed service to businesses and customers willing to pay more for it

netiquette: norms of polite online communication

news aggregation: services that curate news and information from many sources and repackage it for readers or viewers

news avoiders: people who do not seek out news and current events

news teasers: in online and television news, short promotional messages about news stories designed to attract audiences

news values: criteria journalists use to decide what is newsworthy

notice and choice: the legal practice of requiring people to actively consent to terms of service policies before using software

notice-and-takedown provision: the legal requirement that platforms remove potentially infringing content

O

online community: a group of people who participate in social interaction through a digital platform

online disinhibition effect: the lack of restraint some people experience when communicating online

online predators: adults who seek to interact with children and teens for sexual gratification

opt-in: a term used when someone gives a company permission to receive content or advertising.

Overton window: the shifting range of controversial, radical, or taboo ideas that the public gradually comes to tolerate

P

packet switching: a form of data transmission that involves breaking up a message into parts that are sent independently through a network of computers

page views: a way to measure the popularity of a website

paradox of tragedy: the pleasure that audiences experience when seeing bad things happen to characters

paradox of tolerance: a theory that suggests that if society is too tolerant, it will eventually become intolerant and destroy democracy

parasocial relationship: the unequal relationship between a celebrity and an audience

parental mediation: the different strategies, rules, and techniques families use to manage media use in the home

participatory culture: social and technological conditions that encourage people to create and share knowledge and self-expression

partisanship: a type of news reporting or journalism that offers a blend of information and opinion to align with a particular ideology or worldview

pattern recognition: a type of cognitive information processing based on the classification and ordering of features of a media text or other information

peer-to-peer platforms: social media platforms where sharing of content occurs only within a small group of people identified and defined by a user

Pennebaker paradigm: the therapeutic value of expressive writing

perceived reality: in communication theory, the extent to which a person trusts a particular media representation as authentic

performance: a set of behaviors that link an individual to socially perceived expectations

personalization: a way of customizing online content that is displayed to a user using the user's social graph

persuasion: a form of social power where individuals try to influence each other using language, gestures, and other symbols

pitch: in advertising, publishing, and film, a short persuasive communication targeting an editor or journalist about the creation of content for potential publication

platform: a group of technologies used as the base upon which other content, applications, processes, or technologies are developed; a software framework on which user-generated content and applications may be hosted

political economy of mass media: the study of the relationship between media, business, and government

popularity–quality continuum: the relationship between the quality of a media message and its popularity

porn media literacy: educational programs that examine how sexuality is represented in the media

pornography: print or visual communication media designed to produce sexual arousal

power/knowledge: the idea that social control is enacted through political, cultural, and social institutions that reproduce knowledge in ways that reinforce existing forms of power in societies

privacy paradox: the trade-off between the benefits of personalization and the potential harms of data misuse

privacy stewardship: making decisions about privacy on behalf of someone else

professional development: in U.S. education, a term used to describe the continued learning experiences across the life span that teachers engage in

profit motive: the drive to make money

project-based learning: a type of learning experience that involves creating a project or media message

protectionism: an approach to media literacy rooted in the need to protect people from the potential risks and harms of media culture

proximity marketing: reaching consumers with personalized advertising messages based on their specific geographic location

public affairs: a specific form of public relations focused on influencing government officials and policy

public broadcasting: radio and television stations that are noncommercial and rely on donations from audiences, financial support from philanthropies, and government funding

public domain: tangible creative products that are freely available to the public and not subject to copyright restrictions

public interest: a term used to describe the needs of everyone in society

"public interest, convenience, and necessity": the phrase from the 1934 Communications Act that authorized government regulation of broadcasting

public ritual: behaviors done by groups of people in a society that reaffirm shared values and maintain the social order

public sphere: the process of exchanging ideas and opinions in public so as to identify common interests and problems, and of; using imagination and compromise to advance solutions for improvement

publics: in public relations, a synonym for target audiences

purpose: the intention or goal of an author in creating a media message

Q

quasi-experimental design: a type of research employed to measure the effect of a treatment or program, where two or more groups are compared at two or more time periods but participants are not randomly assigned to a particular treatment

query: the term used for the keywords or other information users provide as part of the computer search process

R

raw audio models: using data from sound waves to filter content

reblogging (or re-tweeting): a mechanism that allows users to repost the content of other users' posts in a way that identifies the source

reception theory (also called encoding and decoding): a theory that emphasizes each particular reader's reception or interpretation in making meaning from a text

recommendation engines: created by choice algorithms that filter content based on data audiences provide

reflection: in education, a pedagogical practice that involves considering one's own stance toward a topic or issue using introspection and dialogue

regulation by raised eyebrow: the threat of potential government regulation as a means to influence a media company's socially positive behavior

reliable sources: in journalism, experts and other authorities who provide information to reporters; in research, published information that develops an argument through the use of reasoning and evidence

remix: cultural production using existing media available from the Internet

representation: a term used to describe the constructed nature of media depictions of people, objects, and events

reputation management: a variety of communication and technical practices used to shape messages about a company or an individual in ways that make a favorable impression

resilience: a characteristic of people who leverage whatever assets they have available to them for support and strength; the set of personal and social factors that enable people to resist risks and harms

resistant reading: when a reader or viewer uses an alternative ideological position to interpret a media message in a way the author did not intend

rhetorical agency: the competence to speak or write in a way that will be recognized or heeded by others in one's community

rich snippets: content digital authors create in order to provide a convenient summary that appears in a search engine page of results

right to be forgotten: part of the GDPR law that enables users to request that personal data be erased and removed from search engine results

royalty: in music industry and book publishing, the amount of money that an author receives from the distribution of his or her creative work

rulemaking process: the procedures federal agencies, use to determine whether regulation is needed to address failures of the free market

S

schema: in psychology, the elements of thought and feeling that are patterns of human action

school knowledge: the expectations of students, teachers, and the community about the content and format of instruction that is appropriate for formal education

school–university partnership: a model of implementing innovation in education that connects students and classroom teachers with scholars and researchers

screen time: a term that refers to children's use of TV, movies, video games, the Internet, and social media

script: the planned dialogue, action, and images in a play, film, television program, or other time-based media

search engine optimization: a technical process of increasing the number of website visitors obtaining a high-ranking placement in the search results page of a search engine

search engine page of results (SERP): the list of websites and Web content returned from a search process

Section 230 of the Communications Decency Act (CDA): this law protects Internet service providers who publish content provided by others; platform companies cannot be sued for libelous or fraudulent content on their websites

self-disclosure: the process of revealing information about oneself to another

self-objectification: when people treat themselves or create depictions of themselves not as a person but as an object that provides pleasure to others

self-referential media feedback loop: when media reproduce messages encountered through other media

self-representation: the practices people use to express and share their identity and life experiences

semiotics: the study of how signs and symbols express and share meaning

sensationalism: using content and techniques, including sex, violence, children, animals, and the mysterious or unknown, to attract and hold attention

sexting: sending and receiving sexually explicit text messages or images

shared inquiry: when a group of people engages in exploring a topic through examining different types of media texts, asking questions, and seeking information, using dialogue and discussion

shareholder: people who invest money in a company through the purchase of stock

shipping: in fan fiction, the practice of creating stories that feature romantic or sexual relationships between popular culture characters

situational ethics: in film reviewing, the conflicts of interest that arise as reviewers face pressures from Hollywood to serve business interests

social capital: a form of symbolic wealth based social relationships and family connections

social comparison theory: how people determine their self-worth by making upward or downward comparisons with others

social conformity: the tendency for people to willingly adapt their behavior in ways that reproduce existing power relationships

social conscience: a moral stance that emphasizes the importance of respect for others and integrity in social relationships

social credit system: using social media data to classify people and to reward or punish them based on particular qualities

social graph: the map of relationships between people created as they interact on a digital platform like Facebook, Twitter, or Instagram

social identity: the sense of identity linked to membership in a group

social learning theory: in psychology, the idea that people learn from observation and imitation of role models when their behavior is rewarded

social media: online forms of scalable sociality using digital platforms

social media metrics: data from an individual's social media use that indicate attention, interest, and engagement

social movement: an organized group of people who seek to make social, political, or economic change; the coordinated public actions that address changing social norms and values through political participation

social norms: in psychology, the beliefs and attitudes about what attitudes and behaviors are typical in a peer group

social power: status enacted through the use of symbols and behavior

social stenography: the practice of coding messages in online communication in such a way as to communicate with some audiences while obscuring communication with others

social systems: political, economic, and cultural structures that enable social organization

social validation: feelings of pleasure and power that come from being recognized, seen, or heard by others

society of the spectacle: the positioning of people as passive consumers of superficial entertainment

sock puppet: the use of fake social media accounts to disguise the identity of a communicator

sound bite: a brief spoken-word phrase edited from an interview

spam: messages sent to users without receiving explicit permission

spiders: search software that finds new online content through connecting hyperlinks and copying it to an index.

spin: a term used to refer to all forms of political communication

spreadability: characteristics of a media message that make it likely to be shared on social networks

state standards: in U.S. education, the goals that states set for student learning in math, English, history, science, and other topics

status markers: behaviors and objects that express a particular social class identity

stereotypes: in literature or film, oversimplified ways of expressing key features of people and ideas, or mental representations of the world that reduce complexity

storyboard: a planning tool used in film, television, and video games that uses drawings to sequence the narrative arc

storytelling: the general term for all forms of narrative (in literature, movies, video games, television, journalism, and more)

structuralism: a theory in linguistics, sociology, and anthropology about how social and cultural practices can be defined by their place in a social structure

subjectivity: taking the perspective of the individual self, rather than some neutral or objective perspective

subscription model: a type of economic model for paying for goods and services that involves an ongoing regular monthly or annual fee

surveillance capitalism: using data through computer monitoring and automation to personalize goods and services to users of digital platforms; experimenting on users and consumers without their awareness

symbol: a thing that represents or stands for something else

symbolic interactionism: the theory that communication is the sharing of meaning through symbols and that people actively shape the social world through interpretation

symbolic power: the capacity to intervene in events, to influence the actions of others, and to create events through producing and transmitting symbols

System 1 thinking: fast, intuitive, immediate, and automatic information processing

System 2 thinking: logical, linear, effortful, and strategic processing of information

T

tabloid packaging: a newspaper having a smaller size than a typical broadsheet style, usually dominated by large headlines and photographs of celebrities

taste: a term used to describe the practice of aesthetic judgment

techniques: elements used to construct media messages

telenovela: a serialized television dramatic show focused on family relationships with features like a soap opera

text: a constructed message (in any format) intentionally designed to communicate meaning

third-person effect: the perception that others are more influenced by media than oneself

torrent: this term can refer to downloading a large digital file

tournaments of value: award ceremonies and other public rituals that signal certain cultural values as a form of collective judgment

trading up the chain: a public relations technique where a company's message is shared with a blogger, and then that content is used to persuade a mainstream journalist that the information is newsworthy

transcendence: a special feeling or moment that far surpasses the ordinary experience of life

transformative use: a dimension of fair use that protects the legal rights of creators who use copyrighted content in new work that gives different meaning and purpose to the original

transgression: the state of "going too far" beyond accepted social conventions

transmedia storytelling: telling a story across multiple platforms and formats

transnational media: media companies that work across national borders

trolls: anonymous online contributors who use offensive, mean-spirited, and inappropriate content to annoy or threaten people

tropes: words and other symbols used in a nonliteral sense to communicate ideas

two-step flow of influence: the theory that ideas flow from mass media to opinion leaders, and from them to a wider population

types of reading: the many different strategies readers use as they encounter texts and utilize them for different purposes

U

ubiquitous: a term used to describe media pervasiveness in all aspects of life

user experience (UX): the overall quality of experience of a person using a website or computer application

user-generated content: text, images, and videos people create and share on a digital platform

uses: the ways in which people interact with media messages

uses and gratifications: the theoretical concept that suggests that people choose media that provide the most satisfaction for their basic cognitive, social, and emotional needs

V

vicarious experience: a term used to describe learning through observation

video news release: a short video that mimics the conventions of broadcast television news, created for the purposes of public relations and designed for use by broadcast journalists

violent media effects: the ways in which media violence can influence people's behavior, attitudes, and media use habits

virality: characteristics of news and information that make it likely to reach a large audience, or the conditions that support the widespread dissemination of messages through social media

virtual reality: a computer simulation of a three-dimensional environment that a person can interact with in a seemingly real or physical way by using special equipment

visibility–obscurity continuum: the relative position of one's personal identity along a spectrum from public to private

vlog: a type of video that uses first-person direct address to the camera, a video blog

voice actor: an actor who specializes in recording voice-overs for film and television

W

wi-fi: a technology that allows computers, smartphones, or other devices to connect to the Internet or communicate with one another wirelessly within a particular area

willing suspension of disbelief: the experience of choosing to treat fiction as a kind of real experience

without fear or favor: a phrase that refers to the value of the press being independent of political influence

References

Academy of Interactive Arts and Sciences (2018, March 29). AI for Storytelling. YouTube. https://youtu.be/eqRdCXfnu04

Action Coalition for Media Education (2018). About. https://acmesmartmediaeducation.net

Allen, A. (2016, June 10). Three black teenagers search shows it is society, not Google that is racist. *The Guardian*. www.theguardian.com/commentisfree/2016/jun/10/three-black-teenagers-google-racist-tweet

American Library Association (2013). Digital literacy, libraries and public policy. Office of Information Technology Policy. Retrieved from www.districtdispatch.org/wp-content/uploads/2013/01/2012_OITP_digiliteport_1_22_13.pdf

Anderson, C., Berkowitz, L. Donnerstein, E., Huesmann, L., Johnson, J., Linz, D. & Wartella, E. (2003). The influence of media violence on youth. Psychological Science in the Public Interest, 4(3), 81 – 110.

Anderson, M. (2018, September 27). A majority of teens have experienced some form of cyberbullying. Pew Research Center. www.pewinternet.org/2018/09/27/a-majority-of-teens-have-experienced-some-form-of-cyberbullying

Anderson, R. (2017, June 21). New CAA studt says diverse casting increases box office potential across all budgets. *Los Angeles Times*.

Angier, N. (2006). The cute factor. *The New York Times*, 3.

Antony, M. G., & Thomas, R. J. (2010). "This is citizen journalism at its finest": YouTube and the public sphere in the Oscar Grant shooting incident. *New Media & Society*, 12(8), 1280–1296.

Amos (2020, May 7). Why the movie studios' stance on vod and streaming shouldn't be cause for exhibition panic. *Forbes*.

Appadurai, A. (1998). Full attachment. *Public Culture*, 10(2), 443–449.

Arlen, M. (1997/1969). *Living-room war*. Syracuse University Press.

Association of College and Research Libraries (2015). Framework for information literacy in higher education. www.ala.org/acrl/standards/ilframework

Aubrey, J. S., Behm-Morawitz, E., & Kim, K. (2014). Understanding the effects of MTV's *16 and Pregnant* on adolescent girls' beliefs, attitudes, and behavioral intentions toward teen pregnancy. *Journal of Health Communication*, 19(10), 1145–1160.

Aufderheide, P. (1993). Media literacy. A report of the National Leadership Conference on Media Literacy. Washington, D.C.: Aspen Institute, Communications and Society Program.

Aufderheide, P. & Jaszi P. (2018). *Reclaiming fair use* (2nd ed.). Chicago: University of Chicago Press.

Ayomide, D. (2018, March 17). *Black Panther* raises big questions about identity and loyalty. Medium. https://medium.com/@DocAyomide/black-panther-identity-loyalty-cc5a634d2e02

Baccarin, G. (2017, May 8). Can diversity help AI diversify? TEDxTalks Rome. https://youtu.be/JAxLIu0OXRY

Bagdikian, B., Artz, L., Chitty, N., Cowan, G. He, Z., Karim, K. & Kellner, D. (2004). *War, media, and propaganda: A global perspective*. Lanham, MD: Rowman & Littlefield.

Ball-Rokeach, S. J. (1985). The origins of individual media-system dependency: A sociological framework. *Communication Research*, 12(4), 485–510.

Banaji, M. & Greenwald, A. (2013). *Blind spot: Hidden biases of good people*. New York: Random House.

Band, J., Butler, B., & Morris, C. (2018). Circumventing barriers to education. In R. Hobbs, (Ed.) *The Routledge companion to media education, copyright, and fair use* (XX- XX). New York: Routledge.

Barron, B., Gomez, K., Martin, C. K., & Pinkard, N. (2014). *The digital youth network. Cultivating digital media citizenship in urban communities*. Cambridge, MA: MIT Press.

Barthes, R. (1974). S/Z. Translated by Richard Miller. New York: Hill and Wang.

Bayley, E. (1982). *Joe McCarthy and the press*. Madison: University of Wisconsin Press.

Baym, N. K., & boyd, D. (2012). Socially mediated publicness: An introduction. *Journal of Broadcasting & Electronic Media*, 56(3), 320–329.

Baughman, J. (2011). The rise and fall of partisan journalism. Center for Journalism and Ethics, University of Wisconsin. https://ethics.journalism. wisc.edu/2011/04/20/the-fall-and-rise-of-partisan-journalism/

Beales, H. (2004). Advertising to kids and the FTC: A regulatory retrospective that advises the present. Federal Trade Commission. www.ftc.gov/public-statements/2004/03/advertising-kids-and-ftc-regulatory-retrospective-advises-present

Beers Fägersten, K. (2017). The role of swearing in creating an online persona: The case of YouTuber PewDiePie. *Discourse, Context & Media*, 18, 1–10.

Belshaw, D. (2014, December 1). A brief history of Web literacy and its future potential. Connected Learning Alliance. https://clalliance.org/blog/a-brief-history-of-web-literacy-and-its-future-potential/

Bennett, L. (2016). *News: The politics of illusion*. Chicago: University of Chicago Press.

Bennett, L., & Kidd, J. (2017). Myths about media studies: The construction of media studies education in the British press. *Continuum*, 31(2),163–176.

Bergen, E., Davidson, J., Schulz, A., Schuhmann, P. Johansson, A., Santtila, P., et al. (2014). The effects of using identity deception and suggesting secrecy on the outcomes of adult–adult and adult–child or –adolescent online sexual interactions. *Victims & Offenders*, 9(3), 276–298.

Berman, E. (2016, January 25). Insiders reveal how huge Hollywood's diversity problem is. *Time*. http://time.com/4192594/hollywood-diversity-problem-oscars-academy-awards/

Bernays, E. (2005/1928). *Propaganda*. New York: Ig Publishing.

Better Broadcasts Newsletter (1954). *Better broadcasts, better world*. April 1. Madison, Wisconsin.

Bhargava, R. (2011). The five models of content curation. www.rohitbhargava.com/2011/03/the-5-models-of-content-curation.html

Bhattacharjee, Y. (2015). Why we lie: The science behind our deceptive ways. *National Geographic*. www.nationalgeographic.com/magazine/2017/06/lying-hoax-false-fibs-science

Black, J., Barnes, J., Reiter-Palmon, Roni, & Tinio, Pablo. (2015). Fiction and social cognition: The effect of viewing award-winning television dramas on

Theory of Mind. *Psychology of Aesthetics, Creativity, and the Arts*, 9(4), 423–429.

Blankenhorn, D. (2018, May 16). The top 14 causes of political polarization. *The American Interest*. www.the-american-interest.com/2018/05/16/the-top-14-causes-of-political-polarization/

Bobbitt, D. (2011). Teaching McLuhan: Understanding *Understanding Media*. http://enculturation.net/teaching-mcluhan

Bok, S. (2015, September 24). When lies become the norm in politics. *The New York Times*. Room for Debate. www.nytimes.com/roomfordebate/2012/01/22/why-politicians-get-away-with-lying/when-lies-become-the-norm-in-politics

Bolas, T. (2009). *Screen education: From film appreciation to media studies*. Chicago: Intellect.

Booij, M. (2018) The privacy paradox: The right to be forgotten but the wish to be remembered. *Ad Week*. www.adweek.com/digital/the-privacy-paradox-the-right-to-be-forgotten-but-the-wish-to-be-remembered/

Booker, C. (2004). *The seven basic plots: Why we tell stories*. New York: A&C Black.

Borschke, M. (2011). Rethinking the rhetoric of remix. *Media International Australia*, 141(1), 17–25. https://doi.org/10.1177/1329878X1114100104

Bourdieu, P. (1987). *Distinction: A social critique of the judgment of taste*. Cambridge, MA: Harvard University Press.

Bourdieu, P. (1993). *The field of cultural production*. New York: Columbia University Press.

Bourdieu, P. (2014). *Distinction: A social critique of the judgment of taste*. Cambridge, MA: Harvard University Press.

Bowden, M. (2018, July 8). Why are we obsessed with superhero movies? *New York Times*.

boyd, d. (2008). Why youth (heart) social network sites: The role of networked publics in teenage social life. In D. Buckingham (Ed), *Youth, identity and digital media*. The John D. and Catherine T. MacArthur Foundation Series on Digital Media and Learning (pp. 119–142). Cambridge, MA: MIT Press.

boyd, d. (2016). *It's complicated: The social lives of networked teens*. New Haven CT: Yale University Press.

boyd, d. (2017, January 5). Did media literacy backfire? https://points.datasociety.net/did-media-literacy-backfire-7418c084d88d

boyd, d. (2018, March 9). You think you want media literacy—do you? *Data and Society Blog*. https://points.datasociety.net/you-think-you-want-media-literacy-do-you-7cad6af18ec2

Brady, W. J., Wills, J. A., Jost, J. T., Tucker, J. A., & Van Bavel, J. J. (2017). Emotion shapes the diffusion of moralized content in social networks. *Proceedings of the National Academy of Sciences*, 114(28), 7313–7318.

Braiker, B. (2011, September 26). The next great American consumer. *AdWeek*. www.adweek.com/brand-marketing/next-great-american-consumer-135207/

Braudy, L. (1997). *Fame: The frenzy of renown*. New York: Vintage.

Brown, B. (2015). *Rising strong*. New York: Random House.

Brown, J., el-Toukhy, S. & Ortiz, R. (2014). Growing up sexually in a digital world: The risks and benefits of youths' sexual media use. In A. Jordan & D. Romer (Eds.), *Media and the well-being of children and adolescents* (pp. 90–108). New York: Oxford University Press.

Buckingham, D. (2008). Introducing identity. In D. Buckingham (Ed.), *Youth, identity, and digital media*. The John D. and Catherine T. MacArthur Foundation Series on Digital Media and Learning (pp. 1–24). Cambridge, MA: MIT Press. doi:10.1162/dmal.9780262524834.001

Buchanan, L., Bui, Q. & Patel, J. (2020, July 3). Black Lives Matter may be the largest movement in U.S> history. *The New York Times*. https://www.nytimes.com/interactive/2020/07/03/us/george-floyd-protests-crowd-size.html

Buckingham, D. (2019). *The media education manifesto*. London: Polity Press.

Bulger, M. and Davison, P. (2018). The promises, challenges, and futures of media literacy. *Journal of Media Literacy Education*, 10(1), 1–21.

Burn, A. & Durran, J. (2007). *Media literacy in schools: Practice, production and progression*. London: Chapman.

Burt, S. (2017, August 23). The promise and the potential of fan fiction. *New Yorker*. www.newyorker.com/books/page-turner/the-promise-and-potential-of-fan-fiction

Cain, S. (2017). Ebook sales continue to fall as younger generations drive appetite for print. *The Guardian*, 14.

Callenberger, J. (2016). How to create a reality TV villain. *Vulture*. www.vulture.com/2016/06/reality-tv-villain-how-to-create-one.html

Campbell, K. (2005). Agency: Promiscuous and protean. *Communication and Critical/Cultural Studies*, 2(1), 1–19. doi:10.1080/1479142042000332134

Cappello, G. (2016). Gianna Cappello on Theodor Adorno. In R. Hobbs (Ed.), *Exploring the roots of digital and media literacy through personal narrative* (pp. 107–125). Philadelphia: Temple University Press.

Caramanica, J. (2013, June 26). *Catfish* and the truth about our false online selves. *The New York Times*. https://artsbeat.blogs.nytimes.com/2013/06/26/catfish-and-the-truth-about-our-false-online-selves/

Carnagey, N., Anderson, C., & Bushman, N. (2007). The effect of video game violence on physiological desensitization to real-life violence. *Journal of Experimental Social Psychology* 43(3), 489–496.

Carrington, V. & Robinson, M. (2009). *Digital literacies: Social learning and classroom practices*. Thousand Oaks: Sage.

Carvajal, M., García-Avilés, J. & González, J. (012). Crowdfunding and nonprofit media. *Journalism Practice*, doi:10.1080/17512786.2012.667267

Caswell, Estelle (2018). Earworm. Video Series. www.youtube.com/playlist?list=PLJ8cMiYb3G5fyqfIwGjH2fYC5f-FLfdwW4

Caulfield, M. (2017). Web literacy for student fact checkers. Self-published. https://webliteracy.pressbooks.com/

Cerulo, K. (1998). *Deciphering violence: The cognitive structure of right and wrong*. New York: Psychology Press.

Chandler, D. (2007). *Semiotics: The Basics*. London: Routledge.

Chu, M. T., Blades, M., & Herbert, J. (2014). The development of children's scepticism about advertising. In B. Gunter et al. (Eds.), *Advertising to children* (pp. 38–49). London: Palgrave Macmillan.

Ciocca, S. (2017, October 10). How machine learning finds your new music. *Medium*. https://medium.com/s/story/spotifys-discover-weekly-how-machine-learning-finds-your-new-music-19a41ab76efe

Clancy, E., Klettke, B. & Hallford, D. (2019). The dark side of sexting—Factors predicting the dissemination of sexts. *Computers in Human Behavior*, 92, 266–272.

Clark, R. P. (2018, March 1). Walter Lippmann on liberty and the news. Poynter Institute. www.poynter.org/news/walter-lippmann-liberty-

and-news-century-old-mirror-our-troubled-times

Clogston, J. (2016). The repeal of the Fairness Doctrine and the irony of talk radio: A story of political entrepreneurship, risk, and cover. *Journal of Policy History*, 28(2), 375–396.

Coll, S. (2018, August 20). Alex Jones, the First Amendment and the digital public square. *The New Yorker*. www.newyorker.com/magazine/2018/08/20/alex-jones-the-first-amendment-and-the-digital-public-square

Collins, B. (2017, November 6). Google autocompletes Antifa conspiracy theory after Texas massacre. *Daily Beast*. www.wired.com/story/google-autocomplete-vile-suggestions/

Collins, H., & Evans, R. (2008). *Rethinking expertise*. Chicago: University of Chicago Press.

Comer, J. S., Furr, J. M., Beidas, R. S., Weiner, C. L., & Kendall, P. C. (2008). Children and terrorism-related news: Training parents in coping and media literacy. *Journal of Consulting and Clinical Psychology*, 76, 568–578.

Committee to Protect Journalists (2020). Killed since 1992. https://cpj.org/data/killed/

Convertkit (2017). The state of the blogging industry 2017. https://convertkit.com/reports/blogging/blog/

Cooper, J. (2017, October 9). Sponsored content in the media: Emerging threat or evolution of the industry? *Harvard Political Review*. http://harvardpolitics.com/united-states/sponsored-content-in-the-media-emerging-threat-or-evolution-of-the-industry/

Coscarelli, J. (2016, February 10). The boycott before: Rap and resentment at the 1989 Grammys. *The New York Times*. www.nytimes.com/2016/02/11/arts/music/the-boycott-before-rap-and-resentment-at-the-1989-grammys.html

Costa E. (2018). Affordances-in-practice: An ethnographic critique of social media logic and context collapse. *New Media & Society*, 20(10), 3641–3656. doi:10.1177/146144481875629

Couldry, N. (2012). *Media, society, world: Social theory and digital media practice*. London: Polity.

Couldry, N. & Turow, J. (2014). Advertising, big data, and the clearance of the public realm: Marketers' new approaches to the content subsidy. *International Journal of Communication*, 8, 1710–1726.

Coyne, S., Lindner, J., Rasmussen, E., Nelson, D., & Birkbeck, V. (2016). Pretty as a princess: Longitudinal effects of engagement with Disney princesses on gender stereotypes, body esteem, and prosocial behavior in children. *Child Development*, 87(6), 1909–1925.

Cresci, E. (2016). Lonelygirl15: How one mysterious vlogger changed the internet. *The Guardian*. www.theguardian.com/technology/2016/jun/16/lonelygirl15-bree-video-blog-youtube

Cronk, G. (2015). George Herbert Mead. *Internet Encyclopedia of Philosophy*. www.iep.utm.edu/mead/#H3

Csikszentmihalyi, M. (1997). *Finding flow in everyday life*. New York: Harper Collins.

CSPI TV (2014). Gatorade Bolt! Video. https://youtu.be/-ZqDOJSa7Uo

Culkin, J. M. (1967, March 18). A schoolman's guide to Marshall McLuhan. *Saturday Review*, pp. 51–53, 71–72.

Cunningham, S. (2002). *The idea of propaganda: A reconstruction*. Westport, CT: Praeger.

Dahlgren, P. (2001). The transformation of democracy? In B. Axford & R. Huggins (Eds.), *New media and politics* (pp. 64–88). Thousand Oaks: Sage.

Dance, G., LaForgia, M. & Confessore, N. (2018, December 19). Facebook offered users privacy wall then let tech giants around it. *The New York Times*.

Davis, K. (2012). Friendship 2.0: Adolescents' experiences of belonging and self-disclosure online. *Journal of Adolescence*, 35(6), 1527–1536.

De Vries, D. & Peter, J. (2013). Women on display: The effect of portraying the self online on women's self-objectification. *Computers in Human Behavior*, 29(4), 1483–1489.

Debord, G. (1967/1995). *The society of the spectacle*. Trans: D. Nicholson-Smith. Cambridge: MIT Press.

Delgado, R. (1989). Storytelling for oppositionists and others: A plea for narrative. *Michigan Law Review*, 87(8), 2411–2441.

Deloitte (2018). 2018 Global mobile phone survey: U.S. edition. www2.deloitte.com/us/en/pages/technology-media-and-telecommunications/articles/global-mobile-consumer-survey-us-edition.html

Des Moines Register (2016, September 20). Blurring the lines between news and public relations. www.desmoinesregister.com/story/opinion/editorials/2016/09/20/editorial-blur-ring-lines-between-news-and-public-relations/90750382/

Deuze, M. (2011). Media life. *Media, Culture & Society*, 33(1), 137–148.

DeVolld, T. (2011). *Reality TV: An insider's guide to TV's hottest market*. Studio City, CA: Michael Wiese Productions.

Dewey, J. (1944/2004). *Democracy and education*. New York: Courier.

Dines, G. (2016, April 8). Is porn immoral? That doesn't matter: It's a public health crisis. www.washingtonpost.com/posteverything/wp/2016/04/08/is-porn-immoral-that-doesnt-matter-its-a-public-health-crisis/?noredirect=on&utm_term=.9047bfb6f8ab

Dixon, T. (2017). Good guys are still always in white? Positive change and continued misrepresentation of race and crime on local television news. *Communication Research*, 44(6), 775–792.

DLA Piper (2016). Advertising and marketing to children: Global report. www.lexology.com/library/detail.aspx?g=195d20ef-d179-4556-b572-d9087fd9311b

Dockerman, E. (2013). *Candy Crush Saga*: The science behind our addiction. *Time*. http://business.time.com/2013/11/15/candy-crush-saga-the-science-behind-our-addiction/

Dockter, J., Haug, D. & Lewis, C. (2010). Redefining rigor: Critical engagement, digital media, and the new English/language arts. *Journal of Adolescent & Adult Literacy*, 53(5), 418–420.

Drouin, M., Coupe, M., & Temple, J. (2017). Is sexting good for your relationship? It depends …. *Computers in Human Behavior*, 75, 749–756.

Drumwright, M., & Murphy, P. E. (2004). How advertising practitioners view ethics: Moral muteness, moral myopia, and moral imagination. *Journal of Advertising*, 33(2), 12–13.

DScout (2016, June 26). Putting a finger on our phone obsession. Research by DScout. https://blog.dscout.com/mobile-touches

Dusi, N. (2017). Remixing movies and trailers before and after the digital age. In E. Navas, O. Gallagher & X. Burrough (Eds.), *The Routledge companion to remix studies* (pp. 154–165). New York: Routledge.

e-Marketer (2018, May 18). Total media ad spending will rise 7.4% in 2018. e-Marketer. www.emarketer.com/content/emarketer-total-media-ad-spending-worldwide-will-rise-7-4-in-2018

Easterbrook, G. (2018, December 21) Follow the Monday money. ESPN. www.espn.com/espn/page2/story?page=easterbrook/060912

Economist, (2010, September 2). Putting your money where your mouse is.

Edelstein, D. (2010, September 10). Art of the steal. New York Magazine. https://nymag.com/movies/reviews/68101/index.html

Edgerly, S. (2017). Seeking out and avoiding the news media: Young adults' proposed strategies for obtaining current events information. Mass Communication and Society, 20(3), 358–377.

Edwards, L. (2016). The role of public relations in deliberative systems. Journal of Communication, 66(1), 60–81.

Elgersma, C. (2017, July 25). The facts about online predators that everyone should know. Common Sense Media. www.commonsensemedia.org/blog/the-facts-about-online-predators-every-parent-should-know

Ellemers, N. (2018). Gender steretypes. Annual Review of Psychology, 69(1), 275–298.

Entman, R. (1993). Framing: Toward clarification of a fractured paradigm. Journal of Communication, 43(4), 51–58.

Entman, R. (2005). The nature and sources of news. In G. Overholser & K. Jamieson (Eds.), The press (pp. 48–65). New York: Oxford University Press.

Evans, N., Carlson, L., & Grubbs Hoy, M. (2013). Coddling our kids: Can parenting style affect attitudes toward advergames? Journal of Advertising, 42(2–3), 228–240.

Evers, D., & Deng, N. (2015). Acknowledgement and the paradox of tragedy. Philosophical studies, 173, 337–350.

Ewen, S. (1976). Captains of consciousness advertising and the social roots of the consumer culture. New York: Basic Books.

Fabos, B. (2004). Wrong turn on the Information Superhighway: Education and the commercialization of the Internet. New York: Columbia University Teachers College Press.

Facebook (2017, December 18). Fighting engagement bait on Facebook. https://newsroom.fb.com/news/2017/12/news-feed-fyi-fighting-engagement-bait-on-facebook/

Farid, F. (2017, December 4). Egypt's war on books. The Atlantic. www.theatlantic.com/international/archive/2017/12/egypt-sisi-books-freedom-of-speech/547259/

Fay, S. (2012, April 25). Book reviews: A tortured history. The Atlantic. www.theatlantic.com/entertainment/archive/2012/04/book-reviews-a-tortured-history/256301/

Federal Trade Commission (2017). FTC's endorsement guides: What people are asking. www.ftc.gov/tips-advice/business-center/guidance/ftcs-endorsement-guides-what-people-are-asking

Felini, D. (2014). Quality media literacy education: A tool for teachers and teacher educators of Italian elementary schools. Journal of Media Literacy Education, 6(1), 3–25.

Fellion, M, & Inglis, K. (2017). Censored: A literary history of subversion and control. London: British Library.

Ferguson, Kirby. 2016. Everything is a remix: The Force awakens. [Video.] https://vimeo.com/167069783

Finley, K. (2015, October 8). A brief history of the end of the comments. Wired. www.wired.com/2015/10/brief-history-of-the-demise-of-the-comments-timeline/.

Finucane, M. (2018, February 14). Should you consider letting your teen take a porn literacy class? Boston Globe. www.bostonglobe.com/metro/2018/02/14/should-you-consider-letting-your-teen-take-porn-literacy-class/cTXYCiW48iKNK5A6uprDlK/story.html

Fiske, J. (2010). Understanding popular culture. New York: Routledge.

Fitzgerald, H. (2018, May 18). The decline of Snapchat and the secret joy of Internet ghost towns. The Verge. www.theverge.com/2018/5/18/17366528/snapchat-decline-internet-ghost-towns

Foucault, M. (1991). Discipline and punish: The birth of a prison. London: Penguin.

Franklin, B., Hogan, M., Langley, Q., Mosdell, N., & Pill, E. (2009). Introduction. In B. Franklin et. al. (Eds.), Key concepts in public relations. (pp. 1–12), London: Sage UK.

Frau-Meigs, D. & Torrent, J. (2009). Mapping media education policies in the world: Visions, programmes and challenges. Paris: UNESCO.

Fritz, B. (2018). The big picture: The fight for the future of movies. New York: Houghton Mifflin Harcourt.

Fuller, J. (1996). News values: Ideas for an information age. Chicago: University of Chicago Press.

Gallagher, R. (2018, August 1). Google plans to launch censored search engine in China. The Intercept. https://theintercept.com/2018/08/01/google-china-search-engine-censorship/

Galloway, S. (2018, February 8). Silicon Valley's tax-avoiding, job-killing, soul-sucking machine. Esquire. www.esquire.com/news-politics/a15895746/bust-big-tech-silicon-valley/

Garcia, M. (2017, February 13). How to keep your AI from turning into a racist monster. Wired. https://www.wired.com/2017/02/keep-ai-turning-racist-monster/

Garlitz, D., Smelser, N., & Baltes, P. (2015). Roland Barthes. International encyclopedia of the social and behaviorial sciences (2nd ed., pp. 357–362). New York: Elsevier.

Geertz, Clifford (1973). The interpretation of cultures. New York: Basic Books.

Gelles, D. (2018, September 9). Billionnaires can seem like saviors to media companies, but they come with risks. The New York Times. https://www.nytimes.com/2018/09/19/business/media/newspapers-billionaire-owners-magazines.html

Gelles, D, & Yaffe-Bellany, D. (2019, August 19). Shareholder value is no longer everything, top CEOs say. The New York Times. www.nytimes.com/2019/08/19/business/business-roundtable-ceos-corporations.html

Gerber, J. P., Wheeler, L., & Suls, J. (2018). A social comparison theory meta-analysis 60+ years on. Psychological Bulletin, 144(2), 177–197. http://dx.doi.org/10.1037/bul0000127

Gerbner, G. (1998). Telling stories, or how do we know what we know? The story of cultural indicators and the cultural environment movement. Wide Angle, 20(2), 116–131.

Gerbner, G., Gross, L., Morgan, M., & Signorielli, N. (1980). The "mainstreaming" of America: Violence profile no. 11. Journal of Communication, 30(3), 10–29.

Gerdeman, D. (2017, February 13). Do search ads work? Harvard Business School Working Knowledge. www.forbes.com/sites/hbsworkingknowledge/2017/02/13/do-search-ads-work-harvard-researchers-teamed-up-with-yelp-to-find-out/#42cbe9da4a4d

Giaccardi, S., Ward, L. M., Seabrook, R., Manago, A., & Lippman, J. (2016). Media and modern manhood: Testing associations between media consumption and young men's acceptance of traditional gender ideologies. Sex Roles, 75(3), 151–163.

Girl Scouts USA (2011). Real to me: Girls and reality TV. Retrieved December 1,

2011 from www.girlscouts.org/research/publications/girlsandmedia/real_to_me.asp

Gitlin, T. (2007). *Media unlimited*. New York: Holt.

Gladwell, M. (2008). *Outliers: The story of success*. New York: Little Brown.

Gleiberman, O. (2017, August 20). Healthy tomatoes? The dangers of film critics speaking as one. *Variety*. https://variety.com/2017/film/columns/rotten-tomatoes-the-danger-of-film-critics-speaking-as-one-1202533533/

Global Voices Advox (2013). Facebook's Graph search: Be careful what you "like." https://advox.globalvoices.org/2013/04/06/facebooks-graph-search-be-careful-what-you-like/

Godfrey-Smith, P. & Kerr, B. (2017, October 1). After Charlottesville, how we define tolerance becomes a key question. *The Conversation*. http://theconversation.com/after-charlottesville-how-we-define-tolerance-becomes-a-key-question-83793

Goel, V. (2014, June 29). Facebook tinkers with users' emotions in News Feed experiment, stirring outcry. *The New York Times*. www.nytimes.com/2014/06/30/technology/facebook-tinkers-with-users-emotions-in-news-feed-experiment-stirring-outcry.html

Google (2018). How Google autocomplete works. www.blog.google/products/search/how-google-autocomplete-works-search/

Gorman, S. (2008). NSA's domestic spying grows as agency sweeps up data. *Wall Street Journal*, 10.

Gottfried, J., Barthel, M., Shearer, E., & Mitchell, A. (2016, February 4). The 2016 presidential campaign—A news event that's hard to miss. www.journalism.org/2016/02/04/the-2016-presidential-campaign-a-news-event-thats-hard-to-miss/

Greenberg, D. (2016). *Republic of spin: An inside history of the American presidency*. New York: W. W. Norton.

Greenfield, P. (2004). Inadvertent exposure to pornography on the Internet: Implications of peer-to-peer file-sharing networks for child development and families. *Journal of Applied Developmental Psychology*, 25(6), 741–750.

Greenwood, V. (2018, August 14). Exposing astroturfing as only John Oliver can. Healthy Teens. http://healthyteens.us/exposing-astroturfing-as-only-john-oliver-can/

Grind, K., Schechner, S., McMillan, R., & West, J. (2019, Nov 15). How Google interferes with its search algorithms and changes your results; the internet giant uses blacklists, algorithm tweaks and an army of contractors to shape what you see. *Wall Street Journal*.

Gross, T. (Host) (2012, February 22). How companies are 'defining your worth' online. [Radio broadcast episode.]. https://www.npr.org/transcripts/147189154

Grossman, L. (2011, July 7). The boy who lived forever. *Time*. http://content.time.com/time/arts/article/0,8599,2081784-5,00.html

Grossman, L. (2016, May 26). Here's how PewDiePie reinvented fame. *Time*. https://time.com/4348958/pewdiepie-2/

Grubbs, J., Exline, B., Pargament, J., Volk, J., & Lindberg, K. (2017). Internet pornography use, perceived addiction, and religious/spiritual struggles. *Archives of Sexual Behavior*, 46(6), 1733–1745.

Guernsey, L. (2012). *Screen time: How electronic media—from baby videos to educational software—affects your young child*. London: Hachette UK.

Guess, A., Nyhan, B., & Reifler, J. (2018). *Selective exposure to misinformation: Evidence from the consumption of fake news during the 2016 US presidential campaign*. European Research Council.

Guida, J. (2015, February 4). How movies can change our minds. *The New York Times Blog*. https://op-talk.blogs.nytimes.com/2015/02/04/how-movies-can-change-our-minds/?_r=0

Habermas, J., Lennox, S., & Lennox, F. (1974). The public sphere: An encyclopedia article *New German Critique*, 3, 49–55.

Halavais, A. (2017). *Search engine society* (2nd ed.). New York: Polity/Wiley.

Halim, M., Ruble, D., & Tamis-LeMonda, C. (2013). Four-year-olds beliefs about how others regard males and females. *British Journal of Developmental Psychology*, 31, 128–135.

Hall, S. (1980). Encoding/decoding. In S. Hall, D. Hobson, A. Love, & P. Willis (Eds.), *Culture, media, language* (pp. 128–138). London: Hutchinson.

Hallin, D. C., & Mancini, P. (2004). *Comparing media systems: Three models of media and politics*. Cambridge: Cambridge University Press.

Halpern, S. (2018, October 18). Mind games. *The New Republic*. https://newrepublic.com/article/151548/political-campaigns-big-data-manipulate-elections-weaken-democracy

Hannak, A., Sapiezynski, P., Molavi Kakhki, A., Krishnamurthy, B., Lazer, D., Mislove, A., & Wilson, C. (2013, May). *Measuring personalization of web search*. In Proceedings of the 22nd international conference on World Wide Web (pp. 527–538). ACM.

Harold, C. (2007). *Our space*. Minneapolis: University of Minnesota Press.

Harris, T. (2016, May 18). How technology hijacks people's minds from a magician and Google ethicist. Medium. https://medium.com/thrive-global/how-technology-hijacks-peoples-minds-from-a-magician-and-google-s-design-ethicist-56d62ef5edf3

Harvard Law Review (2018, May 10). Section 230 as First Amendment rule, 131, 7.

Hasinoff, A. (2015). *Sexting panic: Rethinking criminalization, privacy, and consent*. Champaign: University of Illinois Press, 2015.

Hass, N. (1997, January 26). Sex and today's single-minded sitcoms. *The New York Times*. www.nytimes.com/1997/01/26/arts/sex-and-today-s-single-minded-sitcoms.html

HASTAC (2014, September 25). Settings for Trust in Connected Learning. Interview with danah boyd. www.hastac.org/blogs/superadmin/2014/09/25/settings-trust-connected-learning-interview-danah-boyd

Haviland, S., & Clark, H. (1974). What's new? Acquiring new information as a process in comprehension. *Journal of Verbal Learning and Verbal Behavior* 13(5), 512–521.

Head, A., Wihbey, J., Metaxas, T., MacMillan, M., & Cohen, D. (2018). How students engage with news: Five takeaways for educators, journalists, and librarians. Project Information Literacy Research Institute. www.projectinfolit.org/uploads/2/7/5/4/27541717/newsexecutivesummary.pdf

Hebert, C. (2018, January 18). My year of living ignorantly: I entered a news blackout the day Trump was elected. *The Guardian*. www.theguardian.com/lifeandstyle/2018/jan/18/my-year-of-living-ignorantly-i-entered-a-news-blackout-the-day-trump-was-elected

Hjarvard, S. (2008). The mediatization of society. *Nordicom Review*, 29(2), 102–131.

Ho, T. (2015). It's good to talk. *New Scientist*, 226(3023), 38–41.

Hobbs, R. (1998). The seven great debates in the media literacy movement. *Journal of Communication*, 48(1), 16–32.

Hobbs, R. (2006). Reconceptualizing media literacy for the digital age. In A Martin & D. Madigan (Eds.), *Literacies for learning in the digital age* (pp. 99–109). London: Facets Press.

Hobbs, R. (2010a). *Digital and media literacy: A plan of action*. Aspen Institute and the John S. and James L. Knight Foundation, Washington, D.C. www.knightcomm.org/digital-and-media-literacy-a-plan-of-action/

Hobbs, R. (2010b). *Copyright clarity: How fair use supports digital learning*. Thousand Oaks, CA: Corwin/Sage.

Hobbs, R. (2011). The state of media literacy: A response to Potter. *Journal of Broadcasting and Electronic Media* 55(3), 419–430.

Hobbs, R. (2020). *Mind over media: Propaganda education in a digital age*. New York: W. W. Norton.

Hobbs, R., Deslauriers, L., & Steager, P. (2019). *The library screen scene: Film and media literacy education in schools, colleges and communities*. New York: Oxford University Press.

Hobbs, R., & Moore, D.C. (2013). *Discovering media literacy: Digital media and popular culture in elementary school*. Thousand Oaks: Corwin/Sage.

Hobbs, R., & Tuzel, S. (2017). Teacher motivations for digital and media literacy: An examination of Turkish educators. *British Journal of Educational Technology* 48(1), 7–22. doi: 10.1111/bjet.12326

Hobbs, R. (2013). Improvization and strategic risk-taking in informal learning with digital media literacy. *Learning, Media and Technology*, 38(2), 182–197.

Holiday, R. (2013). *Trust me, I'm lying: Confessions of a media manipulator*. New York: Penguin.

Hopkins, N. (2017, May 17). Revealed: Facebook's internal rulebook on sex, terrorism and violence. *The Guardian*. www.theguardian.com/news/2017/may/21/revealed-facebook-internal-rulebook-sex-terrorism-violence

Horovitz, B. (2015, January 15). Consumer group raps Swift's Coke ties. *USA Today*. https://eu.USAToday.com/story/money/2015/01/16/taylor-swift-diet-coke-coca-cola-center-for-science-in-the-public-interest-marketing-soft-drinks/21818157/

Horton, D., & Wohl, R. (1956). Mass communication and para-social interaction: Observations on intimacy at a distance. *Psychiatry* 19(3), 215–229.

Howard, J. (2017, December 11). When kids get their first cell phones around the world. CNN. www.cnn.com/2017/12/11/health/cell-phones-for-kids-parenting-without-borders-explainer-intl/index.html

Hudson, D. (2017). How to leverage social media like Magnum ice cream. Dash Hudson. https://blog.dashhudson.com/magnum-ice-cream-cara-delevingne-model-jeremy-schott-moschino-kendall-jenner/

Hunt, D., Ramon, A., Tran, M., Sargent, A., & Roychouldhury, D. (2018). Hollywood diversity report 2018: Five years of progress and missed opportunities. UCLA Social Sciences. http://bit.ly/2Ox7QQi

Ienca, M., & Vayena, E. (2018). Cambridge Analytica and online manipulation. *Scientific American*. https://blogs.scientificamerican.com/observations/cambridge-analytica-and-online-manipulation/

IFPI (2018). Global music industry report 2017. www.ifpi.org/downloads/GMR2017.pdf

Ingraham, C. (2018, June 29). Leisure reading in the U.S. is at an all-time low. *Washington Post*. www.washingtonpost.com/news/wonk/wp/2018/06/29/leisure-reading-in-the-u-s-is-at-an-all-time-low/

Ito, M., Gutiérrez, K., Livingstone, S., Penuel, B., Rhodes, J., Salen, K., Schor, J., Sefton-Green, J., & Watkins, C. (2013). Connected learning: An agenda for research and design. Digital Media and Learning Research Hub, Irvine, CA. https://dmlhub.net/wp-content/uploads/files/Connected_Learning_report.pdf

Jackson, D. (2017). Environmental justice? Unjust coverage of the Flint water crisis. Shorenstein Center on Media, Politics and Public Policy. https://shorensteincenter.org/environmental-justice-unjust-coverage-of-the-flint-water-crisis/

Jacobs, B. (2017, March 26). Journey: The artistry of game design. YouTube. https://youtu.be/RJyGpVmkewU

Jakupsstovu, G. (2018). Cancel your plans: Remake of Norwegian Internet hit show *Skam* airs in the U.S. today. https://thenextweb.com/socialmedia/2018/04/24/cancel-your-plans-remake-of-norwegian-internet-hit-show-skam-airs-in-the-us-today/

Jeffries, L. (1997). *Mass media effects* (2nd ed.). Prospect Heights: Waveland Press.

Jenkins, H. (2006). *Convergence culture: Where old and new media collide*. New York: NYU Press.

Jenkins, H. (2011, June 20). Acafandom and beyond: Week 2, Part 1. http://henryjenkins.org/blog/2011/06/acafandom_and_beyond_week_two.html

Jenkins, H., Ford, S., & Green, J. (2013). *Spreadable media: Creating value and meaning in a networked culture*. New York: New York University Press.

Jenkins, H., & Kelley, W., eds., with Clinton, K., McWilliams, J., Pitts-Wiley, R., & Reilly, E. (2013). *Reading in a participatory culture: Remixing Moby-Dick in the English classroom*. New York: Teachers College Press.

Jenkins, H., Clinton, K., Purushotma, R., Robison, A. J., & Weigel, M. (2009). *Confronting the challenges of participatory culture: Media education for the 21st century*. The John D. and Catherine T. MacArthur Foundation Reports on Digital Media and Learning. Cambridge: Massachusetts Institute of Technology.

Jenkins, H., Shresthova, S., Gamber-Thompson, L., & Kligler-Vilenchik, N. (2016). Superpowers to the people! How young activists are tapping the civic imagination. In E. Gordon & P. Mihailidis (Eds.), *Civic media: Technology, design, practice* (pp. 295–320). Cambridge, MA: MIT Press.

Jeong, S., Cho, H., & Hwang, Y. (2012). Media literacy interventions: A meta-analytic review. *Journal of Communication* 62(3), 454–472.

Jett, S., & LaPorte, D. (2010). Impact of exposure to pro-eating disorder websites on eating behaviour of college women. *European Eating Disorders Review* 18(5), 410–416.

Jhally, S. (1997), director. *Stuart Hall: Representation and the Media*. [film]. Media Education Foundation.

Johnson, B. (2002). Advertising and the First Amendment. Freedom Forum Institute. www.freedomforuminstitute.org/first-amendment-center/topics/freedom-of-speech-2/advertising-first-amendment-overview/

Johnson, D. R., & Peifer, J. L. (2017). How public confidence in higher education varies by social context. *Journal of Higher Education*, 88(4), 619–644.

Johnson, L. (2018, February 5). Tide's spotless Super Bowl campaign as seen from inside the brand's war room. *AdWeek*. www.adweek.com/digital/tides-spotless-super-bowl-campaign-as-seen-from-inside-the-brands-war-room/

Jones, L. M., Mitchell, K. J., & Finkelhor, D. (2012). Trends in youth Internet victimization: Findings from three youth Internet safety surveys 2000–2010. *Journal of Adolescent Health*, 50(2), 179–186. doi: 10.1016/j.jadohealth.2011.09.015

Jones, M. (2018, February 7). What teenagers are learning from online porn. *The New York Times Magazine*. www.nytimes.com/2018/02/07/magazine/teenagers-learning-online-porn-literacy-sex-education.html

Jones, R., & Hafner, C. (2012). *Understanding digital literacies*. New York: Routledge.

Jowitt, G., & O'Donnell, V. (2012). *Propaganda and persuasion*. Thousand Oaks: Sage.

Kahne, J., & Bowyer, B. (2017). Educating for democracy in a partisan age: Confronting the challenges of motivated reasoning and misinformation. *American Educational Research Journal*, 54(1), 3–34.

Kahne, J., Lee, N., & Feezell, J. (2012). Digital media literacy education and online civic and political participation. *International Journal of Communication*, 6, 24–54.

Kahneman, D. (2011). *Thinking fast and slow*. New York: Farrar, Straus and Giroux.

Kakutani, M. (2008, August 15). Is Jon Stewart the most trusted man in America? *The New York Times*. www.nytimes.com/2008/08/17/arts/television/17kaku.html

Kaminski, M., & Klonick, K. (2017, June 27). Facebook, free expression and the power of a leak. *The New York Times*.

Kashoggi, J. (2018, October 17). What the Arab world needs most is free expression. *Washington Post*. www.washingtonpost.com/opinions/global-opinions/jamal-khashoggi-what-the-arab-world-needs-most-is-free-expression/2018/10/17/

Katz, E., & Lazarsfeld, P. (1955). *Personal influence*. New York: Free Press.

Kavanagh, J. and Rich, M. (2018). *Truth decay: An initial exploration of the diminishing role of facts and analysis in American public life*. Santa Monica: RAND Corporation. www.rand.org/pubs/research_reports/RR2314.html

Kearney, M. S., & Levine, P. B. (2015). Media influences on social outcomes: The impact of MTV's 16 and Pregnant on teen childbearing. *American Economic Review*, 105(12), 3597–3632.

Keen, A. (2007). *The cult of the amateur*. London: Hachette.

Keller, B. (2011). All the aggregation that's fit to aggregate. *The New York Times*. www.nytimes.com/2011/03/13/magazine/mag-13lede-t.html

Kellner, D. (2008). *Guys and guns amok: Domestic terrorism and school shootings from the Oklahoma City bombing to the Virginia Tech massacre*. New York: Routledge.

Kelly, T. M. (2013). *Teaching history in the digital age*. Ann Arbor: University of Michigan Press.

Khamis, S., Ang, L., & Welling, R. (2017). Self-branding, "micro-celebrity" and the rise of social media influencers. *Celebrity Studies*, 8(2), 191–208.

Kilbourne, J. (2012). *Can't buy my love: How advertising changes the way we think and feel*. New York: Simon and Schuster.

Kim, H. S. (2015). Attracting views and going viral: How message features and news-sharing channels affect health news diffusion, *Journal of Communication*, 65(3), 512–534. https://doi-org.uri.idm.oclc.org/10.1111/jcom.12160

Kingson, J. (2016, August 6). How cats took over the Internet. *The New York Times*. www.nytimes.com/2015/08/07/arts/design/how-cats-took-over-the-internet-at-the-museum-of-the-moving-image.html

Kistler, M., Kallman, D., & Austin, E.W. (2017). Media literacy approaches for improving youth and family programs. In B. Abreu, P. Mihailidis, A. Lee, J. Melki, & J. MacDougall (Eds.), *International handbook of media literacy education* (pp. 79–96). London: Routledge.

Klein, E. (2015, April 13). How Vox aggregates. *Vox*. www.vox.com/2015/4/13/8405999/how-vox-aggregates

Klein, I. (2020). "Enemy of the people:" The ghost of the FCC Fairness Doctrine in the age of alternative facts. *Hastings Communication and Entertainment Law Journal*, 42, 45.

Kohler, C. (2009, July 29). July 29, 1994: Videogame makers propose ratings system to Congress. *Wired*. www.wired.com/2009/07/dayintech-0729/

Koop, C., & Goodstein, L. (1987). Report of the Surgeon General's workshop on pornography and public health. *American Psychologist*, 42(10), 944–945.

Kosseff, J. (2019). *The 26 words that created the Internet*. Ithaca, NY: Cornell University Press.

Kovac, M., & Van der Weel, A. (2018). Reading in a post-textual era. *First Monday*, https://firstmonday.org/ojs/index.php/fm/article/view/9416/7592

Kowitt, B. (2019, January 19). Why Tide Pods are even more toxic than regular laundry detergent. *Fortune*. https://fortune.com/2018/01/19/tide-pod-challenge-toxic/

KQED (2018). Media Literacy. https://ww2.kqed.org/education/media-literacy/

Kress, G. R., & Van Leeuwen, T. (1996). *Reading images: The grammar of visual design*. New York: Routledge. Psychology Press.

Kulshrestha, J., Eslami, M., Messias, J., et al. (2018). Search bias quantification: Investigating political bias in social media and Web search. *Information Retrieval Journal* https://doi.org/10.1007/s10791-018-9341-2

Kumar, P., & Schoenebeck, S. (2015, February). The modern day baby book: Enacting good mothering and stewarding privacy on Facebook. In *Proceedings of the 18th ACM Conference on Computer Supported Cooperative Work & Social Computing* (pp. 1302–1312). ACM.

Lancaster, B. (2018, March 7). Glam or sham: How the big brands cash in on YouTube beauty bloggers. *The Guardian*. www.theguardian.com/fashion/2018/mar/08/glam-or-sham-are-youtubes-beauty-vloggers-selling-out

Laposki, I. (2018, February 12). Google autocomplete still makes some vile suggestions. *Wired*. www.wired.com/story/google-autocomplete-vile-suggestions/

Lauzen, M. (2018). Celluloid Ceiling. https://womenintvfilm.sdsu.edu/wp-content/uploads/2018/01/2017_Celluloid_Ceiling_Report.pdf

Lehmann, N. (1989, July 2). Vietnam: The mess and the press. *The New York Times*. www.nytimes.com/1989/07/02/books/vietnam-the-mess-and-the-press.html

Lehrer, J. (2011). The neuroscience of music. *Wired*. www.wired.com/2011/01/the-neuroscience-of-music/

Lenhart, A., Ybarra, M., & Price-Feeney, M. (2016). Non-consensual image sharing: One in 25 Americans has been a victim of "revenge porn." Data and Society Research Institute. https://datasociety.net/pubs/oh/Nonconsensual_Image_Sharing_2016.pdf

Levine, L. (1990). *Highbrow/lowbrow: The emergence of cultural hierarchy in Amer-*

ica. Cambridge, MA:Harvard University Press.

Levitin, D. (2006). *This is your brain on music: The science of a human obsession.* New York: Penguin.

Lippmann, W. (1922). *Public opinion.* New York: Harcourt, Brace and Company.

Livingstone, S. (2014). Developing social media literacy: How children learn to interpret risky opportunities on social network sites. *Communications, 39*(3), 283–303.

Livingstone, S., Blum-Ross, A., Pavlick, J., & Ólafsson, K. (2018). In the digital home, how do parents support their children and who supports them? Parenting for a digital future: Survey Report 1. www.lse.ac.uk/media-and-communications/assets/documents/research/preparing-for-a-digital-future/P4DF-Survey-Report-1-In-the-digital-home.pdf

Livingstone, S., Davidson, J., Bryce, J., Batool, S., Haughton, C., & Nandi, A. (2017). Children's online activities, risks and safety: A literature review by the UKCCIS evidence group.

Loewen, J. (1995/2008). *Lies my teacher told me: Everything your high school history textbook got wrong.* New York: New Press.

Lomas, N. (2017). Verizon's new opt-in rewards program requires users to share personal data for ad targeting. Tech Crunch. https://techcrunch.com/2017/09/06/verizons-new-opt-in-rewards-program-requires-users-to-share-personal-data-for-ad-targeting/

Lopez, G. (2018, December 6). Video game addiction is real, rare, and poorly understood. Vox. www.vox.com/science-and-health/2018/12/6/18050680/video-game-addiction-gaming-disorder-who

Lotz, A. (2014). The television will be revolutionized (2nd ed.). New York: New York University Press.

Luca, M. (2016). Reviews, reputation and revenue: The case of Yelp.com. Harvard Business SchoolWorking Paper 12-016. www.hbs.edu/faculty/Publication%20Files/12-016_a7e4a5a2-03f9-490d-b093-8f951238dba2.pdf

Lucidi, F., Mallia, L., Alivernini, F., Chirico, A., Manganelli, S., Galli, F., Biasi, V., & Zelli, A. (2017). The effectiveness of a new school-based media literacy intervention on adolescents' doping attitudes and supplements use. *Frontiers of Psychology,* 8, 749. doi: 10.3389/fpsyg.2017.00749

Ma, A. (2019, February 22). Hew, AOC, saw your whack tweet. *Business Insider.* www.businessinsider.com/ocasio-cortez-job-creators-network-feud-continues-amazon-hq2-billboard-2019-2

Macnamara, J. (2016). The continuing convergence of journalism and PR: New insights for ethical practice from a three-country study of senior practitioners. Journalism & Mass Communication Quarterly, 93(1), 118–141.

Madden, M. (2016, October 11). If you want to know why privacy matters, the play's the thing. Data & Society. https://points.datasociety.net/if-you-want-to-know-why-privacy-matters-the-plays-the-thing-1be6ef8fef39

Madison, E. (2015). *Newsworthy: Cultivating critical thinkers, readers, and writers in language arts classrooms.* New York: Teachers College Press.

Marantz, A. (2015, January 5). The virologist. *The New Yorker.*

Margulis, E. H. (2014). One more time. Aeon. https://aeon.co/essays/why-repetition-can-turn-almost-anything-into-music

Martens, H. (2010). Evaluating media literacy education: Concepts, theories and future directions. *Journal of Media Literacy Education,* 2(1), 1–22.

Martin, A. (2013, May 30). Online disinhibition and the psychology of trolling. *Wired.* www.wired.co.uk/article/online-aggression.

Martins, N., Weaver, A., Yeshua-Katz, D. Lewis, N. Tyree, N. & Jensen, J. (2013). A content analysis of print news coverage of media violence and aggression research, *Journal of Communication* 63(6), 1070–1087.

Marvin, D., & Meyer, P. (2005). What kind of journalism does the public need? In G. Overholser & K. Jamieson (Eds.), *The press* (pp. 400–412). New York: Oxford University Press.

Marwick, A. E., & boyd, d. (2010). I tweet honestly, I tweet passionately: Twitter users, context collapse, and the imagined audience. *New Media & Society,* 13(1), 114–133.

Marwick, A., Fontaine, C., & boyd, d. (2017). Nobody sees it, nobody gets mad": Social media, privacy, and personal responsibility among low-SES youth. *Social Media+ Society,* 3(2), 1–14 .

Maryland State Department of Education (2010). Library Media Curriculum. http://mdk12.msde.maryland.gov/share/vsc/vsc_librarymedia_grpk8.pdf

Masterman, L. (1985). *Teaching the media.* London: Polity Press.

Masterman, L. (1986). A reply to David Buckingham. *Screen,* 27(5), 96–103.

Matsakis, L. (2018, November 11). What does a fair algorithm look like? *Wired.* www.wired.com/story/what-does-a-fair-algorithm-look-like/

Max, D. T. (2018, June 18). *Skam,* the radical teen drama that unfolds one post at a time. *The New Yorker.* www.newyorker.com/magazine/2018/06/18/skam-the-radical-teen-drama-that-unfolds-one-post-at-a-time

McChesney, R. W. (2006). Freedom of the press for whom: The question to be answered in our critical juncture. *Hofstra Law Review* 35, 1433–1454.

McIntosh, J. (2012). A history of subversive remix video before YouTube: Thirty political video mashups made between World War II and 2005. In F. Coppa & J. Levin Russo (Eds.), *Transformative Works and Cultures,* 9. https://journal.transformativeworks.org/index.php/twc/article/view/371

McKee, R. (1997). *Story: Substance, structure, style, and the principles of screenwriting.* New York: Harper Collins.

McLennan, D., & Miles, J. (2018, March 21). A once-unimaginable scenario: No more newspapers. *Washington Post.* www.washingtonpost.com/news/theworldpost/wp/2018/03/21/newspapers/?noredirect=on&utm_term=.8e82fb4cf24e

McLuhan, M. (1964). *Understanding media: The extensions of man.* New York: McGraw Hill.

McQuail, D. (2010). *McQuail's mass communication theory.* London: Sage.

Mead, G. H. (1913). The social self. *Journal of Philosophy, Psychology and Scientific Methods,* 10, 374–80.

Mead, G. H. (1934). *Mind, self, and society.* Chicago:University of Chicago Press.

Meadows, D. (1987). Bring back the Fairness Doctrine. Sustainability Institute. http://donellameadows.org/archives/bring-back-the-fairness-doctrine/

Media Spot (2016). Students reflect on six years of integrated media literacy. Video: https://vimeo.com/226891930

MEET Tolerance (2018). About. https://meetolerance.eu/#content

Mellissinos, C. (2015, September 22). Video games are one of the most important art forms in history. *Time.* http://time.com/collection-post/4038820/chris-melissinos-are-video-games-art/

Menuey, B. (2009). CIPA: A brief history. *Computers in the Schools*, 26(1), 40–47.

Meyer, R. (2017, August 2). Your smartphone reduces your brain power, even if it's just sitting there. *The Atlantic*. Retrieved from https://theatln.tc/2K7zVul

Mihailidis, P. (2014). *Media literacy & the emerging citizen: Youth, engagement and participation in digital culture*. New York: Peter Lang.

Mihailidis, P. (2018a). Civic media literacies: Re-imagining engagement for civic intentionality. *Learning, Media and Technology*, 43(2), 152–164.

Mihailidis, P. (2018b). *Civic media literacies: Reimagining human connection in an age of digital abundance*. New York: Routledge.

Miller, D., Costa, E., Haynes, N., McDonald, T., Nicolescu, R., Sinanan, J., … & Wang, X. (2016). *How the world changed social media*. London: UCL Press.

Mistreanu, S. (2018, April 8). Life inside China's social credit laboratory. *Foreign Policy*. http://foreignpolicy.com/2018/04/03/life-inside-chinas-social-credit-laboratory/

Mitchell, S. (2018, February 15). Amazon doesn't just dominate the market: It wants to become the market. *The Nation*. www.thenation.com/article/amazon-doesnt-just-want-to-dominate-the-market-it-wants-to-become-the-market/

Mittell, J. (2004). *Genre and television*. New York: Routledge.

Mittell, J. (2015). *Complex TV: The poetics of contemporary television storytelling*. New York: New York University Press.

Moeller, J., & Helberger, N. (2015). Beyond the filter bubble: Concepts, myths, evidence and issues for future debates. University of Amsterdam Institute for Information Law. www.ivir.nl/publicaties/download/Beyond_the_filter_bubble__concepts_myths_evidence_and_issues_for_future_debates.pdf

Molla, R. (2018, Jan 6). America's love-hate relationship with social media, quantified. Recode. Retrieved from www.recode.net/2018/1/6/16846942/social-media-facebook-twitter-hate

Monbiot, G. (2011, February 23). The need to protect people from astroturfing grows ever more urgent. *The Guardian*. www.theguardian.com/environment/georgemonbiot/2011/feb/23/need-to-protect-internet-from-astroturfing

Moorhead, J. (2011, September 5). Carol Ann Duffy: Poems are a form of texting. *The Guardian*. www.theguardian.com/education/2011/sep/05/carol-ann-duffy-poetry-texting-competition

Morgan, J. (2014, May 20). The decline of trust in the United States. *Medium*. https://medium.com/@monarchjogs/the-decline-of-trust-in-the-united-states-fb8ab719b82a

Morville, P. (2014). *Intertwingled: Information changes everything*. Ann Arbor, MI: Semantic Studios.

Muddiman, A. & Stroud, N. (2017). News values, cognitive biases, and partisan incivility in comment sections, *Journal of Communication*, 67(4) 1, 586–609.

Murphy, M. (2017, May 26). Waiting for the credits to end? Movies are naming more names. *The New York Times*. www.nytimes.com/2017/05/26/movies/why-end-credits-in-movies-are-so-long.html

National Association for Media Literacy Education (2007, November). Core principles of media literacy education in the United States. Retrieved from http://namle.net/publications/core-principles

National Center for Education Statistics (NCES) (2016). Fast facts. Dropout Rates. https://nces.ed.gov/fastfacts/display.asp?id=16

National Council of Teachers of English (NCTE) (1970). Resolution on media literacy. www2.ncte.org/statement/medialiteracy/

National Council of Teachers of English (2019, March 3). Resolution on English education for critical literacy in politics and media. https://ncte.org/statement/resolution-english-education-critical-literacy-politics-media/

National Public Radio (NPR) (2018). Audience. www.nationalpublicmedia.com/npr/audience

Neilander, W., & Miller, R. (1951). *Public relations*. New York: Ronald Press.

Nelson, K. M., Eaton, L. A., & Gamarel, K. E. (2016). Preferences for condomless sex in sexually explicit media among black/African American men who have sex with men: Implications for HIV prevention. *Archives of Sexual Behavior*, 46(4), 977–985.

Nelson, N. (2016). The power of a picture. Netflix. https://media.netflix.com/en/company-blog/the-power-of-a-picture

Nelson, R. (1995). *A chronology and glossary of propaganda in the United States*. Westport, CT: Greenwood Press.

Nerdwriter1 (2018, August 15). How music was made on Super Nintendo. YouTube https://youtu.be/jvIzIAgRWV0

Nestle, M. (2010). FTC goes after Kellogg's immunity claim—But why? Food Politics. www.foodpolitics.com/2010/06/ftc-goes-after-kelloggs-immunity-claim-but-why-2/

Neuman, W. R., Park, Y. J., & Panek, E. (2012). Tracking the flow of information into the home: An empirical assessment of the digital revolution in the United States. *International Journal of Communication*, 6, 1022–1041.

New York Times Learning Network (2018). About. www.nytimes.com/section/learning

Newman, N. (2018). Digital news report. Reuters Institute for the Study of Journalism, University of Oxford. www.digitalnewsreport.org/survey/2018/overview-key-findings-2018/

Newman, N., Fletcher, R., Kalogeropoulos, A., Levy, D. A., & Nielsen, R. K. (2017). Reuters Institute digital news report 2017. Oxford, England: Reuters Institute for the Study of Journalism, University of Oxford. Retrieved from www.digitalnewsreport.org/

Newseum (2016). Reporting Vietnam: Cronkite's editorial. Video. www.youtube.com/watch?v=cXg8BbMp1Yg

Nicas, J., Weise, K., & Isaac, M. (2019, September 8). How each big tech company may be targeted by regulators. *The New York Times*. www.nytimes.com/2019/09/08/technology/antitrust-amazon-apple-facebook-google.html

Nichols, T. (2019). *The death of expertise*. New York: Oxford University Press.

Nielsen (2018). Time flies: U.S. adults now spend nearly half a day interacting with media. Neilsen. www.nielsen.com/us/en/insights/news/2018/time-flies-us-adults-now-spend-nearly-half-a-day-interacting-with-media.html

Nightingale, M. (2014). Behind the scenes: Working with Hollywood to make positive change. In A. Jordan & D. Romer (Eds.), *Media and the well-being of children and adolescents* (pp. 201–225). New York: Oxford University Press.

Nimmo, D., & Geyer, G. A. (2017). *Newsgathering in Washington: A study in political communication*. New York: Routledge.

Noble, S. (2016). *Algorithms of oppression: How search engines reinforce racism*. New York: New York University Press.

Norton, T. B. (2016). The non-contractual nature of privacy policies and a new critique of the Notice and Choice privacy protection model. *Fordham Intellectual Property Media & Entertainment Law Journal* 27, 181–210.

Nöth, W., & Bishara, N. (Eds.). (2007). *Self-reference in the media*. Berlin: Walter de Gruyter.

O'Barr, W. (2015) *What is advertising?* Advertising & Society Review, 16(3). Project MUSE. http://muse.jhu.edu/article/594485

O'Neill, B. (2010). Media literacy and communication rights. *International Communication Gazette*, 72(4–5), 323–338.

OFCOM (2016). Children and parents: Media use and attitudes report. www.ofcom.org.uk/__data/assets/pdf_file/0034/93976/Children-Parents-Media-Use-Attitudes-Report-2016.pdf

Ohler, J. (2011). Digital citizenship means character education for the digital age. *Kappa Delta Pi Record*, 47, 25–27.

Oppenheimer, T. (2004). *The flickering mind: Saving education from the false promise of technology*. New York: Random House.

Ortiz De Gortari, A., & Griffiths, M. (2016). Prevalence and characteristics of game transfer phenomena: A descriptive survey study. *International Journal of Human–Computer Interaction*, 32(6), 470–480.

Owens, J., & Smith, B. (2016) Health education and media literacy: A culturally-responsive approach to positive youth development. *Journal of Health Education Research and Development* 4, 169. doi:10.4172/2380-5439.1000169

Pach, C. (2017, May 30). Lyndon Johnson's living room war. *The New York Times*. www.nytimes.com/2017/05/30/opinion/lyndon-johnson-vietnam-war.html

Page, M. (2012). Adventures with text and beyond: Popular culture—the new literacy challenge for English teachers. *English Journal*, 102(2), 129–133.

Palmeri, J. (2012). *Remixing composition: A history of multimodal writing pedagogy*. Carbondale, IL: SIU Press.

Pariser, E. (2011). *The filter bubble: What the Internet is hiding from you*. London: Penguin UK.

Pautz, M. (2015). *Argo and Zero Dark Thirty:* Film, government, and audiences. *PS: Political Science & Politics*, 48(1), 120–128.

Pearson (2018). *Beyond millennials: The next generation of learners*. Global Research & Insights and Harris Polling.

Pearson, A. (2018, March 29). How Vietnam changed journalism. *The New York Times*. www.nytimes.com/2018/03/29/opinion/vietnam-war-journalism.html

Peiser, W., & Peter, J. (2000). Third-person perception of television-viewing behavior. *Journal of Communication*, 50(1), 25–45.

Pérez Tornero, M., & Varis, T. (2011). *Media literacy and new humanism*. Moscow: UNESCO Institute for Information Technologies in Education.

Perloff, R. M. (2002). The third-person effect. In J. Bryant & D. Zillmann (Eds.), *Media effects: Advances in theory and research* (pp. 489–506). Mahwah, NJ: Lawrence Erlbaum.

Perry, S. L., & Schleifer, C. (2018). Till porn do us part? A longitudinal examination of pornography use and divorce. *The Journal of Sex Research*, 55(3), 284–296.

Peter, J., & Valkenburg, P. M. (2009). Adolescents' exposure to sexually explicit Internet material and notions of women as sex objects: Assessing causality and underlying processes. *Journal of Communication*, 59, 407–433.

Pew Research Center (2018, June 6). Digital news fact sheet. https://journalism.org/fact-sheet/digital-news/

Pew Research Center (2019, September 25). One in five Americans now listens to audiobooks. www.pewresearch.org/fact-tank/2019/09/25/one-in-five-americans-now-listen-to-audiobooks/

Picard, R. G. (1985). *The press and the decline of democracy*. Westport, CT: Greenwood Press.

Pierson, R., Hull, D., Forbes, M., & Burian, R. (1994). The epistemic authority of expertise. In *PSA: Proceedings of the Biennial Meeting of the Philosophy of Science Association* (pp. 398–405). Chicago: University of Chicago Press.

Pinkleton, B., Austin, E., Chen, Y., & Cohen, M. (2012). The role of media literacy in shaping adolescents' understanding of and responses to sexual portrayals in mass media. *Journal of Health Communication*, 17(4), 460–476.

Polan, D. (2016). Dana Polan on Roland Barthes. In R. Hobbs (Ed.), *Exploring the roots of digital and media literacy through personal narrative* (pp. 66–76). Philadelphia: Temple University Press.

Popper, K. (1945). *The open society and its enemies*. London: Routledge.

Post, D. (2015, August 27). A bit of Internet history, or how two members of Congress helped create a trillion or so dollars of value. *Washington Post*. https://perma.cc/S4LN-WE9P

Postman, N. (1970). The reformed English curriculum. In A. C. Eurich (Ed.), *High School 1980: The shape of the future in American secondary education* (pp. 160–168). New York: Pitman.

Postman, N. (1979). Propaganda. *ETC: A Review of General Semantics*, 36(2), 128–133.

Postman, N. (1985). *Amusing ourselves to death: Public discourse in an age of show business*. New York: Knopf.

Postman, N. (1992). *Technopoly: The surrender of culture to technology*. New York: Knopf.

Postman, N. (2000, June). The humanism of media ecology. *Proceedings of the Media Ecology Association*, 1(1), 10–16.

Postman, N., & Weingartner, C. (1969) *Teaching as a subversive activity*. New York: Delta.

Potter, J. (2004). *Theory of media literacy: A cognitive approach*. Thousand Oaks: Sage.

Primack, B. A., Gold, M. A., Land, S. R., & Fine, M. J. (2006). Association of cigarette smoking and media literacy about smoking among adolescents. *Journal of Adolescent Health*, 39(4), 465–472.

Quast, C., & Seidel, M. (2018). Introduction: The philosophy of expertise: What is expertise? *Topoi*, 37, 1. https://doi.org/10.1007/s11245-017-9526-0

Radford, C. (1975). How can we be moved by the fate of Anna Karenina? *Proceedings of the Aristotelian Society, Supplemental*, 49, 67–80.

Rangappa, A. (2017, October 4). The social experiment Facebook should run. *The Atlantic*. www.theatlantic.com/technology/archive/2017/10/facebook-zuckerberg-friend-swap/541881/

Ranieri, M. (Ed.). (2016). *Populism, media and education: Challenging discrimination in contemporary digital societies*. New York: Routledge.

Rathje, S. (2017, July 20). The power of framing: It's not what you say it's how you say it. *The Guardian*. www.theguardian.com/science/head-quarters/2017/jul/20/the-power-of-framing-its-not-what-you-say-its-how-you-say-it

Reese, E. (2013, December 9). What kids learn from hearing family stories. *The Atlantic*. www.theatlantic.com/education/archive/2013/12/what-kids-learn-from-hearing-family-stories/282075/

Reese, S. D. (2007). The framing project: A bridging model for media research revisited. *Journal of Communication*, 57(1), 148–154.

Reich, R. (2015, September 18). Big tech has become way too powerful. *The New York Times.* www.nytimes.com/2015/09/20/opinion/is-big-tech-too-powerful-ask-google.html

Reign, A. (2018). #OscarsSoWhite is still relevant this year. *Vanity Fair.* www.vanityfair.com/hollywood/2018/03/oscarssowhite-is-still-relevant-this-year

Reilly, J. (2012, January 22). Living for 90 days without technology. Video. https://youtu.be/dpDQONK5-qI

Reynolds, D. (2011). *Mightier than the sword: Uncle Tom's Cabin and the battle for America.* New York: W. W. Norton.

Rheingold, H. (2012). *Net smart: How to thrive online.* Cambridge, MA: MIT Press.

Rideout, V., Foehr, U., & Roberts, D. (2010). Generation M2: Media in the lives of 8 to 18 year olds. Kaiser Family Foundation. https://files.eric.ed.gov/fulltext/ED527859.pdf

Ritchie, A. (2011). Media literacy standard implementation in Florida: Perceptions of high school principals and language arts curriculum leaders. Dissertation, University of South Florida. http://stars.library.ucf.edu/etd/1706

RobbGrieco, M. (2019). *Making media literacy in America.* New York: Rowman and Littlefield.

Robertson, A. (2016, April 26). The *New York Times* is sending out a second round of Google Cardboards. The Verge. www.theverge.com/2016/4/28/11504932/new-york-times-vr-google-cardboard-seeking-plutos-frigid-heart

Rogers, K. (2018, April 11). Let's talk about Mark Zuckerberg's claim that Facebook does not sell data. Motherboard *Vice.* https://motherboard.vice.com/en_us/article/8xkdz4/does-facebook-sell-data

Romano, A. (2016, June 7). Canon, fanon, shipping and more: Fandom glossary. *Vox.* www.vox.com/2016/6/7/11858680/fandom-glossary-fanfiction-explained

Roose, K. (2018, September 3). Facebook's private groups offer refuge to public figures. *The New York Times.* www.nytimes.com/2018/09/03/technology/facebook-private-groups-alex-jones.html

Rosalind, G., & Kanai, A. (2018). Mediating neoliberal capitalism: Affect, subjectivity and inequality. *Journal of Communication,* 68(2), 318–326.

Rosenkoetter, L. I., Rosenkoetter, S. E., & Acock, A. C. (2009). Television violence: An intervention to reduce its impact on children. *Journal of Applied Developmental Psychology,* 30, 381–397.

Rosenstiel, T., Ivancin, M., Loker, K., Lacy, S., Sonderman, J., & Yaeger, K. (2015). Facing change: The needs, attitudes and experiences of people in media. American Press Institute. www.americanpressinstitute.org/wp-content/uploads/2015/08/Facing-Change-The-needs-attitudes-and-experiences-of-people-in-media-American-Press-Institute.pdf

Rourke, L. (2014). *The phantom of the author: Literary analysis reconsidered.* Doctoral dissertation, Brandeis University.

Ruoff, J. (1996) Can a documentary be made of real life? The reception of *An American Family.* In P. Crawford & S. Hafsteinsson (Eds.), *The construction of the viewer: Media ethnography and the anthropology of audiences* (pp. 270–296). Denmark: Intervention Press in association with the Nordic Anthropological Film Association.

Saettler, P. (2004). *The evolution of American educational technology.* New York: IAP.

Sanchez-Arce, A. (2007). Authenticism, or the authority of authenticity. *Mosaic: An Interdisciplinary Critical Journal,* 40(3), 139–155.

Sandvig, C., Hamilton, K., Karahalios, K., & Langbort, C. (2015). Can an algorithm be unethical? Paper presented to the 65th annual meeting of the International Communication Association, San Juan, Puerto Rico, USA.

Santo, R. (2011). Hacker literacies: Synthesizing critical and participatory media literacy frameworks. *International Journal of Learning and Media,* 3(3), 1–5. DOI: 10.1162/IJLM_a_00075

Scharrer, E. (2006). "I noticed more violence": The effects of a media literacy program on knowledge and attitudes about media violence. *Journal of Mass Media Ethics,* 21(1), 70–87.

Schildkraut, J. (2012). Media and massacre: A comparative analysis of the reporting of the 2007 Virginia Tech shootings. *Fast Capitalism,* 9(1), 1–22.

Schiller, H. I. (1976). *Communication and cultural domination.* White Plains, NY: International Arts and Sciences Press.

Schmidt, H. (2012). Media literacy education at the university level. *Journal of Effective Teaching,* 12(1), 64–77.

Schou, N. (2016, July 14). Operation Tinseltown: How the CIA manipulates Hollywood. *The Atlantic.* www.theatlantic.com/entertainment/archive/2016/07/operation-tinseltown-how-the-cia-manipulates-hollywood/491138/

Schwabach, A. (2018). Legal issues in online fan fiction. In R. Hobbs (Ed.), *The Routledge companion on media education, copyright, and fair use* (pp. 81–92). New York: Routledge.

Schweinitz, J. (2011). Film and stereotype: A challenge for cinema and theory. *Translated by Laura Schleussner.* New York: Columbia University Press.

Scott, A. O. (2009, October 1). Calls to God: Busy signal. *The New York Times.* www.nytimes.com/2009/10/02/movies/02serious.html

Scott, A. O. (2016). *Better living through criticism.* New York: Penguin.

Shanker, P. (2018a, April 11). Why the Apu *Simpsons* controversy bothers me as an Indian American. *National Review.* www.nationalreview.com/2018/04/the-simpsons-apu-controversy-absurd-shallow/

Shanker, P. (2018b, October 29). P C kills an Indian star. *National Review.* www.nationalreview.com/2018/10/simpsons-apu-cut-from-show-pc-culture-wars/

Shapiro, B. (2017, March 20). Is Huda Kattan the most influential beauty blogger in the world? *The New York Times.* www.nytimes.com/2017/03/20/fashion/is-huda-kattan-the-kim-kardashian-west-of-beauty-bloggers.html?_r=0

Shaw, A. (2015). *Gaming at the edge: Sexuality and gender at the margins of gamer culture.* Minneapolis: University of Minnesota Press.

Silver, L. (2019, February 5). Smartphone ownership is growing rapidly around the world, but not always equally. Pew Research Center. www.pewresearch.org/global/2019/02/05/smartphone-ownership-is-growing-rapidly-around-the-world-but-not-always-equally/

Simon, J. (2017). Introduction: The new face of censorship. Committee to Protect Journalists. https://cpj.org/2017/04/introduction-the-new-face-of-censorship.php

Singer, N. (2018, April 30). Creepy or not? Your privacy concerns probably reflect your politics. *The New York Times.* www.nytimes.com/2018/04/30/technology/privacy-concerns-politics.html

Smith, A. (2018, April 30). Declining majority of online adults say the Internet has been good for society. Pew Research Center. www.pewinternet.org/2018/04/30/declining-majority-of-online-adults-say-the-internet-has-been-good-for-society/

Smith, J. (2015). Videos of police killings are numbing us to the spectacle of black death. *The New Republic.* https://newrepublic.com/article/121527/what-does-seeing-black-men-die-do-you

Smith, J. (2018). The revolutionary power of *Black Panther. Time.* http://time.com/black-panther/

Smith, S., Pieper, K. M., Granados, A., & Choueiti, M. (2010). Assessing gender-related portrayals in top-grossing G-rated films. *Sex Roles, 62,* 774–786.

Smyth, J., & Lepore, S. J. (2002). *The writing cure: How expressive writing promotes health and emotional well-being.* Washington, DC: American Psychological Association.

Smythe, D. W. (1977). Communications: Blindspot of Western Marxism. *Critical Theory, 1*(3), 1–27.

Smythe, D. W. (1981). On the audience commodity and its work. In G. Durham & D. Kellner (Eds.), *Media and cultural studies: Keyworks* (pp. 230–256). New York: Wiley.

Solon, O. (2017, May 25). Underpaid and overburdened: The life of a Facebook moderator. *The Guardian.* www.theguardian.com/news/2017/may/25/facebook-moderator-underpaid-overburdened-extreme-content

Sperry, C. (2006). Seeking truth in the social studies classroom: Media literacy, critical thinking and teaching about the Middle East. *Social Education, 70*(1), 37–44.

Starr, P. (2004). *The creation of the media: Political origins of modern communications.* New York: Basic Books.

Steiner, E., & Xu, K. (2018). Binge-watching motivates change: Uses and gratifications of streaming video viewers challenge traditional TV research. *Convergence.* https://doi.org/10.1177/1354856517750365

Stelter, B. (2007, August 27). *To Catch a Predator* is falling prey to advertisers sensibilities. *The New York Times.* www.nytimes.com/2007/08/27/business/media/27predator.html

Stelter, B. (2020). *Hoax: Donald Trump, Fox News, and the dangerous distortion of truth.* New York : One Signal Publishers/Atria.

Stephens-Davidowitz, S. (2014, January 18). Google, tell me: Is my son a genius? *The New York Times.* www.nytimes.com/2014/01/19/opinion/sunday/google-tell-me-is-my-son-a-genius.html

Stephens-Davidowitz, S. (2018, February 10). *The songs that bind. The New York Times.* https://www.nytimes.com/2018/02/10/opinion/sunday/favorite-songs.html

Stewart, J. (2020, May 15). Movie theaters are on the brink: Can wine and cheese save them? *The New York Times.*

Stone, G. R. (1990). Justice Brennan and the freedom of speech: A First Amendment odyssey. *University of Pennsylvania Law Review, 139,* 1333.

Strate, L. (2017). *Media ecology.* New York: Peter Lang.

Suciu, P. (2020, January 3). Is it possible to become the next big YouTube star in 2020? *Forbes.* www.forbes.com/sites/petersuciu/2020/01/03/is-it-possible-to-become-the-next-big-youtube-star-in-2020/#18df75ef2a18

Suler, J. (2016, May 10). The online disinhibition effect, 20 years later. Fifteen Eighty Four. Academic Perspectives from Cambridge University Press. www.cambridgeblog.org/2016/05/the-online-disinhibition-effect-20-years-later/

Sullivan, M. (2016, November 5). Catch and kill gives media one last black eye before the election. *Washington Post.* www.washingtonpost.com/lifestyle/style/catch-and-kill-at-national-enquirer-gives-media-one-last-black-eye-before-election/2016/11/05/

Swanson, E. (2016, August 26). Americans are less trusting than ever before. Washington Post. https://www.washingtonpost.com/news/wonk/wp/2016/08/26/americans-are-less-trusting-than-ever-before-that-could-also-make-us-poor/

Tarrant, S. (2016). *The pornography industry: What everyone needs to know.* London: Oxford University Press.

Tatar, M. (2003). *The hard facts of Grimm fairy tales.* Princeton, NJ: Princeton University Press.

Taub, A. (2017, January 11). The real story about fake news is partisanship. *The New York Times.* www.nytimes.com/2017/01/11/upshot/the-real-story-about-fake-news-is-partisanship.html

Taylor, C. (1984). Foucault on freedom and truth. *Political Theory, 12*(2), 152–183

Taylor, C. (1991). *The ethics of authenticity.* Cambridge, MA: Harvard University Press.

Ter Bogt, T., Delsing, M., Van Zalk, M., Christenson, P., & Meeus, W. (2011). Intergenerational continuity of taste: Parental and adolescent music preferences. *Social Forces, 90*(1), 297–319.

Thacker, K. (2016). *The art of authenticity.* New York: Wiley.

Thevenin, B. (2019). Authorship and participatory culture. In R. Hobbs & P. Mihailidis (Eds.), *The international encyclopedia of media literacy* (pp. 69–76). New York: Wiley.

Thompson, D. (2003). SolPix interviews: An interview with Todd Gitlin. *SolPix.* http://webdelsol.com/SolPix/sp-toddinterview.htm.

Thompson, D. (2016, June 6). Hollywood has a huge Millennial problem. *The Atlantic.* www.theatlantic.com/business/archive/2016/06/hollywood-has-a-huge-millennial-problem/486209/

Thompson, D. (2017, May 1). ESPN is not doomed. *The Atlantic.* www.theatlantic.com/business/archive/2017/05/espn-layoffs-future/524922/

Tien, C. (2020, March 8). I'm Chinese. That doesn't mean I have the virus. *The New York Times,* SR 2.

Tiffany, K. (2019, January 11). Spotify's most personalized playlist is now for sale to brands. *Vox.* www.vox.com/the-goods/2019/1/11/18178701/spotify-discover-weekly-brand-playlists-personalization

Tiku, N. (2017, November 3). How Russia "pushed our buttons" with fake online ads. *Wired.* www.wired.com/story/how-russia-pushed-our-buttons-with-fake-online-ads/

Tiku, N. (2018, March 19). Europe's new privacy law will change the Web and more. *Wired.* www.wired.com/story/europes-new-privacy-law-will-change-the-web-and-more/

Titlow, J. (2017, July 17). How Instagram learns from your likes to keep you hooked. *Fast Company* www.fastcompany.com/40434598/how-instagram-learns-from-your-likes-to-keep-you-hooked

Toff, B., & Nielsen, R. (2018). "I just Google it": Folk theories of distributed discovery. *Journal of Communication, 68*(3), 636–657,

Tracy, M. (2019, October 8). A journalist says he was hounded by a U.S. customs agent. *The New York Times.* www.nytimes.com/2019/10/08/business/journalist-us-customs-border-agent.html

Treece, D. (2013, November 4). Leading change in the game industry: A look at the work of James Portnow and Jesse Schell. Gamasutra. https://gamasutra.com/blogs/DustinTreece/20131104/203918/Leading_Change_in_the_Game_Industry_A_Look_at_the_Work_of_James_Portnow_and_Jesse_Schell.php

Trekels, J., & Eggermont, S. (2017). Beauty is good: The appearance culture, the internalization of appearance ideals, and dysfunctional appearance beliefs among tweens, *Human Communication Research*, 43(2), 173–192.

Tremblay, G. (2012). From Marshall McLuhan to Harold Innis, or From the global village to the world empire. *Canadian Journal of Communication*, 37(4), 561–575.

Tufekci, Z. (2017). *Twitter and tear gas: The power and fragility of networked protest*. New Haven, CT: Yale University Press.

Turow, J. (2012). *The daily you: How the new advertising industry is defining your identity and your worth*. New Haven, CT: Yale University Press.

Turow, J. (2017). *The aisles have eyes: How retailers track your shopping, strip your privacy, and define your power*. New Haven, CT: Yale University Press.

Turnnidge, (2020, October 3). Why are people faking coronavirus stories? Huffington Post www.huffingtonpost.co.uk/entry/coronavirus-fake-news-conspiracy-theories-psychology_uk_

Tushnet, R. (2007). Power without responsibility: Intermediaries and the First Amendment. *George Washington Law Review* 76(4), 101–131.

Tushnet, R. (2018a). Not waving but drowning: Saving the audience from the floods. Knight First Amendment Institute. https://knightcolumbia.org/content/not-waving-drowning-saving-audience-floods

Tushnet, R. (2018b). Mix and match: Transformative purpose in the classroom. In R. Hobbs (Ed.), *The Routledge companion to media education, copyright and fair use* (pp. 22–30). New York: Routledge.

Tyler, G. (2018, May 23). Fake news and the Fairness Doctrine. Social Europe. www.socialeurope.eu/fake-news-and-the-fairness-doctrine

Tyner, K. (2004). Beyond boxes and wires: Literacy in transition. *Television and New Media*, 4(4), 371–388.

U.S. Department of Commerce (2020). Quarterly Retail E-Commerce Sales, 4th Quarter 2019. www.census.gov/retail/mrts/www/data/pdf/ec_current.pdf

U.S. Census (2013). Spotlight on Media and Information. www.bls.gov/spotlight/2013/media/home.htm

U.S. Congress Congressional Executive Committee on China. (n.d.). Freedom of Expression in China. www.cecc.gov/freedom-of-expression-in-china-a-privilege-not-a-right

UNESCO (2013). Global media and information literacy assessment framework: Country readiness and competencies. www.unesco.org/new/en/communication-and-information/resources/publications-and-communication-materials/publications/full-list/global-media-and-information-literacy-assessment-framework/

UNESCO (2018). Global Alliance for Partnerships in Media and Information Literact (GAPMIL). www.unesco.org/new/en/communication-and-information/media-development/media-literacy/global-alliance-for-partnerships-on-media-and-information-literacy/

Vaidhyanathan, S. (2018). *Anti-social media: How Facebook disconnects us and undermines democracy*. New York: Oxford University Press.

Van Syckle, K. (2018, March 26). What it's like to report about the porn industry. *The New York Times*. www.nytimes.com/2018/03/26/insider/reporting-the-porn-industry.html

Vandenbosch, L. & van Oosten, J. (2017). The relationship between online pornography and the sexual objectification of women: The attenuating role of porn literacy education, *Journal of Communication*, 67(6), 1015–1036.

Vanderbes, J. (2013). The evolutionary case for great fiction. *The Atlantic*. https://www.theatlantic.com/entertainment/archive/2013/09/the-evolutionary-case-for-great-fiction/279311/

VanDerWerff (2018, November 20). Why do so many animated films have great stories? One secret: storyboarding. Vox. https://www.vox.com/culture/2018/11/20/18099001/animated-films-storyboards-script-story-ralph-breaks-the-internet

VanEs, B. (2017, January 17). The risks of recommendation engines. *Medium*. https://medium.com/the-thinkerers/the-risks-of-recommendation-engines-ranking-algorithms-and-automated-feeds-e2456367ca20

Vettehen, P., & Kleemans, M. (2017). Proving the obvious? What sensationalism contributes to the time spent on news video. *Electronic News*, 12(2), 113–127. https://doi.org/10.1177/1931243117739947

Vogels, E. (2020, February 6). 10 facts about Americans and online dating. Pew Research Center. https://www.pewresearch.org/fact-tank/2020/02/06/10-facts-about-americans-and-online-dating/

Vonnegut, K. (2010). Kurt Vonnegut on the shapes of stories. YouTube. https://youtu.be/oP3c1h8v2ZQ

Wagner, K. (2018, October 16). It turns out that Facebook could in fact use data collected from its Portal in-home video device to target you with ads. Recode. www.recode.net/2018/10/16/17966102/facebook-portal-ad-targeting-data-collection

Wahl-Jorgenson, K. (2012). The Chicago School of Sociology and Mass Communication Research. *International Encyclopedia of Media Studies*. https://doi.org/10.1002/9781444361506.wbiems027

Wakefield, J. (2014, June 10). Google behind Webdriver Torso mystery. BBC www.bbc.com/news/technology-27778071

Wallace, C. (2018, February 12). Why *Black Panther* is a defining moment for black America. *The New York Times*. www.nytimes.com/2018/02/12/magazine/why-black-panther-is-a-defining-moment-for-black-america.html

Ward, L. M., & Aubrey, J. S. (2017). *Watching gender: How stereotypes in movies and on TV impact kids' development*. San Francisco: Common Sense.

Wargo, J. (2017). "Every selfie tells a story …": LGBTQ youth lifestreams and new media narratives as connective identity texts. *New Media & Society*, 19(4), 560–578.

Wartella, E., & Jennings, N. (2001). New members of the family: The digital revolution in the home. *Journal of Family Communication* 1(1), 59–69.

Waterson, J., & Helmore, E. (2018, August 29). Trump accuses Google of promoting Obama's speeches over his. *The Guardian*. www.theguardian.com/us-news/2018/aug/28/donald-trump-google-news-service-is-rigged-against-me

Watts, D. (2007, April 15). Is Justin Timberlake a product of cumulative advantage? *The New York Times Magazine*. www.nytimes.com/2007/04/15/magazine/15wwlnidealab.t.html

Webb, J., Schirato, T., & Danaher, G. (2002). *Understanding Bourdieu*. Thousand Oaks: Sage.

Weinberger, D. (2012). *Too big to know*. New York: Basic Books.

Wertenbaker, C. (1953, December 26). The world on his back. *The New Yorker*. www.newyorker.com/magazine/1953/12/26/the-world-on-his-back

Williams, R. (1960). The magic system. *New Left Review*, 4, 27.

Wilson, C., Grizzle, A., Tuazon, R., Akyempong, K., & Cheung, C. (2011). *Media and information literacy curriculum for educators*. Paris:UNESCO

Wilson, E. J. (2010). Remarks at the 2010 FOCAS Communications and Society Meeting, Aspen, CO. August 17.

Wiltshire, A. (2016). Why I love video game credits. Eurogamer. www.eurogamer.net/articles/2016-07-02-why-i-love-video-game-credits

Withers, R. (2018, May 8). The dangerous thrill of downvoting "bad comments" on Facebook. Slate. https://slate.com/technology/2018/05/the-facebook-up-vote-and-downvote-experiment-is-a-bust.html

Wojdynski, B. W., & Evans, N. J. (2016). Going native: Effects of disclosure position and language on the recognition and evaluation of online native advertising. *Journal of Advertising*, 45(2), 157–168.

Wolak, J., Finkelhor, D., Mitchell, K. J., & Ybarra, M. L. (2008). Online "predators" and their victims: Myths, realities, and implications for prevention and treatment. *American Psychologist*, 63(2), 111–128.

Wolf, M. (2018, August 1). Skim reading is the new normal. The effect on society is profound. *The Guardian*. www.theguardian.com/commentis-free/2018/aug/25/skim-reading-new-normal-maryanne-wolf

Wong, A. (2018, August 2). How history classes helped create a post-truth America. *The Atlantic*. www.theatlantic.com/education/archive/2018/08/history-education-post-truth-america/566657/

Woodman, S. (2015, October 18). Chris Hansen is back to catching predators. *The New Republic*. https://newrepublic.com/article/123138/chris-hansen-back-catching-predators

Woods, J., & Barna, A. (2010). Defining stereotype. Teaching the Middle East. University of Chicago. http://teachmiddleeast.lib.uchicago.edu/historical-perspectives/middle-east-seen-through-foreign-eyes/islamic-period/framing-the-issues/issue-02.html

World Economic Forum (2016). Digital media and society: Implications in a hyperconnected era. www3.weforum.org/docs/WEFUSA_DigitalMediaAndSociety_Report2016.pdf

World Health Organization (2019). Levels and trends in child mortality. https://childmortality.org/wp-content/uploads/2019/10/UN-IGME-Child-Mortality-Report-2019.pdf

World Health Organization (2016, October 17). Reducing the impact of marketing of foods and non-alcoholic beverages on children. www.who.int/elena/titles/food_marketing_children/en/

Yarrow, T. (2018). Afterword. Mistrust after truth? In F. Muhlfried (Ed.), *Mistrust: Ethnographic approximations* (pp. 219–224). Bielefeld, Germany: Transcript.

Yin, S. (2016, August 27). The accidental plagiarist in all of us. *The New York Times*. www.nytimes.com/2016/08/27/science/cryptomnesia-demi-lovato-plagiarism.html

Zekany, E. (2014). The hauntology of media addiction. *Forum. University of Edinburgh Postgraduate Journal of Culture and the Arts* 19.

Zhou, L. (2019, April 16). Facebook's data sharing politices are called into question, again. *Vox*. www.vox.com/policy-and-politics/2019/4/16/18410932/facebook-user-data-privacy-cambridge-analytica

Zimmer, M. (2008). The gaze of the perfect search engine: Google as an infrastructure of dataveillance. In A. Spink & M. Zimmer (Eds.), *Web search: Disciplinary perspectives* (pp.77–99). Springer, Berlin: Heidelberg.

Zittel, T. (2018, February 18). The dark and bright sides of party polarization. Items: Insights from the social sciences. Social Science Research Council. https://items.ssrc.org/the-dark-and-bright-sides-of-party-polarization

Zuboff, S. (2016, May 3). The secrets of surveillance capitalism. *Frankfurter Allgemeine*. www.faz.net/aktuell/feuilleton/debatten/the-digital-debate/shoshana-zuboff-secrets-of-surveillance-capitalism-14103616.html

Zuboff, S. (2019). *The age of surveillance capitalism*. New York: PublicAffairs.

Index